Taste of Home's
Light & Tasty
Annual Recipes 2003

PICTURED ABOVE AND ON FRONT COVER: Chicken Cacciatore (page 147) and Maple Honey Cheesecake (page 238).

Taste of Home's
Light&Tasty
Annual Recipes 2003

Editor: Julie Schnittka
Art Director: Niki Malmberg
Food Editor: Janaan Cunningham
Associate Editors: Heidi Reuter Lloyd, Jean Steiner, Faithann Stoner
Art Associates: Connie Alenius, Linda Dzik, Maribeth Greinke
Cover Photography: Rob Hagen, Dan Roberts
Senior Food Photography Artist: Stephanie Marchese
Graphic Art Associates: Ellen Lloyd, Catherine Fletcher

Taste of Home's
Light&Tasty

Executive Editor: Kathy Pohl
Food Editor: Janaan Cunningham
Associate Food Editors: Diane Werner RD, Coleen Martin
Managing Editor: Julie Kastello
Art Director: Julie Wagner
Associate Editors: Mark Hagen, Sharon Selz, Barbara Schuetz, Ann Kaiser
Copy Editor: Kristine Krueger
Proofreader: Jean Steiner
Recipe Editor: Janet Briggs
Test Kitchen Director: Karen Johnson RD
Test Kitchen Home Economists: Mark Morgan RD, Wendy Stenman,
Sue Draheim, Tamra Duncan, Peggy Fleming RD, Julie Herzfeldt, Joylyn Jans,
Kristin Koepnick, Pat Schmeling, Karen Wright
Test Kitchen Assistants: Suzanne Kern, Megan Taylor
Editorial Assistants: Ursula Maurer, Joanne Wied, Barb Czysz, Mary Ann Koebernik
Food Photographers: Rob Hagen, Dan Roberts
Senior Food Photography Artist: Stephanie Marchese
Food Photography Artist: Julie Ferron
Photo Studio Manager: Anne Schimmel
Graphic Art Associates: Ellen Lloyd, Catherine Fletcher
Chairman and Founder: Roy Reiman
President: Tom Curl

Taste of Home Books
© 2003 Reiman Media Group, Inc.
5400 S. 60th Street, Greendale WI 53129

International Standard Book Number: 0-89821-374-6
International Standard Serial Number: 1537-3134

To order additional copies of this book, write: *Taste of Home* Books,
P.O. Box 908, Greendale WI 53129; call toll-free 1-800/344-2560 to order
with a credit card. Or visit our Web site at **www.reimanpub.com**.

Contents

513 Dishes Fit for Today's Lifestyle!

IF YOU'RE LIKE most folks these days, you keep an eye on what you eat. You strive to prepare well-balanced meals that are lean on fat and calories but not lean on flavor. All the dishes you serve have to be full-flavored because you don't want your family to feel deprived.

So it's no wonder that *Light & Tasty* magazine became an instant success when it was launched in 2001.

That's because unlike most other food magazines, *Light & Tasty* takes a common sense approach to calorie-wise eating by using fresh and delicious ingredients. It's not a diet magazine, so it doesn't lecture or urge diet and exercise but instead suggests simple options with lighter ingredient choices. *Light & Tasty* is all about good-for-you recipes packed with down-home flavor.

In 2002, the response to our first *Light & Tasty Annual Recipes* cookbook—featuring every recipe from the first year of the magazine—was so positive that we've done it again.

This *2003 Light & Tasty Annual Recipes* cookbook is packed with every recipe published in the magazine during 2002. That's 513 trimmed-down dishes in all!

Many of the recipes are family-favorites of our readers, so they're guaranteed to offer great home-style flavor. The taste is still there... these recipes have just been lightened up a bit with less fat, calories, cholesterol, etc.

Yet, these dishes won't leave you hungry. You'll find lots of great-tasting comfort foods, like Simple Salisbury Steak, Nostalgic Chicken and Dumplings, Jumbo Pineapple Yeast Rolls, Double-Chocolate Cream Roll and much more. Each of these mouth-watering dishes is leaner on fat, calories or sodium...but not leaner on flavor.

Most important, every recipe in this book has been reviewed by a registered dietitian and includes Nutritional Analysis, plus Diabetic Exchanges where appropriate.

Whether you're just cutting back a little or carefully following a weight-loss plan, we think you'll agree *2003 Light & Tasty Annual Recipes* is the right fit for you!

Diane Werner, R.D.

Associate Food Editor, *Light & Tasty*

What's Inside These Recipe-Packed Pages?

AS IF 513 great-tasting, good-for-you recipes aren't enough reasons to love *2003 Light & Tasty Annual Recipes*, the following helpful features will certainly make this big book a valued reference in your kitchen for years to come!

User-Friendly Chapters. We've compiled all 513 recipes from the second year of *Light & Tasty* magazine into 15 convenient chapters, such as Light Bites & Beverages, Beefed-Up Main Dishes, Chicken & Turkey Entrees and Dazzling Desserts. There's even a Trimmed-Down Dishes for Two chapter, which offers foods sized just right for one or two people. (For a complete listing of chapters, turn to page 3.)

Mouth-Watering Meals. You'll find 13 complete menus (including pictures!), which are perfect for either weekend entertaining (page 241) or weekday family dining (page 254).

De-Light-Ful Dinner Planner. It's a challenge to come up with satisfying well-balanced meals throughout the year. So in addition to the meal chapters mentioned above, we've created 27 menu plans that include a main dish and side dish or dessert. (See the De-Light-Ful Dinner Planner on page 7.) Each meal features at least two recipes found inside this book, as well as suggestions for "appealing partners" (side dishes, desserts or beverages) and meal-preparation pointers.

Hundreds of Color Photos. *More than half* of the 513 recipes in this timeless collection are shown in full color. So you can be sure these full-flavored foods not only taste terrific, but are eye-appealing as well.

Easy-to-Use Indexes. Finding all 513 recipes in this cookbook is a snap with two simple-to-use indexes. The general index lists every recipe by food category, major ingredient and/or cooking technique. The alphabetical recipe listing is perfect for folks looking for a specific family-favorite by name.

There's also a reference index that refers you to the many helpful kitchen tips and healthy-eating hints throughout the book. (The indexes begin on page 272.)

Nutritional Analysis Nuggets

EVERY RECIPE in *2003 Light & Tasty Annual Recipes* has been reviewed by a registered dietitian and includes Nutritional Analysis, plus Diabetic Exchanges where appropriate.

The Nutritional Analysis gives you the breakdown for calories, fat, saturated fat, cholesterol, sodium, carbohydrate, fiber and protein.

How we calculated the Nutritional Analysis.

- Whenever a choice of ingredients is given in a recipe (such as 1/3 cup of sour cream or plain yogurt), the first ingredient listed is the one calculated in the Nutritional Analysis.
- When a range is given for an ingredient (such as 2 to 3 teaspoons), we calculate the first amount given.
- Only the amount of marinade absorbed during preparation is calculated.
- Garnishes listed in recipes are generally included in our calculations.

Key ingredients used in our recipe testing.

The following are the standard ingredients we use in recipe testing and in Nutritional Analysis unless otherwise indicated in a recipe:

- Large eggs
- Regular canned chicken broth
- 90% lean ground beef
- Regular long grain white rice
- Stick margarine containing 80% vegetable oil
- Nonstick cooking spray (used on cookware)
- Refrigerated butter-flavored spray (used to enhance flavor in certain dishes). Our Test Kitchen uses I Can't Believe It's Not Butter Spray.
- Baking fat replacement. Our Test Kitchen sometimes uses Smucker's Baking Healthy or Sunsweet's Lighter Bake to replace some of the fat in baked goods.

Food Guide Pyramid Serving Sizes

Bread, cereal, rice and pasta group
(6 to 11 servings a day)
- One slice of bread
- Half of an average bagel (the size of a hockey puck)
- 1 ounce dry cereal (about 2 handfuls)
- 1/2 cup cooked cereal, rice or pasta

Vegetable group
(3 to 5 servings a day)
- 1 cup raw leafy greens
- 1/2 cup of any chopped vegetable, raw or cooked
- 6-ounce glass of vegetable juice

Fruit group
(2 to 3 servings a day)
- 1 medium banana
- One medium apple or orange
- 6-ounce glass of orange juice or any 100% fruit juice

Milk, yogurt and cheese group
(2 to 3 servings a day)
- 8-ounce container of yogurt
- 1 cup cottage cheese
- 1-1/2-ounce chunk of hard cheese (size of two dominoes)
- 8-ounce glass of milk

Meat, poultry, fish and other proteins group
(2 to 3 servings a day)
- 3 ounces cooked lean meat or poultry (size of a deck of cards)
- 3 ounces lean cooked fish (size of a cassette tape)
- Eggs, dry beans, peanut butter, nuts or seeds are also good sources of protein, although they are not always eaten in the quantity required to equal a full serving. These foods are a good way to add a variety of additional protein to your diet.

Daily Nutrition Guide

	Women 25-50	Women over 50	Men over 24
Calories	2,200	1,900 or less	2,900
Fat	73 g or less	63 g or less	96 g or less
Saturated Fat	24 g or less	21 g or less	32 g or less
Cholesterol	300 mg or less	300 mg or less	300 mg or less
Sodium	2,400 mg or less	2,400 mg or less	2,400 mg or less
Carbohydrates	335 g	283 g	446 g
Fiber	20-30 g	20-30 g	20-30 g
Protein	50 g	50 g or less	63 g

This chart is only a general guide. Calorie requirements vary, depending on size, weight and amount of activity. Children's calorie and protein needs vary as they grow.

De-Light-ful Dinner Planner

To make meal planning easy,
turn to these 27 tasty menu suggestions
featuring recipes from this book, "appealing
partners" to round out the dinners and
meal-preparation pointers.

Mexi-Italiana Meal (page 12)

Wonderful Roll-Ups

A delicious ham and Swiss cheese filling gives a special touch to **Breaded Turkey Rolls** (p. 134) from Rita Pearl of Norwalk, Iowa. Prepare the pretty roll-ups for family and company alike.

Accompany them with **Roasted Asparagus with Balsamic Vinegar** (p. 90) shared by Natalie Peterson of Kirkland, Washington. Balsamic vinegar lends distinctive flavor to the springtime side dish that conveniently cooks at the same oven temperature as the turkey rolls.

Appealing Partners

♦ Long grain and wild rice
♦ Apple slices with fat-free caramel dip

Practical Tips

🍎 To cut down on last-minute preparation, assemble the Breaded Turkey Rolls the night before. The next day, coat them with the bread crumb mixture right before baking.

🍎 Use another reduced-fat cheese, such as cheddar, instead of the Swiss cheese called for in the entree recipe.

🍎 If your family is fond of garlic, sprinkle the asparagus with a clove or two of minced garlic before roasting.

Meatless Menu

For a memorable main dish with Tex-Mex taste, prepare **Cheesy Beans and Rice** (p. 186) from Linda Rindels of Littleton, Colorado. The hearty bean-and-rice bake has so much zippy flavor, you won't even miss the meat.

To round out the meal, pair the casserole with a tossed salad topped with **Avocado Salad Dressing** (p. 60). The thick and creamy mixture stirred up by our Test Kitchen complements any combination of greens and vegetables.

Appealing Partners

♦ Baked tortilla chips and salsa
♦ Red grape clusters

Practical Tips

🍎 To hurry along the casserole, use instant brown rice, which cooks more quickly than regular brown rice. Or use up any leftover cooked rice you have in the fridge, such as long grain rice or even a wild rice blend.

🍎 Be sure to pick up extra fixings for your salad drizzled with Avocado Salad Dressing. The grocery list calls for ready-to-serve salad greens, but you may want to jot down other ingredients.

Slow-Cooked Supper

When your family is hungry for a hearty meat-and-potatoes meal, pull out your slow cooker and prepare **Apple and Onion Beef Pot Roast** (p. 114) from Rachel Koistinen of Hayti, South Dakota. The tender slices of beef are wonderful when covered with an apple-flavored gravy.

To complement this meaty main dish, fix **Garlic Potato Wedges** (p. 79) shared by Amy Werner of Grand Ledge, Michigan. Rosemary, garlic and Dijon mustard are among the ingredients that lend terrific taste to this easy oven dish.

Appealing Partners

♦ Broccoli with Roasted Red Peppers (p. 100)
♦ Low-fat brownies

Practical Tips

🍎 Rachel suggests that leftover sliced beef—if there is any—be used in French dip sandwiches, roast beef potpie or sweet-and-sour beef over rice.

🍎 For a tasty variation on traditional potato salad, Amy says you can make the Garlic Potato Wedges ahead of time and serve them chilled.

Down-Home Dinner

Try this crowd-pleasing combination from Lori Gleason of Minneapolis, Minnesota. She came up with **Chicken Noodle Casserole** (p. 132) when guests dropped by and she didn't have much time or many ingredients on hand.

For dessert, pass around a plate of **Cranberry Oat Yummies** (p. 209) from Carol Birkemeier of Nashville, Indiana. The golden treats are bursting with fruity flavor, so they're also good for breakfast or as a snack.

Appealing Partners

♦ Cucumber and onion salad
♦ Tomato vegetable juice

Practical Tips

👉 When assembling the casserole, speed up the cooking time by using frozen vegetables, such as California blend, instead of the carrots and celery called for in the recipe. Then simmer just until the veggies are tender.

🍎 Substitute dried cherries for dried cranberries when making the cookies. Many grocery stores carry dried cherries in the same aisle as other packaged dried fruit.

Pleasing Pork Chops

An impressive meal is just minutes away when you fix **Braised Pork Chops** (p. 156) on your stovetop. Sage, rosemary and garlic season these moist and tender chops from Marilyn Larsen of Port Orange, Florida.

For a refreshing complement to the entree, serve **Fennel Orange Salad** (p. 59) from Nina Hall of Citrus Heights, California. The crisp citrusy salad is especially nice when you're having company for dinner.

Appealing Partners

♦ Hot cooked bow tie pasta
♦ Green beans

Practical Tips

👉 Be sure to grate 1 tablespoon orange peel for the Fennel Orange Salad before sectioning the oranges.

👉 Not familiar with fresh fennel? The white or pale green bulb has overlapping ribs, similar to celery, with feathery dill-like green leaves growing from the middle. Eaten raw, it has a licorice-like flavor and celery-like crunch. It's sold in the produce section of many supermarkets.

Old-Fashioned Appeal

Let your slow cooker help you put **Nostalgic Chicken and Dumplings** (p. 130) on the table. This down-home dish from Brenda Edwards of Hereford, Arizona simmers all afternoon. For the finishing touch, use baking mix to create the fluffy dumplings.

Then serve **Broccoli with Orange Cream** (p. 96) shared by Kathy Samuelson of Omaha, Nebraska. The smooth sauce dresses up this veggie nicely.

Appealing Partners

♦ Honey lemon tea
♦ Fruit medley

Practical Tips

👉 When preparing Nostalgic Chicken and Dumplings, use a dry paper towel to pull the skin from the chicken breasts. It's easier to grip this way.

🍎 Broccoli with Orange Cream calls for grated orange peel. Grate a few oranges and store leftovers in the freezer to use in future recipes.

👉 To bring out the flavor of the walnuts in the side dish, toast them in a dry skillet for a few minutes.

Hearty Ham Dinner

There's no need to turn on the oven when you add **Spiced Pineapple Ham** (p. 162) to your dinner menu. Betty Claycomb of Alverton, Pennsylvania shares the recipe for skillet-warmed ham topped with a sweet pineapple sauce.

Carrot, celery and red pepper lend crispness to **Crunchy Potato Salad** (p. 52) from Janis Plagerman of Lynden, Washington. The salad is a great side dish with ham but also nice for picnics.

Appealing Partners

♦ Steamed brussels sprouts
♦ Raspberry Pie with Oat Crust (p. 220)

Practical Tips

🍎 For the entree, you need 1 cup of pineapple juice so buy a six-pack of 6-ounce cans. Then store the extra cans in your pantry to use later.

🍎 For a pretty presentation, line the bowl that holds the Crunchy Potato Salad with lettuce leaves.

Luscious Lasagna

Shell pasta gives traditional lasagna a tasty twist in this main dish from Mrs. Leo Merchant of Jackson, Mississippi. Her recipe for **Cheesy Shell Lasagna** (p. 112) makes a big pan, so you can feed a crowd—or warm up the leftovers for lunch later in the week.

Round out the meal with a tossed salad topped with **Buttermilk Basil Salad Dressing** (p. 53) shared by Nancy Johnston from San Dimas, California. The creamy dressing has a rich taste but less fat than most bottled dressings.

Appealing Partners

♦ Sesame breadsticks
♦ Mixed melon cup

Practical Tips

🍎 When making the lasagna, feel free to substitute other pasta shapes, such as macaroni, bow ties or spirals.

🍎 Pick up extra fixings for your salad drizzled with Buttermilk Basil Salad Dressing. In the photo above, we used a European blend, but choose your family's favorite. You may also want to jot down other ingredients, such as tomatoes, mushrooms, etc.

Super Sandwiches

Get a head start on dinner when you start marinating the chicken breasts for tonight's casual meal the night before. Once you try the **Ultimate Chicken Sandwiches** (p. 142) from Gregg Voss of Emerson, Nebraska, you're sure to make them again and again.

For a colorful accompaniment, fix **Black-Eyed Pea Salad** (p. 54). Melinda Ewbank of Fairfield, Ohio places servings on lettuce leaves, then garnishes with ripe tomato wedges.

Appealing Partners

♦ Sparkling water with lime
♦ Lemon sherbet

Practical Tips

🍎 If your family prefers pork over chicken, use 1/2-inch-thick boneless pork chops instead of chicken breasts in the sandwich recipe. There's no need to pound them. Just marinate and continue with the rest of the recipe directions. Be sure to cook the pork to 160°.

🍎 To cut down on last-minute preparation, you can assemble the Black-Eyed Pea Salad ahead of time. Cover it and keep it in the fridge until serving.

Easy Oven Entree

You don't need a lot of ingredients to fix Bernice Dean's **Glazed Pork Tenderloin** (p. 161). The Garland, Texas cook serves the meaty main dish with simple seasonings and a swift sauce.

Geri Barr of Calgary, Alberta captures the sunny flavors of fresh citrus in a fruit medley topped with crunchy almonds. With its tangy taste, **Almond Sunshine Citrus** (p. 105) is sure to tantalize your taste buds.

Appealing Partners

◆ Sauteed zucchini
◆ Baked sweet potatoes

Practical Tips

👉 If your grocery store does not stock the pineapple preserves needed for the Glazed Pork Tenderloin, peach or apricot preserves are a nice substitute.

👉 Before grating the citrus peel for the salad, wash all fruit thoroughly. Grate only the top layer of peel; the white pith will give the dish a bitter taste.

👉 To save the time you would spend sectioning grapefruit for the salad, buy a jar of grapefruit sections from the produce department instead.

Beefed-Up Salad

For a refreshing main dish, try **Beefy Broccoli Asparagus Salad** (p. 55) from Betty Rassette of Salina, Kansas. The savory salad is delicious, especially when served with fresh-baked bread.

Anne Smithson of Cary, North Carolina shares her recipe for **Cheddar-Topped English Muffin Bread** (p. 192). Quick-rise yeast hurries along the preparation of these hearty loaves.

Appealing Partners

◆ Iced herbal tea
◆ Fat-free pound cake with sliced strawberries

Practical Tips

👉 In a pinch, you can use frozen vegetables in place of fresh ones in the salad. Buy bags of frozen broccoli florets and asparagus, and measure out the amounts listed. Once thawed, cook the veggies as directed in the recipe.

👉 If you like your bread toasted, eliminate the cheese from the Cheddar-Topped English Muffin Bread before baking. Otherwise, the cheese may burn in the toaster.

Fall Favorite

The classic combo of pork and apple gets an update in **Apple-Topped Pork Chops** (p. 162) from Helen Koehler of Marshalltown, Iowa. Tender chops are browned, then jazzed up with apple slices.

For dessert, enjoy a slice of homemade **Sweet Potato Pie** (p. 221). Our Test Kitchen shares the recipe for this seasonal Southern favorite.

Appealing Partners

◆ Steamed new potatoes
◆ Sauteed zucchini with carrots

Practical Tips

👉 When preparing the pork chops, choose any kind of tart apple, including Granny Smith, Cortland, Braeburn, Jonathan, Winesap and Rome Beauty.

👉 To hurry along the pie, use canned sweet potatoes. Drain them, puree in the food processor until smooth, then use 2-2/3 cups in the recipe.

👉 Try garnishing the pie with miniature marshmallows instead of whipped topping. Place individual pie slices on a microwave-safe plate, then sprinkle with mini marshmallows and zap in the microwave until puffed.

Tried-and-True Casserole

Your family won't know you've lightened up a favorite when you put **Tuna Noodle Casserole** (p. 178) on the table. This better-for-you version from Ruby Wells of Cynthiana, Kentucky is creamy, comforting and tastes just like the traditional recipe.

Pair it with a swift salad like **Plum Tomatoes with Balsamic Vinaigrette** (p. 64) from Ann Sobotka. The Glendale, Arizona cook stirs together a homemade dressing, then tosses it over ripe tomatoes.

Appealing Partners

- Celery sticks
- Sliced peaches with cinnamon

Practical Tips

The casserole recipe calls for 2 cups cooked yolk-free noodles. Don't have leftovers? Cook 4 ounces of uncooked noodles to use in the recipe.

You can easily substitute leftover cooked chicken or turkey for the tuna.

Use homegrown tomatoes in the salad with wonderful results. "Serve them at room temperature for the best flavor," Ann adds.

Mexi-Italiana Meal

Mexican Stuffed Shells (p. 115) from Norma Jean Shaw of Stephens City, Virginia combine two favorite cuisines—Italian and Mexican—to create one memorable main dish. She tucks a flavorful ground beef filling into jumbo pasta shells, then finishes them off with sour cream, olives and other toppings.

You'll need just four ingredients to round out the meal with **Watermelon Slush** (p. 217) from Elizabeth Montgomery of Taylorville, Illinois. Serve the cool treat with a straw as a frosty beverage or with a spoon as a light refreshing dessert.

Appealing Partners

- Parsley rice
- Mixed salad greens

Practical Tips

If you'd like the Mexican Stuffed Shells a little spicier, choose a hotter salsa or use hot turkey Italian sausage.

A 12-ounce box of jumbo pasta shells contains about 35 shells. Since some may break during cooking, cook the entire box. Use whole ones in your main dish, then top broken shells (and extras) with spaghetti sauce for lunch.

Better Burgers

Looking for some casual weekday fare? Give **Hawaiian Turkey Burgers** (p. 146) a try! Babette Watterson of Atglen, Pennsylvania tops the tender burgers with tangy pineapple slices to make the satisfying sandwiches.

You don't have to skip the fries with your burger when you fix **Oven-Baked Country Fries** (p. 84) from LaDonna Reed of Ponca City, Oklahoma. The thick skins-on wedges are covered in a nicely seasoned coating before they're baked to a golden crispness.

Appealing Partners

- Strawberries with Crisp Wontons (p. 208)
- Mixed pepper strips with low-fat dressing

Practical Tips

When buying ground turkey, check the label. The lean ground turkey called for in the burger recipe is 93% lean. Some ground turkey has a higher percentage of fat.

For easy cleanup, line the baking sheet with aluminum foil before cooking the oven-fried potatoes.

Special Supper

Judith McGhan of Perry Hall, Maryland takes advantage of canned soup to prepare the savory sauce for **Dijon Mushroom Beef** (p. 121). The fast-to-fix entree is filling and flavorful.

For a different way to serve veggies, ladle up **Chilled Squash and Carrot Soup** (p. 45) from Elaine Sabacky of Litchfield, Minnesota.

Appealing Partners

◆ Asparagus spears
◆ Angel food cake

Practical Tips

👆 Before preparing Dijon Mushroom Beef, partially freeze the meat to make it easier to slice.

👆 Judith says the leftovers are tasty in other dishes, too. "I used them to make beef potpie, and the mustard added a little zest to the dish."

👆 To give individual bowls of soup a special presentation, use a toothpick to swirl small dollops of reduced-fat sour cream into a pretty pattern.

Favorite French Dip

Ginny Koeppen from Winnfield, Louisiana needs just five ingredients to prepare **Spicy French Dip** (p. 116). The slow-cooked beef simmers in a nicely seasoned broth until deliciously tender.

Try the sandwich alone or topped with **Eggplant Pepper Relish** (p. 94) from Jeanne Vitale of Leola, Pennsylvania. The colorful combo of broiled vegetables can also be served as a side dish.

Appealing Partners

◆ Low-fat potato salad
◆ Sparkling water

Practical Tips

👆 For milder sandwiches, use a can of green chilies in place of jalapenos or strain the broth after cooking to remove the peppers. To please tender palates, eliminate the peppers altogether.

👆 For an authentic French dip, serve the warm cooking juices in a ramekin or custard cup alongside each sandwich for easy dipping.

👆 When weather allows, Jeanne roasts the peppers and eggplant on her outdoor barbecue grill until peppers are blackened and eggplant is soft.

Comforting Casserole

In **Rotini Chicken Casserole** (p. 147) from Ruth Lee of Troy, Ontario, chicken, pasta and vegetables are coated in a creamy sauce, then topped with cornflake crumbs.

It's easy to satisfy a sweet tooth when you serve individual dishes of **Strawberry Mousse** (p. 209). This fluffy dessert from Waydella Hart of Parsons, Kansas is a lovely way to end the meal.

Appealing Partners

◆ Spinach salad with low-fat dressing
◆ Hot apple cider

Practical Tips

👆 You need 3 cups of cooked chicken for the Rotini Chicken Casserole. Purchase a pound of boneless chicken, then poach, microwave or grill it and cube it for the recipe. Or use leftover chicken if you have it on hand.

👆 When preparing the casserole, feel free to use a 13-in. x 9-in. baking dish instead of a 3-quart dish.

👆 For an extra treat, Waydella creates a chocolate topping for the mousse. She melts 1/2 cup of milk chocolate chips and drizzles a bit on each serving.

Traditional Tastes

Ease into your workweek with a comforting classic when you serve **Simple Salisbury Steak** (p. 120) from Elouise Bonar of Hanover, Illinois. It takes about a half hour to prepare, so it can be on the table in no time.

Also easy to fix on the stovetop are **Snappy Green Beans** (p. 89) shared by Tammy Neubauer of Ida Grove, Iowa. Lemon and parsley let the fresh taste of the green beans shine through.

Appealing Partners

♦ Mashed potatoes
♦ Peachy Fruit Salad (p. 74)

Practical Tips

🍎 On occasion, Elouise uses lean ground turkey instead of ground beef in the entree with equally tasty results. You can also use cream of celery soup rather than cream of mushroom soup.

🍎 To cut down on last-minute prep, mix and shape the patties early in the day, then cover and refrigerate until you're ready to cook them.

🍎 Replace the green beans with wax beans if you prefer, or use frozen beans instead of fresh.

Italian Entree

Basil, oregano and white wine dress up **Turkey-Tomato Pasta Sauce** (p. 127) shared by Sherry Hulsman of Louisville, Kentucky. The pasta dish is nice enough for company yet simple enough for busy weeknights.

Mustard lovers and garlic fans are sure to enjoy **Dijon Herb Salad Dressing** (p. 72) from Marge Werner of Broken Arrow, Oklahoma. The robust blend is quick to whip up with on-hand ingredients and serve over salad greens.

Appealing Partners

♦ Italian bread
♦ Broccoli florets

Practical Tips

🍎 We suggest serving the sauce over spaghetti. To save seconds, buy fresh pasta from the dairy section—it cooks more quickly.

🍎 For your salad drizzled with Dijon Herb Salad Dressing, purchase ready-to-serve salad greens and a few extra fixings (mushrooms, cucumbers, tomatoes, etc.).

Classic Combination

For an informal soup and sandwich supper, start with **Pork 'n' Slaw Sandwiches** (p. 157). Our Test Kitchen paired barbecued pork with crunchy coleslaw to create the hearty handheld sandwiches.

Then stir together this cool summery soup that makes the most of zucchini from your garden. **Black Bean Zucchini Gazpacho** (p. 38) from Julie Wilson of Grand Rapids, Ohio is chock-full of good-for-you ingredients.

Appealing Partners

♦ Limeade (from frozen concentrate)
♦ Watermelon slices

Practical Tips

🍎 You can easily substitute turkey tenderloin for the pork tenderloin when making the Pork 'n' Slaw Sandwiches. Just be sure you broil the turkey to 170°.

🍎 To cut down on prep time, use about 2 cups coleslaw mix from your supermarket's produce department rather than shredding the green and red cabbage and carrot.

🍎 If your family prefers a less zippy gazpacho, use regular V8 juice instead of the spicy hot variety.

Delightful Dish

Joyce Unruh of Shipshewana, Indiana shares her recipe for **Wild Rice Chicken Bake** (p. 140), a delicious all-in-one dish that the whole family is sure to love. It features tender chicken, colorful carrots and peas, and an easy-to-prepare wild rice mix.

To round out the meal, fix **Cucumber Salad** (p. 72) from Rose Lauritsen of Orange City, Florida. The refreshing side dish has an old-fashioned taste that complements many entrees.

Appealing Partners

♦ Asparagus spears
♦ Fruit-flavored iced tea

Practical Tips

🍎 In the casserole recipe, use two celery ribs to add crunch in place of the water chestnuts. And if your family isn't fond of peas, use frozen green beans instead.

🍎 When making the cucumber salad, Rose prefers peeling the cucumbers before slicing them.

🍎 Growing dill in your garden? Use 2-1/4 teaspoons minced fresh dill rather than the dill weed called for in the salad.

Great Grilled Salmon

You don't need to heat up your kitchen with this meal that cooks on your outdoor grill. Phyllis Schmalz of Kansas City, Kansas shares her secret for **Firecracker Salmon Steaks** (p. 178).

To complement the fish, serve **Grilled Vegetable Potato Skins** (p. 88). Karen Hemminger of Mansfield, Massachusetts saves time by zapping the potatoes in the microwave, then topping them with colorful grilled veggies.

Appealing Partners

♦ Corn muffins
♦ Orange sherbet

Practical Tips

🍎 Do you favor foods on the spicy side? Be sure to include the crushed red pepper flakes when fixing the sauce for the Firecracker Salmon Steaks.

🍎 You can use salmon fillets instead of steaks. Simply cook skin side down for 8-10 minutes or until fish flakes easily with a fork.

🍎 If the weather isn't conducive to grilling, both the entree and side dish can be cooked in the oven by broiling 4-6 inches from the heat.

Satisfying Stew

In Muncie, Indiana, Jeanette Jones warms cool nights with a steaming kettle of **Tomato Sausage Stew** (p. 142). Brimming with Italian sausage, pasta and beans, the filling fare smells wonderful as it cooks.

To round out the meal, bake a round loaf of this quick bread from Judi Havens of Denton, Texas. With oats sprinkled on top, the tall wedges of **Hearty Oat Loaf** (p. 197) have a rustic look.

Appealing Partners

♦ Tossed salad with Hold-the-Oil French Dressing (p. 74)
♦ Sugar-free vanilla pudding

Practical Tips

🍎 Feel free to substitute a 15-1/2-ounce can of great northern beans for the canned navy beans in the stew recipe.

🍎 Have any leftover stew? Jeanette says it's great reheated for lunch or another dinner. It will keep in the fridge for up to 2 days.

🍎 The Hearty Oat Loaf is best served warm. For a different look, sprinkle the loaf with sesame seeds, poppy seeds or toasted wheat germ before baking.

Microwave Main Dish

This memorable meal-in-one dish of **Microwave Potato Ham Dinner** (p. 157) from Sharon Price of Caldwell, Idaho is a snap to zap in your microwave. It's chock-full of tender chunks of veggies and ham, which are coated with a tasty homemade cheese sauce.

End dinner with a time-saving treat you can stir up on the stovetop with only seven basic ingredients. **No-Bake Chocolate Cookies** (p. 237) shared by Carol Brandon of Uxbridge, Ontario are sure to satisfy a sweet tooth.

Appealing Partners

♦ Warm cranapple juice
♦ Salad greens with low-fat dressing

Practical Tips

👌 When preparing the casserole, feel free to substitute cubed cooked chicken or turkey for the ham.

👌 Carol uses a small ice cream scoop to form the cookies. "It's much faster than using a tablespoon," she says. "If you don't work quickly, the mixture may harden, and you'll end up with one big 'cookie' in your bowl."

Meat-and-Potatoes Menu

In Logan, Utah, Edie DeSpain fixes **Savory Meat Loaf** (p. 123) for all sorts of occasions. The tender-textured loaf, topped with a sweet and tangy sauce, is a real family-pleaser. **Buttermilk Mashed Potatoes** (p. 94) from Stephanie Bremson of Kansas City, Missouri are a lovely accompaniment to the meat loaf. These better-for-you mashed potatoes get a boost of flavor from garlic and buttermilk.

Appealing Partners

♦ Tarragon-Almond Green Beans (p. 84)
♦ Mixed fruit cup

Practical Tips

👌 Get a head start on dinner by mixing up the meat loaf ahead of time and keeping the beef mixture in the fridge. When it's time to bake, shape it into a loaf, top with sauce and cook as directed.

👌 To lighten the entree, substitute lean ground turkey for half the beef.

👌 While you can use most kinds of potatoes when making the Buttermilk Mashed Potatoes, we suggest russets. They're light and fluffy when mashed.

Flavorful Stir-Fry

Extra cooked turkey gets a tasty treatment in **Turkey Stir-Fry** (p. 128) from Kylene Konosky. The Jermyn, Pennsylvania cook creates a simple soy glaze to coat this skillet specialty.

For a light dessert, serve slices of super-moist **Orange Poppy Seed Cake** (p. 230) from Brenda Craig of Spokane, Washington. A boxed cake mix is jazzed up with poppy seeds, orange juice concentrate, almond extract and cinnamon.

Appealing Partners

♦ Phyllo Turkey Egg Rolls (p. 28)
♦ Iced tea

Practical Tips

👌 The Turkey Stir-Fry is a breeze to make with leftover holiday turkey. In case you don't have any, buy a pound of turkey tenderloins. To cook them for this recipe, place them on a rack in a roasting pan and bake in a 350° oven for 20-30 minutes or until a meat thermometer reads 170°.

👌 To round out the stir-fry, serve it with long grain rice.

Light Bites & Beverages

The next time you're in the mood for a satisfying snack or a thirst-quenching beverage, try one of the tempting treats or refreshing drinks on the following pages. They're anything but lightweight in taste!

Beef 'n' Cheese Dip (page 29)

Cauliflower Hors d'oeuvres

These crispy baked tidbits are an appealing alternative to deep-fried fare. A coating of Parmesan cheese, Worcestershire sauce, basil and ground mustard infuses a burst of flavor into each bite. I make these appetizers for parties at our condo, and it's always the first plate to be emptied.
—Dorothy MacNeill, St. Petersburg, Florida

8 cups cauliflowerets (about 3 pounds)
1/2 cup egg substitute
2 tablespoons butter *or* stick margarine, melted
2 teaspoons Worcestershire sauce
1 teaspoon ground mustard
1 cup seasoned bread crumbs
1/3 cup grated Parmesan cheese
1/4 teaspoon dried basil
1/8 teaspoon salt
1/8 teaspoon pepper
1/8 teaspoon paprika
Meatless spaghetti sauce, warmed, optional

Place 1 in. of water and cauliflower in a saucepan; bring to a boil. Reduce heat; cover and simmer for 5 minutes. Drain and immediately place cauliflower in ice water. Drain and pat dry.
   In a small bowl, combine the egg substitute, butter, Worcestershire sauce and mustard. In another bowl, combine bread crumbs, Parmesan cheese, basil, salt, pepper and paprika. Dip cauliflower into the egg mixture, then coat with the crumb mixture. Place in two ungreased 15-in. x 10-in. x 1-in. baking pans. Bake at 350° for 30-35 minutes or until golden. Serve with spaghetti sauce for dipping if desired. **Yield:** 14 servings.

   Nutritional Analysis: One serving (1/2 cup cauliflower) equals 76 calories, 3 g fat (2 g saturated fat), 6 mg cholesterol, 319 mg sodium, 8 g carbohydrate, 2 g fiber, 4 g protein.
   Diabetic Exchanges: 1 vegetable, 1/2 starch, 1/2 fat.

Consider Cauliflower

YOU won't find this flower in a spring bouquet, but it should show up regularly on your dinner plate.
   Cauliflower, which means "cabbage flower", is indeed a flower as well as a member of the cabbage family. Its bunches of tiny florets may not be that lovely to look at, but they pack a pretty punch of vitamin C.
   Here are a few tasty tips to chew on:
● When buying cauliflower, choose a firm heavy head with crisp green leaves and tightly packed florets.
● You can store cauliflower, tightly wrapped, in the refrigerator for up to 5 days. Don't wash it until you're ready to use it.
● Cauliflower can be boiled, baked, sauteed or steamed. Or serve it raw in salads or with dips.
● A cup of cooked florets has 29 calories, 3 grams of fiber, 5 grams of carbohydrate and a trace of fat.

Seafood Nachos

(Pictured above)

I love seafood and sometimes order the seafood nacho appetizer at our local Mexican restaurant as my entree. I've tried many times to duplicate those tasty morsels at home—this recipe comes close!
—Linda McKee, Big Prairie, Ohio

30 baked tortilla chips
1 package (8 ounces) imitation crabmeat, chopped
1/4 cup reduced-fat sour cream
1/4 cup reduced-fat mayonnaise
2 tablespoons finely chopped onion
1/4 teaspoon dill weed
1 cup (4 ounces) shredded reduced-fat cheddar cheese
1/4 cup sliced ripe olives
1/4 teaspoon paprika

Arrange the tortilla chips in a single layer on an ungreased baking sheet. In a bowl, combine the crab, sour cream, mayonnaise, onion and dill; spoon about 1 tablespoon onto each chip. Sprinkle with the cheese, olives and paprika. Bake at 350° for 6-8 minutes or until the cheese is melted. **Yield:** 6 servings.

   Nutritional Analysis: One serving (5 nachos) equals 190 calories, 9 g fat (3 g saturated fat), 25 mg cholesterol, 531 mg sodium, 16 g carbohydrate, 1 g fiber, 13 g protein.
   Diabetic Exchanges: 1 starch, 1 lean meat, 1 fat.

Chili Popcorn

*For munching anytime, this savory snack is a fun
alternative to popcorn with lots of salt and butter.
It gets nice zip from a coating of chili powder,
garlic powder and Parmesan cheese.*
—Mildred Davis, Hagerstown, Maryland

    2 tablespoons grated Parmesan cheese
    2 teaspoons paprika
    2 teaspoons chili powder
1-1/2 teaspoons salt
    1/2 teaspoon garlic powder
    1/8 teaspoon cayenne pepper
2-1/2 quarts popped popcorn
Refrigerated butter-flavored spray*

In a large resealable plastic bag or other 2-qt. airtight container, combine the Parmesan cheese and seasonings; mix well. Add popcorn; spritz with butter-flavored spray. Close bag and shake. Continue spritzing and shaking until popcorn is coated. **Yield:** 5 servings.

   *Editor's Note: This recipe was tested with I Can't Believe It's Not Butter Spray.

   Nutritional Analysis: One serving (2 cups) equals 79 calories, 2 g fat (1 g saturated fat), 2 mg cholesterol, 761 mg sodium, 14 g carbohydrate, 3 g fiber, 3 g protein.
   Diabetic Exchange: 1 starch.

Healthy Snack Mix

*For a crunchy tasty snack mix that's perfect for
parties or to take along to satisfy the "munchies",
give this nutty whole-grain version a try.*
—Cindy Giovanetti, Argyle, Texas

    6 tablespoons egg substitute
    3 tablespoons sesame seeds, toasted
    2 tablespoons Worcestershire sauce
    1 tablespoon seasoned salt
    1 tablespoon fat-free cheese-flavored sprinkles*
1-1/2 teaspoons onion powder
1-1/2 teaspoons garlic powder
    1 teaspoon prepared mustard
    1 package (16 ounces) Wheat Chex
    1/3 cup *each* toasted almonds, salted cashews and
         dry-roasted peanuts

In a large bowl, whisk first eight ingredients. Add cereal and nuts; toss gently until coated. Spread onto two 15-in. x 10-in. x 1-in. baking pans coated with nonstick cooking spray. Bake at 250° for 20 minutes. Stir to break apart large pieces. Bake 30 minutes longer or until dried, stirring every 15 minutes. Spread on waxed paper-lined baking sheets to cool. Store in an airtight container. **Yield:** 18 servings.

   *Editor's Note: This recipe was tested with Molly McButter fat free natural cheese flavor sprinkles. Look for it in the spice aisle of your local grocery store.

   Nutritional Analysis: One serving (1/2 cup) equals 147 calories, 5 g fat (1 g saturated fat), trace cholesterol, 536 mg sodium, 23 g carbohydrate, 4 g fiber, 5 g protein.
   Diabetic Exchanges: 1-1/2 starch, 1 fat.

Fruity Yogurt Ice Pops

(Pictured below)

*Kids will have fun cooling off when temperatures
soar with these sweet treats from our Test
Kitchen. The strawberry-pineapple pops are
so yummy, youngsters won't even guess
that they're good for them, too!*

2 cups (16 ounces) reduced-fat strawberry yogurt
1 can (8 ounces) unsweetened crushed pineapple
1 tablespoon honey
2 to 3 drops red food coloring, optional

In a food processor or blender, combine yogurt, pineapple, honey and food coloring if desired; cover and process until smooth. Pour 1/4 cupfuls into 10 plastic molds or 3-oz. paper cups; top with holders or insert wooden sticks. Freeze until firm, about 8 hours or overnight. **Yield:** 10 servings.

   Nutritional Analysis: One yogurt ice pop equals 61 calories, trace fat (trace saturated fat), 4 mg cholesterol, 24 mg sodium, 13 g carbohydrate, trace fiber, 2 g protein.
   Diabetic Exchange: 1 fruit.

Frank 'n' Swiss Crescents

(Pictured below)

Kids of all ages will enjoy these adorable appetizers from our Test Kitchen. The savory bite-size snacks are quick to assemble with convenient crescent dough, hot dogs and Swiss cheese. Serve additional mustard alongside for dipping.

1 tube (8 ounces) refrigerated reduced-fat crescent rolls
2 tablespoons Dijon mustard
1/2 cup shredded reduced-fat Swiss cheese
1/2 teaspoon salt-free seasoning blend
8 reduced-fat hot dogs

Unroll crescent roll dough and separate into eight triangles. Cut each piece into two triangles. Spread each triangle with mustard; sprinkle with cheese and seasoning blend.

Cut rounded ends from hot dogs (discard or save for another use). Cut hot dogs in half widthwise; place one piece on the end of each triangle and roll up. Place pointed side down 2 in. apart on a baking sheet coated with nonstick cooking spray. Bake at 375° for 15-18 minutes or until golden brown. Serve warm. **Yield:** 16 appetizers.

Nutritional Analysis: One appetizer equals 94 calories, 4 g fat (1 g saturated fat), 15 mg cholesterol, 453 mg sodium, 7 g carbohydrate, trace fiber, 7 g protein.
Diabetic Exchanges: 1/2 starch, 1/2 lean meat.

Granola Fruit Bars

My family prefers these chewy wholesome bars to store-bought granola bars. They combine apple and peanut butter to make a great grab-and-go breakfast or anytime snack.
—Kim Finup, Kalamazoo, Michigan

1/2 cup chopped dried apples
1/3 cup honey
1/4 cup raisins
1 tablespoon brown sugar
1/3 cup reduced-fat peanut butter
1/4 cup apple butter
1/2 teaspoon ground cinnamon
1/2 cup old-fashioned oats
1/3 cup honey crunch *or* toasted wheat germ*
1/4 cup chopped pecans
2-1/2 cups cornflakes

In a large saucepan, combine the apples, honey, raisins and brown sugar. Bring to a boil over medium heat, stirring often. Cook and stir 1 minute longer. Remove from the heat; stir in peanut butter until melted. Add apple butter and cinnamon. Stir in the oats, wheat germ and pecans. Fold in cornflakes.

Press firmly into an 8-in. square pan coated with nonstick cooking spray. Refrigerate for 1 hour or until set. Cut into bars. Store in an airtight container in the refrigerator. **Yield:** 8 servings.

*Editor's Note: This recipe was tested with Kretschmer honey crunch wheat germ.

Nutritional Analysis: One bar equals 239 calories, 7 g fat (1 g saturated fat), 0 cholesterol, 160 mg sodium, 42 g carbohydrate, 3 g fiber, 6 g protein.
Diabetic Exchanges: 2 fruit, 1 starch, 1 fat.

Baked Sausage Wontons

These bite-size appetizers offer a nice change from the usual party fare. It takes a little effort to assemble them, but the shells can be made ahead and frozen to cut party prep time.
—Karen Rolfe, Dayton, Ohio

1/2 pound bulk pork sausage
1/2 cup finely shredded carrot
1/4 cup finely chopped water chestnuts
2 teaspoons cornstarch
1/2 teaspoon ground ginger *or* 2 teaspoons minced fresh gingerroot
1/3 cup chicken broth
1 tablespoon sherry *or* additional chicken broth
1 tablespoon reduced-sodium soy sauce
40 wonton wrappers

In a nonstick skillet, cook sausage over medium heat until no longer pink; drain. Stir in carrot and water chestnuts. In a bowl, combine cornstarch and ginger. Stir in the broth, sherry or additional broth and soy sauce until smooth. Stir into sausage mixture. Bring to a boil; cook and stir for 1-2 minutes or until thickened.

Gently press wonton wrappers into miniature muffin cups coated with nonstick cooking spray. Lightly coat wontons

with nonstick cooking spray. Bake at 350° for 5 minutes. Remove wontons from cups and arrange upside down on baking sheets. Lightly coat with nonstick cooking spray. Bake 5 minutes longer or until light golden. Turn wontons; fill each with about 1 teaspoon sausage mixture. Bake for 2-3 minutes or until filling is heated through. **Yield:** 40 wontons.

Nutritional Analysis: One serving (2 wontons) equals 77 calories, 2 g fat (1 g saturated fat), 10 mg cholesterol, 196 mg sodium, 10 g carbohydrate, trace fiber, 3 g protein.
Diabetic Exchange: 1 starch.

Texas Caviar

(Pictured above)

My neighbor gave me a container of this zippy, tangy salsa one Christmas and I had to have the recipe. I fix it regularly for potlucks and get-togethers and never have leftovers. I take copies of the recipe with me wherever I take the salsa.
—*Kathy Faris, Lytle, Texas*

1 can (15-1/2 ounces) black-eyed peas, rinsed
   and drained
3/4 cup chopped sweet red pepper
3/4 cup chopped green pepper
3 green onions, chopped
1 medium onion, chopped
1/4 cup minced fresh parsley
1 jar (2 ounces) diced pimientos, drained

1 garlic clove, minced
1 bottle (8 ounces) fat-free Italian salad dressing
Baked tortilla chips

In a bowl, combine the first nine ingredients; cover and refrigerate for 24 hours. Serve with tortilla chips. **Yield:** 4 cups.

Nutritional Analysis: One serving (1/2 cup dip with 8 chips) equals 148 calories, 1 g fat (trace saturated fat), 1 mg cholesterol, 661 mg sodium, 30 g carbohydrate, 5 g fiber, 5 g protein.
Diabetic Exchanges: 1-1/2 starch, 1 vegetable.

Banana Mocha Cooler

This thick milk shake-like beverage is delicious, with its big banana and coffee flavor. The recipe makes a cool satisfying snack or a change-of-pace drink to go with a casual meal.
—*Cassandra Corridon, Frederick, Maryland*

1 cup reduced-fat frozen vanilla yogurt
3/4 cup fat-free milk
1 medium ripe banana, sliced
1 teaspoon instant coffee granules
1 cup ice cubes (7 to 8)

In a blender, combine all ingredients. Cover and process for 45-60 seconds or until frothy. Pour into glasses; serve immediately. **Yield:** 3 servings.

Nutritional Analysis: One serving (1 cup) equals 122 calories, 1 g fat (1 g saturated fat), 5 mg cholesterol, 72 mg sodium, 24 g carbohydrate, 1 g fiber, 6 g protein.
Diabetic Exchanges: 1 reduced-fat milk, 1/2 fruit.

Asparagus Spanakopita

(Pictured below)

Fresh asparagus gives traditional Greek spinach pie a tasty twist in this recipe. Served with a mild dill sauce, these crispy light squares make a perfect first course for a special-occasion dinner.
—Dean Paraskeva, La Mesa, California

2 cups cut fresh asparagus (1-inch pieces)
20 sheets phyllo dough
Nonstick cooking spray
Refrigerated butter-flavored spray*
2 cups torn fresh spinach
3 ounces crumbled feta cheese
2 tablespoons butter *or* stick margarine
1/4 cup all-purpose flour
1-1/2 cups fat-free milk
3 tablespoons lemon juice
1 teaspoon dill weed
1 teaspoon dried thyme
1/4 teaspoon salt

Place asparagus in a steamer basket. Place over 1 in. of water in a saucepan; bring to a boil. Cover and steam for 5 minutes or until crisp-tender. Cut phyllo dough sheets into 13-in. x 9-in. rectangles. Place one sheet in a 13-in. x 9-in. x 2-in. baking dish coated with nonstick cooking spray; spritz dough with butter-flavored spray. Repeat layers nine times. Arrange spinach, feta cheese and asparagus over the top. Cover with a sheet of phyllo dough; spritz with butter-flavored spray. Repeat, using remaining phyllo. Cut into 12 pieces. Bake, uncovered, at 350° for 30-35 minutes or until golden brown.

For the sauce, melt butter in a saucepan. Stir in the flour until smooth; gradually add milk. Stir in the lemon juice, dill, thyme and salt. Bring to a boil; cook and stir for 1-2 minutes or until thickened. Serve spanakopita over the sauce.

Yield: 12 servings.
*****Editor's Note:** This recipe was tested with I Can't Believe It's Not Butter Spray.

Nutritional Analysis: *One serving (1 piece with 2 tablespoons sauce) equals 112 calories, 4 g fat (2 g saturated fat), 12 mg cholesterol, 242 mg sodium, 15 g carbohydrate, 1 g fiber, 5 g protein.*
Diabetic Exchanges: *1 starch, 1/2 fat.*

Cinnamon Toasties

These cinnamon squares really hit the spot served hot from the oven. Someone gave my mother the recipe a few years ago, and everyone raves about it. Kids love the cream cheese-filled snacks, especially when they're cut in cookie-cutter shapes.
—Diane Marshall, Winston-Salem, North Carolina

8 slices bread
1/4 cup reduced-fat cream cheese
Refrigerated butter-flavored spray*
3 tablespoons sugar
1-1/2 teaspoons ground cinnamon

Flatten bread with a rolling pin. Spread the cream cheese on one side of half of the slices; top with the remaining bread. Cut each into four squares. Spritz both sides with butter-flavored spray. In a small bowl, combine the sugar and cinnamon; add bread squares and turn to coat both sides. Place on an ungreased baking sheet. Bake at 350° for 8-10 minutes or until puffed and golden. Serve immediately.
Yield: 4 servings.
*****Editor's Note:** This recipe was tested with I Can't Believe It's Not Butter Spray.

Nutritional Analysis: *One serving (4 squares) equals 233 calories, 5 g fat (2 g saturated fat), 9 mg cholesterol, 368 mg sodium, 41 g carbohydrate, 2 g fiber, 7 g protein.*

Berry Fruity Punch

(Pictured above right)

I created this fun punch for a summer boat trip last year...and it was a big hit. Melons and pineapple are a lovely complement to raspberries and strawberries in this refreshing thirst-quencher.
—Phyllis Shaughnessy, Livonia, New York

2 cups unsweetened pineapple juice
2 cups fresh *or* frozen unsweetened raspberries
2 cups fresh strawberries

Transfer to a serving bowl; garnish with reserved oranges. Refrigerate until serving; serve with fruit. **Yield:** 12 servings.

Nutritional Analysis: One serving (1/4 cup dip, calculated without fruit) equals 95 calories, 5 g fat (3 g saturated fat), 16 mg cholesterol, 102 mg sodium, 9 g carbohydrate, trace fiber, 4 g protein.
Diabetic Exchanges: 1 fat, 1/2 reduced-fat milk.

Feta Olive Dip

Feta cheese, garlic and ripe olives, along with a hint of hot sauce, give a Greek salad-like flavor to this distinctive dip. Besides pita chips, it's terrific with crackers, tortilla chips, pita bread, pretzels and carrot and celery sticks.
—Debbie Burton, Callander, Ontario

   4 ounces reduced-fat cream cheese
1/2 cup crumbled feta cheese
1/2 cup reduced-fat sour cream
1/4 cup sliced ripe olives
   2 garlic cloves, minced
   2 teaspoons dried oregano
   1 teaspoon minced fresh parsley
1/4 teaspoon salt
1/4 to 1/2 teaspoon hot pepper sauce
Baked pita chips

In a food processor or blender, combine the first nine ingredients; cover and process until blended. Transfer to a bowl. Cover and refrigerate for at least 1 hour before serving. Serve with pita chips. **Yield:** about 1-1/2 cups.

Nutritional Analysis: One serving (2 tablespoons dip, calculated without pita chips) equals 56 calories, 4 g fat (3 g saturated fat), 14 mg cholesterol, 183 mg sodium, 2 g carbohydrate, trace fiber, 3 g protein.
Diabetic Exchange: 1 fat.

   2 cups cubed honeydew
   1 cup cubed seedless watermelon
3/4 cup sugar
1/2 teaspoon ground ginger
   4 cups diet ginger ale, chilled
   1 cup lime juice, chilled
1/2 cup lemon juice, chilled

In a blender or food processor, process the pineapple juice, berries and melon in batches. Strain and transfer fruit mixture to a punch bowl or large pitcher. Stir in sugar and ginger. Add the ginger ale, lime and lemon juices. Serve immediately over crushed ice. **Yield:** 11 cups.

Nutritional Analysis: One serving (1 cup) equals 121 calories, trace fat (trace saturated fat), 0 cholesterol, 27 mg sodium, 31 g carbohydrate, 3 g fiber, 1 g protein.
Diabetic Exchange: 2 fruit.

Mandarin Orange Fruit Dip

I created this creamy dip to serve to guests at my daughter's first birthday party. It's deliciously different and was a hit with kids and adults. I sometimes layer it with fruit in parfait glasses for a change of pace.
—Nancy LeBano, Stratford, New Jersey

   1 package (8 ounces) reduced-fat cream cheese, cubed
   2 cups (16 ounces) reduced-fat vanilla yogurt
   1 teaspoon vanilla extract
   1 can (11 ounces) mandarin oranges, drained
Assorted fresh fruit

In a mixing bowl, beat cream cheese until creamy. Add yogurt and vanilla; beat until smooth. Set aside three orange segments for garnish. In a small bowl, mash remaining oranges with a fork; drain. Stir into cream cheese mixture.

Cheesy Bagel Bites

Here's a simple recipe that adds zippy flavor to everyday bagels. It's a speedy method for filling up a snack tray in a nutritious way...and emptying it even quicker!
—Becky Ruff, Monona, Iowa

1/3 cup reduced-fat mayonnaise
1/4 cup grated Parmesan cheese
   1 tablespoon prepared mustard
   2 green onions, finely chopped
1/4 teaspoon garlic powder
   3 whole wheat bagels, split and toasted

In a small bowl, combine mayonnaise, Parmesan, mustard, onions and garlic powder. Spread over bagels. Place on a baking sheet. Broil 4-6 in. from the heat for 1-2 minutes or until golden brown and bubbly. Cut each bagel half into six pieces. **Yield:** 12 servings.

Nutritional Analysis: One serving (3 pieces) equals 105 calories, 3 g fat (1 g saturated fat), 4 mg cholesterol, 248 mg sodium, 16 g carbohydrate, 3 g fiber, 4 g protein.
Diabetic Exchanges: 1 starch, 1/2 fat.

Nutritional Analysis: One serving (2 slices of bread with 2 tablespoons pepper mixture) equals 161 calories, 5 g fat (1 g saturated fat), 0 cholesterol, 408 mg sodium, 26 g carbohydrate, 2 g fiber, 4 g protein.
Diabetic Exchanges: 1-1/2 starch, 1 vegetable, 1/2 fat.

Gazpacho Salsa

I combine fresh veggies, garbanzo beans and purchased salsa in this zippy party dip. Served with tortilla chips, it's a surefire crowd-pleaser. I've been making this recipe for years.
—Betty Hatfield, Aurora, Colorado

2 cups V8 juice
1 pound tomatoes, seeded and chopped
1 can (15 ounces) garbanzo beans *or* chickpeas, rinsed and drained
1 cup fresh *or* frozen corn
1 medium green pepper, chopped
1 small cucumber, diced
1/2 cup salsa
1/4 cup chopped green onions
1 tablespoon lime juice
2 garlic cloves, minced
1/2 teaspoon sugar
1/8 teaspoon pepper

In a bowl, combine all ingredients. Cover and refrigerate for at least 1 hour. **Yield:** 14 servings.

Nutritional Analysis: One serving (1/2 cup) equals 69 calories, 1 g fat (trace saturated fat), 0 cholesterol, 221 mg sodium, 14 g carbohydrate, 3 g fiber, 3 g protein.
Diabetic Exchanges: 1 vegetable, 1/2 starch.

Red Pepper Bruschetta

(Pictured above)

Roasted red peppers take the place of tomatoes in this twist on traditional bruschetta developed by our Test Kitchen staff. If your bakery doesn't offer baguettes, buy regular French bread instead, then cut the slices in half to create the crunchy snacks.

1 whole garlic bulb
1 teaspoon plus 2 tablespoons olive *or* canola oil, *divided*
2 medium sweet red peppers, halved and seeded
3 tablespoons minced fresh parsley
2 tablespoons minced fresh basil *or* 2 teaspoons dried basil
1 tablespoon lemon juice
1/2 teaspoon salt
1/4 teaspoon pepper
1 French bread baguette (about 12 ounces)

Remove papery outer skin from garlic bulb (do not peel or separate the cloves). Brush with 1 teaspoon of oil. Wrap in heavy-duty foil. Bake at 425° for 30-35 minutes or until softened. Cool.

Broil red peppers 4 in. from the heat until skins blister, about 10 minutes. Immediately place peppers in a bowl; cover with plastic wrap and let stand for 15-20 minutes. Peel off and discard charred skin. Coarsely chop peppers. Cut top off garlic head, leaving root end intact. Squeeze softened garlic from bulb and finely chop.

In a bowl, combine the parsley, basil, lemon juice, salt, pepper and remaining oil. Add peppers and garlic; mix well. Cut bread into 16 slices, 1/2 in. thick; toast under broiler until lightly browned. Top with pepper mixture. Serve immediately. **Yield:** 8 servings.

🍎 Pineapple Pointers

YOU CAN polish up your pineapple knowledge with these particulars from the Dole Food Company:

● Pineapples are fat- and cholesterol-free, low in sodium and high in vitamin C. A serving size of two slices (3 inches in diameter, 3/4 inch thick) has 60 calories.

● You can purchase fresh-cut pineapple in the refrigerated area of the produce section. It should be stamped with a "use by" date that indicates freshness for at least a week.

● Store whole pineapple in the refrigerator for 2-4 days. Cut pineapple should be kept in an airtight container in the refrigerator.

● To prepare a whole pineapple, cut or twist off the crown, cut the pineapple in half and then into quarters. Trim off both ends and remove core from center of each quarter. Using a thin paring knife, remove shell from fruit. Cut fruit into pieces.

● To make pineapple "boats", leave on the crown and both ends of the pineapple. Cut the pineapple in half lengthwise. Use a thin paring knife to cut out fruit from each half, leaving shell intact. Fill boats with fruit salad, main dish salad or sherbet.

Grilled Pork Appetizers

(Pictured below)

People can't seem to get enough of these tender hors d'oeuvres. Marinated in a sauce that is slightly sweetened with honey, the party starters also make a wonderful entree when served over rice.
—Susan LeBrun, Sulphur, Louisiana

1 pound boneless pork loin roast
3 tablespoons reduced-sodium soy sauce
3 tablespoons honey
1 tablespoon lemon juice
1 tablespoon canola oil
3 garlic cloves, minced
1/2 teaspoon ground ginger

Cut pork into 1/8-in. slices, then cut each slice widthwise in half. In a large resealable plastic bag, combine the remaining ingredients; add the pork. Seal bag and turn to coat; refrigerate for 2-4 hours, turning occasionally.

If grilling the kabobs, coat grill rack with nonstick cooking spray before starting the grill. Drain and discard marinade. Thread pork onto metal or soaked wooden skewers. Grill, uncovered, over medium heat or broil 4-6 in. from the heat for 2-3 minutes on each side or until meat juices run clear, turning once. **Yield:** 8 servings.

Nutritional Analysis: One serving (2 ounces cooked pork) equals 84 calories, 3 g fat (1 g saturated fat), 29 mg cholesterol, 80 mg sodium, 2 g carbohydrate, trace fiber, 11 g protein.
Diabetic Exchange: 2 lean meat.

Tropical Pineapple Smoothies

My children and I often blend "milk shakes" like this tropical refresher. To make the shakes healthier, we substitute fat-free milk and ice cubes for the ice cream. They are fast and nutritious!
—Polly Coumos, Mogadore, Ohio

1 cup fat-free milk
1 can (8 ounces) unsweetened crushed pineapple
1/2 cup unsweetened pineapple juice
3 tablespoons sugar
1/2 teaspoon vanilla extract
1/4 teaspoon coconut extract
6 ice cubes

Place the first six ingredients in a blender; cover and process until smooth. Add ice cubes; cover and process until smooth. **Yield:** 3 servings.

Nutritional Analysis: One serving (1 cup) equals 126 calories, trace fat (trace saturated fat), 2 mg cholesterol, 45 mg sodium, 29 g carbohydrate, 1 g fiber, 3 g protein.
Diabetic Exchanges: 1 fruit, 1/2 fat-free milk, 1/2 starch.

Fabulous Fruit Spread

Our Test Kitchen concocted this citrusy cream cheese spread accented with bits of dried fruit and tangy grated orange peel. Serve it as a snacking spread on low-fat crackers or for breakfast on English muffins or bagels.

1 cup (8 ounces) fat-free cottage cheese
1 package (8 ounces) reduced-fat cream cheese, cubed
1 tablespoon orange juice
1/2 teaspoon grated orange peel
1/2 cup assorted dried fruit, chopped
Toast *or* English muffins

In a food processor, combine the first four ingredients; cover and process until smooth. Stir in fruit. Spread on toast or English muffins. Store leftovers in the refrigerator. **Yield:** 20 servings.

Nutritional Analysis: One serving (2 tablespoons spread) equals 44 calories, 2 g fat (1 g saturated fat), 7 mg cholesterol, 71 mg sodium, 4 g carbohydrate, trace fiber, 3 g protein.
Diabetic Exchange: 1/2 reduced-fat milk.

Fudge Slush

If you're a fan of hot chocolate in winter, you'll crave this creamy "cold cocoa" on a sultry summer's day. Young and old alike will savor every icy sip of the thick fudgy drink created by our Test Kitchen home economists.

3/4 cup sugar
1/2 cup baking cocoa
2-2/3 cups plus 2 tablespoons 1% milk, *divided*

In a saucepan, combine sugar and cocoa. Gradually stir in 2-2/3 cups milk; cook and stir over low heat until sugar is dissolved. Pour into a shallow pan or ice cube trays. Cover and freeze for 6 hours or overnight.

Break frozen mixture into chunks; place in a blender or food processor. Add remaining milk; cover and process until smooth and slushy. **Yield:** 6 servings.

Nutritional Analysis: One serving (1/2 cup) equals 164 calories, 2 g fat (1 g saturated fat), 7 mg cholesterol, 61 mg sodium, 35 g carbohydrate, 2 g fiber, 6 g protein.
Diabetic Exchanges: 2 starch, 1/2 reduced-fat milk.

Saucy Turkey Meatballs

It's easy to turn lean ground turkey into these moist, tender meatballs. Ideal for informal gatherings of family and friends, the appetizers feature a tangy sauce that my guests find delicious.
—Janell Fugitt, Cimarron, Kansas

1 cup old-fashioned oats
3/4 cup fat-free evaporated milk
1 medium onion, chopped
1 teaspoon salt
1 teaspoon chili powder
1/4 teaspoon garlic salt
1/4 teaspoon pepper
1-1/2 pounds lean ground turkey
SAUCE:
2 cups ketchup
1-1/2 cups packed brown sugar
1/4 cup chopped onion
2 tablespoons liquid smoke
1/2 teaspoon garlic salt

In a bowl, combine the first seven ingredients. Crumble turkey over mixture and mix well. Shape into 1-in. balls. Place in a 13-in. x 9-in. x 2-in. baking dish coated with nonstick cooking spray. Bake, uncovered, at 350° for 10-15 minutes. Combine the sauce ingredients; pour over meatballs. Bake 30-35 minutes longer or until meat is no longer pink. **Yield:** 15 servings.

Nutritional Analysis: One serving (3 meatballs) equals 217 calories, 4 g fat (1 g saturated fat), 36 mg cholesterol, 695 mg sodium, 36 g carbohydrate, 1 g fiber, 10 g protein.
Diabetic Exchanges: 2 starch, 1 lean meat.

Turkey Crescent Wreath

(Pictured above)

When hosting a get-together the day after Thanksgiving one year, I prepared this using leftover turkey.
—Jane Jones, Cedar, Minnesota

2 cups diced cooked turkey breast
1 cup (4 ounces) shredded reduced-fat Swiss cheese
1/2 cup dried cranberries
1/2 cup diced celery
1/2 cup fat-free mayonnaise
1/4 cup chopped walnuts
3 tablespoons minced fresh parsley
2 tablespoons honey mustard*
1/2 teaspoon pepper
2 tubes (8 ounces *each***) reduced-fat refrigerated crescent rolls**
1 egg white, lightly beaten

In a large bowl, combine the first nine ingredients. Coat a 14-in. pizza pan with nonstick cooking spray. Separate crescent dough into 16 triangles. Place wide end of 1 triangle 3 in. from edge of prepared pan with point overhanging edge of pan. Repeat with remaining triangles along outer edge of pan, overlapping the wide ends (dough will look like a sun when complete). Lightly press wide ends together.

Spoon turkey mixture over the wide ends of dough. Fold the points of the triangles over the filling and tuck under wide ends (filling will be visible). Brush with egg white. Bake at 375° for 20-25 minutes or until golden brown. **Yield:** 16 servings.

*Editor's Note: As a substitute for honey mustard, combine 1 tablespoon Dijon mustard and 1 tablespoon honey.

Nutritional Analysis: One serving equals 171 calories, 7 g fat (1 g saturated fat), 18 mg cholesterol, 373 mg sodium, 17 g carbohydrate, 1 g fiber, 10 g protein.
Diabetic Exchanges: 1 starch, 1 lean meat, 1 fat.

Blue Cheese Appetizer Pizza

(Pictured below)

This mouth-watering recipe makes enough for two pizzas. Loaded with crumbled blue cheese, slices are always popular at card parties and New Year's Eve gatherings.
—Kathy Stanaway, DeWitt, Michigan

1 loaf (1 pound) frozen bread dough, thawed
3 tablespoons olive *or* canola oil, *divided*
2 teaspoons dried basil
2 teaspoons dried oregano
1 teaspoon garlic powder
1 small red onion, thinly sliced and separated into rings
2 plum tomatoes, chopped
1 cup (4 ounces) shredded part-skim mozzarella cheese, *divided*
3 ounces crumbled blue cheese
2 tablespoons grated Parmesan cheese

Divide bread dough in half. Press each portion onto the bottom of a 12-in. pizza pan coated with nonstick cooking spray; build up edges slightly. Prick dough several times with a fork. Cover and let rise in a warm place for 30 minutes.

Brush dough with oil. Combine the basil, oregano and garlic powder; sprinkle over dough. Bake at 425° for 10 minutes. Arrange onion and tomatoes over crusts; sprinkle with cheeses. Bake 8-10 minutes longer or until golden brown. **Yield:** 2 pizzas (10 slices each).

Nutritional Analysis: One slice equals 118 calories, 5 g fat (2 g saturated fat), 7 mg cholesterol, 228 mg sodium, 13 g carbohydrate, 1 g fiber, 5 g protein.
Diabetic Exchanges: 1 starch, 1 fat.

Mini Rice Cake Snacks

(Pictured below)

Our Test Kitchen staff had a ball dressing up sweet rice cakes with a simple spread and colorful fruits. Try them with a combination of your favorite flavors.

3 ounces reduced-fat cream cheese
1/4 cup orange marmalade
24 miniature honey-nut *or* cinnamon-apple rice cakes
2 medium fresh strawberries, sliced
3 tablespoons fresh blueberries
3 tablespoons mandarin orange segments
3 tablespoons pineapple tidbits

In a small mixing bowl, combine the cream cheese and marmalade until blended. Spread over rice cakes; top with fruit. **Yield:** 2 dozen.

Nutritional Analysis: One serving (3 rice cakes) equals 81 calories, 2 g fat (1 g saturated fat), 6 mg cholesterol, 57 mg sodium, 15 g carbohydrate, 1 g fiber, 2 g protein.
Diabetic Exchanges: 1/2 starch, 1/2 fruit.

No-Bake Almond Bites

To help keep holiday snacking on the skinny side, our Test Kitchen home economists whipped up these simple little sensations. Quick and easy, the chewy no-bake treats are ideal when time is tight.

30 reduced-fat vanilla wafers, finely crushed
1 cup confectioners' sugar, *divided*
1/2 cup chopped almonds
2 tablespoons baking cocoa
2 tablespoons corn syrup
2 tablespoons apple juice
1/4 teaspoon almond extract

In a large bowl, combine the wafer crumbs, 1/2 cup confectioners' sugar, almonds and cocoa. In a small bowl, combine the corn syrup, apple juice and extract. Stir into crumb mixture until well blended. Shape into 1-in. balls; roll in remaining sugar. Store in an airtight container. **Yield:** 1-1/2 dozen.

Nutritional Analysis: One piece equals 81 calories, 2 g fat (trace saturated fat), 0 cholesterol, 25 mg sodium, 15 g carbohydrate, 1 g fiber, 1 g protein.
Diabetic Exchanges: *1 starch, 1/2 fat.*

Mexican Mocha Mix

(Pictured below)

This mix of coffee and cocoa is a wonderful alternative to traditional hot chocolate. It nicely rounds out a spicy meal.
—Maria Regakis, Somerville, Massachusetts

3/4 cup baking cocoa
2/3 cup sugar

2/3 cup packed brown sugar
1/2 cup nonfat dry milk powder
1/3 cup instant coffee granules
3/4 teaspoon ground cinnamon
1/4 teaspoon ground allspice
ADDITIONAL INGREDIENTS (for each serving):
1 cup hot fat-free milk
1 cinnamon stick, optional

In a blender, combine the first seven ingredients; cover and process until mixture forms a powder. Store in an airtight container. **Yield:** about 2-1/4 cups mix.

To prepare mocha drink: In a mug, stir 3 tablespoons mix with 1 cup hot milk until blended. Garnish with a cinnamon stick if desired. **Yield:** 1 serving.

Nutritional Analysis: One serving equals 207 calories, 1 g fat (1 g saturated fat), 6 mg cholesterol, 172 mg sodium, 40 g carbohydrate, 2 g fiber, 12 g protein.

Mock Strawberry Cheesecake Treat

Whenever I have a taste for cheesecake, I know just how to "berry" my craving. I head to the fridge and mix up this pretty strawberry dessert. Sometimes, instead of sprinkling crumbs on top, I'll dip a whole graham cracker in the yummy fluff!
—Kay Dispensire, Baton Rouge, Louisiana

3 tablespoons fat-free whipped topping
2 tablespoons reduced-fat cream cheese
Sugar substitute equivalent to 2 teaspoons sugar
1/4 cup chopped fresh strawberries
1 graham cracker square (2-1/2 inches x 2-1/2 inches), crumbled

In a small dessert dish, combine the whipped topping, cream cheese and sugar substitute until smooth. Stir in the strawberries; sprinkle with the cracker crumbs. **Yield:** 1 serving.

Nutritional Analysis: One serving equals 137 calories, 6 g fat (3 g saturated fat), 17 mg cholesterol, 139 mg sodium, 16 g carbohydrate, 1 g fiber, 4 g protein.
Diabetic Exchanges: *1 starch, 1 fat.*

Phyllo Turkey Egg Rolls

(Pictured at right)

Here's a light twist on traditional egg rolls that are often stuffed with heavy fillings and then deep-fried. Your guests will never guess that these tasty bites are loaded with healthy ingredients.
—Kara De la vega, Suisun City, California

1 pound ground turkey breast
4 cups coleslaw mix (about 8 ounces)
1/4 cup chopped green onions

3 tablespoons reduced-sodium soy sauce
2 garlic cloves, minced
1/2 teaspoon Chinese five-spice powder
1/4 teaspoon ground ginger *or* 1 teaspoon
grated fresh gingerroot
12 phyllo dough sheets (18 inches x 14 inches)
Refrigerated butter-flavored spray*
Sweet-and-sour sauce *and/or* **hot mustard, optional**

Crumble turkey into a large nonstick skillet. Cook over medium heat until no longer pink; drain. Add the coleslaw mix, onions, soy sauce, garlic, five-spice powder and ginger. Cook for 2-3 minutes or until coleslaw is wilted. Remove from the heat.

Place one sheet of phyllo dough on a work surface with a long side facing you; spritz with butter spray and brush to evenly distribute. Repeat with two more sheets of phyllo, spritzing and brushing each layer. (Keep remaining phyllo dough covered with waxed paper to avoid drying out.)

Cut the stack widthwise into four 14-in. x 4-1/2-in. strips. Place 1/4 cup of turkey mixture along one short side of each rectangle. Fold in long sides; starting at the filling edge, roll up tightly. Place seam side down on ungreased baking sheets. Spritz top with butter spray. Repeat with remaining phyllo and filling.

Bake at 350° for 25-30 minutes, then broil 6 in. from the heat for 5 minutes or until golden brown. Serve warm with sweet-and-sour sauce and/or mustard if desired. **Yield:** 16 egg rolls.

***Editor's Note:** This recipe was tested with I Can't Believe It's Not Butter Spray.

Nutritional Analysis: One egg roll equals 108 calories, 4 g fat (1 g saturated fat), 22 mg cholesterol, 236 mg sodium, 12 g carbohydrate, 1 g fiber, 7 g protein.
Diabetic Exchanges: 1 starch, 1 lean meat.

Beef 'n' Cheese Dip

(Pictured above and on page 17)

I combined two favorite recipes and trimmed them down to create this yummy fondue-type dip. It's great for receptions, parties and get-togethers. It was a hit with the guys at our house last Christmas!
—Heather Melnick, Macedon, New York

1 package (8 ounces) reduced-fat cream cheese
1-1/2 cups (6 ounces) shredded reduced-fat cheddar
cheese
1/2 cup fat-free sour cream
2 packages (2-1/2 ounces *each*) thinly sliced
dried beef, diced
1/2 cup chopped green onions
1/2 cup mild pepper rings, drained and chopped*
2 teaspoons Worcestershire sauce
1 loaf (1 pound) unsliced round rye bread
Assorted raw vegetables

In a mixing bowl, combine the cream cheese, cheddar cheese and sour cream. Stir in the beef, onions, peppers and Worcestershire sauce. Cut the top fourth off the loaf of bread; carefully hollow out bottom, leaving a 1-in. shell. Cube removed bread and top of loaf; set aside.

Fill bread shell with beef mixture. Wrap in foil; place on a baking sheet. Bake at 350° for 60-70 minutes or until heated through. Serve with vegetables and reserved bread cubes. **Yield:** 3 cups.

***Editor's Note:** Mild pepper rings come in jars and can be found in the pickle and olive aisle of most grocery stores.

Nutritional Analysis: One serving (3 tablespoons dip) equals 159 calories, 6 g fat (4 g saturated fat), 22 mg cholesterol, 386 mg sodium, 16 g carbohydrate, 2 g fiber, 9 g protein.
Diabetic Exchanges: 1 starch, 1 lean meat, 1/2 fat.

Apple Salsa with Cinnamon Chips

(Pictured below)

For a fun treat that's sure to be requested at all your parties, try this appetizer. The salsa offers good-for-you fruits, and the crunchy home-baked chips are a healthy alternative to commercial snacks.
—*Courtney Fons, Brighton, Michigan*

6 flour tortillas (8 inches)
3 tablespoons sugar
1-1/2 teaspoons ground cinnamon
4 cups finely chopped Granny Smith *or* other tart apples (about 2 medium)
1 cup finely chopped ripe pear
1/2 cup quartered seedless red grapes
1/2 cup chopped celery
1/4 cup chopped walnuts
3 tablespoons orange juice
1 tablespoon brown sugar
2 teaspoons grated orange peel

Coat both sides of each tortilla with nonstick cooking spray. Combine the sugar and cinnamon; sprinkle over both sides of tortillas. Cut each into eight wedges. Place on baking sheets. Bake at 400° for 4-5 minutes or until crisp. Meanwhile, for salsa, combine remaining ingredients in a bowl. Serve with cinnamon chips. **Yield:** 12 servings.

Nutritional Analysis: *One serving (1/2 cup salsa with 4 chips) equals 141 calories, 3 g fat (trace saturated fat), 129 mg sodium, 0 cholesterol, 26 g carbohydrate, 1 g fiber, 3 g protein.*
Diabetic Exchanges: *1 starch, 1 fruit, 1/2 fat.*

🍎 Tips on Delicious Dippers

A GOOD-FOR-YOU dip or spread deserves an equally nutritious dipper. Line a party platter with finger foods like these instead of high-fat crackers and chips:

● Raw veggies are a natural. Try varying celery sticks, baby carrots, mushrooms, cherry tomatoes, red or green pepper slices, steamed whole green beans, steamed asparagus spears, or broccoli and cauliflower florets.
● In-season fruits can be sweet dippers and eye-catching, too. Arrange scooped-out balls of honeydew melon or cantaloupe, whole strawberries, pineapple chunks and apple and banana slices around the dip.
● And don't forget fat-free crackers or pretzels, melba toast rounds, rice cakes, pita triangles, baked tortilla chips and thin-sliced French bread.

Hot Mulled Pineapple Drink

This is a fun way to use pineapple juice. I like to serve this tasty hot beverage in tall mugs and top each drink with a whole clove pressed into a lemon slice.
—*Margaret Wagner Allen, Abingdon, Virginia*

1 can (48 ounces) unsweetened pineapple juice
1 cup reduced-calorie cranberry juice
1/3 cup sugar
1/3 cup packed brown sugar
1 teaspoon ground cinnamon
1/4 teaspoon ground nutmeg
1/8 teaspoon ground cloves
1 medium lemon, sliced
7 cinnamon sticks

In a large saucepan, combine the first seven ingredients. Bring to a boil. Reduce heat; simmer, uncovered, for 15 minutes. Strain. Garnish each serving with a lemon slice and cinnamon stick. **Yield:** 7 servings.

Nutritional Analysis: *One serving (1 cup) equals 192 calories, trace fat (trace saturated fat), 0 cholesterol, 7 mg sodium, 48 g carbohydrate, 1 g fiber, 1 g protein.*
Diabetic Exchanges: *2 fruit, 1 starch.*

Cucumber-Dill Shrimp Dip

(Pictured above right)

This is a favorite standby of mine when I need a quick appetizer. The creamy dill dip, with chunks of shrimp and cucumber, makes a nice change from the standard shrimp and cocktail sauce.
—*Kathyrn Goecke, Montrose, Colorado*

3/4 cup reduced-fat sour cream
4 ounces reduced-fat cream cheese, cubed
1 tablespoon snipped fresh dill *or* 1 teaspoon dill weed

1/4 teaspoon salt
6 ounces cooked medium shrimp, peeled and deveined
3/4 cup diced unpeeled cucumber
Assorted fresh vegetables and crackers

In a mixing bowl, beat the sour cream, cream cheese, dill and salt until smooth. Set aside three shrimp and 2 tablespoons cucumber for garnish. Finely chop the remaining shrimp; add to sour cream mixture. Add remaining cucumber. Garnish with reserved shrimp and cucumbers. Refrigerate for at least 1 hour. Serve with vegetables or crackers. **Yield:** 8 servings.

Nutritional Analysis: One serving (1/4 cup dip) equals 82 calories, 5 g fat (3 g saturated fat), 45 mg cholesterol, 158 mg sodium, 3 g carbohydrate, trace fiber, 5 g protein.
Diabetic Exchanges: 1 lean meat, 1/2 fat.

Ranch Tortilla Roll-Ups

(Pictured at right)

Curb hunger in a hurry with these zesty roll-ups. They are great as picnic nibbles, dinner appetizers and football party munchies. When my husband's co-workers at the state patrol come over for meals, they admit "low-fat" can be delicious.
—Karen Thomas, Berlin, Pennsylvania

**2 packages (8 ounces *each*) fat-free cream cheese, softened
1 envelope ranch salad dressing mix
2 to 3 jalapeno peppers, finely chopped*
1 jar (2 ounces) diced pimientos, drained
8 flour tortillas (8 inches)**

In a small mixing bowl, combine the cream cheese, salad dressing mix, jalapenos and pimientos; mix well. Spread over tortillas. Roll up tightly; wrap each in plastic wrap. Refrigerate for at least 1 hour. Unwrap and cut each tortilla into eight pieces. **Yield:** 16 servings.

*Editor's Note: When cutting or seeding hot peppers, use rubber or plastic gloves to protect your hands. Avoid touching your face.

Nutritional Analysis: One serving (4 pieces) equals 106 calories, 2 g fat (1 g saturated fat), 2 mg cholesterol, 419 mg sodium, 15 g carbohydrate, trace fiber, 6 g protein.
Diabetic Exchanges: 1 starch, 1/2 fat.

Hot Spinach Artichoke Dip

(Pictured above)

No one will ever suspect that this creamy party classic is lower in fat than the much-loved original. The combination of artichoke hearts, spinach and Parmesan cheese gives it great flavor.
—*Michelle Wentz, Fort Polk, Louisiana*

1 small onion, finely chopped
2 packages (10 ounces *each*) frozen chopped
  spinach, thawed and squeezed dry
1 package (8 ounces) fat-free cream cheese,
  cubed
1 cup (8 ounces) reduced-fat sour cream
1 can (14 ounces) water-packed artichoke hearts,
  drained and chopped
3/4 cup grated Parmesan cheese
1/4 teaspoon salt
1/8 teaspoon pepper
1/8 to 1/4 teaspoon crushed red pepper flakes
1/4 cup shredded reduced-fat cheddar cheese
Assorted reduced-fat melba toast *or* pita chips

In a large nonstick skillet coated with nonstick cooking spray, cook and stir onion until tender. Add spinach; cook and stir over medium heat until heated through. Reduce heat to low; stir in cream cheese and sour cream. Add the artichoke hearts, Parmesan cheese, salt, pepper and red pepper flakes; cook for 1-2 minutes or until heated through.
  Transfer to an ungreased 1-1/2-qt. microwave-safe dish; sprinkle with cheddar cheese. Cover and microwave on high for 2-3 minutes or until cheese is melted. Serve warm with melba toast or pita chips. **Yield:** 18 servings.

Nutritional Analysis: One serving (1/4 cup dip) equals 71 calories, 3 g fat (2 g saturated fat), 9 mg cholesterol, 342 mg sodium, 6 g carbohydrate, 2 g fiber, 6 g protein.
  Diabetic Exchanges: 1 lean meat, 1 vegetable.

Cereal Crunchies

Folks can't get enough of this irresistible snack mix. A slightly sweet vanilla coating is the perfect match for the blend of mini pretzels, crispy cereal and salted nuts. It's a real crowd-pleaser.
—*Juanita Carlsen, North Bend, Oregon*

2 cups Multi-Bran Chex
2 cups Corn Chex
2 cups Cheerios
2 cups miniature pretzels
1 cup salted mixed nuts
1/3 cup reduced-fat margarine
1/3 cup packed brown sugar
1/4 cup light corn syrup
  2 to 3 teaspoons butter flavoring
1-1/2 teaspoons salt
  2 tablespoons vanilla extract
1/4 teaspoon baking soda

In a large microwave-safe bowl, combine the cereals, pretzels and nuts; set aside. In a large saucepan, combine the margarine, brown sugar, corn syrup, butter flavoring and salt. Bring to a boil. Boil, uncovered, for 5 minutes. In a small bowl, combine vanilla and baking soda. Remove brown sugar syrup from the heat; stir in vanilla mixture (syrup will foam). Pour over cereal mixture and toss to coat.
  Microwave, uncovered, on high for 3 minutes; stir. Microwave 3 minutes longer; stir. Microwave at 50% power for 3-4 minutes, stirring after 2 minutes. Cool for 3 minutes, stirring well several times. Spread onto waxed paper to cool.
Yield: 8-1/2 cups.
  Editor's Note: This recipe was tested in an 850-watt microwave.

Nutritional Analysis: One serving (1/2 cup) equals 153 calories, 7 g fat (1 g saturated fat), 0 cholesterol, 446 mg sodium, 23 g carbohydrate, 2 g fiber, 3 g protein.
  Diabetic Exchanges: 1-1/2 starch, 1 fat.

Spiced Wassail

This recipe for a delicious blend of fruit juices is perked up with cinnamon, nutmeg and cloves. It appears on many of my holiday menus.
—*Sylvia Ford, Kennett, Missouri*

1 quart unsweetened apple juice
3 cups unsweetened pineapple juice
2 cups reduced-calorie cranberry juice
1 medium navel orange, sliced
1 medium lemon, sliced
1/4 teaspoon ground nutmeg
3 whole cloves
1 cinnamon stick (3 inches), broken

In a saucepan, combine all ingredients; bring to a boil. Reduce heat; simmer, uncovered, for 10 minutes. Discard the orange and lemon slices, cloves and cinnamon stick before serving. **Yield:** 8 servings.

Nutritional Analysis: One serving (1 cup) equals 129 calories, 1 g fat (trace saturated fat), 0 cholesterol, 7 mg sodium, 31 g carbohydrate, 1 g fiber, trace protein.
  Diabetic Exchange: 2 fruit.

Favorite Appetizer Recipe Made Lighter

SUMMER picnics and potlucks would hardly be complete without a platter of creamy deviled eggs. Velma Berger of Nappanee, Indiana has served a classic version of this hearty finger food at many gatherings. Her Deviled Eggs have a mouth-watering filling that includes mustard and mayonnaise.

If you'd like to dig into these "egg-cellent" morsels but would prefer less cholesterol and fat and fewer calories, check out our Test Kitchen's recipe for Makeover Deviled Eggs.

Their revised version uses only half of the egg yolks of the original recipe and calls for soft bread crumbs to help firm up the filling. The mayonnaise was replaced with fat-free mayonnaise and reduced-fat sour cream.

These tempting deviled eggs have all the goodness of the originals but with two-thirds less fat and saturated fat and just half the calories and cholesterol!

Deviled Eggs

    8 hard-cooked eggs
1/2 cup mayonnaise *or* salad dressing
    1 tablespoon milk
    1 teaspoon prepared mustard
1/4 teaspoon salt
Paprika

Cut eggs in half lengthwise; remove yolks and set whites aside. In a small bowl, mash yolks. Add the mayonnaise, milk, mustard and salt; mix well. Stuff or pipe into egg whites. Sprinkle with paprika. **Yield:** 8 servings.

Nutritional Analysis: One serving (2 halves) equals 151 calories, 12 g fat (3 g saturated fat), 217 mg cholesterol, 229 mg sodium, 3 g carbohydrate, trace fiber, 6 g protein.

Makeover Deviled Eggs

(Pictured at left)

    8 hard-cooked eggs
1/4 cup fat-free mayonnaise *or* salad dressing
1/4 cup reduced-fat sour cream
    2 tablespoons soft bread crumbs
    1 tablespoon prepared mustard
1/4 teaspoon salt
Dash white pepper
    3 stuffed olives, sliced

Slice eggs in half lengthwise and remove yolks; refrigerate eight yolk halves for another use. Set whites aside. In a small bowl, mash remaining yolks. Add the mayonnaise, sour cream, bread crumbs, mustard, salt and pepper; mix well. Stuff or pipe into egg whites. Garnish with olives. **Yield:** 8 servings.

Nutritional Analysis: One serving (2 halves) equals 74 calories, 4 g fat (1 g saturated fat), 109 mg cholesterol, 264 mg sodium, 4 g carbohydrate, trace fiber, 6 g protein.
Diabetic Exchanges: 1 lean meat, 1/2 fat.

Meaty Salsa Dip

White corn adds sweetness, and salsa brings a little zip to this hearty meat-and-bean blend. The recipe became an instant family favorite after my daughter served it at a birthday party. It's a snap to make, and guests gobble it up just as fast.
—Bobbe Hart, Holyoke, Massachusetts

1 pound lean ground turkey
1 can (15 ounces) black beans, rinsed and drained
1 package (10 ounces) frozen white corn, thawed
1 jar (16 ounces) chunky salsa
Baked tortilla chips

In a nonstick skillet, cook turkey over medium heat until no longer pink; drain. In a serving bowl, combine the turkey, beans, corn and salsa. Serve with tortilla chips. **Yield:** 12 servings.

Nutritional Analysis: One serving (1/2 cup dip) equals 108 calories, 1 g fat (trace saturated fat), 19 mg cholesterol, 397 mg sodium, 13 g carbohydrate, 3 g fiber, 11 g protein.
Diabetic Exchanges: 1 vegetable, 1 lean meat, 1/2 starch.

Cheesy Pita Crisps

(Pictured below)

I first made these golden wedges when my college roommates and I wanted garlic bread but had only pitas on hand. My husband likes this "skinny" version even better than the original!
—Christine Mattiko, Dallastown, Pennsylvania

2 whole wheat pita breads (6 inches)
1/4 cup reduced-fat margarine, melted
1/2 teaspoon garlic powder
1/2 teaspoon onion powder
1/4 teaspoon salt
1/4 teaspoon pepper

3 tablespoons grated Parmesan cheese
1/2 cup shredded part-skim mozzarella cheese

Split each pita bread into two rounds. Cut each round into four triangles; place inside side up on a baking sheet coated with nonstick cooking spray. In a bowl, combine the margarine, garlic powder, onion powder, salt and pepper; stir in the Parmesan cheese. Spread over triangles. Sprinkle with mozzarella cheese. Bake at 400° for 12-15 minutes or until golden brown. **Yield:** 8 servings.

Nutritional Analysis: One serving (2 triangles) equals 95 calories, 5 g fat (2 g saturated fat), 6 mg cholesterol, 264 mg sodium, 9 g carbohydrate, 1 g fiber, 4 g protein.
Diabetic Exchanges: 1 fat, 1/2 starch.

Creamy Fruit Dip

(Pictured above)

After one taste of this delightful dip, your fruit tray won't seem complete without it. My family enjoys this recipe just as much as they did when I prepared it with full-fat ingredients.
—Judith Reed, Kingsford, Michigan

1 package (8 ounces) fat-free cream cheese
3/4 cup packed brown sugar
1 cup (8 ounces) reduced-fat sour cream
2 teaspoons vanilla extract
1 teaspoon lemon extract
1/2 teaspoon ground cinnamon
1 cup cold 2% milk
1 package (3.4 ounces) instant vanilla pudding mix
Assorted fresh fruit

In a small mixing bowl, beat the cream cheese and brown sugar until smooth. Beat in the sour cream, extracts and cinnamon until smooth. Add milk; mix well. Add pudding mix; beat on low speed for 2 minutes. Cover and refrigerate for at least 1 hour. Serve with fruit. **Yield:** about 3-1/2 cups.

Nutritional Analysis: One serving (1/4 cup dip) equals 118 calories, 2 g fat (2 g saturated fat), 8 mg cholesterol, 211 mg sodium, 21 g carbohydrate, trace fiber, 4 g protein.
Diabetic Exchange: 1-1/2 starch.

Cheese-Stuffed Jalapenos

Folks gobble up these taste-tempting stuffed peppers. They have a crisp golden coating, cheesy center and pleasantly spicy flavor. The best part is that no one realizes they are low in fat, too.
—Gay Nell Nicholas, Henderson, Texas

    1 package (8 ounces) fat-free cream cheese, cubed
    1 cup (4 ounces) shredded reduced-fat cheddar cheese
  1/4 cup fat-free mayonnaise
    1 garlic clove, minced
  1/2 teaspoon dried oregano
   18 jalapeno peppers (about 3 inches long), halved lengthwise and seeded*
    2 egg whites
    1 tablespoon fat-free milk
1-1/2 cups crushed cornflakes

In a small mixing bowl, combine the first five ingredients; beat until blended. Spoon into pepper halves, packing tightly. In a shallow bowl, whisk egg whites and milk. Place cornflakes in another shallow bowl. Dip peppers into egg mixture, then coat with cornflakes. Place on a baking sheet coated with nonstick cooking spray. Bake at 350° for 30 minutes or until browned. **Yield:** 9 servings.

Editor's Note: When cutting or seeding hot peppers, wear rubber or plastic gloves to protect your hands. Avoid touching your face.

Nutritional Analysis: One serving (1 appetizers) equals 127 calories, 3 g fat (2 g saturated fat), 10 mg cholesterol, 441 mg sodium, 17 g carbohydrate, 1 g fiber, 10 g protein.
Diabetic Exchanges: 1 starch, 1 lean meat.

🍎 The Heat's on with Jalapenos

A POPULAR PICK among pepper lovers, the jalapeno is a thumb-sized, tapering, smooth-skinned chili pepper with thick flesh and deep green color. Red versions are jalapenos that have been allowed to ripen and are considerably hotter.

A green jalapeno is moderately hot to hot with its "bite" contained mostly in the seeds and membranes. This is where capsaicin—the compound that gives chilies their fiery flavor—is produced. Since capsaicin's intensity isn't affected by cooking, removing the chilie's seeds and veins is the best way to "turn down the heat".

Fruity Granola

(Pictured below)

When you get a craving for a wholesome snack, go with our Test Kitchen's granola. You'll love the chewy sweetness of the honeyed cereal, fruit and nut mixture. It's great as a snack out of hand or in a parfait glass, layered with low-fat yogurt.

    3 cups old-fashioned oats
  1/2 cup sliced almonds
1-1/4 cups honey
  1/2 cup Grape-Nuts
    1 tablespoon butter *or* stick margarine
    1 teaspoon ground cinnamon
2-1/2 cups Wheaties
  1/2 cup dried cranberries
  1/2 cup raisins
  1/2 cup dried banana chips

Combine oats and almonds; spread evenly in a 15-in. x 10-in. x 1-in. baking pan coated with nonstick cooking spray. Bake at 325° for 15 minutes. In a large bowl, combine the honey, Grape-Nuts, butter and cinnamon. Add oat mixture; stir to combine. Return mixture to the pan. Bake 15-20 minutes longer or until golden. Cool on a wire rack.

When cool enough to handle, break granola into pieces. Place in a large bowl; stir in the Wheaties, cranberries, raisins and banana chips. Store in an airtight container in a cool dry place for up to 2 months. **Yield:** 10 cups.

Nutritional Analysis: One serving (1/2 cup) equals 183 calories, 4 g fat (1 g saturated fat), 2 mg cholesterol, 51 mg sodium, 38 g carbohydrate, 3 g fiber, 3 g protein.
Diabetic Exchanges: 1-1/2 fruit, 1 starch, 1/2 fat.

Crab-Filled Veggie Bites

(Pictured below)

Whenever I go to a party, friends and family hope I bring these appetizers with me. The crab filling is also good piped onto celery or used as a cracker spread.
—Debbie Bloomer, Omaha, Nebraska

- 12 cherry tomatoes
- 12 fresh snow peas
- 1 can (6 ounces) crabmeat, drained, flaked and cartilage removed *or* 1 cup finely chopped imitation crabmeat
- 2 tablespoons reduced-fat cream cheese
- 1 tablespoon finely chopped green onion
- 2 teaspoons reduced-fat sour cream
- 2 teaspoons chili sauce
- 1 teaspoon lemon juice
- 1/2 teaspoon prepared horseradish

Cut the top off each tomato; scoop out the pulp with a small spoon and discard. Invert tomatoes on paper towels to drain; let stand for 1-3 hours.

Place 1 in. of water in a saucepan; add snow peas. Bring to a boil. Reduce heat; cover and simmer for 1-2 minutes or until crisp-tender. Drain and immediately place peas in ice water. Drain and pat dry; refrigerate.

In a bowl, combine the remaining ingredients; mix well. Using a sharp knife, make a slit down the side of each pea pod. Fill peas and tomatoes with crab mixture. Arrange on a serving platter; cover and refrigerate for at least 30 minutes. **Yield:** 4 servings.

Nutritional Analysis: *One serving (3 filled tomatoes and 3 filled snow peas) equals 82 calories, 2 g fat (1 g saturated fat), 43 mg cholesterol, 254 mg sodium, 5 g carbohydrate, 1 g fiber, 10 g protein.*
Diabetic Exchanges: *1 very lean meat, 1 vegetable, 1/2 fat.*

Mediterranean Salsa

(Pictured above)

When entertaining, I rely on this make-ahead dish that's full of peppers, eggplant and zucchini. Low in sodium, it gets its delicious flair from garlic, basil and thyme. We like it on homemade bagel chips.
—Margaret Potempa, Oshkosh, Wisconsin

- 2 cups cubed peeled eggplant (1/2-inch cubes)
- 1 cup cubed sweet red pepper (1/2-inch cubes)
- 1 cup cubed green pepper (1/2-inch cubes)
- 1 cup cubed zucchini (1/2-inch cubes)
- 3 garlic cloves, minced
- 2 tablespoons olive *or* canola oil
- 1 large tomato, cut into 1/2-inch cubes
- 2 tablespoons cider vinegar
- 1 tablespoon dried basil
- 1 teaspoon dried thyme
- 1/2 teaspoon sugar
- 1/2 teaspoon salt
- 1/4 to 1/2 teaspoon coarsely ground pepper
Toasted bread rounds

In a large nonstick skillet, saute the eggplant, peppers, zucchini and garlic in oil for 8 minutes. Add the tomato, vinegar, basil, thyme, sugar, salt and pepper. Cook 4-5 minutes longer or until vegetables are tender. Cover and refrigerate for at least 4 hours. Serve with toasted bread. **Yield:** about 2-1/2 cups.

Nutritional Analysis: *One serving (1/4 cup salsa) equals 45 calories, 3 g fat (trace saturated fat), 0 cholesterol, 121 mg sodium, 5 g carbohydrate, 1 g fiber, 1 g protein.*
Diabetic Exchanges: *1 vegetable, 1/2 fat.*

Simmer Up a Souper Bowl!

Soups are naturally nutritious, oh-so flavorful
and sure to please in any season. Whether
it's a cool soup in summer or a steaming
pot of hearty chowder on a winter's day,
soup is good for the body—and the spirit!

Summer Vegetable Soup (page 42)

Black Bean Zucchini Gazpacho

(Pictured below)

My family enjoys chilled soups during the hot summer months. I came up with this spicy blend when trying to use up our garden zucchini. It's a hit with friends whenever I serve it, too.
—Julie Wilson, Grand Rapids, Ohio

  3 cans (5-1/2 ounces *each*) spicy hot V8 juice
  1 can (15 ounces) black beans, rinsed and drained
  1 medium onion, chopped
  2 large tomatoes, seeded and chopped
  2 medium zucchini, chopped
  2 tablespoons olive *or* canola oil
  2 tablespoons white wine vinegar *or* cider vinegar
  1 garlic clove, minced
1/4 teaspoon salt
1/4 teaspoon pepper
1/4 teaspoon cayenne pepper

In a large bowl, combine all ingredients. Cover and refrigerate for 8 hours or overnight. **Yield:** 6 servings.

Nutritional Analysis: One serving (1 cup) equals 149 calories, 5 g fat (1 g saturated fat), 0 cholesterol, 574 mg sodium, 20 g carbohydrate, 6 g fiber, 6 g protein.
Diabetic Exchanges: 2 vegetable, 1 fat, 1/2 starch.

Tart Cherry Soup

(Pictured above)

A hint of cinnamon spices up this sweet-tart soup. I serve this refreshing chilled concoction as a light first course...or for dessert, topped with a dollop of nonfat yogurt or reduced-fat whipped topping.
—Neva Arthur, New Berlin, Wisconsin

  2 cans (14-1/2 ounces *each*) water-packed pitted tart cherries
1/2 cup orange juice
1/2 cup sugar
  2 tablespoons lime juice
  1 teaspoon grated lime peel
1/2 teaspoon ground cinnamon
  4 lime slices

Place the cherries in a blender or food processor; cover and process until finely chopped. Transfer to a saucepan; add the orange juice, sugar, lime juice, peel and cinnamon. Bring to a boil. Reduce heat; cover and simmer for 10 minutes. Refrigerate until chilled. Garnish with lime slices. **Yield:** 4 servings.

Nutritional Analysis: One serving (1 cup) equals 198 calories, 1 g fat (1 g saturated fat), 0 cholesterol, 15 mg sodium, 49 g carbohydrate, 3 g fiber, 2 g protein.
Diabetic Exchanges: 1-1/2 starch, 1-1/2 fruit.

In a large saucepan or Dutch oven, saute the chicken, onion, celery, carrots and garlic in butter and oil for 5 minutes. Stir in the flour, basil, oregano and pepper until blended. Gradually add broth and tomatoes. Bring to a boil. Reduce heat; cover and simmer for 1 hour. Return to a boil; stir in the pasta. Reduce heat; simmer, uncovered, for 12-15 minutes or until pasta is tender. **Yield:** 9 servings.

Nutritional Analysis: One serving (1 cup) equals 193 calories, 8 g fat (3 g saturated fat), 36 mg cholesterol, 652 mg sodium, 16 g carbohydrate, 2 g fiber, 15 g protein.
Diabetic Exchanges: 1 starch, 1 lean meat, 1 fat.

Curly Noodle Chicken Soup

(Pictured above)

Diners will ladle out praises all around the table when you serve this flavorful soup. My husband and three sons can't get enough of it. I created this recipe for a dinner I hosted for a group of friends. The main course was Italian, and I needed a good soup, so I converted a favorite tortilla soup recipe by substituting pasta and adding different seasonings.
—Maxine Pierson, San Ramon, California

  1 pound boneless skinless chicken breasts,
     cut into 1/2-inch pieces
  1 large onion, chopped
  4 celery ribs, sliced
  2 medium carrots, sliced
  4 garlic cloves, minced
  2 tablespoons butter *or* stick margarine
  2 tablespoons olive *or* canola oil
1/4 cup all-purpose flour
  1 teaspoon dried basil
1/2 teaspoon dried oregano
1/8 teaspoon pepper
  3 cans (14-1/2 ounces *each*) chicken broth
  1 can (14-1/2 ounces) diced tomatoes, undrained
  6 ounces uncooked tricolor spiral pasta

Basil Tomato Soup

Corn dresses up this quick and easy tomato soup. My husband and two sons, who don't always care for soup, like this as much as I do.
—Alice Culberson, Kingsport, Tennessee

1/2 cup uncooked small shell pasta
3/4 cup chopped red onion
3/4 cup diced celery
  3 garlic cloves, minced
  4 teaspoons olive *or* canola oil
3/4 cup fresh *or* frozen corn, thawed
4-1/2 cups vegetable broth
  1 to 2 tablespoons minced fresh basil leaves
3/4 teaspoon salt
1/8 teaspoon pepper
  6 medium firm tomatoes, peeled, seeded and chopped

Cook pasta according to package directions; drain and set aside. In a large saucepan, saute the onion, celery and garlic in oil for 8-10 minutes or until tender. Add corn; saute for 2 minutes. Add broth, basil, salt and pepper. Bring to a boil. Reduce heat; cover and simmer for 15 minutes. Stir in pasta and tomatoes; heat through. **Yield:** 7 servings.

Nutritional Analysis: One serving (1 cup) equals 112 calories, 4 g fat (trace saturated fat), 0 cholesterol, 919 mg sodium, 19 g carbohydrate, 2 g fiber, 4 g protein.
Diabetic Exchanges: 1 vegetable, 1 starch, 1/2 fat.

🍎 The Basics of Basil

THE PEPPERY, almost licorice-like flavor of basil enhances a wide range of foods and is a favorite seasoning around the world.

A few of the most common varieties of this aromatic herb are sweet basil, dwarf basil, Italian or curly basil, purple basil and lemon basil.

To store fresh basil, wrap it in barely damp paper towels, then in a plastic bag for up to 4 days. To keep for a week, place basil stems in a glass of water, cover with a plastic bag and refrigerate. Be sure to change the water daily.

Roasted Chicken Noodle Soup

(Pictured below)

When the weather turns chilly around here, I stock my soup pot with this warmer-upper. The creamy, nicely seasoned broth is chock-full of tender chicken, potatoes, carrots and celery. There's old-fashioned goodness in every spoonful of this thick, hearty soup!
—Julie Wallberg, Reno, Nevada

  1 cup chopped onion
  1 cup chopped carrots
  1 cup chopped celery
  1 garlic clove, minced
  2 teaspoons olive *or* canola oil
1/4 cup all-purpose flour
1/2 teaspoon dried oregano
1/4 teaspoon dried thyme
1/4 teaspoon poultry seasoning
  6 cups reduced-sodium chicken broth
  4 cups diced peeled uncooked potatoes
  1 teaspoon salt
  2 cups diced roasted chicken breast
  2 cups uncooked yolk-free wide noodles
  1 cup fat-free evaporated milk

In a Dutch oven or soup kettle, saute the onion, carrots, celery and garlic in oil for 5 minutes or until tender. Stir in the flour, oregano, thyme and poultry seasoning until blended; saute 1 minute longer. Gradually add broth, potatoes and salt; bring to a boil. Reduce heat; cover and simmer for 15-20 minutes or until potatoes are tender.

Stir in the chicken and noodles; simmer for 10 minutes or until noodles are tender. Reduce heat. Stir in the milk; heat through (do not boil). **Yield:** 8 servings.

Nutritional Analysis: One serving (1-1/2 cups) equals 235 calories, 3 g fat (1 g saturated fat), 31 mg cholesterol, 851 mg sodium, 33 g carbohydrate, 3 g fiber, 20 g protein.
Diabetic Exchanges: 2 very lean meat, 1-1/2 starch, 1 vegetable, 1/2 fat.

Lentil Vegetable Soup

Here is one good-for-you dish that our kids really enjoy. Serve this tasty soup as a hearty meatless entree... or pair it with a favorite sandwich.
—Joy Maynard, St. Ignatius, Montana

1/2 cup lentils, rinsed
  3 cans (14-1/2 ounces *each*) vegetable broth
1/2 cup uncooked long grain brown rice
  1 medium onion, chopped
1/2 cup tomato juice
  1 can (5-1/2 ounces) spicy tomato juice
  1 tablespoon reduced-sodium soy sauce
  1 tablespoon canola oil
  1 medium potato, peeled and diced
  1 medium tomato, diced
  1 medium carrot, sliced
  1 celery rib, sliced

In a saucepan, combine first eight ingredients. Bring to a boil. Reduce heat; cover and simmer for 30 minutes. Add potato, tomato, carrot and celery; simmer 30 minutes longer or until rice and vegetables are tender. **Yield:** 6 servings.

Nutritional Analysis: One serving (1 cup) equals 195 calories, 4 g fat (0 saturated fat), 0 cholesterol, 1,144 mg sodium, 34 g carbohydrate, 6 g fiber, 9 g protein.
Diabetic Exchanges: 2 starch, 1 vegetable, 1/2 fat.

Curry Carrot-Leek Soup

This recipe comes from an old Yorkshire cookbook I picked up in England, where leeks are very popular. The curry powder lends just the right amount of zip. I like to serve the soup with French bread, followed by scones with lemon curd for dessert.
—Valerie Engel, San Jose, California

  1 pound leeks, thinly sliced
  1 pound carrots, coarsely chopped
  2 teaspoons butter *or* stick margarine
  1 medium potato, peeled and diced
1/2 teaspoon curry powder
  4 cups reduced-sodium chicken broth
1/4 teaspoon salt
1/4 teaspoon pepper

In a large saucepan, saute leeks and carrots in butter until leeks are tender. Add potato and curry powder; cook and stir for 2 minutes. Add broth, salt and pepper; bring to a boil. Reduce heat; cover and simmer for 15-20 minutes or until the vegetables are very tender. Cool slightly. Process in

1 teaspoon ground ginger
1/2 teaspoon salt
1/2 cup fat-free milk

In a saucepan, saute onion and sage in butter for 3 minutes or until tender. Add the broth, water and apples; bring to a boil. Reduce heat; cover and simmer for 12 minutes. Add the squash, ginger and salt; return to a boil. Reduce heat; simmer, uncovered, for 10 minutes. Cool until lukewarm.

Process in batches in a blender or food processor until smooth; return to pan. Add milk; heat through. (Do not boil.) **Yield:** 5 servings.

Nutritional Analysis: One serving (1 cup) equals 142 calories, 6 g fat (3 g saturated fat), 13 mg cholesterol, 647 mg sodium, 22 g carbohydrate, 2 g fiber, 3 g protein.
Diabetic Exchanges: 1 fat, 1 starch, 1/2 fruit.

Corn and Pepper Chowder

Chunks of potato, kernels of corn and flecks of red pepper punctuate the creamy broth of this hearty chowder. Cilantro and cumin lend a Southwestern flavor. I got this recipe from someone I work with. It's quick and tasty.
—Donna Hackman, Huddleston, Virginia

1 large onion, chopped
1 medium sweet red pepper, chopped
1 teaspoon canola oil
3 tablespoons all-purpose flour
1/2 teaspoon ground cumin
2 cups water
1-1/3 cups cubed potatoes
1 teaspoon chicken bouillon granules
3/4 teaspoon salt
1/4 teaspoon white pepper
2 cups frozen corn
1 can (12 ounces) fat-free evaporated milk
1/4 cup minced fresh cilantro *or* parsley

In a saucepan, saute onion and red pepper in oil until tender. Stir in flour and cumin until blended. Gradually stir in water. Bring to a boil; cook and stir for 2 minutes or until thickened. Reduce heat; add the potatoes, bouillon, salt and pepper. Cover and cook for 10 minutes or until potatoes are tender. Add corn and milk. Cook, uncovered, 5 minutes longer or until heated through. Garnish with cilantro. **Yield:** 6 servings.

Nutritional Analysis: One serving (1 cup) equals 170 calories, 2 g fat (trace saturated fat), 2 mg cholesterol, 562 mg sodium, 33 g carbohydrate, 3 g fiber, 8 g protein.
Diabetic Exchanges: 1-1/2 starch, 1/2 fat-free milk.

batches in a food processor or blender until pureed. Return to the pan; heat through. **Yield:** 6 servings.

Nutritional Analysis: One serving (1 cup) equals 108 calories, 2 g fat (1 g saturated fat), 3 mg cholesterol, 579 mg sodium, 21 g carbohydrate, 1 g fiber, 1 g protein.
Diabetic Exchanges: 1 starch, 1 vegetable.

Apple Squash Soup

(Pictured above)

This is a new twist on an old favorite—pumpkin soup. I add a little ginger and sage to apples and squash to make this creamy soup. My family loves it when autumn rolls around.
—Crystal Ralph-Haughn, Bartlesville, Oklahoma

1 large onion, chopped
1/2 teaspoon rubbed sage
2 tablespoons butter *or* stick margarine
1 can (14-1/2 ounces) reduced-fat chicken broth
3/4 cup water
2 medium Granny Smith *or* other tart apples, peeled and finely chopped
1 package (12 ounces) frozen mashed squash, thawed

Summer Vegetable Soup

(Pictured below and on page 37)

This vegetable soup is chock-full of garden goodness, from zucchini and green beans to celery and potato, but it's the turmeric that gives it a tasty new twist.
—*Edith Ruth Muldoon, Baldwin, New York*

1 small onion, quartered and thinly sliced
1 tablespoon olive *or* canola oil
4 cups reduced-sodium chicken broth
1 cup sliced zucchini
1 can (15-1/2 ounces) navy beans, rinsed and drained
1/2 cup diced peeled red potato
1/2 cup cut fresh green beans (2-inch pieces)
1/2 cup chopped peeled tomato
1/4 teaspoon pepper
1/8 teaspoon ground turmeric
1/4 cup chopped celery leaves
2 tablespoons tomato paste

In a large saucepan, saute onion in oil until tender. Add the next eight ingredients. Bring to a boil. Reduce heat; cover and simmer for 20-30 minutes or until vegetables are tender. Stir in celery leaves and tomato paste. Cover and let stand for 5 minutes before serving. **Yield:** 4 servings.

Nutritional Analysis: One serving (1-1/2 cups) equals 210 calories, 4 g fat (1 g saturated fat), 0 cholesterol, 1,128 mg sodium, 32 g carbohydrate, 8 g fiber, 13 g protein.
    Diabetic Exchanges: 1-1/2 starch, 1 very lean meat, 1 vegetable, 1/2 fat.

Chilled Peach Soup

Here's a peachy way to begin a lady's luncheon or brunch. This refreshing soup stars my home state's premier fruit crop. The toasted almonds on top are a nice complement to the sweet-tart flavor. A serving of this fruit soup is surprisingly filling.
—*Lane McLoud, Perry, Georgia*

3 cups chopped peeled fresh peaches
1 cup (8 ounces) fat-free plain yogurt
1 teaspoon lemon juice
1/8 to 1/4 teaspoon almond extract
6 tablespoons sliced almonds, toasted
Fresh mint, optional

In a blender or food processor, combine the peaches, yogurt, lemon juice and extract; cover and process until smooth. Refrigerate until chilled. Garnish with almonds and mint if desired. **Yield:** 4 servings.

Nutritional Analysis: One serving (3/4 cup) equals 158 calories, 7 g fat (trace saturated fat), 1 mg cholesterol, 35 mg sodium, 22 g carbohydrate, 4 g fiber, 6 g protein.
    Diabetic Exchanges: 1 fat, 1 fruit, 1/2 fat-free milk.

🍎 Sweet Facts on Fruit Soups

FAVOR fruit smoothies? Then you're sure to savor fruit soups! They're refreshingly delicious and a snap to prepare.

There are two varieties. One version requires precooking, then chilling. The other is simply whirred in a blender or food processor. Both can be prepared in advance and easily modified.

No matter what ingredients you choose, the perfect blend should be a balance of sweet and tart.

Here are a few souped-up suggestions:
● Fruit soups benefit from being chilled overnight. You might have to add more seasoning after the soup sits.
● Chilled soups should be almost too thick to pour.

Favorite Soup Recipe Made Lighter

WHEN she's in the mood for comfort food, Melissa Sherlock of Omaha, Nebraska prepares a pot of Cheesy Ham 'n' Potato Soup. But she asked the home economists in our Test Kitchen to reduce the fat while keeping the great taste.

Their better-for-you version uses lean ham, canola oil, fat-free milk and reduced-fat cheddar cheese.

Additional potatoes, whirred in the food processor, plus dry milk powder help keep the soup's thick creamy texture.

Cheesy Ham 'n' Potato Soup

2 cups cubed potatoes
1-1/2 cups water
1-1/2 cups cubed fully cooked ham
1 large onion, chopped
3 tablespoons butter *or* margarine
3 tablespoons all-purpose flour
1/4 teaspoon pepper
3 cups milk
1-1/2 cups (6 ounces) finely shredded cheddar cheese
1 cup frozen broccoli florets, thawed and chopped

In a saucepan, bring potatoes and water to a boil. Cover and cook for 10-15 minutes or until tender. Drain, reserving 1 cup cooking liquid; set potatoes and liquid aside.

In a large saucepan, saute ham and onion in butter until onion is tender. Stir in the flour and pepper until smooth; gradually add milk and reserved cooking liquid. Bring to a boil; cook and stir for 2 minutes or until thickened. Reduce heat to low. Add the cheese, broccoli and reserved potatoes; cook and stir until cheese is melted and soup is heated through. **Yield:** 7 servings.

Nutritional Analysis: One serving (1 cup) equals 334 calories, 22 g fat (12 g saturated fat), 72 mg cholesterol, 614 mg sodium, 17 g carbohydrate, 1 g fiber, 18 g protein.

Makeover Cheesy Ham 'n' Potato Soup

(Pictured at right)

2-1/4 cups cubed potatoes
1-1/2 cups water
1-1/2 cups cubed fully cooked lean ham
1 large onion, chopped
2 teaspoons canola oil
1/4 cup nonfat dry milk powder
3 tablespoons all-purpose flour
1/4 teaspoon pepper
3 cups fat-free milk
1-1/2 cups (6 ounces) finely shredded reduced-fat cheddar cheese
1 cup frozen broccoli florets, thawed and chopped

In a saucepan, bring potatoes and water to a boil. Cover and cook for 10-15 minutes or until tender. Drain, reserving 1 cup cooking liquid. In a blender or food processor, process reserved liquid and 1/4 cup cooked potatoes until smooth; set aside. Set remaining potatoes aside.

In a large saucepan, saute ham and onion in oil until onion is tender. In a bowl, combine milk powder, flour, pepper, milk and processed potato mixture until smooth. Stir into ham and onion. Bring to a boil; cook and stir for 2 minutes or until thickened. Reduce heat to low. Add the cheese, broccoli and reserved potatoes; cook and stir over low heat until cheese is melted and heated through. Serve immediately. **Yield:** 7 servings.

Nutritional Analysis: One serving (1 cup) equals 228 calories, 8 g fat (4 g saturated fat), 36 mg cholesterol, 616 mg sodium, 21 g carbohydrate, 1 g fiber, 18 g protein.

Diabetic Exchanges: 2 lean meat, 1 starch, 1/2 fat-free milk.

In a large saucepan or Dutch oven, saute the carrots, zucchini, onion and red pepper in oil until crisp-tender. Add the broth, beans, tomatoes, corn, cumin and cayenne; bring to a boil. Reduce heat; simmer, uncovered, for 30-35 minutes or until vegetables are tender, stirring occasionally. Stir in cilantro. **Yield:** 6 servings.

Nutritional Analysis: One serving (1-1/2 cups) equals 285 calories, 5 g fat (trace saturated fat), 0 cholesterol, 1,356 mg sodium, 52 g carbohydrate, 11 g fiber, 13 g protein.
Diabetic Exchanges: 2-1/2 starch, 2 vegetable, 2 very lean meat.

Mushroom Barley Soup

This soup is a variation on one I found years ago in a health cookbook. It tastes so good, no one can believe how low in fat and salt it is! We love it served in a bread bowl...or with oven-fresh corn muffins on the side.
—Laura Christensen, Bountiful, Utah

 6 cups sliced fresh mushrooms
 2 large onions, chopped
 1 cup chopped celery
 1 cup chopped carrots
 5 cups water, *divided*
 4 cups cooked medium pearl barley
 4 cups beef broth
 4 teaspoons Worcestershire sauce
1-1/2 teaspoons salt
 1 teaspoon dried basil
 1 teaspoon dried parsley flakes
 1 teaspoon dill weed
 1 teaspoon dried oregano
 1/2 teaspoon salt-free seasoning blend
 1/2 teaspoon dried thyme
 1/2 teaspoon garlic powder

In a Dutch oven or soup kettle, combine the mushrooms, onions, celery, carrots and 1 cup water. Cook and stir over medium-high heat until vegetables are tender. Add the remaining ingredients; bring to a boil. Reduce heat; cover and simmer for 1 hour. **Yield:** 10 servings.

Nutritional Analysis: One serving (1-1/2 cups) equals 119 calories, 1 g fat (trace saturated fat), 0 cholesterol, 722 mg sodium, 25 g carbohydrate, 4 g fiber, 4 g protein.
Diabetic Exchanges: 2 vegetable, 1 starch.

Vegetable Bean Soup

(Pictured above)

Chock-full of vegetables and beans, this hearty soup is sure to satisfy your hungry bunch on a winter night. This soup is wonderfully easy to make and very tasty. In summer, use fresh produce from the garden or your local farmer's market. In winter, just use frozen or open some cans of veggies—it couldn't be simpler!
—Cathy Seed, Hudson, Ohio

 1 cup sliced carrots
 1 cup thinly sliced zucchini
3/4 cup chopped onion
1/2 cup chopped sweet red pepper
 1 tablespoon olive *or* canola oil
 2 cans (14-1/2 ounces *each*) vegetable broth
 1 can (16 ounces) kidney beans, rinsed and drained
 1 can (16 ounces) chili beans, undrained
 1 can (15 ounces) garbanzo beans *or* chickpeas, rinsed and drained
 1 can (14-1/2 ounces) stewed tomatoes, cut up
 1 cup frozen white *or* shoepeg corn
 4 teaspoons ground cumin
1/4 teaspoon cayenne pepper
 2 tablespoons minced fresh cilantro *or* parsley

Nutritional Analysis: One serving (1 cup) equals 290 calories, 7 g fat (4 g saturated fat), 30 mg cholesterol, 987 mg sodium, 36 g carbohydrate, 9 g fiber, 23 g protein.
Diabetic Exchanges: 2-1/2 starch, 2 lean meat.

Chilled Squash and Carrot Soup

(Pictured below)

This smooth soup is colorful as well as nutritious and filling. Served chilled, it makes an elegant first course when entertaining. But it's also good warm.
—*Elaine Sabacky, Litchfield, Minnesota*

1-1/2 pounds butternut squash, peeled, seeded and
　　　cubed (about 3 cups)
　　1 can (14-1/2 ounces) chicken broth
　　2 medium carrots, sliced
　　1 medium onion, chopped
　1/4 teaspoon salt
　1/2 cup fat-free evaporated milk
　　3 tablespoons reduced-fat sour cream

In a large saucepan, combine the squash, broth, carrots, onion and salt. Bring to a boil. Reduce heat; cover and simmer for 15-20 minutes or until vegetables are very tender. Remove from the heat; cool. In a blender or food processor, puree squash mixture in batches. Transfer to a bowl; stir in milk. Cover and chill until serving. Garnish with sour cream. **Yield:** 4 servings.

Nutritional Analysis: One serving (1-1/4 cups) equals 127 calories, 1 g fat (1 g saturated fat), 5 mg cholesterol, 637 mg sodium, 25 g carbohydrate, 5 g fiber, 6 g protein.
Diabetic Exchanges: 2 vegetable, 1 starch.

Skinny Tortilla Soup

(Pictured above)

Chock-full of healthy ingredients, this tasty soup makes a warming lunch or dinner. Plus, it's so quick and easy to fix. Family and friends will be surprised to hear that refried beans are the base of this slightly spicy soup.
—*Sharon Adams, Columbus, Ohio*

　　1 can (16 ounces) fat-free refried beans
　　1 can (15 ounces) black beans, rinsed and
　　　drained
　　1 can (14-1/2 ounces) reduced-sodium chicken
　　　broth
1-1/2 cups frozen corn
　3/4 cup chunky salsa
　3/4 cup cubed cooked chicken breast
　1/2 cup water
　　2 cups (8 ounces) reduced-fat shredded cheddar
　　　cheese, *divided*
　　28 baked tortilla chips, *divided*

In a large saucepan, combine the beans, broth, corn, salsa, chicken and water. Bring to a boil. Reduce heat; cover and simmer for 10 minutes. Add 1 cup cheese; cook and stir over low heat until melted. Crumble half of the tortilla chips into soup bowls. Ladle soup over chips. Top each serving with two crumbled chips; sprinkle with remaining cheese. **Yield:** 7 servings.

In a large saucepan, cook sausage, beef, onion, green pepper and garlic over medium heat until meat is no longer pink; drain. Stir in the remaining ingredients. Bring to a boil. Reduce heat; cover and simmer for 30-40 minutes or until heated through. **Yield:** 8 servings.

*Editor's Note: When cutting or seeding hot peppers, use rubber or plastic gloves to protect your hands. Avoid touching your face.

Nutritional Analysis: One serving (1-1/3 cups) equals 222 calories, 9 g fat (3 g saturated fat), 41 mg cholesterol, 1,153 mg sodium, 18 g carbohydrate, 2 g fiber, 18 g protein.
Diabetic Exchanges: 2 lean meat, 1 starch, 1/2 vegetable, 1/2 fat.

Rich Onion Beef Soup

When you're in the mood for soup that's big on beef flavor, reach for this robust recipe. Guests agree that this quick and easy version rivals any restaurant's French onion soup.
—*Nina Hall, Citrus Heights, California*

 2 cups thinly sliced onions
 1 tablespoon butter *or* stick margarine
 2 cups cubed cooked lean beef
 2 cans (14-1/2 ounces *each*) beef broth
 3 tablespoons all-purpose flour
1/2 teaspoon ground mustard
1/2 teaspoon sugar
1/2 cup dry red wine *or* additional beef broth
 1 teaspoon browning sauce

In a large saucepan, cook onions in butter over medium-low heat for 15-20 minutes or until tender and golden brown, stirring occasionally. Add beef and broth. Bring to a boil. Reduce heat; cover and simmer for 10 minutes.

In a small bowl, combine the flour, mustard and sugar; stir in the wine or additional broth and browning sauce until smooth. Stir into the soup. Bring the soup to a boil; cook and stir for 1-2 minutes or until slightly thickened. **Yield:** 5 servings.

Nutritional Analysis: One serving (1 cup) equals 165 calories, 6 g fat (3 g saturated fat), 43 mg cholesterol, 631 mg sodium, 9 g carbohydrate, 1 g fiber, 16 g protein.
Diabetic Exchanges: 2 lean meat, 1/2 starch, 1/2 fat.

Spice It Up Soup

(Pictured above)

Turkey Italian sausage and jalapeno peppers add kick to this chunky soup. The original recipe called for a lot of butter and three cooking pots. I eliminated the butter and tossed the ingredients together in just one pot. My husband really enjoys this meaty soup, so I make plenty and freeze what's left over in individual servings for his lunches.
—*Guyla Cooper, Enville, Tennessee*

 1 **pound uncooked hot turkey Italian sausage links, sliced**
1/2 **pound lean ground beef**
 1 **large onion, chopped**
 1 **medium green pepper, chopped**
 3 **garlic cloves, minced**
 2 **cans (14-1/2 ounces *each*) beef broth**
 2 **cups water**
 2 **cups fresh *or* frozen corn**
 1 **can (14-1/2 ounces) diced tomatoes with green chilies, undrained**
 1 **cup diced carrots**
1/3 **cup minced fresh cilantro *or* parsley**
 2 **jalapeno peppers, seeded and chopped***
1/2 **teaspoon salt**
1/2 **teaspoon ground cumin**

Lemon Lentil Soup

Loaded with protein-rich lentils, this hearty soup is rooted in the old-fashioned goodness of leeks, parsnips, celery and carrots. The addition of lemon juice transforms what might otherwise be an everyday soup into something out of the ordinary.
—Jean Rawlings, Saskatoon, Saskatchewan

    1 cup chopped leeks (white portion only)
    2 tablespoons canola oil
    1 can (15 ounces) tomato puree
    1 cup chopped celery
    1 cup chopped carrots
    1/4 cup chopped peeled parsnips
    2 tablespoons dried basil
    8 cups water
1-1/2 cups lentils, rinsed
    2 bay leaves
    1 tablespoon grated lemon peel
1-1/2 teaspoons salt
    1 teaspoon dill weed
    1/2 teaspoon pepper
    2 to 3 tablespoons lemon juice

In a large saucepan, saute leeks in oil until tender. Add the tomato puree, celery, carrots, parsnips and basil; saute for 3-4 minutes. Add water; bring to a boil. Add lentils and bay leaves. Reduce heat; cover and simmer for 30 minutes. Stir in lemon peel, salt, dill and pepper; simmer 30 minutes longer or until lentils are tender. Discard bay leaves. Stir in lemon juice. **Yield:** 6 servings.

Nutritional Analysis: One serving (1-1/2 cups) equals 248 calories, 5 g fat (1 g saturated fat), 0 cholesterol, 637 mg sodium, 39 g carbohydrate, 14 g fiber, 14 g protein.
Diabetic Exchanges: 2 vegetable, 1-1/2 starch, 1 very lean meat, 1 fat.

Mexican Chicken Soup

(Pictured below)

This zesty dish is loaded with chicken, corn and black beans in a mildly spicy red broth. As a busy mom of three young children, I'm always looking for dinner recipes that can be prepared in the morning. The kids love the taco-like taste of this easy soup.
—Marlene Kane, Lainesburg, Michigan

1-1/2 pounds boneless skinless chicken breasts, cubed
    2 teaspoons canola oil
    1/2 cup water
    1 envelope reduced-sodium taco seasoning
    1 can (32 ounces) V8 juice
    1 jar (16 ounces) salsa
    1 can (15 ounces) black beans, rinsed and drained
    1 package (10 ounces) frozen corn, thawed
    6 tablespoons reduced-fat cheddar cheese
    6 tablespoons reduced-fat sour cream
    2 tablespoons chopped fresh cilantro *or* parsley

In a large nonstick skillet, saute chicken in oil until no longer pink. Add water and taco seasoning; simmer until chicken is well coated. Transfer to a slow cooker. Add V8 juice, salsa, beans and corn; mix well. Cover and cook on low for 3-4 hours or until heated through. Serve with cheese, sour cream and cilantro. **Yield:** 6 servings.

Nutritional Analysis: One serving (1-1/2 cups with 1 tablespoon each cheese and sour cream and 1 teaspoon cilantro) equals 345 calories, 6 g fat (2 g saturated fat), 75 mg cholesterol, 1,385 mg sodium, 35 g carbohydrate, 7 g fiber, 36 g protein.
Diabetic Exchanges: 4 very lean meat, 2 vegetable, 1-1/2 starch, 1/2 fat.

Fresh Corn Chowder

This creamy corn and potato dish is perfect when you yearn for a full-bodied soup with lots of down-home flavor. I discovered the recipe in a fresh fruit and vegetable cookbook. It really hits the spot on a chilly day, ladled up for lunch or dinner.
—Margaret Olien, New Richmond, Wisconsin

    4 **large ears sweet corn, husks removed**
    1 **large onion, chopped**
    1 **celery rib, chopped**
    1 **tablespoon butter *or* stick margarine**
1-1/2 **cups diced peeled potatoes**
    1 **cup water**
    2 **teaspoons chicken bouillon granules**
  1/4 **teaspoon dried thyme**
  1/4 **teaspoon pepper**
    6 **tablespoons all-purpose flour**
    3 **cups 2% milk**

Cut corn off the cob; set aside. In a large saucepan, saute onion and celery in butter until tender. Add the potatoes, water, bouillon, thyme, pepper and corn. Bring to a boil. Reduce heat; cover and simmer for 15 minutes or until potatoes are tender. Combine the flour and milk until smooth; gradually stir into soup. Bring to a boil; cook and stir for 2 minutes or until thickened. **Yield:** 7 servings.

Nutritional Analysis: One serving (1 cup) equals 204 calories, 5 g fat (3 g saturated fat), 13 mg cholesterol, 410 mg sodium, 35 g carbohydrate, 4 g fiber, 8 g protein.
Diabetic Exchanges: 2 starch, 1/2 reduced-fat milk.

Pumpkin Vegetable Soup

This golden-toned soup is wonderfully warming on crisp autumn days. Unlike most creamy pumpkin soups, this one is especially hearty, with additional vegetables such as potatoes, carrots and corn. For fun autumn flair, serve the soup in hollowed-out pumpkin shells. My boys love it that way.
—Joan Conover, Easton, Pennsylvania

  1 **large onion, chopped**
  2 **tablespoons butter *or* stick margarine**
  4 **cups reduced-sodium chicken broth**
  2 **medium potatoes, peeled and cubed**
  2 **large carrots, chopped**
  2 **celery ribs, chopped**
  1 **cup cooked fresh *or* frozen lima beans**
  1 **cup fresh *or* frozen corn**
  1 **can (15 ounces) solid-pack pumpkin**
1/2 **teaspoon salt**
1/4 **teaspoon white pepper**
1/4 **teaspoon ground nutmeg**

In a large saucepan, saute onion in butter until tender. Add the broth, potatoes, carrots, celery, lima beans and corn. Bring to a boil. Reduce heat; cover and simmer for 25-30 minutes or until vegetables are tender. Stir in the pumpkin, salt, pepper and nutmeg. Cook 5-10 minutes longer or until heated through. **Yield:** 7 servings.

Nutritional Analysis: One serving (1-1/2 cups) equals 153 calories, 4 g fat (2 g saturated fat), 9 mg cholesterol, 583 mg sodium, 27 g carbohydrate, 7 g fiber, 7 g protein.
Diabetic Exchanges: 1-1/2 starch, 1 vegetable, 1/2 fat.

Lentil Chili

Cumin and chili powder perk up this saucy lentil and ground turkey blend. Fans of traditional chili featuring ground beef and beans will gobble up this good-for-you version.
—Noel Egert Diebe, Richland, Washington

  1 **pound lean ground turkey**
  1 **can (49 ounces) reduced-sodium chicken broth**
  2 **cups lentils, rinsed**
  1 **can (15 ounces) tomato sauce**
  1 **can (14-1/2 ounces) diced tomatoes, undrained**
  1 **medium onion, chopped**
  1 **tablespoon chili powder**
  1 **teaspoon ground cumin**
1/4 **teaspoon pepper**

In a Dutch oven, cook turkey over medium heat until no longer pink; drain. Add the remaining ingredients; bring to a boil. Reduce heat; cover and simmer for 25-30 minutes or until lentils are tender. **Yield:** 8 servings.

Nutritional Analysis: One serving (1-1/2 cups) equals 278 calories, 5 g fat (1 g saturated fat), 45 mg cholesterol, 918 mg sodium, 35 g carbohydrate, 12 g fiber, 25 g protein.
Diabetic Exchanges: 3 very lean meat, 1-1/2 starch, 1 vegetable, 1/2 fat.

Step Up to The Salad Bar

Whether you're looking for a standout side dish to accompany a main course, a tangy take-along for the neighborhood barbecue or an appealing addition to your lunchtime lineup, nothing beats garden-fresh salads!

Pasta Salad Plus (page 71)

Gingered Citrus-Avocado Salad

(Pictured at right)

A citrusy dressing served over a combination of fruits makes this salad so refreshing. We enjoy the mix of flavors—mellow avocado, tangy grapefruit and toasted pecans.
—Ruby Williams, Bogalusa, Louisiana

 2 large navel oranges, peeled and sliced 1/4 inch thick
 1 medium grapefruit, peeled and sectioned
 1 can (20 ounces) unsweetened pineapple chunks, undrained
 1/2 cup fat-free sour cream
 2 tablespoons fat-free milk
 1 tablespoon brown sugar
 1 teaspoon grated orange peel
 1/4 teaspoon ground ginger
 1/8 teaspoon ground nutmeg
 6 cups torn leaf lettuce
 1 large avocado, peeled and sliced
 1/4 cup chopped pecans, toasted

In a large bowl, combine oranges, grapefruit and pineapple; cover and refrigerate until serving. In another bowl, combine sour cream, milk, brown sugar, orange peel, ginger and nutmeg. Cover and refrigerate for at least 1 hour. Divide lettuce and avocado between six salad plates. Using a slotted spoon, arrange fruit over lettuce. Drizzle with dressing. Sprinkle with nuts. **Yield:** 6 servings.

Nutritional Analysis: One serving equals 206 calories, 9 g fat (1 g saturated fat), trace cholesterol, 45 mg sodium, 32 g carbohydrate, 8 g fiber, 4 g protein.
Diabetic Exchanges: 1-1/2 fruit, 1-1/2 fat, 1/2 starch.

Tomato-Sesame Pasta Toss

(Pictured at right)

This hearty warm pasta salad features so many flavors and textures, it's amazing they all fit in one bowl! The sesame oil and soy sauce give it an Oriental flair.
—Betty Mitchem, Satsuma, Alabama

 4 quarts water
 8 ounces uncooked angel hair pasta, broken in half
 2 cups broccoli florets
 14 to 16 cherry tomatoes, halved
 1 cup sliced fresh mushrooms
 1 cup torn fresh spinach
 3 green onions, thinly sliced
 1/4 cup cashews
 1/4 cup reduced-sodium soy sauce
 2 tablespoons sesame seeds, toasted
 2 tablespoons brown sugar
 2 tablespoons sesame oil
 2 teaspoons lime juice
 1 garlic clove, minced
 1 teaspoon finely chopped jalapeno pepper*

In a Dutch oven, bring water to a boil. Add pasta; boil for 4 minutes. Add broccoli; boil 2 minutes longer or until pasta is tender. Drain and place in a large bowl. Add tomatoes, mushrooms, spinach, onions and cashews; toss. In a jar with a tight-fitting lid, combine the remaining ingredients; shake well. Pour over pasta mixture and toss gently. **Yield:** 7 servings.
 *Editor's Note: When cutting or seeding hot peppers, use rubber or plastic gloves to protect your hands. Avoid touching your face.
 Nutritional Analysis: One serving (1 cup) equals 260 calories, 10 g fat (2 g saturated fat), 0 cholesterol, 399 mg sodium, 37 g carbohydrate, 4 g fiber, 8 g protein.
 Diabetic Exchanges: 2 starch, 2 fat, 1 vegetable.

Barley Radish Salad

My family loves barley, so I try to work it into everyday menus—including picnics and packed lunches. Cooked barley gives this salad a chewy texture, while radishes, celery and green onions add a pleasant crunch.
—Maude Chuba, Chardon, Ohio

 1 cup finely chopped radishes
 2 celery ribs, finely chopped
 1/4 cup finely chopped green onions
 1 cup medium pearl barley, cooked
 2 tablespoons olive *or* canola oil
 2 tablespoons cider vinegar
 1/2 teaspoon salt
 1/2 teaspoon dried basil
 1/4 teaspoon pepper

In a bowl, combine radishes, celery, onions and barley. In a jar with a tight-fitting lid, combine the remaining ingredients; shake well. Pour over barley mixture and toss to coat. Cover and refrigerate for at least 2 hours before serving. **Yield:** 4 servings.

Nutritional Analysis: One serving (3/4 cup) equals 140 calories, 7 g fat (1 g saturated fat), 0 cholesterol, 319 mg sodium, 18 g carbohydrate, 5 g fiber, 2 g protein.
Diabetic Exchanges: 1-1/2 fat, 1 starch.

Herbed Cottage Cheese

When I switched from regular to low-fat cottage cheese, I was disappointed with the taste. So I pulled out this recipe my mother gave me years ago. With this jazzed-up version of light cottage cheese, I don't miss the fat at all.
—Traci Hirstein, Western Springs, Illinois

 2 cups (16 ounces) 1% cottage cheese
 1 tablespoon minced chives
 1/4 teaspoon garlic powder
 1/4 teaspoon onion powder
 1/4 teaspoon salt
 1/8 teaspoon celery seed
 1/8 teaspoon pepper

In a bowl, combine all of the ingredients. Serve immediately. **Yield:** 4 servings.

Nutritional Analysis: One serving (1/2 cup) equals 83 calories, 1 g fat (1 g saturated fat), 5 mg cholesterol, 607 mg sodium, 3 g carbohydrate, trace fiber, 14 g protein.
Diabetic Exchange: 2 very lean meat.

Crunchy Potato Salad

(Pictured below)

Dill and mustard pep up the tangy dressing that coats this combination of crunchy vegetables and tender potato chunks. We try to eat healthy, and recipes like this one fit right in with our goals.
—Janis Plagerman, Lynden, Washington

1-1/2 pounds red potatoes, cubed
1 celery rib, chopped
1/4 cup chopped sweet red pepper
1 medium carrot, shredded
1 green onion, chopped
1/4 cup reduced-fat mayonnaise
1/4 cup reduced-fat plain yogurt
1 tablespoon sweet pickle relish
3/4 teaspoon prepared mustard
1/2 teaspoon salt
1/2 teaspoon lemon-pepper seasoning
1/2 teaspoon dill weed
Lettuce leaves, optional

Place potatoes in a saucepan and cover with water; bring to a boil. Reduce heat; cover and simmer for 15-20 minutes or until tender. Drain and cool; place in a bowl. Add the celery, red pepper, carrot and onion.

In a small bowl, combine the mayonnaise, yogurt, pickle relish, mustard, salt, lemon-pepper and dill; pour over vegetables and toss to coat. Cover and refrigerate for at least 1 hour. Serve in a lettuce-lined bowl if desired. **Yield:** 6 servings.

Nutritional Analysis: One serving (3/4 cup) equals 143 calories, 4 g fat (1 g saturated fat), 4 mg cholesterol, 371 mg sodium, 25 g carbohydrate, 3 g fiber, 3 g protein.
Diabetic Exchanges: 1-1/2 starch, 1/2 fat.

Fire and Ice Tomatoes

(Pictured above)

You won't miss the salt in this refreshing tomato salad! It's well-seasoned with cayenne pepper, mustard seed and vinegar but not the least bit spicy.
—Nan Rickey, Yuma, Arizona

5 large tomatoes, cut into wedges
1 medium onion, sliced
3/4 cup white vinegar
6 tablespoons sugar
1/4 cup water
1 tablespoon mustard seed
1/4 teaspoon cayenne pepper
1 large cucumber, sliced

In a large bowl, combine the tomatoes and onion; set aside. In a small saucepan, combine the vinegar, sugar, water, mustard seed and cayenne. Bring to a boil; boil for 1 minute. Pour over tomatoes and onion; toss to coat. Cover and refrigerate for at least 2 hours. Add cucumber; toss to coat. Refrigerate overnight. Serve with a slotted spoon. **Yield:** 8 servings.

Nutritional Analysis: One serving (3/4 cup) equals 72 calories, 1 g fat (trace saturated fat), 0 cholesterol, 11 mg sodium, 17 g carbohydrate, 2 g fiber, 2 g protein.
Diabetic Exchanges: 2 vegetable, 1/2 starch.

Grilled Salmon Salad

For a cool summer supper, try this fresh-tasting salmon salad created by our Test Kitchen staff. Lightly dressed with tangy raspberry vinegar, it gets a little crunch from onion and celery.

2 salmon fillets (about 1-1/2 pounds)
2 celery ribs, chopped

1/2 cup finely chopped red onion
2 tablespoons snipped fresh dill *or* 2 teaspoons dill weed
DRESSING:
1/4 cup raspberry vinegar
1 tablespoon olive *or* canola oil
1-1/2 teaspoons sugar
1/2 teaspoon salt
1/4 teaspoon pepper

Coat grill rack with nonstick cooking spray before starting the grill. Cut salmon fillets widthwise into 4-in. pieces; place skin side down on grill. Grill, covered, over medium-hot heat for 12-15 minutes or until fish flakes easily with a fork. Cover and refrigerate for 1 hour.

Bone, skin and flake salmon; place in a bowl. Add celery, onion and dill. Combine the dressing ingredients; pour over salad and gently toss to coat. Serve or refrigerate; stir before serving. **Yield:** 4 servings.

Nutritional Analysis: One serving (1 cup) equals 278 calories, 13 g fat (2 g saturated fat), 88 mg cholesterol, 376 mg sodium, 5 g carbohydrate, 1 g fiber, 34 g protein.
Diabetic Exchanges: 4 lean meat, 1 fat.

Carrot-Pineapple Gelatin Salad

My grandma frequently fixed this salad when she was asked to bring a dish to a family gathering. Now I make it often since it's a favorite of our kids. It's a fun way for them to get a fruit and vegetable.
—Sue Gronholz, Beaver Dam, Wisconsin

1 can (8 ounces) unsweetened crushed pineapple
1 package (.3 ounce) sugar-free lemon gelatin
1 cup boiling water
1/2 cup cold water
1 teaspoon white vinegar
1/8 teaspoon salt
2 medium carrots, grated

Drain pineapple, reserving 1/2 cup juice; set pineapple and juice aside. In a bowl, dissolve gelatin in boiling water. Stir in cold water, vinegar, salt and reserved juice. Chill until partially thickened, about 45 minutes. Stir in carrots and reserved pineapple. Pour into a 3-cup mold coated with nonstick cooking spray. Chill until firm. Unmold to serve. **Yield:** 4 servings.

Nutritional Analysis: One serving equals 59 calories, 0 fat (0 saturated fat), 0 cholesterol, 158 mg sodium, 12 g carbohydrate, 2 g fiber, 1 g protein.
Diabetic Exchanges: 1 vegetable, 1/2 fruit.

Buttermilk Basil Salad Dressing

(Pictured above)

My husband can't eat greasy or spicy foods, and none of us like mayonnaise, so I created this creamy dressing we all enjoy. It gets its pleasant flavor from fresh basil and Parmesan cheese.
—Nancy Johnston, San Dimas, California

1 cup 1% buttermilk
1 cup reduced-fat sour cream
1/4 cup plus 2 teaspoons grated Parmesan cheese
3 tablespoons minced fresh basil (no substitutes)
1 teaspoon onion salt
2 garlic cloves, minced
Torn mixed salad greens

In a bowl, combine buttermilk and sour cream. Stir in Parmesan cheese, basil, onion salt and garlic. Cover and refrigerate for at least 1 hour. Serve over salad greens. **Yield:** 2 cups.

Nutritional Analysis: One serving (2 tablespoons dressing) equals 35 calories, 2 g fat (1 g saturated fat), 7 mg cholesterol, 173 mg sodium, 2 g carbohydrate, trace fiber, 2 g protein.
Diabetic Exchange: 1/2 fat.

Barbecue BLT Chicken Salad

My family requests this satisfying salad often. Barbecue sauce gives the dressing an unexpected tang.
—*Kathleen Williams, Maryville, Tennessee*

1/4 cup reduced-fat mayonnaise
1/4 cup barbecue sauce
1 tablespoon lemon juice
1/2 teaspoon pepper
1/4 teaspoon salt
2 cups chopped cooked chicken breast
2 medium tomatoes, chopped
1 celery rib, sliced
5 cups torn salad greens
4 bacon strips, cooked and crumbled

In a small bowl, combine the mayonnaise, barbecue sauce, lemon juice, pepper and salt. Cover and refrigerate for at least 1 hour. Just before serving, combine the chicken, tomatoes and celery; stir in dressing. Serve over salad greens; sprinkle with bacon. **Yield:** 5 servings.

Nutritional Analysis: One serving (3/4 cup) equals 191 calories, 9 g fat (2 g saturated fat), 56 mg cholesterol, 457 mg sodium, 7 g carbohydrate, 2 g fiber, 20 g protein.
Diabetic Exchanges: 2 lean meat, 1 vegetable, 1 fat.

Black-Eyed Pea Salad

(Pictured above)

To create a more interesting pasta salad, I added pasta to my favorite black-eyed pea salad. The result is different and delicious. Cucumber and green pepper give this picnic side dish its satisfying crunch.
—*Melinda Ewbank, Fairfield, Ohio*

6 ounces small shell pasta, cooked and drained
1 can (15 ounces) black-eyed peas, rinsed and drained
1 cup sliced green onions
3/4 cup diced seeded peeled cucumber
3/4 cup diced green pepper
3/4 cup diced seeded tomato
1 small jalapeno pepper, seeded and finely chopped*
DRESSING:
3 tablespoons canola oil
1/4 cup red wine vinegar *or* cider vinegar
1 teaspoon sugar
1 teaspoon dried basil
1 teaspoon chili powder
1 teaspoon hot pepper sauce
1/2 teaspoon seasoned salt

In a salad bowl, combine the first seven ingredients. In a jar with a tight-fitting lid, combine the oil, vinegar, sugar, basil, chili powder, hot pepper sauce and seasoned salt; shake well. Pour the dressing over salad and stir to coat. Cover and refrigerate for at least 2 hours before serving. **Yield:** 6 servings.

*Editor's Note: When cutting or seeding hot peppers, use rubber or plastic gloves to protect your hands. Avoid touching your face.

Nutritional Analysis: One serving (1 cup) equals 186 calories, 6 g fat (1 g saturated fat), 0 cholesterol, 269 mg sodium, 28 g carbohydrate, 4 g fiber, 6 g protein.
Diabetic Exchanges: 1-1/2 starch, 1 vegetable, 1 fat.

Dressing It Up

TRY DRIZZLING a homemade dressing on your next veggie or fruit salad. When you whisk together your own blend, you control the amount of oil and can alter the taste to your liking.

Here are a few salad-making suggestions:

- Cut down on the oil in dressing by replacing some of the oil with wine, fat-free broth, vegetable or tomato juice, fruit nectar or water.
- Prepared or ground mustard not only adds great flavor, it also helps keep the dressing from separating.
- It's best to make salad dressing with fresh ingredients in small quantities, since homemade dressings usually keep for only a few days in the refrigerator.
- Onion or garlic powder perks up the flavor in any salad dressing without adding salt and helps keep it emulsified.
- Next time your dressing recipe calls for lemon juice or vinegar, try lime juice—it's wonderful on salad greens or fruits.
- For a more robust flavor, add fresh lemon juice, basil, marjoram and oregano to your dressing.
- The classic ratio of 1 part vinegar or lemon juice to 3 parts oil in dressings can differ depending on personal preferences. Many people add more vinegar for zip.
- Dress salad greens lightly just before serving so they won't become wilted and limp. Too much dressing will weigh down the ingredients and mask the natural flavors.

Beefy Broccoli Asparagus Salad

(Pictured above)

Colorful veggies provide this make-ahead main dish with crispness, while soy sauce and sesame oil flavor the homemade dressing.
—Betty Rassette, Salina, Kansas

    3/4 pound boneless beef sirloin steak
      8 cups water
      4 cups cut fresh asparagus (1-inch pieces)
      2 cups fresh broccoli florets
    1/4 cup reduced-sodium soy sauce
      2 tablespoons white wine vinegar *or* white
        vinegar
  4-1/2 teaspoons sesame oil
    1/4 teaspoon ground ginger *or* 1 teaspoon minced
        fresh gingerroot
      2 teaspoons sugar
Dash pepper

Place steak on a broiler pan coated with nonstick cooking spray. Broil 3-4 in. from the heat for 6-10 minutes on each side or until meat reaches desired doneness (for rare, a meat thermometer should read 140°; medium, 160°; well-done, 170°); cool completely.

In a large saucepan, bring water to a boil. Add asparagus and broccoli; cover and cook for 3 minutes. Drain and immediately place vegetables in ice water. Drain and pat dry; refrigerate.

For dressing, in a jar with a tight-fitting lid, combine the soy sauce, vinegar, oil, ginger, sugar and pepper; shake well. Thinly slice beef and place in a bowl; add dressing and toss to coat. Cover and refrigerate for 1 hour. Just before serving, add vegetables and toss to coat. **Yield:** 4 servings.

Nutritional Analysis: One serving (1-1/4 cups) equals 229 calories, 10 g fat (2 g saturated fat), 56 mg cholesterol, 670 mg sodium, 11 g carbohydrate, 3 g fiber, 24 g protein.
Diabetic Exchanges: 2 lean meat, 2 vegetable, 1 fat.

Pineapple Chicken Paradise

(Pictured below)

You'll think you've traveled to the tropics when you bite into this inviting chicken salad, served in an attractive pineapple "boat". This salad blends a variety of tastes and textures, including coconut, peanuts, mandarin oranges and green grapes.
—Dorothy Anderson, Ottawa, Kansas

      2 fresh pineapples with tops
  1-1/2 cups cubed cooked chicken breast
    3/4 cup chopped celery
    1/3 cup reduced-fat mayonnaise
    1/3 cup fat-free plain yogurt
      2 tablespoons chutney
    1/2 teaspoon salt
    1/4 cup dry roasted peanuts
    1/4 cup flaked coconut, toasted
      1 can (11 ounces) mandarin oranges, drained
    1/2 cup halved green grapes

Cut each pineapple in half lengthwise, then cut in half lengthwise again, making four shells with part of the leaves. Remove fruit; cut into cubes. Turn pineapple shells cut side down on paper towels to drain; set aside.

In a bowl, combine the pineapple cubes, chicken and celery; cover and refrigerate. In another bowl, combine the mayonnaise, yogurt, chutney and salt; cover and refrigerate for at least 30 minutes.

Before serving, drain the chicken mixture; toss with mayonnaise mixture and peanuts. Using a slotted spoon, fill pineapple shells. Sprinkle with coconut; top with oranges and grapes. **Yield:** 8 servings.

Nutritional Analysis: One serving (3/4 cup) equals 203 calories, 8 g fat (2 g saturated fat), 26 mg cholesterol, 300 mg sodium, 25 g carbohydrate, 3 g fiber, 11 g protein.
Diabetic Exchanges: 2 fruit, 1 lean meat, 1 fat.

Honey-Mustard Salad Dressing

(Pictured at right)

Pair sweet honey with zippy Dijon mustard in this quick-to-fix recipe. The creamy yellow blend nicely coats mixed salad greens with a mildly tangy flavor. No one would ever guess this is low in fat.
—Terri Webber, Miami, Florida

    1 cup (8 ounces) fat-free plain yogurt
1/3 cup reduced-fat mayonnaise
1/3 cup honey
1/4 cup Dijon mustard
    2 tablespoons prepared mustard
4-1/2 teaspoons white wine vinegar *or* cider vinegar

In a bowl, whisk together all ingredients. Refrigerate for at least 1 hour before serving. **Yield:** 2 cups.

Nutritional Analysis: One serving (2 tablespoons) equals 50 calories, 2 g fat (trace saturated fat), 2 mg cholesterol, 165 mg sodium, 8 g carbohydrate, trace fiber, 1 g protein.
Diabetic Exchanges: 1/2 fruit, 1/2 fat.

Wild Rice Chicken Salad

(Pictured at right)

Juicy red grapes, crunchy cashews and water chestnuts and a touch of tarragon made this wild rice salad a big hit at our family reunion. I fix it often at home and for potluck dinners.
—Mary Ann Morgan, Powder Springs, Georgia

2-1/2 cups cubed cooked chicken breast
    3 cups cooked wild rice
    1 can (8 ounces) sliced water chestnuts, drained
1/3 cup thinly sliced green onions
2/3 cup reduced-fat mayonnaise
1/3 cup fat-free milk
    2 to 3 tablespoons lemon juice
1/2 teaspoon salt
1/4 teaspoon dried tarragon
1/8 teaspoon pepper
    1 cup halved seedless red grapes
1/4 cup salted cashew halves

In a large bowl, combine the chicken, rice, water chestnuts and green onions. In a small bowl, combine the mayonnaise, milk, lemon juice, salt, tarragon and pepper. Pour over chicken mixture; toss to coat. Cover and refrigerate for 2-3 hours. Just before serving, fold in grapes and sprinkle with cashews. **Yield:** 7 servings.

Nutritional Analysis: One serving (1 cup) equals 303 calories, 13 g fat (2 g saturated fat), 51 mg cholesterol, 435 mg sodium, 28 g carbohydrate, 3 g fiber, 20 g protein.
Diabetic Exchanges: 2 lean meat, 1-1/2 starch, 1-1/2 fat.

Floret Cabbage Slaw

For a salad that's on the crunchy side, try this simple slaw. With its blend of broccoli, cauliflower and cabbage, this side dish goes well with most any meal. I often take it to church functions.
—Arlene Hole, Mebane, North Carolina

    2 cups shredded cabbage
    2 cups broccoli florets
1-1/2 cups cauliflowerets
    1 medium red onion, thinly sliced
1/4 cup reduced-fat mayonnaise
1/4 cup fat-free plain yogurt
1/4 cup reduced-fat sour cream
1/4 cup shredded Parmesan cheese
    2 tablespoons plus 1-1/2 teaspoons sugar

In a salad bowl, combine the cabbage, broccoli, cauliflower and onion. In a small bowl, combine the remaining ingredients. Pour over vegetables and toss to coat. Cover and refrigerate until serving. **Yield:** 6 servings.

Nutritional Analysis: One serving (3/4 cup) equals 118 calories, 6 g fat (2 g saturated fat), 10 mg cholesterol, 189 mg sodium, 13 g carbohydrate, 2 g fiber, 5 g protein.
Diabetic Exchanges: 1 vegetable, 1 fat, 1/2 starch.

Greek Tomatoes

This recipe is quick and easy, and especially good if you use homegrown tomatoes. I like to serve this savory side at family barbecues or on camping trips. The tomatoes are delicious with grilled steak and roasted corn on the cob.
—Marilyn Morel, Keene, New Hampshire

    4 medium tomatoes, cut into 1/4-inch slices
    1 small red onion, thinly sliced and separated into rings
3/4 cup crumbled feta cheese
1/4 cup minced fresh parsley
1/2 teaspoon salt
1/2 teaspoon coarsely ground pepper
    1 tablespoon olive *or* canola oil

Arrange tomato and onion slices on a plate. Sprinkle with the feta cheese, parsley, salt and pepper. Drizzle with oil. Cover and refrigerate for 15 minutes. **Yield:** 6 servings.

Nutritional Analysis: One serving equals 91 calories, 7 g fat (3 g saturated fat), 17 mg cholesterol, 416 mg sodium, 5 g carbohydrate, 1 g fiber, 4 g protein.
Diabetic Exchanges: 1-1/2 fat, 1 vegetable.

Fruity Coleslaw

(Pictured below)

This tangy sweet side dish is a favorite at picnics and potlucks. For fun, try varying the fruits by substituting apples, cherries or raisins.
—*Susan Skinner-Martin, Sandusky, Ohio*

- 1 cup (8 ounces) fat-free plain yogurt
- 1/2 cup honey
- 1/4 cup white vinegar
- 3 tablespoons lemon juice
- 1/2 teaspoon salt
- 1/8 teaspoon pepper
- 1 can (16 ounces) reduced-sugar fruit cocktail, drained
- 2 cups blueberries
- 1 cup sliced fresh strawberries
- 1 medium ripe banana, sliced
- 1 package (16 ounces) coleslaw mix

In a large bowl, combine the yogurt, honey, vinegar, lemon juice, salt and pepper. Add the fruit cocktail, blueberries, strawberries and banana. Stir in the coleslaw mix. Serve immediately. **Yield:** 12 servings.

Nutritional Analysis: One serving (3/4 cup) equals 109 calories, trace fat (trace saturated fat), trace cholesterol, 121 mg sodium, 28 g carbohydrate, 2 g fiber, 2 g protein.
Diabetic Exchanges: 1-1/2 fruit, 1 vegetable.

Dijon Four-Bean Salad

(Pictured above)

Dress up traditional bean salad with a tangy Dijon mustard vinaigrette. I'm a busy home-schooling mom, so I love how easy this colorful side dish is to prepare. It's also perfect for bring-a-dish-to-pass dinners.
—*Karen Riordan, Fern Creek, Kentucky*

- 1 package (10 ounces) frozen baby lima beans
- 1 package (10 ounces) frozen cut green beans
- 2 cans (16 ounces *each*) red kidney beans, rinsed and drained
- 1 can (15 ounces) white kidney *or* cannellini beans, rinsed and drained
- 1/3 cup white wine vinegar *or* cider vinegar
- 1/4 cup sugar
- 3 tablespoons Dijon mustard
- 2 tablespoons canola oil
- 1/2 teaspoon salt

Cook lima and green beans according to package directions; drain. Place in a large serving bowl; cool. Add kidney beans. In a jar with a tight-fitting lid, combine the vinegar, sugar, mustard, oil and salt; shake well. Pour over beans and stir gently to coat. Cover and refrigerate overnight. Serve with a slotted spoon. **Yield:** 10 servings.

Nutritional Analysis: One serving (3/4 cup) equals 195 calories, 4 g fat (trace saturated fat), 0 cholesterol, 644 mg sodium, 33 g carbohydrate, 7 g fiber, 9 g protein.
Diabetic Exchanges: 2 starch, 1 very lean meat, 1/2 fat.

Beef 'n' Black-Eyed Pea Salad

When I want a light yet hearty meal, I fix this refreshing main-dish salad. My husband loves the beef and the zippy flavor. As a busy mom, I appreciate that it doesn't take long to put this entree on the table.
—Bonnie Wittekind, Higley, Arizona

2 to 3 garlic cloves, minced
1 to 2 teaspoons chili powder
12 ounces boneless beef sirloin steak
8 cups torn romaine
1 can (15-1/2 ounces) black-eyed peas, rinsed and drained
1 large sweet red pepper, julienned
1/2 cup sliced ripe olives
1 can (4 ounces) chopped green chilies, drained
2 green onions, chopped
2 tablespoons minced fresh cilantro *or* parsley
3 tablespoons lime juice
2 tablespoons canola oil
2 teaspoons sugar
1 teaspoon salt
1 teaspoon grated lime peel
1/4 teaspoon pepper

Combine garlic and chili powder; rub over both sides of steak. If grilling the steak, coat grill rack with nonstick cooking spray before starting the grill. Grill steak, covered, over medium heat or broil 4 in. from the heat for 5-7 minutes on each side or until meat reaches desired doneness (for rare, a meat thermometer should read 140°; medium, 160°; well-done, 170°).

When cool enough to handle, slice meat across the grain into thin strips; place in a large bowl. Add the romaine, peas, red pepper, olives, chilies, onions and cilantro. In a small bowl, combine the remaining ingredients. Pour over salad and toss to coat. **Yield:** 6 servings.

Nutritional Analysis: *One serving (1-2/3 cups) equals 223 calories, 10 g fat (2 g saturated fat), 33 mg cholesterol, 823 mg sodium, 18 g carbohydrate, 6 g fiber, 17 g protein.*
Diabetic Exchanges: *2 lean meat, 1 vegetable, 1 fat, 1/2 starch.*

🍎 Turning Over a New Leaf

WHETHER it is starring in salads, casseroles, soups or stews, cilantro adds a unique and flavorful twist to dishes.

What we call "cilantro" is actually the bright green leaves and stems of the coriander plant. Sometimes also known as Chinese Parsley, cilantro has a lively distinctive flavor and strong aroma that lends itself well to highly spiced foods.

It can be found fresh in bunches in the produce or herb section of many grocery stores or at farmer's markets. Look for evenly colored leaves and no wilting. Store cilantro in a plastic bag in the refrigerator for up to one week.

Fennel Orange Salad

(Pictured above)

You'll need just a few ingredients to fix this fresh-tasting salad. The combination of crisp fennel and juicy oranges is delightful. To reduce last-minute prep, make it the day before you plan to serve it.
—Nina Hall, Citrus Heights, California

1 fennel bulb with fronds (about 3/4 pound)
4 medium navel oranges, peeled and sectioned
1/3 cup orange juice
4 teaspoons olive *or* canola oil
1 tablespoon grated orange peel
1/4 teaspoon salt
1/8 teaspoon pepper

Finely chop enough fennel fronds to measure 1/4 cup; set aside. Cut fennel bulb in half lengthwise; remove and discard the tough outer layer, fennel core and any green stalks. Cut widthwise into thin slices and measure 3 cups; place in a large bowl. Add orange sections.

In a jar with a tight-fitting lid, combine the orange juice, oil, orange peel, salt and pepper; shake well. Pour over fennel and oranges; toss gently. Sprinkle with reserved fronds. **Yield:** 4 servings.

Nutritional Analysis: *One serving (1 cup) equals 143 calories, 5 g fat (1 g saturated fat), 0 cholesterol, 193 mg sodium, 25 g carbohydrate, 6 g fiber, 3 g protein.*
Diabetic Exchanges: *1 fruit, 1 vegetable, 1 fat.*

Avocado Salad Dressing

(Pictured above)

Buttermilk and plain yogurt create the base for our Test Kitchen's thick dressing, which gets its color from avocado and parsley. The mild mixture is refreshing when dolloped over a tossed green salad.

1 cup 1% buttermilk
1/2 cup fat-free plain yogurt
1 ripe avocado, peeled and sliced
2 green onions, chopped
1/4 cup minced fresh parsley
1/2 teaspoon salt
1/2 teaspoon garlic powder
1/4 teaspoon dill weed
1/8 teaspoon pepper
Salad greens and vegetables of your choice

In a food processor, combine the first nine ingredients; cover and process until smooth. Serve over salad. Store in the refrigerator. **Yield:** 2 cups.

Nutritional Analysis: One serving (2 tablespoons dressing) equals 31 calories, 2 g fat (trace saturated fat), 1 mg cholesterol, 96 mg sodium, 3 g carbohydrate, 1 g fiber, 1 g protein.
Diabetic Exchange: 1/2 fat.

Sausage Bow Tie Salad

I made this flavorful entree salad for a first date. My boyfriend liked it so much, he took the leftovers home and his roommates raved about it, too! For a change of pace, substitute turkey sausage for the kielbasa.
—Christina Campeau, Simi Valley, California

1 pound fully cooked reduced-fat kielbasa *or* Polish sausage, cut into 1/4-inch slices
1 large onion, finely chopped
1 tablespoon water
1-1/2 teaspoons minced garlic, *divided*
1/2 cup balsamic vinegar
1 to 3 teaspoons fennel seed, crushed
5 cups cooked bow tie pasta
7 plum tomatoes, diced
1/4 cup minced fresh basil *or* 4 teaspoons dried basil
1 cup (4 ounces) crumbled feta cheese

In a large nonstick skillet, cook the sausage, onion, water and 3/4 teaspoon garlic over medium heat for 10 minutes. Add the vinegar and fennel seed. Reduce heat; cover and simmer for 5 minutes. Remove from the heat. Stir in pasta until coated. Add the tomatoes, basil and remaining garlic; stir gently. Cover and refrigerate until serving. Sprinkle with feta cheese. **Yield:** 9 servings.

Nutritional Analysis: One serving (1 cup) equals 235 calories, 5 g fat (2 g saturated fat), 29 mg cholesterol, 582 mg sodium, 35 g carbohydrate, 2 g fiber, 13 g protein.
Diabetic Exchanges: 2 starch, 1 lean meat, 1 vegetable.

Seven Fruit Salad

(Pictured below)

This refreshing fruit medley, lightly coated with cherry pie filling, makes a great picnic dish. You can substitute other fruits, such as red grapes or bananas, and use strawberry pie filling instead of cherry.
—Martha Cutler, Willard, Missouri

1 can (29 ounces) reduced-sugar sliced peaches, drained
2 cans (11 ounces *each*) mandarin oranges, drained

**1 can (20 ounces) unsweetened pineapple
chunks, drained
1 cup reduced-sugar cherry pie filling
1 cup halved fresh strawberries
1 cup green grapes
1/2 cup fresh *or* frozen blueberries**

In a large bowl, combine the peaches, oranges, pineapple and pie filling. Add the strawberries, grapes and blueberries; stir gently. Store leftovers in the refrigerator. **Yield:** 10 servings.

Nutritional Analysis: One serving (3/4 cup) equals 104 calories, trace fat (trace saturated fat), 0 cholesterol, 6 mg sodium, 25 g carbohydrate, 2 g fiber, 1 g protein.
Diabetic Exchange: 1-1/2 fruit.

Paradise Rice Salad

Toss together this satisfying salad starring rice and other healthy ingredients such as spinach, almonds and oranges. A little citrus makes this a fruitful change of pace from plain lettuce and dressing.
—Esther Conrad, Overland Park, Kansas

**1/3 cup orange juice
1/4 cup reduced-fat Italian salad dressing
1 tablespoon grated orange peel
2 teaspoons honey
1/2 teaspoon salt
4 cups cooked rice
2 cups torn fresh spinach
2 small navel oranges, peeled and sectioned
1 celery rib, chopped
1/4 cup slivered almonds, toasted**

In a large bowl, combine the orange juice, Italian dressing, orange peel, honey and salt. Add rice; toss to coat. Cover and refrigerate for 2 hours. Just before serving, add the spinach, oranges, celery and almonds; toss to coat. **Yield:** 8 servings.

Nutritional Analysis: One serving (3/4 cup) equals 171 calories, 4 g fat (trace saturated fat), trace cholesterol, 218 mg sodium, 31 g carbohydrate, 2 g fiber, 4 g protein.
Diabetic Exchanges: 1 starch, 1 fruit, 1/2 fat.

Raspberry Chicken Salad

(Pictured above)

This pretty summer salad is a snap to make, but it looks as though you fussed. The slightly tart dressing also serves as a basting sauce, which gives the thin slices of tender chicken breast a nice fruity flavor.
—Sue Zimonick, Green Bay, Wisconsin

**1 cup 100% raspberry spreadable fruit
1/3 cup raspberry vinegar
4 boneless skinless chicken breasts (4 ounces each)
8 cups torn mixed salad greens
1 small red onion, thinly sliced
24 fresh raspberries**

In a small bowl, combine spreadable fruit and vinegar; set aside 3/4 cup for dressing. Broil chicken 4 in. from the heat for 5-7 minutes on each side or until juices run clear, basting occasionally with remaining raspberry mixture. Cool for 10 minutes. Meanwhile, arrange greens and onion on salad plates. Slice chicken; place over greens. Drizzle with reserved dressing. Garnish with raspberries. **Yield:** 4 servings.

Nutritional Analysis: One serving (2 cups greens with 1 chicken breast half and 3 tablespoons dressing) equals 320 calories, 3 g fat (1 g saturated fat), 63 mg cholesterol, 97 mg sodium, 48 g carbohydrate, 3 g fiber, 25 g protein.
Diabetic Exchanges: 3 very lean meat, 3 fruit, 1 vegetable.

Orange Cucumber Tossed Salad

(Pictured at right)

This salad has been a family favorite for as long as I can remember. It's prettiest when it's served in a glass bowl, with orange and cucumber slices lining the sides.
—*Betty Tobias, Nashua, New Hampshire*

- 2 medium navel oranges, peeled and sliced
- 1 medium cucumber, sliced
- 4 cups torn romaine
- 4 cups torn leaf lettuce
- 1 small red onion, sliced and separated into rings
- 1/4 cup orange juice
- 2 tablespoons balsamic vinegar
- 1-1/2 teaspoons sugar
- 1/4 teaspoon salt
- 1/8 teaspoon pepper
- 3 tablespoons canola oil
- 1 cup seasoned salad croutons

Place orange and cucumber slices around the bottom sides of a straight-sided glass salad bowl. Cut any remaining orange and cucumber slices in half; place in another bowl. Add the lettuce and onion. In a jar with a tight-fitting lid, combine the orange juice, vinegar, sugar, salt, pepper and oil; shake well. Pour over lettuce mixture and toss gently to coat; carefully spoon into salad bowl. Sprinkle with croutons. Serve immediately. **Yield:** 8 servings.

Nutritional Analysis: One serving (1 cup) equals 111 calories, 6 g fat (1 g saturated fat), trace cholesterol, 141 mg sodium, 13 g carbohydrate, 3 g fiber, 2 g protein.
Diabetic Exchanges: 1 vegetable, 1 fat, 1/2 fruit.

Marinated Vegetable Salad

(Pictured at right)

Crisp and refreshing, this lovely veggie salad takes center stage. I like to toss it together for large gatherings and parties. I always place it in the middle of the table so folks have easy access. Before I know it, my "centerpiece" bowl is empty!
—*Hindy Silberstein, Highland Mills, New York*

- 3 medium yellow summer squash, sliced 1/4 inch thick
- 1 *each* medium sweet red, yellow, orange and green pepper, sliced *or* chopped
- 1 small red onion, thinly sliced and separated into rings
- 1 can (15 ounces) whole baby corn, rinsed and drained *or* 3/4 cup frozen corn, thawed
- 1 medium carrot, thinly sliced
- 1/4 cup white vinegar
- 2 tablespoons sugar
- 2 tablespoons water
- 2 tablespoons olive *or* canola oil
- 1 teaspoon salt

In a large bowl, combine the squash, peppers, onion, corn and carrot. In a jar with a tight-fitting lid, combine the re-maining ingredients; shake well. Pour over vegetables and toss to coat. Cover and refrigerate for 2 hours or until chilled. Serve with a slotted spoon. **Yield:** 10 servings.

Nutritional Analysis: One serving (3/4 cup) equals 89 calories, 3 g fat (trace saturated fat), 0 cholesterol, 243 mg sodium, 15 g carbohydrate, 3 g fiber, 2 g protein.
Diabetic Exchanges: 3 vegetable, 1/2 fat.

Creamy Pea Salad

This salad, which stars plenty of peas and crumbled bacon in a light dressing, is a delicious alternative to potato or pasta salad.
—*Candy Snyder, Salem, Oregon*

- 1/2 cup fat-free sour cream
- 2 bacon strips, cooked and crumbled
- 1 green onion, chopped
- 1 teaspoon white wine vinegar *or* cider vinegar
- 1/2 teaspoon salt
- 1/8 teaspoon pepper
- 3 cups fresh *or* frozen peas, thawed

In a bowl, combine the first six ingredients; mix well. Add peas; toss to coat. Refrigerate for at least 1 hour before serving. **Yield:** 4 servings.

Nutritional Analysis: One serving (3/4 cup) equals 142 calories, 2 g fat (1 g saturated fat), 3 mg cholesterol, 496 mg sodium, 22 g carbohydrate, 5 g fiber, 9 g protein.
Diabetic Exchanges: 1 starch, 1/2 fat-free milk, 1/2 fat.

Pineapple Waldorf Salad

This pretty salad is a staple at my house. I've shared the recipe with many satisfied guests. It's easily divided for smaller portions, too—I often make just "one apple's worth". If you don't like pineapple, try substituting canned mandarin oranges and juice instead.
—*Lois Kinneberg, Phoenix, Arizona*

- 1 can (20 ounces) unsweetened pineapple tidbits
- 6 cups chopped red apples (about 4 medium)
- 1-1/2 cups chopped celery
- 1/2 cup golden raisins
- 1/4 cup dry-roasted sunflower kernels
- 1/2 cup reduced-fat mayonnaise
- 1/2 cup plain fat-free yogurt
- 1/4 cup sugar

Drain pineapple, reserving 1/2 cup juice (discard remaining juice or save for another use). In a bowl, combine the pineapple, apples, celery, raisins and sunflower kernels. In another bowl, combine the mayonnaise, yogurt, sugar and reserved pineapple juice. Pour over fruit mixture and toss to coat. Refrigerate until serving. **Yield:** 13 servings.

Nutritional Analysis: One serving (3/4 cup) equals 131 calories, 5 g fat (1 g saturated fat), 3 mg cholesterol, 113 mg sodium, 24 g carbohydrate, 2 g fiber, 1 g protein.
Diabetic Exchanges: 1-1/2 fruit, 1 fat.

Step Up to the Salad Bar 63

Roasted Tomato Pasta Salad

*Herb-roasted plum tomatoes star in this pleasing
pasta dish. For added taste and texture, I mix
in chunks of creamy mozzarella and crunchy green
pepper, then tosses it all with a tangy dressing.*
—Ruth Barron, Mt. Pleasant, Pennsylvania

  10 plum tomatoes
   1 tablespoon olive *or* canola oil
 3/4 teaspoon salt, *divided*
 1/2 teaspoon dried basil
 1/4 teaspoon dried thyme
 1/4 teaspoon pepper
   1 medium green pepper, chopped
   4 ounces part-skim mozzarella cheese, cubed
 1/4 cup chopped onion
 1/4 cup fat-free red wine vinaigrette dressing
   3 cups cooked spiral pasta

Core tomatoes and cut in half lengthwise. Place cut side up
on a broiler pan; brush with oil. Combine 1/4 teaspoon of
salt, basil, thyme and pepper; sprinkle over tomatoes. Turn
tomatoes cut side down. Bake at 425° for 30-35 minutes
or until edges are well browned. Cool slightly.

Peel off skins and discard. Chop tomatoes; combine with
green pepper, cheese, onion, dressing and remaining salt.
Place pasta in a serving bowl; add tomato mixture and
toss to coat. **Yield:** 4 servings.

*Nutritional Analysis: One serving (1 cup) equals 326 calories,
10 g fat (4 g saturated fat), 15 mg cholesterol, 826 mg sodium,
46 g carbohydrate, 4 g fiber, 15 g protein.*
Diabetic Exchanges: 2 starch, 2 vegetable, 1 lean meat, 1 fat.

 1/8 teaspoon garlic powder
 1/8 teaspoon pepper
   4 fresh basil leaves, snipped

In a bowl, gently combine the tomatoes and onion. In a jar
with a tight-fitting lid, combine the vinegar, oil, sugar, salt,
garlic powder and pepper; shake well. Pour over tomato
mixture; toss gently to coat. Sprinkle with basil. Serve at
room temperature with a slotted spoon. **Yield:** 4 servings.

*Nutritional Analysis: One serving (1 cup) equals 114 calories,
7 g fat (1 g saturated fat), 0 cholesterol, 93 mg sodium, 12 g carbohydrate, 2 g fiber, 2 g protein.*
Diabetic Exchanges: 2 vegetable, 1-1/2 fat.

Plum Tomatoes with
Balsamic Vinaigrette

(Pictured above right)

*Sliced plum tomatoes and red onion are tossed with a
homemade vinaigrette to create this summery salad.
Fresh basil adds the flavorful finishing touch.*
—Ann Sobotka, Glendale, Arizona

   6 medium plum tomatoes, sliced
 1/2 cup sliced red onion
   3 tablespoons balsamic vinegar
   2 tablespoons olive *or* canola oil
 1/2 teaspoon sugar
 1/8 teaspoon salt

Green Shell Salad

*Pasta provides the base for this palate-pleasing salad.
I lightened up a friend's version of this recipe.
Seasoned with garden-fresh herbs, it tastes,
looks and smells wonderful. It's always a big hit
at cookouts and family gatherings.*
—Janet Bernard, Twinsburg, Ohio

 12 ounces small shell pasta
 1/2 cup fat-free plain yogurt
 1/2 cup reduced-fat mayonnaise
 1/2 cup minced fresh parsley
 1/2 cup minced fresh basil
   2 tablespoons olive *or* canola oil
   3 green onions, sliced
   2 teaspoons lemon juice
   2 garlic cloves, peeled
 1/2 teaspoon salt
 1/8 teaspoon pepper
 1/3 cup grated Parmesan cheese

Cook pasta according to package directions; drain and rinse
in cold water. Place in a serving bowl; set aside. In a blender

or food processor, combine the next 10 ingredients; cover and process until smooth. Pour over pasta and toss to coat. Sprinkle with Parmesan cheese. Serve immediately. **Yield:** 9 servings.

Nutritional Analysis: One serving (1/2 cup) equals 147 calories, 9 g fat (2 g saturated fat), 8 mg cholesterol, 303 mg sodium, 14 g carbohydrate, 1 g fiber, 4 g protein.
Diabetic Exchanges: 1-1/2 fat, 1 starch.

Tabbouleh

(Pictured below)

This cool refreshing salad is perfect to serve in warm weather. Bulgur blends deliciously with parsley, mint, tomatoes, onions and lemon juice. My brother brought this great grain dish to a family gathering. I loved the taste and texture so much, I had to have his recipe.
—Wanda Watson, Irving, Texas

    1 cup bulgur*
    2 cups boiling water
    3 tablespoons lemon juice
    2 tablespoons olive *or* canola oil
    2 tablespoons sliced green onions (tops only)
    1 tablespoon minced fresh parsley
    1 teaspoon salt
    1 teaspoon minced fresh mint
    1 medium tomato, seeded and diced
    6 romaine leaves

Place bulgur in a bowl; stir in water. Cover and let stand for 30 minutes or until liquid is absorbed. Drain and squeeze dry. Stir in lemon juice, oil, onions, parsley, salt and mint. Cover and refrigerate for 1 hour. Just before serving, stir in

Take Tabbouleh to the Table

TABBOULEH is a centuries-old Middle Eastern dish that has gained a healthy following worldwide. Its key ingredients include bulgur and fresh herbs (typically parsley and mint) in a lemony dressing.

Bulgur is parboiled whole-grain wheat that's been cracked or crushed and comes in coarse, medium or fine grinds. For tabbouleh, the fine grind is best, but medium is acceptable.

Be creative with tabbouleh. Popular add-ins range from chopped cucumbers, zucchini and red peppers to feta cheese, chickpeas and grilled fish, meat or poultry. Barley or rice can replace the bulgur.

In summer, tabbouleh makes a perfect pack-along picnic food. Simply put it in a pita pocket, scoop it up with veggies such as celery, carrots or sweet pepper strips, or eat it with a fork like a salad.

tomato. Serve in a lettuce-lined bowl. **Yield:** 6 servings.
*Editor's Note: Look for bulgur in the cereal, rice or organic food aisle of your grocery store.

Nutritional Analysis: One serving (3/4 cup) equals 129 calories, 5 g fat (1 g saturated fat), 0 cholesterol, 399 mg sodium, 20 g carbohydrate, 5 g fiber, 3 g protein.
Diabetic Exchanges: 1 starch, 1 fat.

Grilled Corn Salad

Our family and friends always rave over this dish at Sunday afternoon barbecues. We usually grill the corn the night before. I especially like this recipe because it lets me share the cooking with my husband, Rich. We call him "King of the Grill"!
—Patty Cook, West Palm Beach, Florida

    1 bottle (16 ounces) fat-free Italian salad dressing
    1 to 2 tablespoons minced fresh rosemary
      or 1 to 2 teaspoons dried rosemary, crushed
    7 medium ears sweet corn, husks removed
    7 plum tomatoes, sliced
    7 cups torn fresh spinach

Coat grill rack with nonstick cooking spray before starting the grill. In a large resealable plastic bag, combine the dressing and rosemary; add corn. Seal bag and turn to coat; remove corn from marinade. Seal bag and refrigerate marinade. Grill corn, covered, over medium heat for 15-18 minutes or until tender, turning occasionally. Return corn to the marinade; add tomatoes. Seal bag and turn to coat; refrigerate for at least 4 hours or overnight.

Drain corn and tomatoes, reserving marinade. Cut corn off the cob. Arrange spinach on salad plates; top with tomatoes and corn. Drizzle with reserved marinade. **Yield:** 7 servings.

Nutritional Analysis: One serving equals 141 calories, 2 g fat (trace saturated fat), 2 mg cholesterol, 873 mg sodium, 29 g carbohydrate, 5 g fiber, 5 g protein.
Diabetic Exchanges: 1-1/2 starch, 1 vegetable

Sesame Seed Veggie Salad

(Pictured below)

*This colorful combo will perk up any picnic,
potluck or holiday gathering.*
—*Bob Lesburg, Mount Pleasant, South Carolina*

1 pound fresh green beans, cut into 1-inch pieces
1 can (15-1/2 ounces) black-eyed peas, rinsed
   and drained
1 cup grape *or* cherry tomatoes
1 small red onion, chopped
2 tablespoons balsamic vinegar
1 tablespoon olive *or* canola oil
3 garlic cloves, minced
1/2 teaspoon salt
1/4 to 1/2 teaspoon crushed red pepper flakes
1/4 teaspoon ground mustard
2 tablespoons sesame seeds, toasted

Place beans in a saucepan and cover with water. Bring to
a boil. Reduce heat; simmer, uncovered, for 5-7 minutes or
until crisp-tender. Drain and rinse with cold water; pat dry.

In a large bowl, combine the beans, peas, tomatoes
and onion. In a small bowl, whisk the vinegar, oil, garlic, salt,
red pepper flakes and mustard; pour over bean mixture.
Sprinkle with sesame seeds. Toss to coat. Let stand for 1
hour at room temperature before serving. **Yield:** 8 servings.

*Nutritional Analysis: One serving (3/4 cup) equals 97 calo-
ries, 2 g fat (trace saturated fat), 0 cholesterol, 259 mg sodium, 13
g carbohydrate, 4 g fiber, 4 g protein.*
Diabetic Exchanges: 1 vegetable, 1/2 starch, 1/2 fat.

Apple Salad

*This is a delightfully refreshing salad. With only
six ingredients, it's simple to assemble and quick
to serve. A creamy dressing coats the crunchy
apples, celery and chewy dates.*
—*Beverly Little, Marietta, Georgia*

3 celery ribs, finely chopped
4 medium apples, peeled and chopped
1 cup fat-free whipped topping
1/4 cup chopped dates *or* raisins
2 tablespoons chopped pecans
4 teaspoons reduced-fat mayonnaise

In a bowl, combine all ingredients. Cover and refrigerate until serving. **Yield:** 6 servings.

*Nutritional Analysis: One serving (2/3 cup) equals 121 calo-
ries, 3 g fat (trace saturated fat), 1 mg cholesterol, 51 mg sodium,
23 g carbohydrate, 3 g fiber, 1 g protein.*
Diabetic Exchanges: 1-1/2 fruit, 1/2 fat.

Cranberry Couscous Salad

*This satisfying salad has an
interesting mix of good-for-you ingredients.
It's a favorite of ours in fall.*
—*Carol Miller, Northumberland, New York*

1 cup water
3/4 cup uncooked couscous
3/4 cup dried cranberries
1/2 cup chopped carrots
1/2 cup chopped seeded cucumber
1/4 cup thinly sliced green onions
3 tablespoons balsamic vinegar
1 tablespoon olive *or* canola oil
2 teaspoons Dijon mustard
1/2 teaspoon salt
1/8 teaspoon pepper
1/4 cup slivered almonds, toasted

In a saucepan, bring water to a boil. Stir in couscous. Remove from the heat; cover and let stand for 5 minutes.
Fluff with a fork. Cool for 10 minutes.

In a bowl, combine the couscous, cranberries, carrots,
cucumber and green onions. In a small bowl, combine the
vinegar, oil, mustard, salt and pepper. Pour over couscous
mixture; mix well. Cover and refrigerate. Just before serving, stir in almonds. **Yield:** 6 servings.

*Nutritional Analysis: One serving (1/2 cup) equals 199 calo-
ries, 6 g fat (1 g saturated fat), 0 cholesterol, 247 mg sodium, 33
g carbohydrate, 3 g fiber, 4 g protein.*
Diabetic Exchanges: 1 starch, 1 fruit, 1 fat.

Spiced Fruit

(Pictured above)

*Cinnamon, cloves, rosemary and
lemon juice turn canned fruit into something
special. With its festive flavor, this sunny
dish is perfect for a Christmas brunch.*
—Sue Gronholz, Beaver Dam, Wisconsin

**1 can (20 ounces) unsweetened pineapple
chunks**
1 can (16 ounces) reduced-sugar pear halves
1 can (15 ounces) mandarin oranges, drained
1 tablespoon lemon juice
3 cinnamon sticks (3 inches *each*), broken
3 sprigs fresh rosemary (2 inches *each*)
4 whole cloves

Drain pineapple and pears, reserving 1-1/2 cups juice.
Place the pineapple, pears and oranges in a bowl; set aside.
In a saucepan, combine the lemon juice, cinnamon sticks,
rosemary, cloves and reserved juices; bring to a boil. Reduce heat; simmer, uncovered, for 3-4 minutes. Remove
from the heat; cool to room temperature. Pour over fruit.
Cover and refrigerate overnight. Discard cinnamon sticks,
rosemary and cloves before serving. **Yield:** 5 servings.

*Nutritional Analysis: One serving (3/4 cup) equals 129 calo-
ries, trace fat (0 saturated fat), 0 cholesterol, 13 mg sodium, 32 g
carbohydrate, 2 g fiber, 1 g protein.*
Diabetic Exchange: *2 fruit.*

Italian Broccoli Salad

(Pictured above)

*Brighten up your winter meals with this crisp and
colorful salad. Tomatoes, broccoli, mushrooms and
red onions mingle with crunchy water chestnuts,
all draped in a zesty bottled dressing.*
—Dorothy Myrick, Kent, Washington

4 cups broccoli florets
1 small red onion, sliced and separated into rings
1 can (8 ounces) sliced water chestnuts, drained
1/2 cup sliced fresh mushrooms
3/4 cup reduced-fat Italian salad dressing
1-1/2 cups halved cherry tomatoes

In a large bowl, combine the broccoli, onion, water chestnuts and mushrooms. Pour dressing over vegetables; toss
to coat. Cover and refrigerate for at least 2 hours. Add tomatoes; gently toss. **Yield:** 9 servings.

*Nutritional Analysis: One serving (3/4 cup) equals 38 calo-
ries, 1 g fat (trace saturated fat), 1 mg cholesterol, 295 mg sodium, 7 g carbohydrate, 2 g fiber, 2 g protein.*
Diabetic Exchange: *1 vegetable.*

Whipped Carrot Salad

(Pictured at right)

Carrots and pineapple give this fluffy gelatin salad its refreshing taste. A friend gave me the recipe. I serve this side dish often, whether I'm entertaining guests or my family. Lovely and light, it's perfect with almost any menu.
—Jean Smith, Crossville, Tennessee

1 package (6 ounces) orange gelatin
2 cups boiling water
1 package (8 ounces) reduced-fat cream cheese, cubed
2 cans (8 ounces *each*) unsweetened crushed pineapple, drained
1 cup finely grated carrots
1 carton (8 ounces) frozen reduced-fat whipped topping, thawed

In a bowl, dissolve gelatin in boiling water. Place cream cheese in a food processor or blender; cover and process until smooth. While processing, gradually add dissolved gelatin; process until smooth. Pour into a large bowl. Stir in pineapple and carrots; fold in whipped topping. Pour into a serving bowl. Refrigerate for 2 hours or until firm. **Yield:** 12 servings.

Nutritional Analysis: One serving (2/3 cup) equals 158 calories, 6 g fat (4 g saturated fat), 11 mg cholesterol, 92 mg sodium, 22 g carbohydrate, 1 g fiber, 4 g protein.
Diabetic Exchanges: *1-1/2 starch, 1 fat.*

Asparagus Avocado Medley

(Pictured at right)

This pretty blend of garden-fresh vegetables and zesty herb dressing tastes as good as it looks!
—Patricia Alderete, Lowell, Indiana

1 pound fresh asparagus, trimmed and cut into 1-1/2-inch pieces
8 medium fresh mushrooms, sliced
1 large ripe avocado, peeled and cubed
1 medium zucchini, diced
1 large tomato, seeded and chopped
1 medium red onion, sliced
2 tablespoons lemon juice
2 tablespoons olive *or* canola oil
1 tablespoon balsamic vinegar
1 teaspoon Dijon mustard
1 garlic clove, minced
1/2 teaspoon dried basil
1/2 teaspoon dried thyme
1/4 teaspoon salt
1/4 teaspoon pepper

Place asparagus and 2 tablespoons water in a microwave-safe dish. Cover and microwave on high for 3-6 minutes or until crisp-tender, stirring once; drain and cool.
In a large bowl, combine the asparagus, mushrooms, avocado, zucchini, tomato and onion; toss gently. In a jar with a tight-fitting lid, combine the remaining ingredients; shake well. Pour over salad and toss gently to coat. Cover and refrigerate until serving. **Yield:** 7 servings.

*Editor's Note: This recipe was tested in an 850-watt microwave.

Nutritional Analysis: One serving (1 cup) equals 122 calories, 9 g fat (1 g saturated fat), 0 cholesterol, 111 mg sodium, 11 g carbohydrate, 4 g fiber, 4 g protein.
Diabetic Exchanges: *2 vegetable, 1-1/2 fat.*

Summertime Yogurt Salad

Vanilla yogurt, with a touch of ginger and lime, coats the colorful summer fruits in this cool-tasting salad from our Test Kitchen.

2 cups cubed cantaloupe
1 cup cubed watermelon
1 medium fresh peach, sliced
1 medium pear, sliced
1/2 cup halved green grapes
1 cup (8 ounces) fat-free vanilla yogurt
1 tablespoon lime juice
1 teaspoon grated lime peel
1/4 teaspoon ground ginger

In a bowl, combine the fruit. In another bowl, combine the yogurt, lime juice, peel and ginger. Pour over fruit and stir gently to coat. Serve immediately. **Yield:** 8 servings.

Nutritional Analysis: One serving (3/4 cup) equals 75 calories, trace fat (trace saturated fat), 1 mg cholesterol, 21 mg sodium, 17 g carbohydrate, 1 g fiber, 2 g protein.
Diabetic Exchanges: *1/2 starch, 1/2 fruit.*

Fruit 'n' Feta Tossed Salad

This is an adaptation of a salad I tasted at a restaurant. The combination of cheese and apples is delicious. I came up with the dressing recipe, which has a fruity flavor and creamy texture.
—Debbie Blackburn, Camp Hill, Pennsylvania

CREAMY RASPBERRY VINAIGRETTE:
1 package (10 ounces) frozen sweetened raspberries, thawed
1 cup (8 ounces) reduced-fat plain yogurt
2 tablespoons cider vinegar
1/2 teaspoon dried tarragon
SALAD:
9 cups torn mixed salad greens
1-1/2 cups shredded carrots
2 Red Delicious apples, chopped
1 Golden Delicious apple, chopped
3/4 cup crumbled feta cheese

Strain raspberries, reserving juice; discard seeds and pulp. In a small bowl, whisk the yogurt, vinegar, tarragon and raspberry juice until smooth. In a large bowl, toss the salad greens, carrots and apples. Sprinkle with feta cheese. Serve with dressing. **Yield:** 12 servings.

Nutritional Analysis: One serving (1 cup salad with 2 tablespoons dressing) equals 94 calories, 2 g fat (2 g saturated fat), 10 mg cholesterol, 126 mg sodium, 16 g carbohydrate, 3 g fiber, 3 g protein.
Diabetic Exchanges: *1 fruit, 1/2 fat.*

*from church potlucks and family functions
to bridal luncheons.*
—Fran Thompson, Tarboro, North Carolina

6 ounces uncooked spiral pasta
1/4 cup reduced-sodium soy sauce
1/3 cup white wine vinegar *or* cider vinegar
2 tablespoons canola oil
2 tablespoons sugar
2 tablespoons sesame seeds, toasted
1/2 teaspoon salt
1/4 teaspoon pepper
3 cups chopped cooked chicken breast
2 cups torn fresh spinach
1/2 cup sliced green onions
1/4 cup minced fresh parsley

Cook pasta according to package directions. In a jar with a tight-fitting lid, combine the soy sauce, vinegar, oil, sugar, sesame seeds, salt and pepper; shake well. Drain pasta and rinse in cold water; place in a bowl. Add chicken and half of the dressing; toss to coat. Cover and refrigerate for at least 4 hours. Set remaining dressing aside.

Just before serving, add the spinach, onions, parsley and remaining dressing; toss to coat. **Yield:** 8 servings.

Nutritional Analysis: One serving (1 cup) equals 181 calories, 7 g fat (1 g saturated fat), 45 mg cholesterol, 496 mg sodium, 11 g carbohydrate, 1 g fiber, 19 g protein.
Diabetic Exchanges: 2 very lean meat, 1 starch, 1 fat.

Strawberry Salad Dressing

(Pictured above)

A bit of honey perfectly balances puckery raspberry vinegar with sweet strawberries in this homemade dressing. Drizzle it over mixed salad greens of your choice and enjoy!
—Rebekah Hubbard, Las Vegas, Nevada

1 package (20 ounces) frozen unsweetened
  strawberries, thawed
1/2 cup water
3 tablespoons raspberry vinegar
2 tablespoons honey
2 teaspoons canola oil
1 teaspoon reduced-sodium soy sauce
1/4 teaspoon salt
1/4 teaspoon dried thyme
1/4 teaspoon pepper
Torn mixed salad greens and sliced onion

In a blender or food processor, combine the first nine ingredients. Cover and process until smooth. Serve over greens and onion. Store in the refrigerator. **Yield:** 3 cups.

Nutritional Analysis: One serving (2 tablespoons dressing) equals 17 calories, trace fat (trace saturated fat), 0 cholesterol, 33 mg sodium, 4 g carbohydrate, 1 g fiber, trace protein.
Diabetic Exchange: Free food.

Sesame Chicken Pasta Salad

This tasty chicken salad tops my list of most-requested recipes. I've made it for countless occasions,

Cranberry-Chutney Turkey Salad

(Pictured below)

Dried cranberries give this refreshing salad sweetness while chopped pecans lend a pleasant crunch. Whether served on a lettuce leaf or stuffed inside

a pita, it makes a perfect lunch or midday snack.
—Andrea Yacyk, Brigantine, New Jersey

 3 cups diced cooked turkey breast
 1/2 cup dried cranberries
 1/3 cup chopped pecans
 1/3 cup diced onion
 1/3 cup diced green pepper
 1/2 cup fat-free mayonnaise
 1/2 cup reduced-fat sour cream
 1 tablespoon lemon juice
 1/2 teaspoon ground ginger
 1/8 teaspoon cayenne pepper
Leaf lettuce

In a large bowl, combine the turkey, cranberries, pecans, onion and green pepper. In a small bowl, combine the mayonnaise, sour cream, lemon juice, ginger and cayenne. Pour over turkey mixture; stir gently to coat. Cover and refrigerate until serving. Serve in a lettuce-lined bowl. **Yield:** 6 servings.

Nutritional Analysis: One serving (2/3 cup) equals 226 calories, 8 g fat (2 g saturated fat), 69 mg cholesterol, 214 mg sodium, 15 g carbohydrate, 2 g fiber, 23 g protein.
Diabetic Exchanges: 3 very lean meat, 1 fat, 1/2 starch, 1/2 fruit.

Tarragon Turkey Salad

Mandarin oranges complement tender turkey and bow tie pasta in this summery salad. My family loves the combination of citrus and tarragon.
—Shannon Bitenc, Scottsdale, Arizona

 4 cups uncooked bow tie pasta
 2 cups cubed cooked turkey breast
 3/4 cup sliced celery
 1 can (11 ounces) mandarin oranges, drained
 1/2 cup reduced-fat mayonnaise
 1 tablespoon orange juice
 1 tablespoon Dijon mustard
 2 teaspoons minced fresh tarragon or 3/4
 teaspoon dried tarragon
 1 teaspoon grated orange peel
 3/4 teaspoon salt
 1/8 teaspoon white pepper
Lettuce leaves

Cook pasta according to package directions; rinse with cold water and drain. Place in a large bowl; add turkey, celery and oranges. In a small bowl, combine mayonnaise, orange juice, mustard, tarragon, orange peel, salt and pepper. Pour over pasta mixture and toss to coat. Cover and refrigerate for 1 hour. Serve over lettuce. **Yield:** 8 servings.

Nutritional Analysis: One serving (1 cup) equals 234 calories, 6 g fat (1 g saturated fat), 41 mg cholesterol, 421 mg sodium, 27 g carbohydrate, 1 g fiber, 17 g protein.
Diabetic Exchanges: 2 starch, 2 lean meat.

Pasta Salad Plus

(Pictured below and on page 49)

When it comes to pleasing a crowd at a picnic, this colorful pasta and veggie salad does the trick.
—Taunja Roberts, Amity, Oregon

 12 ounces uncooked spiral pasta
 4 medium carrots, sliced
 3 celery ribs, sliced
 1 can (16 ounces) kidney beans, rinsed and drained
 1 can (15 ounces) garbanzo beans or chickpeas, rinsed and drained
 1 large onion, halved and thinly sliced
 1 cup sliced fresh mushrooms
 1 medium green pepper, julienned
 1 can (6 ounces) pitted ripe olives, drained and sliced
 1 jar (4-1/2 ounces) marinated artichoke hearts, drained and coarsely chopped
DRESSING:
 1/2 cup white wine vinegar or cider vinegar
 1/2 cup canola oil
 1/3 cup sugar
 2 tablespoons grated Parmesan cheese
 3/4 to 1 teaspoon garlic powder
 3/4 teaspoon salt
 1/8 teaspoon pepper

Cook pasta according to package directions; drain and rinse in cold water. Place in a large bowl; add the next nine ingredients. In a jar with a tight-fitting lid, combine the dressing ingredients; shake well. Pour over salad and toss to coat. **Yield:** 15 servings.

Nutritional Analysis: One serving (1 cup) equals 267 calories, 10 g fat (1 g saturated fat), 1 mg cholesterol, 474 mg sodium, 38 g carbohydrate, 5 g fiber, 7 g protein.
Diabetic Exchanges: 1-1/2 starch, 1-1/2 fat, 1 lean meat, 1 vegetable.

Dijon Herb Salad Dressing

(Pictured above)

Mustard and garlic lend plenty of flavor to this thick dressing for green salads. I also like to drizzle it over fresh sliced tomatoes when they're at their peak.
—Marge Werner, Broken Arrow, Oklahoma

2/3 cup fat-free mayonnaise
1/4 cup white wine vinegar *or* cider vinegar
2 tablespoons minced fresh parsley
2 tablespoons Dijon mustard
1 tablespoon sugar
1 garlic clove, minced
1 teaspoon dried thyme
1/8 teaspoon pepper
Salad greens and vegetables of your choice

In a small bowl, whisk together the first eight ingredients. Cover and refrigerate for at least 1 hour. Serve over salad. Refrigerate leftovers. **Yield:** 1 cup.

Nutritional Analysis: One serving (2 tablespoons dressing) equals 27 calories, 1 g fat (trace saturated fat), 2 mg cholesterol, 255 mg sodium, 5 g carbohydrate, 1 g fiber, trace protein.
Diabetic Exchange: 1/2 starch.

Tomato Corn Salad

I have a remedy for those same-old lettuce salad blues—red vine-ripe tomatoes mixed with white and yellow corn. This salad is great for backyard barbecues, especially when there's a harvest of fresh corn in your garden. Or use frozen corn for other occasions year-round.
—Wendy Ann Wood, Portland, Oregon

2-1/4 cups cooked fresh *or* frozen white corn, thawed

2-1/4 cups cooked fresh *or* frozen yellow corn, thawed
1 medium cucumber, diced
2 medium tomatoes, chopped
1/4 cup chopped red onion
1/4 cup reduced-fat sour cream
2 tablespoons reduced-fat mayonnaise
1 tablespoon white wine vinegar *or* cider vinegar
1/2 teaspoon salt
1/4 teaspoon celery seed
1/4 teaspoon ground mustard

In a bowl, combine the corn, cucumber, tomatoes and onion. In another bowl, whisk together the remaining ingredients. Pour over vegetable mixture; toss gently to coat. Refrigerate for at least 2 hours. **Yield:** 9 servings.

Nutritional Analysis: One serving (3/4 cup) equals 93 calories, 2 g fat (1 g saturated fat), 3 mg cholesterol, 164 mg sodium, 19 g carbohydrate, 3 g fiber, 3 g protein.
Diabetic Exchange: 1 starch.

Cucumber Salad

(Pictured below)

My family just loves this cool cucumber salad well dressed with sour cream and vinegar. It's a refreshing side dish that's quick to fix with everyday ingredients.
—Rose Lauritsen, Orange City, Florida

1/2 cup reduced-fat sour cream
2 tablespoons cider vinegar
1 teaspoon sugar
3/4 teaspoon garlic powder
3/4 teaspoon dill weed
1/2 teaspoon salt
3 medium cucumbers, sliced
1/2 cup sliced onion

In a bowl, combine the sour cream, vinegar, sugar, garlic powder, dill and salt. Add cucumbers and onion; toss to

coat. Cover and refrigerate for at least 1 hour. Serve with a slotted spoon. **Yield:** 6 servings.

Nutritional Analysis: One serving (3/4 cup) equals 58 calories, 2 g fat (1 g saturated fat), 7 mg cholesterol, 211 mg sodium, 8 g carbohydrate, 2 g fiber, 3 g protein.
Diabetic Exchanges: 1 vegetable, 1/2 fat.

Simply Fruit

Young and old alike will enjoy this fun fruit medley featuring banana, kiwifruit, oranges and grapes. A dollop of yogurt with brown sugar tops off this nourishing sweet treat from our Test Kitchen.

2 medium navel oranges, peeled and sliced
2 kiwifruit, peeled and cubed
1 medium firm banana, sliced
1 cup seedless red grapes
1/2 cup reduced-fat vanilla yogurt
2 tablespoons plus 2 teaspoons brown sugar

In a bowl, combine the oranges, kiwi, banana and grapes. Divide among six serving bowls. Combine the yogurt and brown sugar; dollop over the fruit. Serve immediately. **Yield:** 6 servings.

Nutritional Analysis: One serving (2/3 cup) equals 107 calories, 1 g fat (trace saturated fat), 1 mg cholesterol, 15 mg sodium, 27 g carbohydrate, 4 g fiber, 2 g protein.
Diabetic Exchange: 2 fruit.

🍎 Kiwifruit Cues

FAMILIAR with kiwifruit? If not, don't be put off by its odd exterior. This brown, fuzzy egg-sized fruit is nutritious...and delicious! Some say its flavor is a blend of strawberry and pineapple.

Here are a few kiwifruit facts to snack on:

- Kiwifruit is packed with vitamin C and is a good source of potassium.
- When shopping, choose kiwifruit that is somewhat firm and heavy. Avoid those that are soft or bruised.
- Most kiwifruit comes from either New Zealand or Italy, although Chile and California are also producers.
- Kiwifruit will keep in the refrigerator for 3 to 4 weeks.
- It's easy to eat kiwifruit—just peel and slice. You can also add it to fruit salads, cereal, coleslaw and blender drinks.
- Kiwifruit can be used as a garnish on pies, cakes, meat dishes or in punch. It's also a great meat tenderizer.
- And don't confuse kiwifruit with kiwi, the long-beaked bird that's native to New Zealand!

Creamy Bean Salad

This hearty no fuss salad is perfect for a family gathering. Dill pickles bring puckery flavor to the kidney beans that are dressed with sour cream...and celery adds a satisfying crunch.
—Dorothy Poch, Concord, New Hampshire

2 cans (16 ounces *each*) kidney beans, rinsed and drained
2 celery ribs, sliced
1 cup (8 ounces) reduced-fat sour cream
1 small onion, finely chopped
2 large dill pickles, chopped
1/2 teaspoon salt
1/4 teaspoon pepper
2 hard-cooked eggs, sliced

In a large bowl, combine the beans, celery, sour cream, onion, pickles, salt and pepper; mix well. Cover and refrigerate for at least 1 hour. Just before serving, top with the eggs. **Yield:** 8 servings.

Nutritional Analysis: One serving (1/2 cup) equals 149 calories, 4 g fat (2 g saturated fat), 63 mg cholesterol, 764 mg sodium, 19 g carbohydrate, 4 g fiber
Diabetic Exchanges: 1 starch, 1 lean meat.

Warm Chicken Spinach Salad

I enjoy cooking but don't always have time to prepare elaborate meals, so I love this pretty salad because it's so fast to fix.
—Cheryl Arnold, Lake Zurich, Illinois

1/2 pound boneless skinless chicken breasts, cut into thin strips
3 teaspoons olive *or* canola oil, *divided*
1/4 teaspoon cornstarch
1/4 teaspoon salt
1/8 teaspoon pepper
2 tablespoons orange juice
2 tablespoons white wine vinegar *or* cider vinegar
3 cups torn fresh spinach
1 medium navel orange, peeled and sectioned
2 thin slices red onion, halved
2 tablespoons chopped walnuts, toasted

In a skillet, saute chicken in 1 teaspoon oil for 5 minutes or until no longer pink. In a small bowl, combine the cornstarch, salt, pepper, orange juice, vinegar and remaining oil until smooth; stir into skillet. Bring to a boil; cook and stir for 1 minute or until thickened. In a large bowl, combine the spinach, orange, onion and walnuts; add chicken mixture and toss. Serve immediately. **Yield:** 2 servings.

Nutritional Analysis: One serving equals 298 calories, 13 g fat (2 g saturated fat), 66 mg cholesterol, 406 mg sodium, 16 g carbohydrate, 4 g fiber, 30 g protein.
Diabetic Exchanges: 3 lean meat, 1 vegetable, 1 fat, 1/2 fruit.

Western Broccoli Salad

(Pictured at right)

The broccoli, kidney beans, tomato and cheddar cheese give this colorful salad a unique flavor that's absolutely delicious. You'll love this make-ahead dish.
—Carol Rumsey, Jacksonville, Florida

- 4 cups fresh broccoli florets
- 1 medium tomato, chopped
- 1 can (16 ounces) kidney beans, rinsed and drained
- 3/4 cup chopped sweet onion
- 1 cup (4 ounces) shredded reduced-fat cheddar cheese
- 1/4 teaspoon salt
- 3/4 cup fat-free ranch salad dressing

Place 1 in. of water and broccoli in a skillet; bring to a boil. Boil for 1 minute. Cover and remove from the heat; let stand for 3-4 minutes or until crisp-tender. Drain and pat dry. In a serving bowl, toss the broccoli, tomato, beans, onion, cheese and salt. Drizzle with dressing; toss to coat. Cover and refrigerate until serving. **Yield:** 8 servings.

Nutritional Analysis: One serving (3/4 cup) equals 138 calories, 3 g fat (2 g saturated fat), 8 mg cholesterol, 633 mg sodium, 21 g carbohydrate, 4 g fiber, 9 g protein.
Diabetic Exchanges: 1 vegetable, 1 starch, 1 lean meat.

Hold-the-Oil French Dressing

(Pictured at right)

The first time I served this dressing, my husband thought I had bought a new brand and commented on how good it was. No one would guess that this zesty salad topping starts with a can of tomato soup.
—Ruth Koberna, Brecksville, Ohio

- 1 can (10-3/4 ounces) reduced-fat reduced-sodium condensed tomato soup, undiluted
- 1/3 cup sugar
- 1/3 cup cider vinegar
- 1 tablespoon Worcestershire sauce
- 1 tablespoon grated onion
- 1 teaspoon salt
- 1/2 teaspoon ground mustard
- 1 garlic clove, minced
- 1/2 teaspoon paprika
- 1/4 teaspoon pepper
- Salad greens and vegetables of your choice

In a bowl, whisk the first 10 ingredients until blended. Serve with a tossed salad. Refrigerate leftover dressing. **Yield:** 14 servings (1-3/4 cups).

Nutritional Analysis: One serving (2 tablespoons dressing) equals 38 calories, trace fat (trace saturated fat), 0 cholesterol, 260 mg sodium, 9 g carbohydrate, trace fiber, trace protein.
Diabetic Exchange: 1/2 starch.

Mediterranean Lentil Salad

A light refreshing dressing lends a lemony lift to this Mediterranean mix of lentils, tomatoes, olives and feta cheese. This good-for-you side dish tastes terrific and goes together in a jiffy. My family loves it served with homemade bread.
—Melissa Nichols, Shorewood, Minnesota

- 5 cups water
- 1 cup lentils, rinsed
- 1/4 cup lemon juice
- 3 tablespoons olive *or* canola oil
- 2 garlic cloves, minced
- 2 teaspoons sugar
- 2 teaspoons minced fresh thyme *or* 1 teaspoon dried thyme
- 1 teaspoon salt
- 1/8 teaspoon pepper
- 1-1/2 cups chopped tomato (about 4 medium)
- 3 celery ribs, chopped
- 1/2 cup crumbled feta cheese
- 1/4 cup sliced ripe olives
- 2 tablespoons chopped fresh parsley

In a saucepan, bring water and lentils to a boil. Reduce heat; cover and simmer for 20-25 minutes or until tender. Rinse under cold water; drain. Place in a large bowl to cool. Meanwhile, in a jar with a tight-fitting lid, combine the lemon juice, oil, garlic, sugar, thyme, salt and pepper; shake well. Add tomato, celery, cheese and olives to lentils; toss to combine. Add dressing and gently toss to coat. Sprinkle with parsley. **Yield:** 6 servings.

Nutritional Analysis: One serving (2/3 cup) equals 231 calories, 11 g fat (3 g saturated fat), 11 mg cholesterol, 614 mg sodium, 25 g carbohydrate, 11 g fiber, 12 g protein.
Diabetic Exchanges: 1-1/2 starch, 1 lean meat, 1 fat.

Peachy Fruit Salad

I came up with this quick salad when I wanted a cool treat on a hot day. It's fun for breakfast, as a side dish or dessert. The pie filling provides all the extra sweetening it needs.
—Lori Daniels, Beverly, West Virginia

- 2 medium fresh peaches, peeled and sliced
- 1 medium red apple, chopped
- 1 cup halved seedless red grapes
- 1 medium ripe mango *or* additional peach, peeled and sliced
- 1 medium firm banana, sliced
- 1-1/2 cups apple pie filling

In a large bowl, combine the fruit. Add pie filling and toss to coat. Refrigerate until serving. **Yield:** 8 servings.

Nutritional Analysis: One serving (3/4 cup) equals 103 calories, trace fat (trace saturated fat), 0 cholesterol, 6 mg sodium, 26 g carbohydrate, 2 g fiber, 1 g protein.
Diabetic Exchange: 2 fruit.

Chicken Rice Salad

I start this salad by poaching chicken breasts in a mixture of white wine, garlic and lemon juice. It gives them great flavor and helps keep them moist. The cubed chicken, veggies and cooked rice are tossed with a tasty homemade dressing.
—Janne Rowe, Wichita, Kansas

    1 cup dry white wine *or* chicken broth
    1 tablespoon lemon juice
    1 garlic clove, minced
  3/4 teaspoon ground ginger *or* 3 teaspoons minced
        fresh gingerroot, divided
1-1/4 pounds boneless skinless chicken breasts
    3 cups chicken broth
1-1/2 cups uncooked long grain rice
    1 package (10 ounces) frozen peas, thawed
  1/2 cup sliced green onions
  1/2 cup diced celery
    2 tablespoons diced sweet red pepper
    2 tablespoons diced green pepper
DRESSING:
  1/4 cup cider vinegar
    2 tablespoons Dijon mustard
    1 tablespoon reduced-sodium soy sauce
    1 tablespoon olive *or* canola oil
    1 tablespoon sesame *or* canola oil
    2 teaspoons honey
    1 garlic clove, minced
Dash ground ginger *or* 1/4 teaspoon minced fresh
    gingerroot

In a large nonstick skillet, combine the wine or broth, lemon juice, garlic and 1/4 teaspoon ground ginger or 1 teaspoon gingerroot. Bring to a boil; reduce heat. Add chicken; poach, uncovered, over medium-low heat for 15 minutes or until juices run clear. Remove chicken from cooking liquid and chill.

In a saucepan, bring broth and remaining ginger to a boil. Stir in rice; reduce heat. Cover; simmer for 15-20 minutes or until liquid is absorbed and rice is tender. Transfer to a large bowl; cool. Add peas, onions, celery and peppers. Cut chicken into bite-size pieces; add to rice mixture and toss. In a jar with a tight-fitting lid, combine dressing ingredients; shake well. Pour over salad and toss to coat. **Yield:** 7 servings.

Nutritional Analysis: One serving (1-1/2 cups) equals 350 calories, 6 g fat (1 g saturated fat), 47 mg cholesterol, 704 mg sodium, 43 g carbohydrate, 3 g fiber, 25 g protein.
Diabetic Exchanges: 2-1/2 starch, 2 lean meat, 1 fat.

Creamy Herb Dressing

(Pictured below)

This dressing is part of a turkey salad recipe I found in a cookbook published by members of the gym I go to. It's flecked with herbs and has a mild ranch-Dijon flavor.
—Tracy Powers, Cedar Springs, Michigan

  1/2 cup reduced-fat mayonnaise
    1 carton (8 ounces) fat-free plain yogurt
  1/2 teaspoon dried thyme
  1/2 teaspoon dried tarragon
    1 teaspoon Dijon mustard
  1/4 teaspoon salt
  1/8 teaspoon dried rosemary, crushed
  1/8 teaspoon pepper

In a bowl, whisk together all of the ingredients. Refrigerate until serving. **Yield:** 10 servings.

Nutritional Analysis: One serving (2 tablespoons) equals 51 calories, 4 g fat (1 g saturated fat), 5 mg cholesterol, 180 mg sodium, 3 g carbohydrate, trace fiber, 1 g protein.
Diabetic Exchange: 1 fat.

Side Dishes & Condiments

In this chapter, you'll find just the right accompaniment for your meals...from fresh vegetables, pleasing pasta and hearty potatoes to satisfying rice, mouth-watering relishes and perfectly seasoned spices.

Bacon 'n' Veggie Pasta (page 91)

Kohlrabi with Honey Butter

If you're not acquainted with kohlrabi, this recipe will serve as a pleasant introduction. Honey and lemon lend a sweet, citrusy taste to the turnip-like veggie. I found the recipe several years ago and gave it a try. It remains one of our favorite dishes.
—*Wanda Holoubek, Salina, Kansas*

> 1 pound kohlrabi (4 to 5 small), peeled and cut into 1/4-inch strips
> 1 medium carrot, cut into 1/8-inch strips
> 1 tablespoon minced chives
> 1 tablespoon lemon juice
> 1 tablespoon butter *or* stick margarine, melted
> 2 teaspoons honey
> 1/4 teaspoon grated lemon peel
> 1/8 teaspoon pepper
> 4 lemon slices

In a large skillet, bring 1 in. of water, kohlrabi and carrot strips to a boil. Reduce heat; cover and simmer for 10-12 minutes or until crisp-tender. In a small bowl, combine the chives, lemon juice, butter, honey, lemon peel and pepper; mix well. Drain vegetables; add honey butter and toss to coat. Garnish with lemon slices. **Yield:** 4 servings.

Nutritional Analysis: One serving (1/2 cup) equals 77 calories, 3 g fat (2 g saturated fat), 8 mg cholesterol, 62 mg sodium, 12 g carbohydrate, 5 g fiber, 2 g protein.
Diabetic Exchanges: 2 vegetable, 1/2 fat.

Grilled Vegetable Skewers

(Pictured above)

My mother and I love to eat vegetables the most flavorful way—grilled! Seasoned with fresh herbs, these colorful kabobs showcase the best of summer's bounty.
—*Susan Bourque, Danielson, Connecticut*

> 1 medium ear fresh *or* frozen sweet corn, thawed and quartered
> 1 small zucchini, quartered
> 1/4 small red onion, halved
> 4 cherry tomatoes
> 1/4 teaspoon dried basil
> 1/4 teaspoon dried rosemary, crushed
> 1/4 teaspoon dried thyme
> 1/8 teaspoon garlic powder
> 1/8 teaspoon salt
> 1/8 teaspoon pepper

Place the corn on a microwave-safe plate. Cover with waxed paper. Microwave on high for 2 minutes. If grilling the kabobs, coat grill rack with nonstick cooking spray before starting the grill. On two metal or soaked wooden skewers, alternately thread the corn, zucchini, onion and tomatoes. Lightly coat vegetables with nonstick cooking spray. In a small bowl, combine the seasonings; sprinkle over vegetables. Grill, covered, over medium heat or broil 4-6 in. from the heat for 3 minutes on each side or until vegetables are tender, turning three times. **Yield:** 2 servings.

Nutritional Analysis: One serving (1 kabob) equals 69 calories, 1 g fat (trace saturated fat), 0 cholesterol, 131 mg sodium, 16 g carbohydrate, 3 g fiber, 3 g protein.
Diabetic Exchanges: 1 vegetable, 1/2 starch.

🍎 Getting to Know Kohlrabi

KOHLRABI ("cabbage turnip" in German) might look strange, what with its unusual bulb-like stem, but don't let that stop you from trying this nutritious vegetable. Kohlrabi is an excellent source of potassium, calcium, fiber and vitamin C.

Like a turnip, kohlrabi's greens and stem are both edible. Its taste has been compared to turnips, cabbage and broccoli. The cooked leaves mimic collards or kale.

You can prepare kohlrabi a number of ways. Steam or saute the leaves for soups and stews. Cut the bulb into cubes or slices and saute, steam or stir-fry them. Or hollow out the bulb and stuff it. Both the bulb and leaves can be added raw to salads also. Take these additional cues when using kohlrabi:

- Look for kohlrabi in your grocery store from mid-spring to mid-fall; its peak months are June and July.
- When buying, choose a bulb that is heavy with firm, dark green leaves.
- Wrapped in plastic, kohlrabi can keep in the refrigerator for 4 to 5 days.
- There's no need to peel kohlrabi; just trim away any tough or woody skin.

Onion Pepper Medley

This crisp-tender combination is a quick-and-easy way to dress up an everyday sandwich. It also helps us use up the abundance of fresh vegetables from our annual garden.
—Loretta Hill, Westminster, Maryland

4 large green peppers, julienned
1 large onion, sliced
4-1/2 teaspoons canola oil
1 teaspoon dried oregano
1/2 teaspoon salt

In a microwave-safe bowl, combine all ingredients. Cover and microwave on high for 7-10 minutes or until peppers and onion are crisp-tender. Serve warm. **Yield:** 3 cups.
   Editor's Note: This recipe was tested in an 850-watt microwave.

   Nutritional Analysis: One serving (1/3 cup) equals 47 calories, 2 g fat (trace saturated fat), 0 cholesterol, 132 mg sodium, 6 g carbohydrate, 2 g fiber, 1 g protein.
   Diabetic Exchanges: 1 vegetable, 1/2 fat.

Carrot Raisin Pilaf

The raisins in this colorful rice pilaf add a touch of natural sweetness, while almonds add fun crunch. A hint of curry boosts the flavor, too.
—Lauretta Musser, Apollo, Pennsylvania

1 medium onion, chopped
2 tablespoons butter *or* stick margarine
2-1/2 cups water
2 medium carrots, cut into 1-inch julienne strips
1 cup uncooked long grain rice
1/2 cup raisins
1 tablespoon chicken bouillon granules
1/2 teaspoon curry powder
1/4 teaspoon salt
1/4 teaspoon dried thyme
1/4 cup slivered almonds, toasted

In a saucepan, saute onion in butter until tender. Stir in the water, carrots, rice, raisins, bouillon, curry powder, salt and thyme. Bring to a boil. Reduce heat; cover and simmer for 15-20 minutes or until rice is tender. Sprinkle with almonds before serving. **Yield:** 6 servings.

   Nutritional Analysis: One serving (2/3 cup) equals 243 calories, 7 g fat (3 g saturated fat), 11 mg cholesterol, 733 mg sodium, 41 g carbohydrate, 3 g fiber, 5 g protein.
   Diabetic Exchanges: 1-1/2 starch, 1 fruit, 1 vegetable, 1 fat.

Garlic Potato Wedges

(Pictured above)

Looking for a change from run-of-the-mill potatoes? Try these tender wedges that are generously seasoned with garlic, rosemary and other flavorful ingredients. They complement any meal.
—Amy Werner, Grand Ledge, Michigan

4 pounds small red potatoes, cut into wedges
1/3 cup olive *or* canola oil, *divided*
16 unpeeled garlic cloves
2 tablespoons minced fresh rosemary
   or 2 teaspoons dried rosemary, crushed
1 teaspoon salt
1/3 cup white wine vinegar *or* cider vinegar
4 teaspoons Dijon mustard
3 teaspoons sugar
1/4 teaspoon pepper
1/3 cup chopped green onions

In a large bowl, combine the potatoes, 1 tablespoon of oil, garlic, rosemary and salt. Pour into two 15-in. x 10-in. x 1-in. baking pans coated with nonstick cooking spray. Bake, uncovered, at 450° for 25-30 minutes or until potatoes are tender, stirring every 10 minutes.
   In a small bowl, combine the vinegar, mustard, sugar, pepper and remaining oil until smooth. Squeeze the roasted garlic into the vinegar mixture (discard skins). Pour over the potatoes and toss to coat. Sprinkle with onions. **Yield:** 8 servings.

   Nutritional Analysis: One serving (1 cup) equals 299 calories, 9 g fat (1 g saturated fat), 0 cholesterol, 374 mg sodium, 51 g carbohydrate, 5 g fiber, 5 g protein.
   Diabetic Exchanges: 3 starch, 2 fat.

6 medium ears sweet corn in husks
1 tablespoon butter *or* stick margarine
2 garlic cloves, minced
1/4 cup steak sauce
3/4 teaspoon chili powder
1/4 teaspoon ground cumin

Soak corn in cold water for 1 hour. Meanwhile, in a microwave-safe dish, combine butter and garlic. Cover and microwave on high for 2 minutes or until garlic is softened, stirring once. Stir in the steak sauce, chili powder and cumin; set aside.

Carefully peel back husks from corn to within 1 in. of bottom; remove silk. Brush corn with sauce. Rewrap corn in husks and secure with kitchen string. Coat grill rack with nonstick cooking spray before starting the grill. Grill corn, covered, over medium heat for 25-30 minutes, turning occasionally. **Yield:** 6 servings.

Nutritional Analysis: One ear of corn equals 107 calories, 3 g fat (1 g saturated fat), 5 mg cholesterol, 223 mg sodium, 20 g carbohydrate, 3 g fiber, 3 g protein.
Diabetic Exchanges: 1 starch, 1/2 fat.

Three-Berry Sauce

(Pictured above)

I combined cranberries with strawberries and raspberries for a tasty twist on the traditional holiday sauce. Cinnamon and cloves spice up this fruity topping that's great over poultry or pork.
—*Suzanne Ganatta, Mammoth Lakes, California*

2 cups fresh *or* frozen cranberries
1/2 cup honey
1/4 cup orange juice
1 tablespoon grated orange peel
1/4 teaspoon salt
1/4 teaspoon ground cinnamon
1/8 teaspoon ground cloves
1/8 teaspoon ground allspice
2/3 cup frozen sweetened sliced strawberries, thawed
2/3 cup frozen sweetened raspberries, thawed

n a saucepan, combine the first eight ingredients. Cook, uncovered, over medium heat for 10 minutes or until the cranberries pop, stirring occasionally. Reduce heat; add the strawberries and raspberries. Cook until heated through. Remove from the heat; cool. Store in the refrigerator. **Yield:** 2-1/4 cups.

Nutritional Analysis: One serving (1/4 cup) equals 108 calories, trace fat (trace saturated fat), 0 cholesterol, 67 mg sodium, 29 g carbohydrate, 2 g fiber, trace protein.
Diabetic Exchange: 2 fruit.

Santa Fe Corn on the Cob

Corn is my all-time favorite food, and this is the best way I've found to fix it. The zesty grilling sauce has Southwestern flair, but it's not too hot or spicy. My family loves corn served this way.
—*Laurie Meaike, Audubon, Iowa*

Spinach Supreme

Showcase spinach at its best in this satisfying side dish. Mushrooms, onion and crunchy walnuts enhance the good-for-you greens. With so much flavor, you won't even miss the butter!
—*Clara Coulston, Washington Court House, Ohio*

1 cup sliced fresh mushrooms
1 medium onion, chopped
1/4 cup reduced-sodium chicken broth
8 cups chopped fresh spinach
1/2 teaspoon garlic powder
1/4 teaspoon salt
1/8 teaspoon pepper
2 tablespoons chopped walnuts, toasted

In a large saucepan, cook mushrooms and onion in broth over medium-low heat until tender. Stir in the spinach, garlic powder, salt and pepper; cover and cook for 2-3 minutes or until spinach is wilted. Stir in walnuts. Serve with a slotted spoon. **Yield:** 2 servings.

Nutritional Analysis: One serving (3/4 cup) equals 108 calories, 5 g fat (trace saturated fat), 0 cholesterol, 469 mg sodium, 12 g carbohydrate, 5 g fiber, 7 g protein.
Diabetic Exchanges: 2 vegetable, 1 fat.

Italian Rice

(Pictured above right)

Bring a bit of Italy to the table without the usual pasta and sauce. This colorful side dish blends fluffy rice, fresh spinach and roasted red peppers. The amount of garlic can be adjusted to fit your personal taste. For me, the more garlic, the better!
—*Michelle Armistead, Marlboro, New Jersey*

2 garlic cloves, minced
2 teaspoons olive *or* canola oil

Nutritional Analysis: One serving (1 filled squash half) equals 261 calories, 6 g fat (4 g saturated fat), 16 mg cholesterol, 268 mg sodium, 54 g carbohydrate, 5 g fiber, 2 g protein.

Barbecued Lima Beans

(Pictured below)

Surprise! This lively lima bean dish has the great flavor of old-fashioned baked beans. Sweet and savory, they're a crowd-pleasing addition to picnics and barbecues.
—*Lois Johnson, South Hill, Virginia*

      1 pound dried lima beans
      6 cups water
  1-1/2 cups chopped onions
      1 teaspoon salt
      1 cup ketchup
    0/4 cup packed brown sugar
    1/3 cup pancake syrup
    1/4 teaspoon hot pepper sauce
      4 bacon strips, cooked and crumbled

Place beans in a large saucepan; add water to cover by 2 in. Bring to a boil; boil for 2 minutes. Remove from the heat; cover and let stand for 1 hour. Drain and rinse beans, discarding water. Return beans to the saucepan. Add 6 cups water, onions and salt; mix well. Bring to a boil. Reduce heat; cover and simmer for 1-1/2 to 1-3/4 hours or until beans are tender.

Drain and discard liquid. Stir in the ketchup, brown sugar, syrup, hot pepper sauce and bacon. Transfer to an ungreased 2-qt. baking dish or bean pot. Cover and bake at 350° for 30 minutes. Uncover and bake 30 minutes longer or until bubbly. **Yield:** 12 servings.

Nutritional Analysis: One serving (1/2 cup) equals 163 calories, 1 g fat (trace saturated fat), 2 mg cholesterol, 480 mg sodium, 35 g carbohydrate, 3 g fiber, 4 g protein.
Diabetic Exchange: 2 starch.

---

      8 cups fresh spinach (about 10 ounces), chopped
      1 tablespoon balsamic vinegar
    1/2 teaspoon salt
    1/8 teaspoon pepper
      2 cups hot cooked rice
    1/2 cup chopped roasted sweet red peppers

In a large nonstick skillet, saute garlic in oil for 1 minute. Stir in spinach. Cover and cook for 3-4 minutes or until tender; drain well. Add the vinegar, salt and pepper. Stir in the rice and red peppers until combined. Cook and stir until heated through. **Yield:** 4 servings.

Nutritional Analysis: One serving (3/4 cup) equals 151 calories, 3 g fat (trace saturated fat), 0 cholesterol, 398 mg sodium, 29 g carbohydrate, 2 g fiber, 4 g protein.
Diabetic Exchanges: 1-1/2 starch, 1 vegetable, 1/2 fat.

Cherry-Stuffed Acorn Squash

Sweet dried cherries, brown sugar and tangy lemon juice spruce up tender squash halves in this special wintertime side dish. Instead of sweet potatoes, I make this delicious recipe for holiday dinners.
—*Christa Beard, Jacksonville, Florida*

      3 medium acorn squash
    2/3 cup dried cherries *or* cranberries
    1/2 cup packed brown sugar
      1 teaspoon grated lemon peel
    1/4 teaspoon ground nutmeg
    1/2 teaspoon salt
    1/4 cup lemon juice
      3 tablespoons butter *or* stick margarine

Cut squash in half; discard seeds. Place squash cut side up in two 13-in. x 9-in. x 2-in. baking dishes coated with nonstick cooking spray. Combine the cherries, brown sugar, lemon peel, nutmeg and salt; spoon into squash halves. Sprinkle with lemon juice; dot with butter. Bake, uncovered, at 350° for 45-55 minutes or until squash is tender. **Yield:** 6 servings.

Three-Bean Casserole

(Pictured below)

This recipe came from a family reunion of mostly Mennonites and is over 30 years old. You can choose different beans, according to your family's tastes, but keep the pork and beans as a base. I often take a big pot of these to large gatherings or pitch-in suppers, and everyone enjoys them.
—Jane Bone, Cape Coral, Florida

2 bacon strips, diced
1 large green pepper, chopped
1 medium onion, chopped
1 can (31 ounces) pork and beans
1 can (16 ounces) kidney beans, rinsed and drained
1 can (15-1/4 ounces) lima beans, rinsed and drained
1/2 cup ketchup
1 jar (4 ounces) diced pimientos
1/4 cup packed brown sugar
1 tablespoon Worcestershire sauce
1 teaspoon ground mustard

In a large nonstick skillet, cook bacon over medium heat until crisp. Remove to paper towels; drain, reserving 1 tablespoon drippings. In the drippings, saute green pepper and onion until tender.

Combine the beans in a large bowl. Gently stir in pepper mixture and bacon. Stir in the ketchup, pimientos, brown sugar, Worcestershire sauce and mustard until combined.

Transfer to a 2-qt. baking dish coated with nonstick cooking spray. Cover and bake at 350° for 50-60 minutes or until bubbly. **Yield:** 9 servings.

Nutritional Analysis: One serving (3/4 cup) equals 238 calories, 3 g fat (1 g saturated fat), 5 mg cholesterol, 864 mg sodium, 46 g carbohydrate, 10 g fiber, 10 g protein.
Diabetic Exchanges: 2-1/2 starch, 1 very lean meat.

Confetti Couscous

Couscous prepared this way makes a fun and colorful side dish alongside chicken, pork or fish. I've even stirred in pineapple chunks and cooked chicken for a great lunch.
—Marla Stewart, Kirby, Arkansas

1 can (14-1/2 ounces) chicken broth
2 tablespoons water
2 tablespoons lemon juice
1 teaspoon grated lemon peel
1/2 teaspoon salt
1 package (10 ounces) couscous
2 cups fresh *or* frozen peas, thawed
1/2 cup slivered almonds, toasted
1 jar (4 ounces) diced pimientos, drained

In a saucepan, bring the broth, water, lemon juice, peel and salt to a boil. Stir in couscous and peas. Cover; remove from the heat and let stand for 5 minutes. Stir in almonds and pimientos. **Yield:** 6 servings.

Nutritional Analysis: One serving (3/4 cup) equals 294 calories, 6 g fat (trace saturated fat), 0 cholesterol, 570 mg sodium, 47 g carbohydrate, 6 g fiber, 12 g protein.
Diabetic Exchanges: 3 starch, 1 fat.

Broccoli-Stuffed Tomatoes

I'm a recent college graduate who's starting to become an everyday cook. This is one of my childhood favorites and a nice alternative to stuffed peppers.
—Ruth Schleusener, Stockton, Kansas

1-1/2 cups chopped fresh broccoli
4 medium tomatoes
1 teaspoon lemon juice
1 small onion, chopped
1 tablespoon butter *or* stick margarine
2 tablespoons all-purpose flour
1/2 cup 2% milk
1/4 cup chicken broth
2 tablespoons grated Parmesan cheese
1 tablespoon minced fresh basil *or* 1/2 teaspoon dried basil
1/4 teaspoon salt
1/8 teaspoon pepper
1 egg white

In a saucepan, bring broccoli and 1 in. of water to a boil. Reduce heat; cover and simmer for 3-4 minutes or until crisp-tender. Drain and set aside. Cut a 1/2-in. slice off the top of each tomato; with a spoon or melon baller, hollow out each tomato, leaving a 1/2-in. shell. Discard pulp. Sprinkle 1/4 teaspoon lemon juice into each tomato; place upside down on paper towel for 10 minutes to drain.

Meanwhile, in a skillet, saute onion in butter until tender. In a bowl, combine the flour, milk and broth until smooth. Stir into onion mixture. Bring to a boil; cook and stir for 2 minutes or until thickened. Remove from the heat; stir in Parmesan cheese, basil, salt, pepper and reserved broccoli. In a mixing bowl, beat the egg white until stiff peaks form. Fold into broccoli mixture.

Place the tomatoes in an ungreased 8-in. square baking dish. Spoon the broccoli mixture into each tomato, mounding in the center. Bake, uncovered, at 350° for 30-35 minutes or until a knife inserted near the center comes out clean and the tops are golden brown. **Yield:** 4 servings.

Nutritional Analysis: One serving (1 tomato) equals 118 calories, 5 g fat (3 g saturated fat), 13 mg cholesterol, 345 mg sodium, 14 g carbohydrate, 2 g fiber, 6 g protein.
Diabetic Exchanges: 2 vegetable, 1 fat, 1/2 starch.

Cantina Pinto Beans

Cumin, cilantro and red pepper flakes lend a Southwestern flair to tender pinto beans in this recipe. This dish was inspired by one served at a Dallas, Texas restaurant. The chef added chunks of ham, but my version is meatless. It makes a great Tex-Mex side or a filling lunch when served with corn bread.
—Mrs. L.R. Larson, Sioux Falls, South Dakota

  2 cups dry pinto beans (1 pound)
  2 cans (14-1/2 ounces *each*) reduced-sodium
    chicken broth
  2 celery ribs, diced
1/4 cup diced onion
1/4 cup diced green pepper
  1 teaspoon ground cumin
1/2 teaspoon rubbed sage
1/4 teaspoon crushed red pepper flakes
  2 bay leaves
  1 garlic clove, minced
  2 cans (14-1/2 ounces *each*) Mexican diced
    tomatoes, drained
1/2 teaspoon salt
Minced fresh cilantro *or* parsley

Place beans in a Dutch oven or soup kettle; add water to cover by 2 in. Bring to a boil; boil for 2 minutes. Remove from the heat; cover and let stand for 1 hour. Drain and rinse beans, discarding liquid. Return beans to the pan.

Stir in broth, celery, onion, green pepper, cumin, sage, pepper flakes, bay leaves and garlic. Bring to a boil. Reduce heat; simmer, uncovered, for 1 hour or until beans are very tender. Discard bay leaves. Stir in tomatoes and salt. Simmer, uncovered, for 30 minutes or until heated through. Sprinkle with cilantro. **Yield:** 10 servings.

Nutritional Analysis: One serving (3/4 cup) equals 164 calories, 1 g fat (trace saturated fat), 0 cholesterol, 605 mg sodium, 32 g carbohydrate, 10 g fiber, 10 g protein.
Diabetic Exchanges: 1-1/2 starch, 1 very lean meat, 1 vegetable.

Sunny Snow Peas

(Pictured above)

Turn crispy snow peas into something special by tossing them with a lovely honey-orange sauce. I enjoy serving fresh vegetables, especially when I can prepare a sauce like this.
—Kathleen Bailey, Chester Springs, Pennsylvania

1/2 cup orange juice
  2 tablespoons honey
  1 tablespoon butter *or* stick margarine
  1 to 2 teaspoons grated orange peel
1/2 teaspoon salt
1/8 teaspoon ground cardamom
  1 pound fresh snow peas *or* sugar snap peas

In a small saucepan, combine the first six ingredients; bring to a boil. Reduce heat; simmer, uncovered, until mixture is reduced by half, about 15 minutes. Meanwhile, in another saucepan, bring 1 in. of water and peas to a boil. Reduce heat; simmer, uncovered, for 5-6 minutes or until crisp-tender. Drain and place in a serving bowl. Pour sauce over peas and toss to coat. **Yield:** 6 servings.

Nutritional Analysis: One serving (2/3 cup) equals 81 calories, 2 g fat (1 g saturated fat), 5 mg cholesterol, 218 mg sodium, 14 g carbohydrate, 2 g fiber, 2 g protein.
Diabetic Exchanges: 2 vegetable, 1/2 fat.

Oven-Baked Country Fries

(Pictured above)

*Looking for an alternative to French fries? Try these
lightly crisped potato wedges. You can have fun with the
coating. Add some garlic powder, Cajun seasoning
or whatever spices your family prefers.*
—LaDonna Reed, Ponca City, Oklahoma

>   2 egg whites
> 1/4 cup all-purpose flour
> 1/3 cup dry bread crumbs
>   2 tablespoons grated Parmesan cheese
> 1-1/2 teaspoons onion salt
> 1-1/2 teaspoons Italian seasoning
>   1 teaspoon paprika
> 1/4 teaspoon pepper
>   3 medium unpeeled baking potatoes (1 pound)

In a shallow bowl, beat egg whites until foamy. In another
shallow bowl, combine the flour, bread crumbs, Parmesan
cheese and seasonings. Cut each potato lengthwise into
eight wedges. Dip potatoes into egg whites, then coat with
crumb mixture. Place in a single layer on a baking sheet
coated with nonstick cooking spray. Spray wedges evenly
with nonstick cooking spray. Bake, uncovered, at 375° for
40-45 minutes or until golden brown. **Yield:** 4 servings.

*Nutritional Analysis: One serving (6 wedges) equals 185
calories, 1 g fat (1 g saturated fat), 3 mg cholesterol, 822 mg
sodium, 36 g carbohydrate, 3 g fiber, 7 g protein.*
Diabetic Exchange: *2-1/2 starch.*

Sweet Potato Pancakes

*Folks are sure to flip over these tastefully different
pancakes! They're a twist on the traditional potato
pancake. Sour cream, onion and red pepper give them a
unique flavor that everyone seems to love. I usually
double the recipe because they disappear so quickly.*
—Mari Krajec, Lindenhurst, Illinois

>   1 pound sweet potatoes, peeled and shredded
>   2 green onions, chopped
>   2 eggs, lightly beaten
> 1/4 cup all-purpose flour
> 1/2 teaspoon salt
> 1/2 teaspoon pepper
>   5 tablespoons reduced-fat sour cream
> **Finely chopped sweet red pepper and sliced green
> onions, optional**

In a bowl, combine sweet potatoes, onions, eggs, flour,
salt and pepper; mix well. Drop batter by 1/4 cupfuls onto
baking sheets coated with nonstick cooking spray; flatten
slightly. Bake at 400° for 8 minutes; turn pancakes over.
Bake 8-10 minutes longer or until potatoes are tender and
pancakes are golden brown. Top with sour cream; garnish
with red pepper and onions if desired. **Yield:** 5 servings.

*Nutritional Analysis: One serving (2 pancakes with 1 table-
spoon sour cream) equals 171 calories, 4 g fat (2 g saturated
fat), 90 mg cholesterol, 283 mg sodium, 29 g carbohydrate, 2 g
fiber, 6 g protein.*
Diabetic Exchange: *2 starch.*

Tarragon-Almond Green Beans

*A hint of balsamic vinegar gives a fresh taste to this
simple side. Sliced almonds dress up green beans
tastefully when company's coming. I can't think of an
entree this dish doesn't complement.*
—Glenda Malan, Lake Forest, California

> 1-1/2 pounds fresh green beans, trimmed
> 1/3 cup sliced green onions
>   1 garlic clove, minced
>   2 teaspoons olive *or* canola oil
> 1/4 cup balsamic vinegar
>   4 teaspoons sugar
> 1-1/2 teaspoons minced fresh tarragon
>   *or* 1/2 teaspoon dried tarragon
> 1/8 teaspoon salt
> 1/4 cup sliced almonds, toasted

Place beans in a saucepan and cover with water. Bring to
a boil; cook, uncovered, for 8-10 minutes or until tender.
Meanwhile, in a nonstick skillet, saute onions and garlic in
oil until onions are tender. Add the vinegar, sugar, tarragon and salt. Bring to a boil; cook until liquid is reduced
by half. Drain beans; add to onion mixture. Cook and stir until heated through. Sprinkle with almonds. **Yield:** 6 servings.

*Nutritional Analysis: One serving (3/4 cup) equals 93 calo-
ries, 4 g fat (trace saturated fat), 0 cholesterol, 54 mg sodium, 13
g carbohydrate, 5 g fiber, 3 g protein.*
Diabetic Exchanges: *1 vegetable, 1/2 starch, 1/2 fat.*

Some Crantastic Facts

- Cranberries can be frozen for up to 9 months when stored in a heavy-duty freezer bag or container. Do not thaw before using in recipes.
- You can substitute frozen cranberries in most recipes calling for fresh.
- To prepare cranberries for cooking, sort out bruised, soft or shriveled berries and discard. Rinse remaining berries in cold water.
- Cook cranberries by boiling gently in water and waiting until the berries "pop" (when the outer skin expands until it bursts).
- A 12-ounce bag of cranberries yields about 3 cups.
- For quick results, chop cranberries in a food processor.
- For some fast and berry tasty results, try these easy ideas. Mix a little cranberry juice with some hot apple cider for a zingy beverage. Add a half cup (or more) of chopped cranberries to your favorite bread, muffin or stuffing mix. Add variety to baked apples by filling the center with cranberries and a dash of sugar and cinnamon.

Parmesan Spinach and Noodles

I love this dish because it's so quick to fix…and it's versatile, too. Sometimes I'll dress it up by stirring in cooked shrimp, crab, chicken or turkey for an elegant company meal.
—Merrie Fischer, Glen Arm, Maryland

  6 ounces uncooked yolk-free noodles
1/2 cup chopped onion
  1 package (10 ounces) frozen chopped spinach
  1 can (10-3/4 ounces) reduced-fat reduced-sodium condensed cream of chicken soup, undiluted
  4 ounces reduced-fat cream cheese, cubed
1/2 cup grated Parmesan cheese
1/3 cup fat-free milk
1/2 teaspoon dried parsley flakes
1/8 teaspoon dried basil
1/8 teaspoon ground nutmeg
1/8 teaspoon pepper

Cook noodles according to package directions. Meanwhile, place onion in a 2-qt. microwave-safe bowl. Cover and microwave on high for 3 minutes or until tender. Add spinach; cover and cook on high for 5 minutes or until spinach is thawed; stir.
   Add the soup, cream cheese, Parmesan cheese, milk and seasonings; mix well. Cover and microwave at 50% power for 8 minutes or until heated through, stirring once. Drain noodles; add to spinach mixture and stir to coat. **Yield:** 5 servings.
   *Editor's Note: This recipe was tested in an 850-watt microwave.

Nutritional Analysis: One serving (1 cup) equals 286 calories, 9 g fat (5 g saturated fat), 29 mg cholesterol, 544 mg sodium, 36 g carbohydrate, 4 g fiber, 14 g protein.
Diabetic Exchanges: 2 starch, 1 lean meat, 1 vegetable, 1 fat.

Gingered Squash Saute

(Pictured below)

This vibrant veggie saute puts summer's bounty in the spotlight. The recipe comes from a 20-year-old cookbook, but I still use it, especially when produce from our garden is plentiful.
—Ruth Andrewson, Peck, Idaho

  1 pound yellow summer squash
1/2 pound small zucchini, sliced
  1 medium onion, thinly sliced
  1 medium green pepper, julienned
  4 teaspoons butter *or* stick margarine
  3 medium tomatoes, peeled and quartered
3/4 teaspoon salt
1/2 to 1 teaspoon ground ginger

Cut yellow squash in half lengthwise, then into 1/2-in. slices. In a large skillet, saute squash, zucchini, onion and green pepper in butter for 1 minute. Cover and cook over medium heat for 3 minutes. Add tomatoes, salt and ginger. Cover and cook 2-3 minutes or until heated through. **Yield:** 9 servings.

Nutritional Analysis: One serving (3/4 cup) equals 48 calories, 2 g fat (1 g saturated fat), 5 mg cholesterol, 219 mg sodium, 7 g carbohydrate, 2 g fiber, 2 g protein.
Diabetic Exchanges: 1 vegetable, 1/2 fat.

Chili-Cheese Spoon Bread

This versatile casserole can serve as a snappy side dish or a meatless meal with mass appeal. My family raves about it.
—Patricia Barkman, Riverton, Manitoba

1/2 cup egg substitute
1 egg
1 can (8-3/4 ounces) whole kernel corn, drained
1 can (8-1/4 ounces) cream-style corn
1 cup (8 ounces) reduced-fat sour cream
1 cup (4 ounces) shredded reduced-fat cheddar cheese
1 cup (4 ounces) shredded reduced-fat Mexican cheese blend *or* part-skim mozzarella cheese
1 can (4 ounces) chopped green chilies, drained
1/2 cup cornmeal
2 tablespoons butter *or* stick margarine, melted
1/2 teaspoon salt
1/2 teaspoon Worcestershire sauce
1/8 teaspoon cayenne pepper

In a large bowl, beat egg substitute and egg. Add the remaining ingredients; mix well. Pour into a 9-in. square baking dish coated with nonstick cooking spray. Bake at 350° for 35-40 minutes or until a knife inserted near the center comes out clean. Serve warm. **Yield:** 9 servings.

Nutritional Analysis: One serving equals 213 calories, 10 g fat (6 g saturated fat), 53 mg cholesterol, 525 mg sodium, 19 g carbohydrate, 2 g fiber, 13 g protein.
Diabetic Exchanges: 1-1/2 lean meat, 1 starch, 1 fat.

Herbed Mushroom Sauce

Our Test Kitchen team dreamed up this savory sauce that's chock-full of fresh mushrooms and a variety of herbs. It's especially good spooned over pork chops, beef tenderloin, chicken or even pasta.

1 pound fresh mushrooms, sliced
3 to 4 garlic cloves, minced
2 tablespoons butter *or* stick margarine
2-1/2 cups chicken broth, *divided*
2 to 3 teaspoons minced fresh rosemary *or* 3/4 to 1 teaspoon dried rosemary, crushed
1 teaspoon minced fresh thyme *or* 1/4 teaspoon dried thyme
1/4 cup dry sherry *or* additional chicken broth
1 tablespoon reduced-sodium teriyaki sauce
1/8 to 1/4 teaspoon hot pepper sauce
3 tablespoons nonfat dry milk powder
2 tablespoons cornstarch
2 cups fat-free milk
3 tablespoons grated Parmesan cheese
2 tablespoons spicy brown mustard
2 teaspoons minced fresh oregano *or* 1/2 teaspoon dried oregano

In a large nonstick skillet, saute mushrooms and garlic in butter until tender. Add 1-1/4 cups broth, rosemary and thyme. Bring to a boil; cook until mixture is reduced by two-thirds. Add 2/3 cup broth, sherry or additional broth, teriyaki and hot pepper sauce; cook and stir over high heat until mixture is reduced by two-thirds. Add remaining broth. Reduce heat; simmer for 5 minutes.

In a bowl, combine milk powder and cornstarch; gradually stir in milk until blended. Stir into sauce. Bring to a boil; cook and stir for 2 minutes or until thickened. Reduce heat; add the cheese, mustard and oregano. Stir until cheese is melted. **Yield:** 7 servings.

Nutritional Analysis: One serving (1/2 cup) equals 123 calories, 5 g fat (3 g saturated fat), 13 mg cholesterol, 577 mg sodium, 12 g carbohydrate, 1 g fiber, 8 g protein.
Diabetic Exchanges: 1 fat-free milk, 1 fat.

Asparagus Tomato Stir-Fry

(Pictured at right)

Last spring, when asparagus was in the stores, my sister found this recipe, tried it and thought I might like it, too. This fast-to-fix side dish is perfect after a busy day at work.
—Elizabeth MacAulay
Charlottetown, Prince Edward Island

2 teaspoons cornstarch
1/4 cup chicken broth
4 teaspoons reduced-sodium soy sauce
2 teaspoons minced fresh gingerroot, *divided*
1 teaspoon canola oil
3/4 pound fresh asparagus, cut into 1-inch pieces
4 green onions, cut into 1-inch pieces
1-1/2 cups sliced fresh mushrooms
2 small plum tomatoes, cut into thin wedges
1 teaspoon sesame oil

In a small bowl, combine the cornstarch, broth, soy sauce and 1/2 teaspoon ginger until blended; set aside. In a nonstick skillet or wok, stir-fry the remaining ginger in canola oil for 30 seconds. Add asparagus and onions; stir-fry for 3 minutes. Add mushrooms; stir-fry for 1 minute.

Stir cornstarch mixture and add to skillet. Bring to a boil; cook and stir for 1 minute or until thickened. Reduce heat. Add tomatoes and sesame oil; cook 1 minute longer. **Yield:** 4 servings.

Nutritional Analysis: One serving (3/4 cup) equals 68 calories, 3 g fat (trace saturated fat), 0 cholesterol, 268 mg sodium, 9 g carbohydrate, 3 g fiber, 3 g protein.
Diabetic Exchanges: 2 vegetable, 1/2 fat.

etables; sprinkle with remaining salt. Grill 5 minutes longer or until cheese is melted. **Yield:** 4 servings.

Editor's Note: This recipe was tested in an 850-watt microwave.

Nutritional Analysis: One serving (1 stuffed potato half) equals 107 calories, 6 g fat (2 g saturated fat), 4 mg cholesterol, 497 mg sodium, 11 g carbohydrate, 3 g fiber, 4 g protein.
Diabetic Exchanges: 1 vegetable, 1 fat, 1/2 starch.

Grilled Vegetable Potato Skins

(Pictured above)

People just love these stuffed spuds in the summer as an alternative to heavier grilled fare. Topped with a colorful vegetable medley, the tender potato skins are light yet satisfying.
—Karen Hemminger, Mansfield, Massachusetts

2 large baking potatoes
1 cup sliced yellow summer squash
1 cup sliced zucchini
1/2 large sweet red pepper, julienned
1/2 large green pepper, julienned
1 small red onion, cut into 1/4-inch wedges
1/4 cup reduced-fat olive oil and vinegar salad dressing *or* Italian salad dressing
1-1/2 teaspoons olive *or* canola oil
1/2 teaspoon salt, *divided*
1/4 cup shredded reduced-fat cheddar cheese

Pierce potatoes several times with a fork and place on a microwave-safe plate. Microwave on high for 18-20 minutes or until tender, rotating the potatoes once. Let stand until cool enough to handle.

Meanwhile, in a large resealable plastic bag, combine the summer squash, zucchini, peppers and onion. Pour salad dressing over vegetables. Seal bag and turn to coat; marinate for 20 minutes.

Cut each potato in half lengthwise. Scoop out pulp, leaving a thin shell (discard pulp or save for another use). Brush inside of shells with oil and sprinkle with 1/4 teaspoon salt.

Coat grill rack with nonstick cooking spray. Place potato shells skin side up on grill rack. Grill, covered, over indirect medium heat for 10 minutes or until golden brown.

Drain vegetables, reserving marinade. Grill vegetables in a grill basket, uncovered, over medium heat for 10 minutes or until tender, basting with reserved marinade.

Sprinkle potato skins with cheese. Fill with grilled veg-

Brown Sugar Baked Beans

If you must be stingy with salt, you're sure to appreciate this flavor-rich bean dish. These beans are well-received by folks who love hot and spicy foods and those with a more conservative palate, too. It's requested for all our family reunions.
—Debra Hogenson, Brewster, Minnesota

1-2/3 cups dried pinto beans
1 medium onion, chopped
1 cup chunky salsa
1/2 cup packed brown sugar
1/2 teaspoon garlic powder
1/2 teaspoon ground cumin
1/4 teaspoon dried oregano
1/8 to 1/4 teaspoon cayenne pepper

Place beans in a Dutch oven or soup kettle; add water to cover by 2 in. Bring to a boil; boil for 2 minutes. Remove from the heat; cover and let stand for 1 hour.

Drain and rinse beans, discarding liquid. Return beans to Dutch oven; add onion and enough water to cover by 2 in. Bring to a boil. Reduce heat; cover and simmer for 60-70 minutes or until the beans are tender.

Drain beans and place in an ungreased 2-qt. baking dish. Add the remaining ingredients. Cover and bake at 350° for 25 minutes or until heated through. **Yield:** 8 servings.

Nutritional Analysis: One serving (1/2 cup) equals 202 calories, 1 g fat (trace saturated fat), 0 cholesterol, 159 mg sodium, 42 g carbohydrate, 9 g fiber, 9 g protein.
Diabetic Exchange: 2-1/2 starch.

Cheesy Zucchini Rounds

Here's a fun way to serve zucchini…and provide a low-fat alternative to high-calorie nachos. Our Test Kitchen sprinkled zucchini slices with cheese, seasonings and bacon bits, then heated them in the microwave. Even kids will eat their veggies when you serve these as a side dish or snack.

1 medium zucchini, sliced
1/8 to 1/4 teaspoon dried basil
1/8 teaspoon onion powder
1/4 cup shredded reduced-fat cheddar cheese
1 bacon strip, cooked and crumbled
2 teaspoons grated Parmesan cheese

Place zucchini on a microwave-safe plate; sprinkle with basil and onion powder. Microwave, uncovered, on high for 1 minute or until hot. Sprinkle with the cheddar cheese, bacon and Parmesan cheese; microwave on high for 30-60 seconds or until cheese is melted. **Yield:** 2 servings.

*Editor's Note: This recipe was tested in an 850-watt microwave.

Nutritional Analysis: One serving equals 71 calories, 4 g fat (2 g saturated fat), 12 mg cholesterol, 240 mg sodium, 4 g carbohydrate, 1 g fiber, 7 g protein.
Diabetic Exchanges: 1 lean meat, 1 vegetable.

Chili-Scented Seasoning

This pleasantly mild seasoning blend is a great way to perk up fish, poultry and meat. Shake a little of it on at the table, just as you would salt.
—Millie Osburn, Winona, Missouri

6 tablespoons onion powder
3 tablespoons poultry seasoning
3 tablespoons paprika
2 tablespoons ground mustard
1 tablespoon garlic powder
2 teaspoons dried oregano, crushed
1 teaspoon chili powder
1 teaspoon black pepper
1/4 teaspoon cayenne pepper

In a bowl, combine all ingredients. Store in an airtight container. **Yield:** 1 cup.

Nutritional Analysis: One serving (1/2 teaspoon) equals 4 calories, trace fat (trace saturated fat), 0 cholesterol, 1 mg sodium, 1 g carbohydrate, trace fiber, trace protein.
Diabetic Exchanges: Free food.

Grilled Sweet Potatoes

Sweet potato wedges are seasoned to please in this savory side dish. My husband and I love the sweet spuds any way they are cooked. This recipe from a friend is not only different, it's delicious, too.
—Gay Nell Nicholas, Henderson, Texas

2 pounds sweet potatoes, peeled and cut into wedges
3 tablespoons reduced-sodium soy sauce
2 tablespoons sherry *or* apple juice
2 tablespoons honey
2 tablespoons water
1 garlic clove, minced
1 tablespoon sesame oil *or* canola oil

Place sweet potatoes in a steamer basket; place in a saucepan over 1 in. of water. Bring to a boil; cover and steam for 5-7 minutes. Place potatoes in a large bowl. In another bowl, combine the soy sauce, sherry or juice, honey, water and garlic; pour over potatoes and toss gently.

Drain sweet potatoes, reserving soy sauce mixture. Arrange sweet potatoes in a single layer in a grill basket coated with nonstick cooking spray. Brush potatoes with oil. Grill, covered, over medium heat for 8-10 minutes or until tender, basting with reserved soy sauce mixture and turning occasionally. **Yield:** 8 servings.

Nutritional Analysis: One serving equals 158 calories, 2 g fat (trace saturated fat), 0 cholesterol, 242 mg sodium, 33 g carbohydrate, 2 g fiber, 2 g protein.
Diabetic Exchange: 2 starch.

Snappy Green Beans

(Pictured below)

This streamlined side dish is a great way to serve fresh beans from the garden. It's simple yet looks elegant. With its mild seasonings, it complements most any main dish.
—Tammy Neubauer, Ida Grove, Iowa

2 pounds fresh green beans
2 teaspoons butter *or* stick margarine
2 tablespoons minced fresh parsley
2 teaspoons lemon juice
1/2 teaspoon salt
1/8 teaspoon pepper

Place beans in a large saucepan; cover with water. Bring to a boil. Reduce heat; simmer, uncovered, for 10-15 minutes or until crisp-tender. Drain.

In a large nonstick skillet, melt butter. Add beans; cook and stir until heated through. Remove from the heat. Add the parsley, lemon juice, salt and pepper; toss to coat. Serve immediately. **Yield:** 6 servings.

Nutritional Analysis: One serving (3/4 cup) equals 58 calories, 2 g fat(1 g saturated fat), 3 mg cholesterol, 213 mg sodium, 11 g carbohydrate, 4 g fiber, 3 g protein.
Diabetic Exchange: 2 vegetable.

1 pound fresh green beans, trimmed
1/4 cup water
1 tablespoon butter *or* stick margarine, melted
3 garlic cloves, minced
1/8 teaspoon salt
1/8 teaspoon pepper
1/3 cup minced fresh parsley

Place beans and water in a 2-qt. microwave-safe dish. Cover and microwave on high for 6-8 minutes or until tender. Drain and keep warm. In a small microwave-safe bowl, combine the butter, garlic, salt and pepper. Microwave, uncovered, on high for 1 minute. Pour over beans; toss to coat. Stir in parsley. **Yield:** 4 servings.

Editor's Note: This recipe was tested in an 850-watt microwave.

Nutritional Analysis: One serving (3/4 cup) equals 66 calories, 3 g fat (2 g saturated fat), 8 mg cholesterol, 113 mg sodium, 9 g carbohydrate, 4 g fiber, 2 g protein.
Diabetic Exchanges: 2 vegetable, 1/2 fat.

Roasted Asparagus with Balsamic Vinegar

(Pictured above)

Since my husband and I both work full-time, I'm always looking for fast nutritious recipes. The whole family loves this tasty treatment for asparagus. I can't make it often enough.
—Natalie Peterson, Kirkland, Washington

1-1/2 pounds fresh asparagus, trimmed
2 teaspoons olive *or* canola oil
1/2 tcaspoon salt
1/8 teaspoon white pepper
3 tablespoons balsamic vinegar

Place the asparagus in a 13-in. x 9-in. x 2-in. baking dish. Sprinkle with oil, salt and pepper; toss to coat. Bake, uncovered, at 425° for 10-15 minutes or until lightly browned. Drizzle with vinegar just before serving. **Yield:** 4 servings.

Nutritional Analysis: One serving equals 47 calories, 3 g fat (trace saturated fat), 0 cholesterol, 305 mg sodium, 5 g carbohydrate, 1 g fiber, 2 g protein.
Diabetic Exchanges: 1 vegetable, 1/2 fat.

Garlic Green Beans

Dress up garden-fresh green beans in minutes, thanks to this easy microwave recipe. The tender beans are delicious served with baked ham or grilled salmon.
—Margaret Wagner Allen, Abingdon, Virginia

Savory Lemon Limas

Lima beans get a lemony lift with this treatment. If you are a lima bean lover like I am, this recipe just makes them even more delicious. If you simply tolerate the beans, like my husband does, you might actually find these quite tasty.
—Cathy Attig, Jacobus, Pennsylvania

1/2 cup water
1 package (10 ounces) frozen lima beans
1 tablespoon butter *or* stick margarine, melted
1 tablespoon lemon juice
1 teaspoon sugar
1/2 to 3/4 teaspoon ground mustard
1/4 teaspoon salt

In a saucepan, bring water to a boil. Add lima beans; return to a boil. Reduce heat; cover and simmer for 8-10 minutes or until tender. Drain. Combine the butter, lemon juice, sugar, mustard and salt; pour over beans and toss to coat. **Yield:** 4 servings.

🍎 The Line on Limas

THE MILD-MANNERED lima bean, first "discovered" in Peru, has been pleasing palates for more than 500 years. If you haven't discovered its smooth, creamy taste, it's time to give it a try.

This pale green or whitish bean is full of protein. It's also rich in calcium, iron and vitamins, making it one of the most nutritious members of the legume family.

The bean comes in two varieties: baby lima and Fordhook. Baby limas have a delicate, almost sweet, taste. Fordhooks are a bit more flavorful than their smaller kin. In the American South, the larger lima is better known as the butter bean.

Nutritional Analysis: One serving (1/3 cup) equals 107 calories, 3 g fat (2 g saturated fat), 8 mg cholesterol, 197 mg sodium, 15 g carbohydrate, 3 g fiber, 5 g protein.
Diabetic Exchange: 1 starch.

Tomato Broccoli Bake

I've been making this comforting noodle and vegetable side dish for more than 10 years. It travels well and is always popular.
—Ellie Marsh, Lewistown, Pennsylvania

3/4 cup uncooked elbow macaroni
1 medium onion, thinly sliced
1 garlic clove, minced
2 teaspoons butter *or* stick margarine
2 cups chopped fresh broccoli
2 cups chopped seeded peeled tomatoes
  (about 6 medium)
1/2 cup minced fresh parsley
1 teaspoon chicken bouillon granules
1/4 teaspoon salt
1/4 teaspoon dried oregano
1/4 teaspoon dried basil
1 cup (4 ounces) shredded reduced-fat cheddar
  cheese, *divided*

Cook macaroni according to package directions; drain and set aside. In a saucepan, saute onion and garlic in butter until tender. Add the broccoli, tomatoes, parsley, bouillon, salt, oregano and basil; bring to a boil. Reduce heat; cover and simmer for 3 minutes. Stir in macaroni and 3/4 cup cheese.

Transfer to an 8-in. square baking dish coated with non-stick cooking spray. Cover and bake at 375° for 20 minutes or until heated through. Uncover; sprinkle with remaining cheese. Bake 5 minutes longer or until cheese is melted. **Yield:** 6 servings.

Nutritional Analysis: One serving (1 cup) equals 143 calories, 5 g fat (3 g saturated fat), 14 mg cholesterol, 436 mg sodium, 18 g carbohydrate, 2 g fiber, 9 g protein.
Diabetic Exchanges: 1 starch, 1 lean meat, 1 vegetable.

Bacon 'n' Veggie Pasta

(Pictured at right and on page 77)

When the weather turns chilly, our daughter, who is an inventive cook, transforms her favorite cold pasta salad into this warm, hearty side dish. I love recipes like this one that bring compliments and don't keep me in the kitchen too long.
—Muriel Hollenbeck, Sedalia, Colorado

2 cans (14-1/2 ounces *each*) stewed tomatoes
2 cups broccoli florets
2 medium carrots, thinly sliced
1/2 teaspoon salt

1/2 teaspoon Italian seasoning
1/2 teaspoon dried oregano
1/4 teaspoon dried basil
4 bacon strips, diced
1/2 pound fresh mushrooms, sliced
1/3 cup chopped green pepper
1/4 cup chopped onion
2 garlic cloves, minced
16 ounces uncooked medium shell pasta
1/4 cup shredded Parmesan cheese

In a large saucepan, combine the first seven ingredients. Bring to a boil. Reduce heat; cover and simmer for 25-30 minutes or until broccoli and carrots are tender.

In a skillet, cook bacon over medium heat until crisp. Remove to paper towels; drain, reserving 1 tablespoon drippings. In the drippings, saute the mushrooms, green pepper, onion and garlic until tender; add to tomato mixture and heat through. Meanwhile, cook the pasta according to package directions. Drain and place in a serving bowl; top with vegetable mixture. Sprinkle with bacon and Parmesan cheese. **Yield:** 13 servings.

Nutritional Analysis: One serving (3/4 cup) equals 205 calories, 3 g fat (1 g saturated fat), 4 mg cholesterol, 289 mg sodium, 36 g carbohydrate, 3 g fiber, 8 g protein.
Diabetic Exchanges: 2 starch, 1 vegetable, 1/2 fat.

Barley and Rice Pilaf

If you're tired of potatoes, try this quick-and-easy pilaf for a change of taste. I put it together while trying to use up leftover rice. I've experimented with many variations, such as adding broccoli and asparagus.
—*Marilyn Bazant, Albuquerque, New Mexico*

1/2 cup finely chopped celery
1/2 cup finely chopped sweet red pepper
1/2 cup finely chopped green onions
1 garlic clove, minced
1 tablespoon canola oil
3 cups cooked long grain rice
1 cup cooked medium pearl barley
2 bacon strips, cooked and crumbled
1/2 teaspoon salt
1/8 teaspoon pepper

In a skillet, saute the celery, red pepper, onions and garlic in oil until crisp-tender. Stir in the rice, barley, bacon, salt and pepper; cook and stir until heated through. **Yield:** 6 servings.

Nutritional Analysis: One serving (3/4 cup) equals 187 calories, 4 g fat (1 g saturated fat), 2 mg cholesterol, 236 mg sodium, 34 g carbohydrate, 3 g fiber, 4 g protein.
Diabetic Exchanges: 2 starch, 1/2 fat.

Orange Cream Cheese Spread

Here's a smooth fluffy spread that couldn't be easier to make—it has only four ingredients. Try it as a topper on oven-fresh muffins or pumpkin bread.
—*Lois Gelzer, Cape Elizabeth, Maine*

1 package (8 ounces) reduced-fat cream cheese, softened
3 tablespoons sugar
2 teaspoons vanilla extract
1 teaspoon grated orange peel

In a bowl, beat all ingredients until smooth. Store in the refrigerator. **Yield:** 1 cup.

Nutritional Analysis: One serving (2 tablespoons) equals 84 calories, 5 g fat (3 g saturated fat), 16 mg cholesterol, 84 mg sodium, 7 g carbohydrate, trace fiber, 3 g protein.
Diabetic Exchanges: 1 fat, 1/2 starch.

Maple Baked Beans

When my son developed diabetes at age 3, I found myself converting a lot of our favorite recipes. He always liked these saucy beans. They get their sweet maple flavor from sugar-free pancake syrup.
—*Laura Fisher, Glendale, Arizona*

1 can (28 ounces) pork and beans
1/4 cup sugar-free pancake syrup
2 tablespoons ketchup
2 tablespoons prepared mustard
2 bacon strips, cooked and crumbled
1 onion slice, separated into rings

In a bowl, combine the pork and beans, syrup, ketchup and mustard. Pour into an 8-in. square baking dish coated with nonstick cooking spray. Sprinkle with bacon; top with onion. Bake, uncovered, at 350° for 40-45 minutes or until bubbly. **Yield:** 6 servings.

Nutritional Analysis: One serving (1/2 cup) equals 161 calories, 3 g fat (1 g saturated fat), 7 mg cholesterol, 603 mg sodium, 29 g carbohydrate, 6 g fiber, 6 g protein.
Diabetic Exchanges: 2 starch, 1/2 fat.

Zucchini with Basil Cream

I enjoy cooking and have a big garden every year. I like to fix this colorful side dish that makes the most of fresh zucchini and carrots.
—*Annabelle Erhart, Missoula, Montana*

1 cup chicken broth
2 garlic cloves, minced
Dash cayenne pepper
2 small carrots, julienned
4 medium zucchini, cut into 2-inch julienne strips
1 teaspoon cornstarch
1/4 cup 2% milk
1/4 cup grated Parmesan cheese
1 tablespoon minced fresh basil *or* 1 teaspoon dried basil
1/4 cup shredded part-skim mozzarella cheese

In a large saucepan, bring the broth, garlic and cayenne to a boil; cook, uncovered, until mixture is reduced by a third. Add carrots. Reduce heat; cover and cook for 4-5 minutes or until tender. Add zucchini; cover and cook for 8-10 minutes or until tender. Drain.

Combine the cornstarch and milk until smooth; stir into vegetables. Bring to a boil; cook and stir for 2 minutes or until thickened. Add Parmesan cheese and basil; stir gently. Sprinkle with mozzarella cheese. **Yield:** 6 servings.

Nutritional Analysis: One serving (3/4 cup) equals 72 calories, 2 g fat (1 g saturated fat), 7 mg cholesterol, 277 mg sodium, 8 g carbohydrate, 2 g fiber, 5 g protein.
Diabetic Exchanges: 2 vegetable, 1/2 fat.

Favorite Casserole Recipe Made Lighter

SERVE Creamy Broccoli Casserole at any gathering, and there's no doubt guests will ask for seconds of the rich side dish. Carolyn Creasman of Gastonia, North Carolina shared the scrumptious recipe, but this creative cook also included her own slimmed-down version to share with readers.

"I have to watch my fat intake, so I'm always looking for ways to make my cooking as healthy as possible," she explains. "I adapted this family favorite to fit my diet."

When our Test Kitchen staff reviewed Carolyn's makeover, they decided they couldn't have done it better themselves! Her better-for-you broccoli bake takes advantage of several fat-free or reduced-fat products. It calls for fat-free mayonnaise, reduced-fat cheese, reduced-fat crackers and reduced-fat reduced-sodium condensed soup.

It also uses egg substitute instead of eggs and less than half the butter called for in the original.

Creamy Broccoli Casserole

- 2 packages (10 ounces *each*) frozen chopped broccoli
- 2 eggs, lightly beaten
- 1 can (10-3/4 ounces) condensed cream of mushroom soup, undiluted
- 1 cup mayonnaise
- 1 cup (4 ounces) shredded cheddar cheese
- 1 small onion, finely chopped
- 1/2 cup butter *or* margarine, melted
- 1/3 cup crushed butter-flavored crackers (about 8 crackers)

Place 1 in. of water and broccoli in a large saucepan; bring to a boil. Reduce heat; cover and simmer for 5-8 minutes or until crisp-tender. Meanwhile, in a bowl, combine the eggs, soup, mayonnaise, cheese, onion and butter. Drain broccoli; gently stir into soup mixture.

Pour into a greased 2-qt. baking dish. Sprinkle with crushed crackers. Bake, uncovered, at 350° for 25-30 minutes or until heated through. **Yield:** 9 servings.

Nutritional Analysis: One serving equals 453 calories, 40 g fat (14 g saturated fat), 107 mg cholesterol, 688 mg sodium, 16 g carbohydrate, 3 g fiber, 8 g protein.

Makeover Creamy Broccoli Casserole

(Pictured below left)

- 2 packages (10 ounces *each*) frozen chopped broccoli
- 1 can (10-3/4 ounces) reduced-fat reduced-sodium condensed cream of mushroom soup, undiluted
- 1 cup fat-free mayonnaise
- 1 cup (4 ounces) shredded reduced-fat cheddar cheese
- 1/2 cup egg substitute
- 1 small onion, finely chopped
- 3 tablespoons butter *or* stick margarine, melted
- 1/4 cup crushed reduced-fat butter-flavored crackers (about 8 crackers)

Refrigerated butter-flavored spray*

Place 1 in. of water and broccoli in a large saucepan; bring to a boil. Reduce heat; cover and simmer for 5-8 minutes or until crisp-tender. Meanwhile, in a bowl, combine the soup, mayonnaise, cheese, egg substitute, onion and butter. Drain broccoli; gently stir into soup mixture.

Pour into a 1-1/2-qt. baking dish coated with non-stick cooking spray. Sprinkle with crushed crackers. Spritz crumbs with butter-flavored spray. Bake, uncovered, at 350° for 25-30 minutes or until heated through. **Yield:** 9 servings.

***Editor's Note:** This recipe was tested with I Can't Believe It's Not Butter Spray.

Nutritional Analysis: One serving equals 145 calories, 8 g fat (5 g saturated fat), 25 mg cholesterol, 422 mg sodium, 12 g carbohydrate, 3 g fiber, 7 g protein.
Diabetic Exchanges: 1 lean meat, 1 vegetable, 1 fat, 1/2 starch.

Buttermilk Mashed Potatoes

(Pictured below)

My sister-in-law, who is a dietitian, shared this recipe with me. Buttermilk and garlic flavor these smooth mashed potatoes that are better for you than typical versions that include lots of butter.
—Stephanie Bremson, Kansas City, Missouri

   2 pounds potatoes, peeled and cut into 1-inch cubes
   2 cups water
   1 cup chicken broth
   6 garlic cloves, peeled
1/2 cup 1% buttermilk
1/4 cup thinly sliced green onions
   1 teaspoon salt
1/8 teaspoon pepper

In a large saucepan, combine the potatoes, water, broth and garlic. Bring to a boil. Reduce heat; cover and simmer for 12-15 minutes or until potatoes are tender. Meanwhile, in a small saucepan, heat buttermilk until warm. Drain potatoes and garlic; mash with buttermilk. Stir in onions, salt and pepper. **Yield:** 6 servings.

Nutritional Analysis: *One serving (2/3 cup) equals 133 calories, trace fat (trace saturated fat), 1 mg cholesterol, 575 mg sodium, 30 g carbohydrate, 3 g fiber, 4 g protein.*
Diabetic Exchange: *2 starch.*

Eggplant Pepper Relish

(Pictured above)

This colorful combination of broiled peppers and eggplant is nicely seasoned with garlic and oregano. Serve it warm or cold, as a side dish, sandwich topper or on toasted bread rounds as an appetizer.
—Jeanne Vitale, Leola, Pennsylvania

   3 medium sweet red peppers, cut in half lengthwise
   3 medium sweet yellow peppers, cut in half lengthwise
   1 medium eggplant, cut in half lengthwise
   2 tablespoons olive *or* canola oil
   1 garlic clove, minced
1/4 cup minced fresh parsley
   1 tablespoon minced fresh oregano
      or 1 teaspoon dried oregano
3/4 teaspoon salt
1/4 teaspoon pepper

Place peppers skin side up on a broiler pan. Broil for 10-15 minutes or until tender and skin is blistered. Place in a bowl; cover and let stand for 15-20 minutes. Peel off and discard charred skin.

Broil eggplant skin side up for 5-7 minutes or until tender and skin is blistered. Place in a bowl; cover and let stand for 15-20 minutes. Peel off and discard charred skin. Cut peppers into strips and eggplant into cubes.

In a large bowl, combine the oil and garlic. Add peppers, eggplant, parsley, oregano, salt and pepper. Toss to coat. Serve at room temperature. **Yield:** 12 servings.

Nutritional Analysis: *One serving (1/3 cup) equals 55 calories, 3 g fat (trace saturated fat), 0 cholesterol, 150 mg sodium, 8 g carbohydrate, 2 g fiber, 1 g protein.*
Diabetic Exchanges: *1 vegetable, 1/2 fat.*

Roasted Spicy Mustard Potatoes

Even mild red potatoes can be a standout side dish when they're tossed with this mustard and spice coating, then baked. They perk up any meal.
—*Shirley Glaab, Hattiesburg, Mississippi*

1/4 cup Dijon mustard
2 teaspoons paprika
1 teaspoon ground cumin
1 teaspoon chili powder
1/2 teaspoon salt
1/8 teaspoon cayenne pepper
2 pounds small red potatoes

Spray a shallow roasting pan with nonstick cooking spray three times to coat well; set aside. In a large bowl, whisk the mustard, paprika, cumin, chili powder, salt and cayenne. Pierce potatoes with a fork several times; add to mustard mixture and toss to coat. Place in prepared pan. Bake, uncovered, at 375° for 30-40 minutes or until tender. **Yield:** 8 servings.

Nutritional Analysis: One serving equals 138 calories, 1 g fat (trace saturated fat), 0 cholesterol, 353 mg sodium, 30 g carbohydrate, 3 g fiber, 3 g protein.
Diabetic Exchange: 2 starch.

Ginger Broccoli Stir-Fry

Are you looking for an appetizing way to enhance a nutritious vegetable? Try this eye-catching stir-fry. The broccoli keeps its bright color and crispness, while ginger and soy sauce help to spice it up nicely.
—*Marie Rossey, Creston, Ohio*

4 cups broccoli florets
2 tablespoons water
2 teaspoons canola oil
2 garlic cloves, minced
1 teaspoon reduced-sodium soy sauce
1/8 teaspoon ground ginger *or* 1/2 teaspoon minced fresh gingerroot

Place broccoli and water in a 1-1/2-qt. microwave-safe dish. Cover and microwave on high for 2 minutes; drain. In a nonstick skillet or wok, stir-fry broccoli in oil for 6-7 minutes. Add garlic, soy sauce and ginger; stir-fry 1-2 minutes longer or until broccoli is crisp-tender. **Yield:** 4 servings.

Nutritional Analysis: One serving (1/2 cup) equals 41 calories, 3 g fat (trace saturated fat), 0 cholesterol, 70 mg sodium, 4 g carbohydrate, 2 g fiber, 2 g protein.
Diabetic Exchanges: 1 vegetable, 1/2 fat.

Southwestern Rice

(Pictured below)

I created this zippy side dish after eating something similar at a restaurant. It complements any Tex-Mex meal wonderfully. Sometimes I add cubes of grilled chicken breast to the rice to make it a meal in itself.
—*Michelle Dennis, Clarks Hill, Indiana*

1 medium green pepper, diced
1 medium onion, chopped
2 garlic cloves, minced
1 tablespoon olive *or* canola oil
1 can (14-1/2 ounces) reduced-sodium chicken broth
1 cup uncooked long grain rice
1/2 teaspoon ground cumin
1/8 teaspoon ground turmeric
1 can (15 ounces) black beans, rinsed and drained
1 can (10 ounces) diced tomatoes and green chilies, undrained
1 package (10 ounces) frozen corn, thawed

In a large nonstick skillet, saute the green pepper, onion and garlic in oil for 3 minutes. Stir in the broth, rice, cumin and turmeric; bring to a boil. Reduce heat; cover and simmer for 15 minutes or until rice is tender. Add beans, tomatoes and corn, heat through. **Yield:** 8 servings.

Nutritional Analysis: One serving (3/4 cup) equals 198 calories, 3 g fat (1 g saturated fat), 1 mg cholesterol, 339 mg sodium, 37 g carbohydrate, 5 g fiber, 7 g protein.
Diabetic Exchanges: 2 starch, 1 vegetable.

Broccoli with Orange Cream

(Pictured below)

I received the recipe for this broccoli side dish from a good friend in North Carolina. I like to use fresh thyme from my herb garden. The creamy orange sauce is even better than hollandaise.
—Kathy Samuelson, Omaha, Nebraska

1-1/2 pounds fresh broccoli, cut into florets
   6 ounces fat-free cream cheese, cubed
  1/4 cup fat-free milk
    1 teaspoon minced fresh thyme *or* 1/4 teaspoon dried thyme
  1/4 teaspoon salt
  1/4 teaspoon grated orange peel
  1/4 cup orange juice
    2 tablespoons chopped walnuts

Place broccoli in a steamer basket over 1 in. of boiling water in a saucepan. Cover and steam for 5-8 minutes or until crisp-tender. Meanwhile, in a small saucepan, combine the cream cheese, milk, thyme, salt and orange peel. Cook and stir over medium-low heat until blended. Stir in orange juice until combined. Place broccoli in a serving dish; top with orange cream and nuts. **Yield:** 6 servings.

Nutritional Analysis: One serving (3/4 cup) equals 126 calories, 4 g fat (1 g saturated fat), 4 mg cholesterol, 433 mg sodium, 14 g carbohydrate, 2 g fiber, 12 g protein.
Diabetic Exchanges: *2 vegetable, 1/2 fat.*

Sweet Potato Apple Scallop

My cousin, Ann Smith, gave me the recipe for this wonderful dish, which makes traditional Thanksgiving sweet potatoes a bit more special. Apple slices and a crunchy pecan topping dress up the seasonal spuds.
—Sarah Joyce, Bedford, Texas

  2 pounds sweet potatoes (about 3 medium)
  2 medium apples, peeled and cored
  1 tablespoon lemon juice
1/2 cup packed brown sugar
1/4 cup chopped pecans
1/2 teaspoon ground cinnamon
1/2 teaspoon pumpkin pie spice
1/2 teaspoon orange extract
  2 tablespoons butter *or* stick margarine

Place sweet potatoes in a saucepan and cover with water. Bring to a boil; cook for 20-25 minutes or until tender. Drain and cool. Peel potatoes and cut into 1/4-in. slices. Place in a 13-in. x 9-in. x 2-in. baking dish coated with nonstick cooking spray.

Cut apples into 1/4-in. rings; cut in half. Arrange over sweet potatoes. Sprinkle with lemon juice. Combine the brown sugar, pecans, cinnamon, pumpkin pie spice and orange extract; sprinkle over apples. Dot with butter. Bake, uncovered, at 350° for 25-30 minutes or until apples are tender. **Yield:** 7 servings.

Nutritional Analysis: One serving (2/3 cup) equals 221 calories, 7 g fat (2 g saturated fat), 9 mg cholesterol, 48 mg sodium, 41 g carbohydrate, 4 g fiber, 2 g protein.
Diabetic Exchanges: *1-1/2 starch, 1 fruit, 1 fat.*

Taco Seasoning

Our Test Kitchen developed this spicy, salt-free alternative to packaged taco seasoning. Stir it into dips or ground beef, sprinkle on chicken or wherever you want a Southwestern flair.

4 teaspoons dried minced onion
3 teaspoons chili powder*
1 teaspoon cornstarch
1 teaspoon garlic powder
1 teaspoon ground cumin
1/2 teaspoon dried oregano
1/8 teaspoon cayenne pepper

In a small bowl, combine all of the ingredients. Store in an airtight container in a cool dry place for up to 1 year. **Yield:** 3 tablespoons.

***Editor's Note:** Not all chili powders are alike, and salt levels vary greatly. Ingredients are listed in descending order on package labels. Check your chili powder label to ensure that salt is not listed as one of the first three ingredients.

Nutritional Analysis: One serving (1/4 teaspoon) equals 7 calories, trace fat (0 saturated fat), 0 cholesterol, 15 mg sodium, 1 g carbohydrate, trace fiber, trace protein.
Diabetic Exchanges: *Free food.*

Roasted Rosemary Cauliflower

Roasting the cauliflower really brings out its flavor in this side dish. Even folks who aren't cauliflower lovers like it this way.
—Joann Fritzler, Belen, New Mexico

1 head cauliflower (2-1/2 pounds), cut into 1-inch florets
4-1/2 teaspoons olive *or* canola oil
2 teaspoons minced fresh rosemary
** *or* 3/4 teaspoon dried rosemary, crushed**
1/2 teaspoon salt

In a bowl, toss cauliflower with oil, rosemary and salt until well coated. Arrange in a single layer in an ungreased 15-in. x 10-in. x 1-in. baking pan. Roast, uncovered, at 450° for 25-30 minutes or until cauliflower is lightly browned and tender, stirring occasionally. **Yield:** 8 servings.

Nutritional Analysis: One serving (3/4 cup) equals 44 calories, 3 g fat (trace saturated fat), 0 cholesterol, 161 mg sodium, 4 g carbohydrate, 3 g fiber, 2 g protein.
Diabetic Exchanges: 1 vegetable, 1/2 fat.

Cranberry Pear Relish

Tart and tempting, this relish is a traditional part of our holiday menu. It's pleasant with both poultry and pork. My husband, children and grandkids like the pairing of fall fruits and the hint of ginger and cinnamon. It tastes just like autumn.
—Kathie Theis, Monticello, Minnesota

1 medium navel orange
4 medium pears, peeled and coarsely chopped
1 package (12 ounces) fresh *or* frozen cranberries
1 cup packed brown sugar
1 teaspoon grated orange peel
1/2 teaspoon ground cinnamon
1/4 teaspoon ground ginger *or* 1 teaspoon minced fresh gingerroot
1/8 teaspoon ground allspice

Squeeze juice from the orange; add enough water to measure 1/2 cup. Pour into a saucepan; add the remaining ingredients. Bring to a boil. Reduce heat; simmer, uncovered, for 25-30 minutes or until the cranberries pop and mixture is thickened. Cool. Cover and store in the refrigerator. **Yield:** 4 cups.

Nutritional Analysis: One serving (1/4 cup) equals 95 calories, trace fat (trace saturated fat), 0 cholesterol, 6 mg sodium, 24 g carbohydrate, 2 g fiber, trace protein.
Diabetic Exchanges: 1 fruit, 1/2 starch.

Meatless Hopping John

(Pictured above)

I traditionally make this black-eyed pea dish for New Year's celebrations. This version has more seasonings and veggies than the classic Southern dish.
—Ann Buckendahl, Benton, Kansas

3/4 cup uncooked long grain rice
1 cup frozen corn
3 medium carrots, thinly sliced
1/2 cup *each* chopped green, sweet red and yellow pepper
1/4 cup chopped onion
4 garlic cloves, minced
1 tablespoon canola *or* vegetable oil
1 can (15-1/2 ounces) black-eyed peas, rinsed and drained
1 can (14-1/2 ounces) diced tomatoes, drained
2 tablespoons minced fresh parsley
1 teaspoon dried thyme
1/2 teaspoon salt
1/4 teaspoon pepper
1/4 teaspoon crushed red pepper flakes

Cook rice according to package directions. Meanwhile, in a large nonstick skillet, saute the corn, carrots, peppers, onion and garlic in oil for 6-8 minutes or until crisp-tender. Stir in the rice, peas and tomatoes; bring to a boil. Reduce heat; cover and simmer for 5 minutes or until heated through, stirring occasionally. Add the seasonings; cook 2-3 minutes longer. **Yield:** 10 servings.

Nutritional Analysis: One serving (3/4 cup) equals 149 calories, 2 g fat (trace saturated fat), 0 cholesterol, 313 mg sodium, 29 g carbohydrate, 4 g fiber, 5 g protein.
Diabetic Exchanges: 1-1/2 starch, 1 vegetable.

Southwest Skillet Corn

(Pictured below)

This colorful stir-fried side complements any Mexican menu nicely.
—Marilyn Smudzinski, Peru, Illinois

1 medium sweet red pepper, chopped
1 tablespoon finely chopped seeded jalapeno pepper*
1 tablespoon butter *or* stick margarine
1-1/2 teaspoons ground cumin
1 package (16 ounces) frozen corn, thawed
1/3 cup minced fresh cilantro *or* parsley

In a large nonstick skillet, saute red pepper and jalapeno in butter until tender. Add cumin; cook for 30 seconds. Add corn and cilantro; saute 2 minutes longer or until heated through. **Yield:** 4 servings.
*Editor's Note: When cutting or seeding hot peppers, use rubber or plastic gloves to protect your hands. Avoid touching your face.

Nutritional Analysis: One serving (3/4 cup) equals 138 calories, 4 g fat (2 g saturated fat), 8 mg cholesterol, 37 mg sodium, 26 g carbohydrate, 4 g fiber, 4 g protein.
Diabetic Exchanges: *1-1/2 starch, 1/2 fat.*

Baby Carrots with Curry Sauce

Curry gives bold flavor to sweet baby carrots in this quick-and-easy side dish.
—Pat Patty, Spring, Texas

1 package (16 ounces) baby carrots
1/4 cup reduced-fat mayonnaise
2 tablespoons fat-free sour cream
1 teaspoon lemon juice
1 teaspoon fat-free milk
1 teaspoon honey
1/2 to 1 teaspoon curry powder
1/4 teaspoon salt

Place carrots in a steamer basket over 1 in. of boiling water in a saucepan. Cover and steam for 12-14 minutes or until crisp-tender. Meanwhile, combine the remaining ingredients in a small saucepan; cook and stir over medium-low heat until heated through (do not boil). Drain carrots; add sauce and toss to coat. **Yield:** 4 servings.

Nutritional Analysis: One serving (3/4 cup) equals 110 calories, 6 g fat (1 g saturated fat), 5 mg cholesterol, 313 mg sodium, 14 g carbohydrate, 2 g fiber, 2 g protein.
Diabetic Exchanges: *1 starch, 1 vegetable.*

Lemon-Maple Butternut Squash

My mother discovered this healthy recipe that's become a family favorite. We enjoy its bright color, smooth texture and flavorful combination of tangy lemon and sweet maple.
—Barbara Ballast, Grand Rapids, Michigan

1 large butternut squash (2-1/2 pounds), halved lengthwise and seeded
1/4 cup water
1/4 cup maple syrup
1 tablespoon butter *or* stick margarine, melted
1 tablespoon lemon juice
1/2 teaspoon grated lemon peel

Place squash cut side down in an ungreased 13-in. x 9-in. x 2-in. baking dish. Add water. Cover and bake at 350° for 50-60 minutes or until tender. Scoop out the squash and place in a mixing bowl. Add the syrup, butter, lemon juice and peel; beat until smooth. **Yield:** 4 servings.

Nutritional Analysis: One serving (3/4 cup) equals 186 calories, 3 g fat (2 g saturated fat), 8 mg cholesterol, 41 mg sodium, 42 g carbohydrate, 8 g fiber, 2 g protein.
Diabetic Exchanges: *2-1/2 starch, 1/2 fat.*

Sweet 'n' Savory Apple Stuffing

(Pictured above)

*After a few dozen Thanksgivings, I began to
search for a new stuffing recipe. With its bits of fruit
and nuts, this one has become my favorite.*
—Karen Horne Staab, New Rochelle, New York

  1 medium tart apple, peeled and chopped
  2 celery ribs, chopped
  1 medium onion, chopped
1/4 cup minced fresh parsley
  3 green onions, thinly sliced
  2 tablespoons chopped celery leaves
  2 tablespoons butter *or* stick margarine
1/2 cup tropical medley dried fruit mix
1/4 cup dried cranberries
1/4 cup chopped pecans
  1 teaspoon poultry seasoning
1/2 teaspoon salt
1/2 teaspoon rubbed sage
1/4 teaspoon pepper
  1 can (14-1/2 ounces) reduced-sodium chicken
    broth
1-1/2 cups water
  1 package (12 ounces) unseasoned stuffing
    croutons

In a skillet, cook the apple, celery, onion, parsley, green
onions and celery leaves in butter until tender. Stir in the fruit
mix, cranberries, pecans, poultry seasoning, salt, sage and
pepper; mix well. Stir in broth, water and stuffing. Toss to
coat evenly.

Transfer to a 13-in. x 9-in. x 2-in. baking dish coated
with nonstick cooking spray. Cover and bake at 350° for 20

minutes. Uncover; bake 10-15 minutes longer or until
heated through and lightly browned. **Yield:** 12 servings.

*Nutritional Analysis: One serving (3/4 cup) equals 183 calo-
ries, 5 g fat (2 g saturated fat), 5 mg cholesterol, 671 mg sodium,
31 g carbohydrate, 2 g fiber, 4 g protein.*
Diabetic Exchanges: 1 starch, 1 fat, 1/2 fruit.

Dutch Beets

*You can give a rosy complexion to most any meal by
adding these sure-to-be-relished roots. Even people who
typically shy away from beets will polish these off.
They're quick to make, too, since they start
with convenient canned beets.*
—Marie Hattrup, The Dalles, Oregon

  2 cans (13-1/4 ounces *each*) sliced beets
  1 tablespoon finely chopped onion
  1 tablespoon butter *or* stick margarine
  2 tablespoons all-purpose flour
  2 tablespoons cider vinegar
  1 tablespoon sugar
1/2 teaspoon salt
1/8 teaspoon pepper

Drain beets, reserving 1 cup liquid (discard remaining liquid); set beets aside. In a saucepan, saute onion in butter
until tender. Stir in flour until blended. Gradually add the
reserved beet liquid. Bring to a boil; cook and stir for 2
minutes or until thickened. Stir in the vinegar, sugar, salt,
pepper and beets; heat through. **Yield:** 4 servings.

*Nutritional Analysis: One serving (3/4 cup) equals 107 calo-
ries, 3 g fat (2 g saturated fat), 8 mg cholesterol, 728 mg sodium,
19 g carbohydrate, 3 g fiber, 2 g protein.*
Diabetic Exchanges: 2 vegetable, 1/2 starch, 1/2 fat.

Scalloped Squash and Apples

*This recipe is a tasty variation on traditional squash
with brown sugar and butter. Orange juice and apple
chunks lend a subtle sweetness to the pleasing side dish.*
—Jeanne Bunders, Wauzeka, Wisconsin

  2 pounds butternut squash, peeled, seeded and
    cut into 1-inch pieces
  2 large apples, peeled and cut into 1-inch pieces
1/4 cup packed brown sugar
  2 tablespoons corn syrup
  2 tablespoons orange juice
  1 tablespoon butter *or* stick margarine, melted
  2 teaspoons grated orange peel
1/2 teaspoon salt

Layer squash and apples in an 11-in. x 7-in. x 2-in. baking
dish coated with nonstick cooking spray. In a bowl, combine
the remaining ingredients. Pour over squash and apples.
Cover and bake at 350° for 35-40 minutes or until tender.
Yield: 6 servings.

*Nutritional Analysis: One serving (3/4 cup) equals 161 calo-
ries, 2 g fat (1 g saturated fat), 5 mg cholesterol, 228 mg sodium,
38 g carbohydrate, 6 g fiber, 1 g protein.*
Diabetic Exchanges: 1-1/2 fruit, 1 starch.

Broccoli with Roasted Red Peppers

(Pictured below)

Here's an easy and appetizing way to dress up broccoli. Our Test Kitchen staff teamed up that garden-fresh vegetable with roasted red peppers and garlic in this colorful combination. It tastes so good, you won't believe it's good for you, too!

5 cups broccoli florets (about 1 large bunch)
1 to 2 garlic cloves, minced
1 tablespoon butter *or* stick margarine
1/4 cup diced roasted red peppers
1 tablespoon minced fresh parsley
1/2 teaspoon salt
1/8 teaspoon pepper

Place broccoli in a steamer basket. Place in a saucepan over 1 in. of water; bring to a boil. Cover and steam for 5-8 minutes or until crisp-tender. Meanwhile, in a nonstick skillet, saute garlic in butter. Stir in the red peppers, parsley, salt and pepper. Transfer broccoli to a large bowl; add red pepper mixture and toss to coat. **Yield:** 6 servings.

Nutritional Analysis: One serving (2/3 cup) equals 41 calories, 2 g fat (1 g saturated fat), 5 mg cholesterol, 235 mg sodium, 5 g carbohydrate, 1 g fiber, 2 g protein.
Diabetic Exchange: 1-1/2 vegetable.

Orzo and Peppers

I love green peppers but my husband does not, so I created this dish one night when he wasn't home. When the two of us are here, I leave out the peppers and add the veggies my husband prefers.
—Jennifer Tarr, Baltimore, Maryland

6 cups water
2 teaspoons beef bouillon granules
1 package (8 ounces) orzo pasta
1 large sweet red pepper, cut into thin 1-inch-long pieces
1 large green pepper, cut into thin 1-inch-long pieces
1 medium onion, chopped
1 tablespoon olive *or* canola oil
2 garlic cloves, minced
1/4 cup shredded Romano cheese
2 tablespoons balsamic vinegar

In a large saucepan, bring water and bouillon to a boil. Add orzo. Cook according to package directions; drain. In a large nonstick skillet, saute peppers and onion in oil for 3-4 minutes or until crisp-tender. Add garlic; saute 2 minutes longer. Add the orzo, cheese and vinegar; toss to coat. **Yield:** 6 servings.

Nutritional Analysis: One serving (3/4 cup) equals 208 calories, 4 g fat (1 g saturated fat), 4 mg cholesterol, 344 mg sodium, 36 g carbohydrate, 2 g fiber, 7 g protein.
Diabetic Exchanges: 2 starch, 1 vegetable, 1/2 fat.

Balsamic Roasted Red Potatoes

Well-seasoned with garlic, thyme, nutmeg and rosemary, plus balsamic vinegar, these potatoes are sure to stand out at any meal.
—Bev Bosveld, Waupun, Wisconsin

2 tablespoons olive *or* canola oil
2 pounds small red potatoes, quartered
1 tablespoon finely chopped green onion
1 tablespoon minced garlic
1 teaspoon dried thyme
1 teaspoon dried rosemary, crushed
1/8 teaspoon ground nutmeg
1/4 cup balsamic vinegar
3/4 teaspoon salt
1/4 teaspoon pepper

In a large nonstick skillet, heat oil over medium-high heat. Add the potatoes, onion and garlic; toss to combine. Add the thyme, rosemary and nutmeg; toss well. Cook and stir for 2-3 minutes or until potatoes are hot.

Transfer to a 15-in. x 10-in. x 1-in. baking pan coated with nonstick cooking spray. Bake at 400° for 25-30 minutes or until potatoes are golden and almost tender. Add the vinegar, salt and pepper; toss well. Bake 5-8 minutes longer or until potatoes are tender. **Yield:** 6 servings.

Nutritional Analysis: One serving (3/4 cup) equals 184 calories, 5 g fat (1 g saturated fat), 0 cholesterol, 306 mg sodium, 33 g carbohydrate, 3 g fiber, 3 g protein.
Diabetic Exchanges: 2 starch, 1 fat.

Breakfast & Brunch

Breakfast boosts your energy level, which is bound to give you a sunny outlook on the day and help you perform your best. So open your family's eyes to good eating with these day-brightening recipes.

Makeover Sausage Pinwheels with Herb Gravy (page 104)

Ham and Corn Souffle

(Pictured at right)

Breakfast is bound to be the most memorable meal of the day with this attractive souffle. The ham and corn enhance the cheesy egg flavor. A puffed golden top makes it look too pretty to eat...but nobody can resist.
—Pat Patty, Spring, Texas

> 2 teaspoons dry bread crumbs
> 1-1/2 cups fresh *or* frozen corn
> 1/3 cup thinly sliced green onions
> 2/3 cup diced fully cooked lean ham
> 1/4 cup all-purpose flour
> 1/4 teaspoon salt
> 1/8 teaspoon cayenne pepper
> 1 cup fat-free milk
> 1/2 cup shredded reduced-fat sharp cheddar
>   cheese
> 2 egg yolks
> 4 egg whites
> 1/2 teaspoon cream of tartar

Coat a 1-1/2-qt. baking dish with nonstick cooking spray; sprinkle with bread crumbs and set aside. In a large nonstick skillet coated with nonstick cooking spray, saute corn and onions for 5 minutes or until tender. Remove from the heat. Stir in ham; set aside.

In a small saucepan, combine the flour, salt and cayenne; gradually whisk in milk until smooth. Bring to a boil; cook and stir for 2 minutes or until thickened. Remove from the heat; stir in cheese until melted. In a small mixing bowl, beat egg yolks until thick and lemon-colored, about 5 minutes. Gradually add to cheese sauce, stirring constantly. Stir in corn mixture; set aside.

In another mixing bowl, beat egg whites on medium speed until foamy. Add cream of tartar; beat on high until stiff peaks form. Fold into corn mixture. Pour into prepared baking dish. Bake, uncovered, at 325° for 50-55 minutes or until puffed and golden. **Yield:** 4 servings.

Nutritional Analysis: *One serving (1 cup) equals 248 calories, 7 g fat (3 g saturated fat), 123 mg cholesterol, 577 mg sodium, 28 g carbohydrate, 2 g fiber, 20 g protein.*
Diabetic Exchanges: *2 lean meat, 2 starch.*

Spiced Tomato Drink

(Pictured at right)

I was looking for a different beverage to serve when I remembered a tomato drink I'd sampled in New Guinea. I experimented until I came up with this spicy concoction. It's delicious hot or cold any time of day. If you're watching your salt, use reduced-sodium tomato juice and skip the salt.
—Dorothy Anne Schultz, Dallas, Oregon

> 1 can (46 ounces) tomato juice
> 1/4 cup packed brown sugar
> 1 teaspoon ground cinnamon
> 1/2 teaspoon ground allspice
> 1/4 teaspoon salt
> 1/4 teaspoon pepper
> 1 tablespoon lemon juice

In a large saucepan, combine the first six ingredients. Bring to a boil. Reduce heat; simmer, uncovered, for 20 minutes. Remove from the heat; stir in lemon juice. Serve warm or cold. **Yield:** 8 servings.

Nutritional Analysis: *One serving (3/4 cup) equals 62 calories, trace fat (trace saturated fat), 0 cholesterol, 653 mg sodium, 13 g carbohydrate, 1 g fiber, 1 g protein.*
Diabetic Exchanges: *1 vegetable, 1/2 starch.*

Anise Raisin Bread

My yummy yeast bread tastes as special as the holidays. The festive blend of anise, citrus and raisins makes it perfect for a Christmas or Easter brunch. I've even used leftover slices to make a bread pudding dessert.
—Linda Hoza, Poland, Ohio

> 1 package (1/4 ounce) active dry yeast
> 1/3 cup warm fat-free milk (110° to 115°)
> 2/3 cup sugar
> 1/2 cup orange juice
> 1/3 cup butter *or* stick margarine, softened
> 2 eggs
> 2 egg whites
> 3 tablespoons lemon juice
> 1 tablespoon grated orange peel
> 1 teaspoon salt
> 1 teaspoon grated lemon peel
> 1 teaspoon anise extract
> 4-1/2 to 5-1/2 cups all-purpose flour
> 1 cup golden raisins

In a mixing bowl, dissolve yeast in warm milk. Add the sugar, orange juice, butter, eggs, egg whites, lemon juice, orange peel, salt, lemon peel, extract and 2 cups flour. Beat until smooth. Stir in raisins and enough remaining flour to form a soft dough. Turn onto a floured surface; knead until smooth and elastic, about 6-8 minutes. Place dough in a bowl coated with nonstick cooking spray; turn once to grease top. Cover and let rise in a warm place until doubled, about 1-1/4 hours.

Punch dough down. Turn onto a lightly floured surface; divide in half. Shape into loaves. Place in two 8-in. x 4-in. x 2-in. loaf pans coated with nonstick cooking spray. Cover and let rise in a warm place until doubled, about 45 minutes. Bake at 350° for 45-50 minutes or until golden brown. Remove from pans to cool on wire racks. **Yield:** 2 loaves (12 slices each).

Nutritional Analysis: *One slice equals 170 calories, 3 g fat (2 g saturated fat), 25 mg cholesterol, 137 mg sodium, 31 g carbohydrate, 1 g fiber, 4 g protein.*
Diabetic Exchanges: *1-1/2 starch, 1/2 fruit, 1/2 fat.*

Favorite Recipe Made Lighter

FOR a down-home way to start the day, Elizabeth Tonn of Waukesha, Wisconsin serves Sausage Pinwheels with Herb Gravy. Our Test Kitchen home economists modified her recipe to create Makeover Sausage Pinwheels with Herb Gravy.

Sausage Pinwheels With Herb Gravy

2-1/4 cups all-purpose flour, *divided*
1 tablespoon baking powder
1-1/4 teaspoons minced chives, *divided*
1-1/4 teaspoons dried parsley flakes, *divided*
1 teaspoon seasoned salt
3/4 teaspoon dried tarragon, *divided*
1/2 teaspoon sugar
5 tablespoons cold butter *or* margarine, *divided*
2 tablespoons shortening
2-3/4 cups milk, *divided*
1 pound bulk spicy *or* breakfast pork sausage
1/4 teaspoon pepper
Dash crushed red pepper flakes
2 teaspoons chicken bouillon granules

In a bowl, combine 2 cups flour, baking powder, 3/4 teaspoon chives, 3/4 teaspoon parsley, seasoned salt, 1/2 teaspoon tarragon and sugar. Cut in 2 tablespoons butter and shortening until mixture resembles coarse crumbs. Stir in 3/4 cup milk. On a floured surface, roll or pat dough into a 14-in. x 10-in. rectangle.

Between two sheets of waxed paper, roll or pat sausage into a 14-in. x 8-in. rectangle. Peel off top sheet of waxed paper. Invert sausage onto dough, lining up sausage along one long edge of dough. Peel off remaining waxed paper. Starting with the long side covered with sausage, roll up jelly-roll style; pinch seam to seal. Wrap in waxed paper. Refrigerate for 45 minutes.

Remove waxed paper; cut roll into 1-in. slices. Place cut side down in a greased 13-in. x 9-in. x 2-in. baking pan. Bake at 400° for 30-35 minutes or until golden.

For gravy, melt remaining butter in a saucepan over medium heat. Add the remaining flour, chives, parsley, tarragon, and the pepper and pepper flakes; stir until blended. Gradually add remaining milk. Bring to a boil; cook and stir 1-2 minutes or until thickened. Add bouillon; cook and stir over medium heat until dissolved. Serve immediately with pinwheels. **Yield:** 7 servings.

Nutritional Analysis: One serving (2 pinwheels with 1/4 cup gravy) equals 585 calories, 42 g fat (18 g saturated fat), 79 mg cholesterol, 1,209 mg sodium, 37 g carbohydrate, 1 g fiber, 15 g protein.

Makeover Sausage Pinwheels With Herb Gravy

(Pictured below left and on page 101)

2-1/4 cups all-purpose flour, *divided*
2 teaspoons baking powder
1-1/4 teaspoons snipped chives, *divided*
1-1/4 teaspoons dried parsley flakes, *divided*
3/4 teaspoon dried tarragon, *divided*
1/2 teaspoon seasoned salt
1/2 teaspoon sugar
1/4 teaspoon baking soda
2 tablespoons plus 2 teaspoons cold butter *or* stick margarine, *divided*
3/4 cup 1% buttermilk
12 ounces reduced-fat bulk pork sausage
2 cups fat-free half-and-half
2 teaspoons chicken bouillon granules
1/4 teaspoon pepper
Dash crushed red pepper flakes

In a bowl, combine 2 cups flour, baking powder, 3/4 teaspoon chives, 3/4 teaspoon parsley, 1/2 teaspoon tarragon, seasoned salt, sugar and baking soda. Cut in 2 tablespoons butter until mixture resembles coarse crumbs. Stir in buttermilk. On a floured surface, roll or pat dough into a 14-in. x 10-in. rectangle.

Between two sheets of waxed paper, roll or pat sausage into a 14-in. x 8-in. rectangle. Peel off top sheet of waxed paper. Invert sausage onto dough, lining up sausage along one long edge of dough. Peel off remaining waxed paper. Starting with the long side covered with sausage, roll up jelly-roll style; pinch seam to seal. Wrap in waxed paper. Refrigerate for 45 minutes.

Remove waxed paper; cut roll into 1-in. slices. Place cut side down in a 13-in. x 9-in. x 2-in. baking pan coated with nonstick cooking spray. Bake at 400° for 30-35 minutes or golden brown.

For gravy, place remaining flour in a saucepan. Gradually stir in half-and-half, bouillon, pepper, pepper flakes and remaining chives, parsley and tarragon until smooth. Bring to a boil over medium-low heat; cook and stir for 1-2 minutes or until thickened. Remove from the heat; stir in remaining butter. Serve immediately with pinwheels. **Yield:** 7 servings.

Nutritional Analysis: One serving (2 pinwheels with 1/4 cup gravy) equals 363 calories, 14 g fat (6 g saturated fat), 13 mg cholesterol, 999 mg sodium, 40 g carbohydrate, 1 g fiber, 16 g protein.
Diabetic Exchanges: 2 starch, 2 fat, 1 lean meat, 1/2 fat-free milk.

Almond Sunshine Citrus

(Pictured below)

I adapted this recipe from one I found in a newspaper. The tangy combination of citrus fruits is welcome as a light dessert after a big meal or as a refreshing addition to a brunch. Friends and family rave about it.
—Geri Barr, Calgary, Alberta

   3 **large navel oranges**
   1 **medium red grapefruit**
   1 **medium white grapefruit**
   1 **small lemon**
   1 **small lime**
1/3 **cup sugar**
1/8 **teaspoon almond extract**
   2 **tablespoons sliced almonds, toasted**

Grate enough peel from the oranges, grapefruit, lemon and lime to measure 1 tablespoon of mixed citrus peel; set peel aside. To section citrus fruit, cut a thin slice off the bottom and top of the oranges, grapefruit, lemon and lime. Place each fruit cut side down on a cutting board. With a sharp knife, remove peel and white pith. Holding fruit over a bowl, slice between the membrane of each section and the fruit until the knife reaches the center; remove sections and place in a glass bowl. Set 1/2 cup juice aside.

In a small saucepan, combine the sugar and reserved peel and juice. Bring to a boil. Reduce heat; simmer, uncovered, for 10 minutes. Cool; stir in extract. Pour over fruit. Refrigerate overnight. Just before serving, sprinkle with almonds. **Yield:** 4 servings.

Nutritional Analysis: *One serving (3/4 cup fruit and juice) equals 203 calories, 3 g fat (trace saturated fat), 0 cholesterol, 1 mg sodium, 46 g carbohydrate, 6 g fiber, 3 g protein.*
Diabetic Exchanges: *3 fruit, 1/2 fat.*

Asparagus Frittata

(Pictured above)

You would never guess that egg substitute takes the place of eggs in this frittata. Chock-full of fresh asparagus, this is perfect for a light springtime lunch or brunch.
—James Bates, Hermiston, Oregon

    1 **cup water**
 2/3 **pound fresh asparagus, trimmed and cut into 1-inch pieces**
    1 **medium onion, chopped**
    2 **teaspoons olive** *or* **canola oil**
    2 **tablespoons minced fresh parsley**
1-1/2 **cups egg substitute**
    5 **tablespoons shredded Parmesan cheese, divided**
 1/4 **teaspoon salt**
 1/8 **teaspoon pepper**
 1/4 **cup shredded reduced-fat cheddar cheese**

In a saucepan, bring water to a boil. Add asparagus; cover and boil for 3 minutes. Drain and immediately place asparagus in ice water; drain and pat dry. In a 10-in. ovenproof skillet, saute onion in oil until tender. Add parsley and asparagus; toss to coat.

In a bowl, combine the egg substitute, 3 tablespoons of Parmesan cheese, salt and pepper. Pour over the asparagus mixture; cover and cook for 8-10 minutes or until eggs are nearly set. Sprinkle with remaining Parmesan. Place uncovered skillet in the broiler, 6 in. from the heat, for 2 minutes or until eggs are set. Sprinkle with cheddar cheese. Cut into quarters. Serve immediately. **Yield:** 4 servings.

Nutritional Analysis: *One serving equals 146 calories, 5 g fat (2 g saturated fat), 8 mg cholesterol, 533 mg sodium, 9 g carbohydrate, 2 g fiber, 16 g protein.*
Diabetic Exchanges: *2 lean meat, 1 vegetable.*

Breakfast Pizza

(Pictured at right)

Eggs and hash browns have extra pizzazz when they're served up on a pizza pan. My family requests this fun breakfast often, and it's a snap to make with the prebaked crust. I adjust the "heat index" of the toppings to suit the taste buds of my diners.
—Christy Hinrichs, Parkville, Missouri

    2 cups frozen shredded hash brown potatoes
  1/4 teaspoon ground cumin
  1/4 teaspoon chili powder
    2 tablespoons canola oil, *divided*
    1 cup egg substitute
    2 tablespoons fat-free milk
  1/4 teaspoon salt
    2 green onions, chopped
    2 tablespoons diced sweet red pepper
    1 tablespoon finely chopped jalapeno pepper*
    1 garlic clove, minced
    1 prebaked Italian bread shell crust (16 ounces)
  1/2 cup salsa
  3/4 cup shredded reduced-fat cheddar cheese

In a nonstick skillet, cook hash browns, cumin and chili powder in 1 tablespoon oil over medium heat until golden. Remove and keep warm. In a bowl, beat egg substitute, milk and salt; set aside. In the same skillet, saute the onions, peppers and garlic in remaining oil until tender. Add egg mixture. Cook and stir over medium heat until almost set. Remove from the heat.

Place crust on an ungreased 14-in. pizza pan. Spread salsa over crust. Top with egg mixture. Sprinkle with hash browns and cheese. Bake at 375° for 8-10 minutes or until cheese is melted. **Yield:** 6 slices.

***Editor's Note**: When cutting or seeding hot peppers, use rubber or plastic gloves to protect your hands. Avoid touching your face.

Nutritional Analysis: One slice equals 375 calories, 12 g fat (2 g saturated fat), 10 mg cholesterol, 748 mg sodium, 50 g carbohydrate, 1 g fiber, 19 g protein.
Diabetic Exchanges: 3 starch, 2 fat, 1 lean meat.

Honeydew Kiwi Cooler

(Pictured at right)

Our Test Kitchen staff suggests you make a big pitcher of this thick, fruity beverage because guests are sure to ask for a second glass! The colorful quencher has a refreshing melon flavor and gets its creamy consistency from fat-free yogurt. Serve it at breakfasts throughout the year.

    3 cups cubed honeydew
    2 kiwifruit, peeled and cubed
  1/2 cup fat-free plain yogurt
    2 tablespoons honey
    1 cup ice cubes
    2 to 3 drops green food coloring, optional

In a blender, combine all ingredients; cover and process until blended. Pour into chilled glasses; serve immediately. **Yield:** 4 servings.

Nutritional Analysis: One serving (1 cup) equals 113 calories, trace fat (trace saturated fat), 1 mg cholesterol, 32 mg sodium, 28 g carbohydrate, 2 g fiber, 2 g protein.
Diabetic Exchange: 2 fruit.

Strawberry Breakfast Spread

This recipe comes from my mother, Helen Orman, who is on a restricted diet. She makes this yummy fruity spread often and uses it in place of jellies and syrups.
—Theresa Brown, Mountain Home, Idaho

    2 teaspoons unflavored gelatin
  1/4 cup orange juice
 1-3/4 cups unsweetened strawberries, mashed
Sugar substitute equivalent to 1/2 cup sugar*
  1/4 teaspoon grated orange peel

In a small saucepan, sprinkle gelatin over orange juice; let stand for 1 minute. Cook and stir over low heat until gelatin is dissolved. Remove from the heat; stir in remaining ingredients. Transfer to a container; cover and refrigerate for 3-4 hours or until firm. Store in the refrigerator. **Yield:** 1-1/4 cups.

***Editor's Note:** This recipe was tested with Equal Sweetener.

Nutritional Analysis: One serving (2 tablespoons) equals 16 calories, trace fat (trace saturated fat), 0 cholesterol, 1 mg sodium, 3 g carbohydrate, 1 g fiber, 1 g protein.
Diabetic Exchange: Free food.

Orange Whole Wheat Pancakes

Friends and family will flip over these light whole wheat pancakes with a sunny twist of citrus, which I adapted from a traditional pancake recipe. Feel free to mix raisins or dried cranberries into the batter to add a bit of chewy sweetness.
—Earl Brunner, Las Vegas, Nevada

    3 egg whites
    1 cup orange juice
  1/3 cup unsweetened applesauce
  1/4 teaspoon orange extract
 1-1/4 cups whole wheat flour
    2 tablespoons sugar
    2 teaspoons baking powder
  1/2 teaspoon salt
  1/2 cup orange marmalade

In a blender, place the first four ingredients. Cover and process until smooth. In a bowl, combine the flour, sugar, baking powder and salt; make a well. Add orange juice mixture; stir just until moistened.

Pour batter by 2 tablespoonfuls onto a hot griddle coated with nonstick cooking spray. Turn when bubbles form on top of pancake; cook until second side is golden brown. Serve with marmalade. **Yield:** 16 pancakes.

Nutritional Analysis: One serving (2 pancakes with 1 tablespoon marmalade) equals 150 calories, trace fat (trace saturated fat), 0 cholesterol, 238 mg sodium, 35 g carbohydrate, 3 g fiber, 4 g protein.
Diabetic Exchanges: 1-1/2 starch, 1/2 fruit.

Blueberry 'n' Spice Sauce

Our family enjoys this sweet fruity sauce on French toast, angel food cake, fat-free frozen yogurt or most anything we can drizzle it over.
—Mary Jo Carlton, Montrose, Pennsylvania

1/2 cup sugar
1 tablespoon cornstarch
1/2 teaspoon ground cinnamon
1/4 teaspoon ground nutmeg
1/2 cup water
2 cups fresh *or* frozen blueberries

In a saucepan, combine sugar, cornstarch, cinnamon and nutmeg. Gradually stir in water until smooth. Bring to a boil; cook and stir for 1 minute or until thickened. Stir in blueberries; return to a boil. Reduce heat; cook and stir for 5 minutes. Serve warm. **Yield:** 1-3/4 cups.

Nutritional Analysis: One serving (1/4 cup) equals 83 calories, trace fat (trace saturated fat), 0 cholesterol, 3 mg sodium, 21 g carbohydrate, 1 g fiber, trace protein.
Diabetic Exchange: *1-1/2 fruit.*

Raisin Cinnamon Rolls

(Pictured at right)

It's easy to get on a roll in the morning when these cinnamony treats greet you at the table. These tender rolls have the same sweet aroma and glistening glaze as bakery rolls...only without the guilt.
—Carolyn Wolbers, Loveland, Ohio

2 medium potatoes, peeled and diced
1 package (1/4 ounce) active dry yeast
1/2 teaspoon plus 1/4 cup sugar, *divided*
1/2 cup evaporated fat-free milk
1/4 cup honey
3 tablespoons canola oil
1 teaspoon salt
1/2 teaspoon butter flavoring
5 cups all-purpose flour
2 egg whites, lightly beaten, *divided*
1-1/4 cups packed brown sugar
1/2 cup raisins
2 teaspoons ground cinnamon
GLAZE:
1-1/2 cups confectioners' sugar
3 tablespoons fat-free milk
1/2 teaspoon vanilla extract

In a saucepan, cook potatoes in 1-1/2 cups water until very tender; drain, reserving 3/4 cup cooking liquid. Mash potatoes; set aside 1 cup (refrigerate any remaining potatoes for another use). Heat reserved cooking liquid to 110°-115° if necessary. In a mixing bowl, dissolve yeast in warm liquid. Add 1/2 teaspoon sugar; let stand for 5 minutes.

Add the milk, honey, oil, salt, butter flavoring, remaining sugar, 2 cups flour and reserved potatoes. Beat until smooth. Stir in enough remaining flour to form a soft dough. Turn onto a floured surface; knead until smooth and elastic, about 6-8 minutes. Place in a greased bowl, turning once to grease top. Cover and let rise in a warm place until doubled, about 1-1/2 hours.

Punch dough down. Turn onto a lightly floured surface; roll into an 18-in. x 13-in. rectangle. Brush with some of the egg whites. Combine brown sugar, raisins and cinnamon; sprinkle over dough to within 1 in. of edges. Roll up jelly-roll style, starting with a long side; pinch seam to seal. Cut into 18 slices. Place cut side down in two 9-in. square baking pans coated with nonstick cooking spray. Brush with remaining egg white. Cover and let rise until doubled, about 30 minutes.

Bake at 350° for 20-25 minutes or until golden brown. Cool on a wire rack. Combine glaze ingredients; drizzle over rolls. **Yield:** 18 rolls.

Nutritional Analysis: One roll equals 288 calories, 2 g fat (trace saturated fat), trace cholesterol, 184 mg sodium, 64 g carbohydrate, 1 g fiber, 5 g protein.

Pecan Waffles

(Pictured at right)

Your bunch will say a big "yes" to breakfast when these wonderful nutty waffles are on the menu.
—Susan Bell, Spruce Pine, North Carolina

1-1/4 cups all-purpose flour
1/4 cup wheat bran
1 tablespoon sugar
2-1/2 teaspoons baking powder
1/2 teaspoon salt
1 egg
1 egg white
1-1/2 cups fat-free milk
2 tablespoons canola oil
1/3 cup chopped pecans

In a bowl, combine the flour, bran, sugar, baking powder and salt. In another bowl, combine the egg, egg white, milk and oil; add to the dry ingredients. Fold in the pecans. Bake in a preheated waffle iron according to manufacturer's directions until golden brown. **Yield:** 6 waffles (6-1/2-inch diameter).

Nutritional Analysis: One waffle equals 233 calories, 11 g fat (1 g saturated fat), 37 mg cholesterol, 344 mg sodium, 28 g carbohydrate, 2 g fiber, 8 g protein.
Diabetic Exchanges: *2 starch, 2 fat.*

● Breakfast Bonus

- Set up a bagel buffet for breakfasts on the fly. Put out a variety of bagels (such as whole wheat, cinnamon and pumpernickel), along with an array of low-fat toppings.
- Stir up a bowl of instant cooked cereal, then top with honey or cinnamon or a sprinkling of wheat germ.

Jumbo Pineapple Yeast Rolls

(Pictured above)

Believe it or not, these big breakfast treats will fit right into a light eating plan. A friend gave me the recipe for these yummy yeast rolls. I sometimes use the pineapple filling as a dressing for fruit salad, too. Delicious!
—Pat Walter, Pine Island, Minnesota

- 2 packages (1/4 ounce *each*) active dry yeast
- 2 cups warm fat-free milk (110° to 115°), *divided*
- 1 cup sugar, *divided*
- 2 eggs
- 6 tablespoons butter *or* stick margarine, softened
- 1 teaspoon salt
- 7 to 8 cups all-purpose flour

FILLING:
- 1 tablespoon butter *or* stick margarine
- 1 tablespoon all-purpose flour
- 1/2 cup orange juice
- 1 can (8 ounces) unsweetened crushed pineapple, drained
- 1/3 cup sugar
- 1 tablespoon grated orange peel
- 1/4 teaspoon salt
- 15 maraschino cherries

GLAZE:
- 1-1/2 cups confectioners' sugar
- 2 tablespoons fat-free milk
- 1/4 teaspoon vanilla extract

In a large mixing bowl, dissolve yeast in 1/2 cup warm milk. Stir in 1 tablespoon sugar; let stand for 5 minutes. Add the eggs, butter, salt, and remaining milk and sugar. Beat in 4 cups flour until smooth. Stir in enough remaining flour to form a soft dough. Turn onto a floured surface; knead until smooth and elastic, about 6-8 minutes. Place in a greased bowl, turning once to grease top. Cover and let rise in a warm place until doubled, about 1 hour.

For filling, melt butter in a small saucepan. Stir in flour until smooth. Add the orange juice, pineapple, sugar, orange peel and salt. Bring to a boil; cook and stir over medium heat for 2 minutes or until thickened. Remove from the heat; cool.

Punch dough down. Turn onto a lightly floured surface. Roll out into a 24-in. x 12-in. rectangle. Spread filling over dough to within 1/2 In. of edges. Roll up jelly-roll style, starting with a long side; pinch seam to seal. Cut into 15 slices. Place cut side down in a 13-in. x 9-in. x 2-in. baking pan and a 9-in. square baking pan coated with nonstick cooking spray. Top each roll with a cherry.

Bake at 350° for 35-40 minutes or until golden. Remove from pans to wire racks to cool. Combine glaze ingredients; drizzle over rolls. **Yield:** 15 rolls.

Nutritional Analysis: One roll equals 417 calories, 7 g fat (4 g saturated fat), 44 mg cholesterol, 279 mg sodium, 81 g carbohydrate, 2 g fiber, 9 g protein.

Breakfast Sundaes

Kids of all ages will love the layers of creamy yogurt, crunchy granola, banana slices and mandarin oranges in this dish. It sweetens the morning meal but also serves as a healthful dessert or after-school snack. Spooned into clear parfait glasses, this yummy treat makes a pretty presentation.
—Linda Franceschi, Eldred, New York

- 2 cartons (8 ounces *each*) fat-free raspberry yogurt *or* flavored yogurt of your choice
- 1 cup reduced-fat granola cereal
- 2 medium firm bananas, sliced
- 1 can (15 ounces) mandarin oranges, drained

In four parfait glasses or bowls, layer 2 tablespoons each of yogurt, granola, bananas and oranges. Repeat layers. Serve immediately. **Yield:** 4 servings.

Nutritional Analysis: One serving equals 266 calories, 2 g fat (trace saturated fat), 3 mg cholesterol, 130 mg sodium, 57 g carbohydrate, 6 g fiber, 9 g protein.
Diabetic Exchanges: 2 fruit, 1 starch, 1 fat-free milk.

Beefed-Up Main Dishes

Even folks watching their diets can indulge in a meaty entree. The secret is to select lean beef cuts and to trim down the accompanying sauces. No one will guess you cheated these dishes out of fat and calories!

Pita Pizzas (page 118)

Cheesy Shell Lasagna

(Pictured above)

This zesty layered casserole is a real crowd-pleaser. It was one of our children's favorites when they were young...now our grandchildren love it! Plus, it's easier to make than traditional lasagna.
—Mrs. Leo Merchant, Jackson, Mississippi

1-1/2 pounds lean ground beef
2 medium onions, chopped
1 garlic clove, minced
1 can (14-1/2 ounces) stewed tomatoes, cut up
1 jar (14 ounces) meatless spaghetti sauce
1 can (4 ounces) mushroom stems and pieces, undrained
8 ounces uncooked small shell pasta
2 cups (16 ounces) reduced-fat sour cream
11 slices (8 ounces) reduced-fat provolone cheese
1 cup (4 ounces) shredded part-skim mozzarella cheese

In a nonstick skillet, cook the beef, onions and garlic over medium heat until meat is no longer pink; drain. Stir in tomatoes, spaghetti sauce and mushrooms. Bring to a boil. Reduce heat; simmer, uncovered, for 20 minutes. Meanwhile, cook pasta according to package directions; drain.

Place half of the pasta in an ungreased 13-in. x 9-in. x 2-in. baking dish. Top with half of the meat sauce, sour cream and provolone cheese. Repeat layers. Sprinkle with mozzarella cheese.

Cover and bake at 350° for 35-40 minutes. Uncover; bake 10 minutes longer or until the cheese begins to brown. Let stand for 10 minutes before cutting. **Yield:** 12 servings.

Nutritional Analysis: One serving equals 346 calories, 15 g fat (8 g saturated fat), 50 mg cholesterol, 515 mg sodium, 29 g carbohydrate, 2 g fiber, 27 g protein.
Diabetic Exchanges: 3 lean meat, 1-1/2 starch, 1 vegetable, 1 fat.

Herbed Beef Stew

(Pictured below)

This is one of the tastiest stews I have ever made. It's hearty and especially good for folks on restricted diets because most of its flavor comes from herbs and spices.
—Dixie Terry, Marion, Illinois

6 tablespoons all-purpose flour, *divided*
1 teaspoon paprika
1/4 teaspoon pepper
1-1/2 pounds beef stew meat, cut into 1-inch cubes
1 tablespoon canola oil
2 cups water
3 tablespoons tomato paste
2 teaspoons beef bouillon granules
2 teaspoons dried basil, *divided*
1 teaspoon dried thyme, *divided*
1 teaspoon garlic powder, *divided*
2 bay leaves
3 cups cubed peeled potatoes
3 cups quartered peeled small onions
2 cups sliced carrots
2 tablespoons minced fresh parsley
1/4 teaspoon salt
1/4 cup cold water

In a large resealable plastic bag, combine 4 tablespoons flour, paprika and pepper. Add beef, a few pieces at a time, and shake to coat. In a Dutch oven, brown beef in oil over medium heat. Add the water, tomato paste, bouillon, 1-1/2 teaspoons basil, 3/4 teaspoon thyme, 3/4 teaspoon garlic powder and bay leaves. Bring to a boil. Reduce heat; cover and simmer for 1-1/2 hours or until meat is almost tender.

Add the potatoes, onions and carrots. Cover and simmer 30 minutes longer or until the meat and vegetables are tender. Discard bay leaves. In a small bowl, combine the parsley, salt, and the remaining flour, basil, thyme and gar-

lic powder. Add cold water; stir until smooth. Stir into stew. Bring to a boil; cook and stir for 2 minutes or until thickened. **Yield:** 6 servings.

Nutritional Analysis: One serving (1-1/2 cups) equals 336 calories, 11 g fat (3 g saturated fat), 71 mg cholesterol, 512 mg sodium, 34 g carbohydrate, 5 g fiber, 26 g protein.
Diabetic Exchanges: 3 lean meat, 2 vegetable, 1-1/2 starch.

Oriental Steak Skewers

(Pictured at right)

I'm always on the lookout for light meals that will satisfy my family, and these stuffed kabobs fit the bill. Served with a creamy mustard sauce, the colorful bundles are special enough for company.
—Gina Hatchell, Mickleton, New Jersey

 1 pound boneless beef sirloin tip roast
1/3 cup reduced-sodium soy sauce
1/4 cup sugar
1/2 teaspoon ground ginger *or* 2 teaspoons grated
    fresh gingerroot
 1 cup water
 4 medium carrots, julienned
1/2 pound fresh green beans
 1 large sweet red pepper, julienned
1/2 cup reduced-fat sour cream
 2 tablespoons Dijon mustard
1-1/4 teaspoons prepared horseradish

Cut beef widthwise into 16 slices, 1/4 in. thick. In a large resealable plastic bag, combine the soy sauce, sugar and ginger; add the beef. Seal bag and turn to coat; refrigerate for 4 hours.

In a saucepan, bring water and carrots to a boil. Reduce heat; cover and simmer for 3 minutes. Add the beans and red pepper; cover and simmer for 3-5 minutes or until vegetables are crisp-tender. Drain and immediately place vegetables in ice water. Drain and pat dry.

Drain and discard marinade from beef. Arrange three beans, one carrot strip and one pepper strip down the center of each beef slice; roll up. For each kabob, use metal or soaked wooden skewers and thread two bundles on two parallel skewers.

If grilling the kabobs, coat grill rack with nonstick cooking spray before starting the grill. Grill kabobs, covered, over medium heat or broil 4-6 in. from the heat for 2-3 minutes on each side or until beef reaches desired doneness, turning once.

In a bowl, combine the sour cream, mustard and horseradish. Serve with kabobs. **Yield:** 4 servings.

Nutritional Analysis: One serving (4 bundles with 2 tablespoons sauce) equals 304 calories, 10 g fat (5 g saturated fat), 87 mg cholesterol, 542 mg sodium, 21 g carbohydrate, 5 g fiber, 31 g protein.
Diabetic Exchanges: 4 lean meat, 3 vegetable, 1/2 fat.

The Skinny on Skewers

NOT ONLY are shish kabobs an ideal way to serve a healthy, satisfying and fun meal, but throwing them together is a cinch as well. The next time you have a craving for kabobs, consider the following "pointers" and start stacking!

- To help prevent wooden skewers from burning or splintering, soak them in water for 15-30 minutes. Remove them from the water and then pile on the ingredients.
- Items such as mushrooms, chunks of zucchini and pieces of meat may spin on kabobs, making it difficult to cook them evenly on all sides. To avoid this, pierce the food with two parallel skewers (as Oriental Steak Skewers are prepared, shown above right).
- Not able to grill? Simply broil your kabobs 4-6 in. from the heat. Broil until poultry is no longer pink or until meat reaches the desired doneness.

Apple and Onion Beef Pot Roast

(Pictured above)

Rely on your slow cooker to help prepare this moist pot roast. I thicken the juices to make a pleasing apple gravy that's wonderful over the beef slices and onions.
—Rachel Koistinen, Hayti, South Dakota

    1 boneless beef sirloin tip roast (3 pounds),
        cut in half
    1 cup water
    1 teaspoon seasoned salt
    1/2 teaspoon reduced-sodium soy sauce
    1/2 teaspoon Worcestershire sauce
    1/4 teaspoon garlic powder
    1 large tart apple, quartered
    1 large onion, sliced
    2 tablespoons cornstarch
    2 tablespoons cold water
    1/8 teaspoon browning sauce

In a large nonstick skillet coated with nonstick cooking spray, brown roast on all sides. Transfer to a 5-qt. slow cooker. Add water to the skillet, stirring to loosen any browned bits; pour over roast. Sprinkle with seasoned salt, soy sauce, Worcestershire sauce and garlic powder. Top with apple and onion. Cover and cook on low for 5-6 hours or until the meat is tender.

Remove roast and onion; let stand for 15 minutes before slicing. Strain cooking liquid into a saucepan, discarding apple. Bring liquid to a boil; cook until reduced to 2 cups, about 15 minutes. Combine cornstarch and cold water until smooth; stir in browning sauce. Stir into cooking liquid. Bring to a boil; cook and stir for 2 minutes or until thickened. Serve over beef and onion. **Yield:** 8 servings with leftovers.

Nutritional Analysis: One serving (3 ounces cooked beef with 3 tablespoons gravy) equals 173 calories, 6 g fat (2 g saturated fat), 69 mg cholesterol, 262 mg sodium, 4 g carbohydrate, trace fiber, 25 g protein.
Diabetic Exchange: 3 lean meat.

Pepper Steak

When I need a speedy skillet supper, this pepper steak comes to my rescue. The tender meat is slightly sweet, with a hint of brown sugar and molasses. It's a delectable way to beef up your dinner menu without piling on the calories.
—Monica Williams, Burleson, Texas

    2 tablespoons cornstarch
    2 tablespoons brown sugar
1-1/2 teaspoons ground ginger *or* 2 tablespoons
        minced fresh gingerroot
    3/4 teaspoon garlic powder
    1 can (14-1/2 ounces) beef broth
    3 tablespoons reduced-sodium soy sauce
    1 tablespoon molasses
1-1/2 pounds boneless beef sirloin steak, cut into
        1/4-inch strips
    1 tablespoon canola oil
    2 large green peppers, cut into 1/2-inch strips
1-1/2 cups sliced celery
    3 green onions, chopped
    4 teaspoons lemon juice
Hot cooked noodles, optional

In a bowl, combine the cornstarch, brown sugar, ginger and garlic powder. Stir in broth until smooth. Add soy sauce and molasses; set aside.

In a nonstick skillet or wok, stir-fry steak in oil for 4-5 minutes; remove and keep warm. Stir-fry peppers, celery and onions for 5 minutes or until crisp-tender. Stir broth mixture and add to the vegetables. Return meat to the pan. Bring to a boil; cook and stir for 2 minutes or until thickened. Stir in lemon juice. Serve over noodles if desired. **Yield:** 6 servings.

Nutritional Analysis: One serving (3/4 cup beef mixture, calculated without noodles) equals 257 calories, 9 g fat (3 g saturated fat), 75 mg cholesterol, 679 mg sodium, 16 g carbohydrate, 2 g fiber, 28 g protein.
Diabetic Exchanges: 3 lean meat, 1 vegetable, 1/2 starch, 1/2 fat.

Mexican Stuffed Shells

(Pictured below)

*My husband and I both love Mexican food—
the hotter the better. But since our children and
friends like milder dishes, I created this recipe.
It's delicious, inexpensive and quick to fix.*
—Norma Jean Shaw, Stephens City, Virginia

  24 uncooked jumbo pasta shells
    1 pound lean ground beef
    2 cups salsa
    1 can (8 ounces) tomato sauce
    1 cup frozen corn
  1/2 cup canned black beans, rinsed and drained
    1 cup (4 ounces) shredded reduced-fat Mexican
       cheese blend *or* cheddar cheese
TOPPINGS:
    8 tablespoons reduced-fat sour cream
    8 tablespoons salsa
  1/4 cup sliced ripe olives
  1/4 cup sliced green onions

Cook pasta shells according to package directions; drain.
In a nonstick skillet, cook beef over medium heat until no
longer pink; drain. Stir in the salsa, tomato sauce, corn
and beans. Spoon into pasta shells.

Place in a 13-in. x 9-in. x 2-in. baking dish coated with
nonstick cooking spray. Sprinkle with cheese. Cover and
bake at 350° for 25-30 minutes or until heated through. Top
with sour cream, salsa, olives and onions. **Yield:** 8 servings.

*Nutritional Analysis: One serving (3 stuffed shells with 1 ta-
blespoon each sour cream and salsa and 1-1/2 teaspoons each
olives and onions) equals 323 calories, 10 g fat (5 g saturated
fat), 36 mg cholesterol, 787 mg sodium, 35 g carbohydrate, 4 g
fiber, 23 g protein.*
Diabetic Exchanges: 2 lean meat, 2 starch, 1 vegetable, 1 fat.

Oven Beef Stew

(Pictured above)

*No one ever guesses that this traditional combination
is low in fat. A thick flavorful sauce makes this hearty
dish one that will be requested time and again.
I know your family will enjoy it.*
—Debbie Patton, Westchester, Illinois

    2 pounds boneless beef round roast, cut into
       1-1/2-inch cubes
    2 medium potatoes, peeled and cut into 1/2-inch
       cubes
    2 medium onions, cut into eighths
    3 celery ribs, cut into 1-inch pieces
    4 medium carrots, cut into 1-inch slices
    1 can (11-1/2 ounces) tomato juice
  1/3 cup dry sherry *or* water
  1/3 cup quick-cooking tapioca
    1 tablespoon sugar
    1 teaspoon salt
  1/2 teaspoon dried basil
  1/4 teaspoon pepper
    2 cups fresh green beans, cut into 1-inch pieces

In a Dutch oven, combine the beef, potatoes, onions, celery and carrots; set aside. In a bowl, combine the tomato
juice, sherry or water, tapioca, sugar, salt, basil and pepper.
Let stand for 15 minutes. Pour over the beef mixture. Cover and bake at 325° for 2 to 2-1/2 hours or until meat is almost tender.

Add the beans; cook 30 minutes longer or until beans
and meat are tender. **Yield:** 8 servings.

*Nutritional Analysis: One serving (1 cup) equals 268 calories,
7 g fat (2 g saturated fat), 70 mg cholesterol, 519 mg sodium, 25
g carbohydrate, 4 g fiber, 25 g protein.*
Diabetic Exchanges: 3 lean meat, 2 vegetable, 1 starch.

2 tablespoons sugar
1 tablespoon grated orange peel
3/4 pound boneless beef sirloin steak, cut into thin strips
1 tablespoon canola oil
3 cups fresh green beans, cut into 2-inch pieces
2 tablespoons water
1 teaspoon cornstarch
1 teaspoon ground ginger
1/8 teaspoon pepper
1/4 cup reduced-sodium soy sauce
3 tablespoons orange juice

In a large bowl, combine the sugar and orange peel; mix well. Add beef; toss to coat. In a large nonstick skillet, stir-fry beef in oil for 5 minutes or until browned. In a microwave-safe dish, cover and cook beans in water for 3-5 minutes on high; drain. Add the beans to skillet; cook, stirring constantly, until tender.

In a bowl, combine the cornstarch, ginger and pepper. Stir in the soy sauce and orange juice until smooth. Pour the sauce over beef and beans; toss to coat. Bring to a boil; cook and stir for 1 minute or until thickened. Serve immediately. **Yield:** 4 servings.

Nutritional Analysis: *One serving (1 cup) equals 225 calories, 8 g fat (2 g saturated fat), 53 mg cholesterol, 653 mg sodium, 16 g carbohydrate, 3 g fiber, 21 g protein.*
Diabetic Exchanges: *3 lean meat, 1 vegetable, 1/2 starch.*

Spicy French Dip

(Pictured above)

If I'm cooking for a party or family get-together,
I can put this beef in the slow cooker in the morning
and then concentrate on other preparations.
It's a great time-saver and never fails to get rave reviews.
—Ginny Koeppen, Winnfield, Louisiana

1 boneless beef sirloin tip roast (about 3 pounds), cut in half
1/2 cup water
1 can (4 ounces) diced jalapeno peppers, drained
1 envelope Italian salad dressing mix
12 crusty rolls (5 inches)

Place beef in a 5-qt. slow cooker. In a small bowl, combine the water, jalapenos and dressing mix; pour over beef. Cover and cook on low for 8-10 hours or until meat is tender. Remove beef and shred using two forks. Skim fat from cooking juices. Serve beef on buns with juice. **Yield:** 12 servings.

Nutritional Analysis: *One serving (one sandwich with 3 tablespoons juice) equals 357 calories, 9 g fat (4 g saturated fat), 68 mg cholesterol, 877 mg sodium, 37 g carbohydrate, 2 g fiber, 31 g protein.*
Diabetic Exchanges: *3 lean meat, 2 starch.*

Orange Beef and Beans

Green beans are one of my all-time favorite vegetables.
I can cook them more ways than ground beef, and this
dish showcases them beautifully. Orange juice adds
zesty flavor to the sirloin steak and garden-fresh beans.
—Sundra Hauck, Bogalusa, Louisiana

Chuck Wagon Wraps

(Pictured below)

If you like baked beans, you'll savor this robust wrap. I
combine canned baked beans, ground beef and corn,
then roll it up in tortillas. I was wondering what to
fix for dinner one night and came up with this. My

husband raved about it! It's fast and easy to make, too.
—Wendy Conger, Winfield, Illinois

   1 pound lean ground beef
   1 can (28 ounces) barbecue-flavored baked
     beans
   1 package (10 ounces) frozen corn, thawed
4-1/2 teaspoons Worcestershire sauce
   1 cup (4 ounces) shredded reduced-fat cheddar
     cheese
  12 flour tortillas (8 inches), warmed
   3 cups shredded lettuce
1-1/2 cups chopped fresh tomatoes
  3/4 cup reduced-fat sour cream

In a large nonstick skillet, cook beef over medium heat until no longer pink; drain. Stir in the beans, corn and Worcestershire sauce; mix well. Bring to a boil. Reduce heat; simmer, uncovered, for 4-5 minutes or until heated through. Sprinkle with cheese; cook 1-2 minutes longer. Spoon about 1/2 cup off center on each tortilla; top with lettuce, tomatoes and sour cream. Roll up. **Yield:** 12 servings.

Nutritional Analysis: One wrap equals 373 calories, 11 g fat (4 g saturated fat), 27 mg cholesterol, 605 mg sodium, 50 g carbohydrate, 4 g fiber, 20 g protein.
Diabetic Exchanges: 3 starch, 2 lean meat, 1/2 fat.

Creamy Beef and Mushroom Skillet

Our Test Kitchen staff stirred up this light rendition of classic Stroganoff. The saucy stovetop supper combines lean ground beef, mushrooms and onions in a flavorful brown gravy.

  1 pound lean ground beef
  2 medium onions, sliced
  1 jar (12 ounces) fat-free beef gravy
1/3 cup reduced-fat sour cream
1/3 cup fat-free plain yogurt
  1 tablespoon Worcestershire sauce
1/4 teaspoon dried thyme
1/4 teaspoon pepper
1/4 teaspoon browning sauce
Hot cooked noodles or rice
1/4 cup minced fresh parsley

In a large nonstick skillet, cook the beef, mushrooms and onions over medium heat until meat is no longer pink; drain. In a bowl, combine gravy, sour cream, yogurt, Worcestershire sauce, thyme, pepper and browning sauce; mix well. Stir into meat mixture; heat through. Serve over noodles or rice. Sprinkle with parsley. **Yield:** 5 servings.

Nutritional Analysis: One serving (1 cup beef mixture, calculated without noodles or rice) equals 239 calories, 10 g fat (4 g saturated fat), 44 mg cholesterol, 475 mg sodium, 16 g carbohydrate, 2 g fiber, 22 g protein.
Diabetic Exchanges: 3 lean meat, 1 starch.

Gaucho Casserole

(Pictured below)

When our daughters graduated from college, my husband and I made recipe books for their closest friends. This dish was a big hit.
—Dianne Hennis, King George, Virginia

   1 pound lean ground beef
   1 medium onion, chopped
   1 small green pepper, chopped
   1 can (16 ounces) kidney beans, rinsed and
     drained
   1 can (14-1/2 ounces) diced tomatoes, undrained
   1 can (8 ounces) tomato sauce
1/4 cup water
   1 envelope reduced-sodium taco seasoning
   1 teaspoon chili powder
1-1/3 cups uncooked instant rice
   1 cup (4 ounces) shredded reduced-fat Mexican
     cheese blend

Crumble the beef into an ungreased 2-1/2-qt. microwave-safe dish. Add onion and green pepper; mix well. Cover and microwave on high for 6 minutes or until meat is no longer pink, stirring every 2 minutes; drain.

Stir in the next six ingredients. Cover and microwave on high for 5-6 minutes or until bubbly, stirring every 2 minutes. Stir in rice.

Transfer to a shallow 2-1/2-qt. microwave-safe dish coated with nonstick cooking spray. Cover and let stand for 6-8 minutes or until liquid is absorbed. Sprinkle with cheese. Cover and microwave on high for 1-2 minutes or until cheese is melted. **Yield:** 8 servings.

Editor's Note: This recipe was tested in an 850-watt microwave.

Nutritional Analysis: One serving (1 cup) equals 304 calories, 9 g fat (4 g saturated fat), 31 mg cholesterol, 670 mg sodium, 34 g carbohydrate, 7 g fiber, 22 g protein.
Diabetic Exchanges: 2 starch, 2 lean meat, 1 vegetable, 1/2 fat.

3 cups broccoli florets
2 cups sliced fresh mushrooms
1 tablespoon cornstarch
1/8 teaspoon pepper
1 cup beef broth
2 tablespoons balsamic vinegar
Hot cooked rice, optional

In a large nonstick skillet or wok, stir-fry the onion, green onion and garlic in oil over low heat until tender. Add beef; stir-fry over medium heat for 5-7 minutes or until meat is no longer pink and onions are golden. Using a slotted spoon, remove meat and onions; set aside.

Add wine or broth to the pan; stir to loosen browned bits. Add broccoli and mushrooms; stir-fry over high heat until broccoli is tender. In a bowl, combine cornstarch and pepper; stir in broth and vinegar until smooth. Add to the pan. Bring to a boil; cook and stir for 2 minutes or until thickened. Stir in beef and onions; heat through. Serve over rice if desired. **Yield:** 4 servings.

Nutritional Analysis: One serving (1 cup beef mixture, calculated without rice) equals 248 calories, 9 g fat (3 g saturated fat), 67 mg cholesterol, 297 mg sodium, 11 g carbohydrate, 2 g fiber, 28 g protein.
Diabetic Exchanges: 3 lean meat, 2 vegetable, 1/2 fat.

Pita Pizzas

(Pictured above and on page 111)

This recipe is great when time is of the essence. Purchased pita bread makes an easy crust for ground beef, refried beans, salsa and cheese.
—Jeanette McMahon, Colorado Springs, Colorado

1/2 pound lean ground beef
5 whole pita breads (6 inches)
1 can (16 ounces) fat-free refried beans
1 cup chunky salsa
1/2 cup shredded reduced-fat Mexican cheese blend
5 tablespoons fat-free sour cream
2 green onions, sliced

In a nonstick skillet, cook beef over medium heat until no longer pink; drain. Place pitas on a baking sheet. Spread with refried beans; top with beef, salsa and cheese. Broil 4 in. from the heat for 3-5 minutes or until cheese is melted. Top with sour cream and onions. **Yield:** 5 servings.

Nutritional Analysis: One pizza equals 379 calories, 8 g fat (4 g saturated fat), 26 mg cholesterol, 1,022 mg sodium, 52 g carbohydrate, 7 g fiber, 24 g protein.
Diabetic Exchanges: 3 starch, 2 lean meat, 1 vegetable, 1/2 fat.

Beef 'n' Broccoli Stir-Fry

Our Test Kitchen combined tender strips of beef and fresh vegetables to come up with this delicious skillet dish.

1/2 cup thinly sliced onion
2 tablespoons chopped green onion
2 garlic cloves, minced
2 teaspoons olive *or* canola oil
1 pound boneless beef sirloin steak, cut into thin strips
1/3 cup dry white wine *or* beef broth

Bulgur Barbecue

I'm happy to share my secret for stretching ground beef into saucy and satisfying sloppy joes. I add bulgur to my tangy barbecue sandwiches for a healthy measure of fiber.
—Jackie Blankenship, Sherwood, Oregon

2-3/4 cups water, *divided*
2/3 cup bulgur*
1-1/2 pounds lean ground beef
1-1/2 cups chopped celery
1 large onion, chopped
1 can (8 ounces) tomato sauce
1/2 cup packed brown sugar
1/2 cup ketchup
1 tablespoon white vinegar
1/2 teaspoon prepared mustard
1/4 teaspoon salt
1/4 teaspoon pepper
12 hamburger buns, split

In a saucepan, bring 2 cups water to a boil. Stir in bulgur. Reduce heat; cover and simmer for 15 minutes. Remove from the heat. Drain and squeeze dry; set aside.

In a large nonstick skillet, cook the beef, celery and onion over medium heat until meat is no longer pink; drain. Add the tomato sauce, brown sugar, ketchup, vinegar, mustard, salt, pepper and remaining water. Stir in reserved bulgur. Transfer to a 2-qt. baking dish. Cover and bake at 350° for 50-60 minutes or until heated through. Serve on buns. **Yield:** 12 servings.

Editor's Note: Look for bulgur in the cereal, rice or organic food aisle of your grocery store.

Nutritional Analysis: One sandwich equals 289 calories, 7 g fat (2 g saturated fat), 21 mg cholesterol, 521 mg sodium, 41 g carbohydrate, 5 g fiber, 17 g protein.
Diabetic Exchanges: 2-1/2 starch, 2 lean meat.

Garden Bounty Beef Kabobs

(Pictured below)

We make these kabobs to use up our garden harvest. Have everyone fix their own skewers for an all-in-one dinner.
—*Christine Klessig, Amherst Junction, Wisconsin*

1/4 cup reduced-sodium soy sauce
2 tablespoons olive *or* canola oil
1 tablespoon molasses
3 garlic cloves, minced
1 teaspoon ground ginger
1 teaspoon ground mustard
1 pound boneless beef sirloin steak, cut into 1-inch cubes
1 large sweet onion, cut into 1-inch pieces
1 large green *or* sweet red pepper, cut into 1-inch pieces
1 medium zucchini, cut into 1-inch slices
1 pint cherry tomatoes
1/2 pound large fresh mushrooms

DIPPING SAUCE:
1 cup (8 ounces) reduced-fat sour cream
1/4 cup fat-free milk
3 tablespoons dry onion soup mix
2 tablespoons Dijon mustard
1/8 teaspoon pepper

In a large resealable plastic bag, combine first six ingredients; add beef. Seal bag, turn to coat. Refrigerate for 1 hour.

If grilling the kabobs, coat grill rack with nonstick cooking spray before starting the grill. Drain and discard marinade. On eight metal or soaked wooden skewers, alternately thread beef and vegetables. Grill, covered, over medium heat or broil 4-6 in. from the heat for 3-4 minutes on each side or until beef reaches desired doneness, turning three times.

In a saucepan, combine the dipping sauce ingredients; mix well. Cook over low heat until heated through. Serve with kabobs. **Yield:** 4 servings.

Nutritional Analysis: One serving (2 kabobs with 5 tablespoons of sauce) equals 369 calories, 15 g fat (7 g saturated fat), 97 mg cholesterol, 856 mg sodium, 24 g carbohydrate, 4 g fiber, 35 g protein.
Diabetic Exchanges: 4 lean meat, 3 vegetable, 1 fat, 1/2 starch.

Simple Salisbury Steak

*Fresh mushrooms and cream of mushroom soup
create the speedy simmered sauce that covers
these ground beef patties. The family-pleasing
entree is perfect for a busy weeknight.*
—Elouise Bonar, Hanover, Illinois

1 egg
1/3 cup dry bread crumbs
1 can (10-3/4 ounces) reduced-fat reduced-
 sodium condensed cream of mushroom soup,
 undiluted, *divided*
1/4 cup finely chopped onion
1 pound lean ground beef
1/2 cup fat-free milk
1/4 teaspoon browning sauce, optional
1/4 teaspoon salt
1-1/2 cups sliced fresh mushrooms

In a bowl, combine the egg, bread crumbs, 1/4 cup soup
and onion. Crumble the beef over mixture and mix
well. Shape into six patties. In a large nonstick skillet, brown
the patties on both sides; drain.

In a bowl, combine the milk, browning sauce if desired,
salt and remaining soup; stir in mushrooms. Pour over patties. Reduce heat; cover and simmer for 15-20 minutes or
until meat is no longer pink. **Yield:** 6 servings.

*Nutritional Analysis: One serving (1 patty with 1/4 cup sauce)
equals 212 calories, 9 g fat (3 g saturated fat), 67 mg cholesterol,
599 mg sodium, 11 g carbohydrate, trace fiber, 20 g protein.*
Diabetic Exchanges: *3 lean meat, 1/2 starch, 1/2 fat.*

Southwest Beef Stew

(Pictured above)

*Add your family's favorite picante sauce to
ground beef, black beans and corn, then watch
how quickly they empty their bowls.*
—Janet Brannan, Sidney, Montana

2 pounds lean ground beef
1-1/2 cups chopped onions
1 can (28 ounces) diced tomatoes, undrained
1 package (16 ounces) frozen corn, thawed
1 can (15 ounces) black beans, rinsed and
 drained
1 cup picante sauce
3/4 cup water
1 teaspoon ground cumin
3/4 teaspoon salt
1/2 teaspoon garlic powder
1/2 teaspoon pepper
1/2 cup shredded reduced-fat cheddar cheese

In a Dutch oven, cook beef and onions over medium heat
until meat is no longer pink; drain. Stir in the tomatoes, corn,
beans, picante sauce, water, cumin, salt, garlic powder and
pepper. Bring to a boil. Reduce heat; cover and simmer for
15 minutes or until corn is tender. Garnish with cheese.
Yield: 8 servings.

*Nutritional Analysis: One serving (1-1/3 cups) equals 344
calories, 12 g fat (5 g saturated fat), 45 mg cholesterol, 847 mg
sodium, 28 g carbohydrate, 7 g fiber, 31 g protein.*
Diabetic Exchanges: *4 lean meat, 1-1/2 starch, 1 vegetable.*

Paprika Chili Steak

*Marinade seasoned with chili powder and paprika
gives grilled flank steak a robust flavor. This treasured
recipe from a German neighbor opened up my
taste buds to a whole new world.*
—DiAnn Mallehan, Grand Rapids, Michigan

1 medium onion, chopped
1/2 cup ketchup
1/4 cup cider vinegar
1 tablespoon paprika
1 tablespoon canola oil
2 teaspoons chili powder
1 teaspoon salt
1/8 teaspoon pepper
1-1/2 pounds beef flank steak

In a large resealable plastic bag, combine the first eight ingredients; add steak. Seal bag and turn to coat; refrigerate
for 3 hours or overnight, turning occasionally.

Coat grill rack with nonstick cooking spray before starting the grill. Drain and discard marinade. Grill steak, covered, over medium-hot heat for 6-8 minutes on each side or
until meat reaches desired doneness (for rare, a meat
thermometer should read 140°; medium, 160°; well-done,
170°). **Yield:** 6 servings.

*Nutritional Analysis: One serving (3 ounces cooked beef)
equals 200 calories, 10 g fat (4 g saturated fat), 59 mg cholesterol,
253 mg sodium, 3 g carbohydrate, trace fiber, 24 g protein.*
Diabetic Exchange: *3 lean meat.*

Dijon Mushroom Beef

(Pictured below)

Coated in a mild Dijon mustard sauce, the beef strips and sliced mushrooms in this dish are delicious over noodles or rice. This was a hit with my family when I served it with broccoli and fresh tomatoes.
—Judith McGhan, Perry Hall, Maryland

   1/2 **pound fresh mushrooms, sliced**
     1 **medium onion, sliced**
     2 **teaspoons olive** *or* **canola oil**
     1 **pound boneless beef sirloin steak, thinly sliced**
     1 **can (10-3/4 ounces) reduced-fat reduced-sodium condensed cream of mushroom soup, undiluted**
   3/4 **cup fat-free milk**
     2 **tablespoons Dijon mustard**
Hot cooked yolk-free noodles, optional

In a large nonstick skillet, saute mushrooms and onion in oil until tender. Remove and set aside. In the same skillet, cook beef until no longer pink. Add the soup, milk, mustard and mushroom mixture. Bring to a boil. Reduce heat; cook and stir until thickened. Serve over hot cooked noodles if desired. **Yield:** 4 servings.

Nutritional Analysis: *One serving (1 cup beef mixture, calculated without noodles) equals 281 calories, 11 g fat (3 g saturated fat), 82 mg cholesterol, 567 mg sodium, 15 g carbohydrate, 2 g fiber, 30 g protein.*
Diabetic Exchanges: *3 lean meat, 1 vegetable, 1/2 starch, 1/2 fat.*

Soft Taco Burgers

(Pictured above)

I love to grill these sandwiches for quick summer meals or impromptu get-togethers around the pool. They're a snap to prepare, and no one ever guesses that they're low in fat.
Joan Hallford, North Richland Hills, Texas

     1 **cup fat-free refried beans**
     1 **can (4 ounces) chopped green chilies,** *divided*
   1/4 **cup chopped onion**
   1/4 **teaspoon salt**
1-1/2 **pounds lean ground beef**
     1 **cup (4 ounces) shredded reduced-fat cheddar cheese**
     8 **flour tortillas (6 inches), warmed**
     1 **cup chopped lettuce**
     1 **medium tomato, chopped**
   1/2 **cup salsa**

In a bowl, combine the beans, 2 tablespoons green chilies, onion and salt. Crumble the beef over mixture and mix well. Shape into eight 5-in. patties. Top each patty with 2 tablespoons cheddar cheese; fold in half and press edges to seal, forming a half-moon.

If grilling the burgers, coat grill rack with nonstick cooking spray before starting the grill. Grill burgers, uncovered, over medium heat or broil 4 in. from the heat for 7-9 minutes on each side or until meat is no longer pink and a meat thermometer reads 160°. Serve on tortillas with lettuce, tomato, salsa and remaining chilies. **Yield:** 8 servings.

Nutritional Analysis: *One sandwich equals 322 calories, 12 g fat (5 g saturated fat), 38 mg cholesterol, 656 mg sodium, 26 g carbohydrate, 3 g fiber, 26 g protein.*
Diabetic Exchanges: *3 lean meat, 1-1/2 starch, 1 vegetable, 1/2 fat.*

Tortilla Pie

(Pictured at right)

My husband and I especially like this delicious layered entree because it's lighter tasting than some of the traditional lasagnas made with pasta. Even our two young daughters enjoy the pleasantly mild flavor.
—Lisa King, Caledonia, Michigan

1/2 pound lean ground beef
1/4 cup chopped onion
  1 garlic clove, minced
  1 can (14-1/2 ounces) Italian *or* Mexican diced
    tomatoes, drained
1/2 teaspoon chili powder
1/4 teaspoon ground cumin
3/4 cup part-skim ricotta cheese
1/4 cup shredded part-skim mozzarella cheese
  3 tablespoons minced fresh cilantro *or* parsley,
    divided
  4 flour tortillas (8 inches)
1/2 cup shredded reduced-fat cheddar cheese

In a nonstick skillet, cook beef, onion and garlic over medium heat until meat is no longer pink; drain. Stir in tomatoes, chili powder and cumin. Bring to a boil; remove from the heat. In a bowl, combine the ricotta cheese, mozzarella cheese and 2 tablespoons cilantro.

Place one tortilla in a 9-in. round cake pan coated with nonstick cooking spray. Layer with half of the meat sauce, one tortilla, all of the ricotta mixture, another tortilla and the remaining meat sauce. Top with remaining tortilla; sprinkle with cheddar cheese and remaining cilantro. Cover and bake at 400° for 15 minutes or until heated through and cheese is melted. **Yield:** 6 servings.

Nutritional Analysis: One piece equals 250 calories, 9 g fat (4 g saturated fat), 28 mg cholesterol, 439 mg sodium, 22 g carbohydrate, 1 g fiber, 19 g protein.
Diabetic Exchanges: 2 lean meat, 1-1/2 starch, 1/2 fat.

Southwestern Beef Stew

My husband and I enjoy this hearty stew often. It's the perfect way to warm up on a cool evening. Sometimes I add a can of chopped green chilies for a little more heat.
—Betty Jean Howard, Prineville, Oregon

1-1/2 pounds boneless beef round steak, cut into
    1/2-inch cubes
  1 can (14-1/2 ounces) beef broth
  1 cup cubed peeled potatoes
  1 cup sliced carrots
  1 cup chopped onion
1/4 cup chopped sweet red pepper
  1 jalapeno pepper, seeded and chopped*
  1 garlic clove, minced
1-1/2 teaspoons chili powder
1/2 teaspoon salt
  1 can (14-1/2 ounces) diced tomatoes, undrained
  2 tablespoons all-purpose flour
  2 tablespoons water
  2 tablespoons minced fresh cilantro *or* parsley

In a Dutch oven coated with nonstick cooking spray, brown meat on all sides over medium-high heat. Add the broth, potatoes, carrots, onion, red pepper, jalapeno, garlic, chili powder and salt. Bring to a boil. Reduce heat; cover and simmer for 30 minutes or until potatoes and carrots are tender. Add tomatoes; cover and cook 1 hour longer or until meat is tender.

Combine flour and water until smooth; stir into pot. Stir in cilantro. Bring to a boil; cook and stir for 2 minutes or until thickened. **Yield:** 6 servings.

*Editor's Note: When cutting or seeding hot peppers, use rubber or plastic gloves to protect your hands. Avoid touching your face.

Nutritional Analysis: One serving (1 cup) equals 222 calories, 6 g fat (2 g saturated fat), 72 mg cholesterol, 600 mg sodium, 16 g carbohydrate, 3 g fiber, 26 g protein.
Diabetic Exchanges: 3 lean meat, 2 vegetable, 1/2 starch.

Slow-Cooked Steak Fajitas

We enjoy the flavors of Mexican food, so I was glad when I spotted the recipe for this spicy entree. I simmer the beef in my slow cooker...and it always comes out nice and tender.
—Twila Burkholder, Middleburg, Pennsylvania

  1 beef flank steak (1-1/2 pounds)
  1 can (14-1/2 ounces) diced tomatoes with garlic
    and onion, undrained
  1 jalapeno pepper, seeded and chopped*
  2 garlic cloves, minced
  1 teaspoon ground coriander
  1 teaspoon ground cumin
  1 teaspoon chili powder
1/2 teaspoon salt
  1 medium onion, sliced
  1 medium green pepper, julienned

1 medium sweet red pepper, julienned
1 tablespoon minced fresh cilantro *or* parsley
2 teaspoons cornstarch
1 tablespoon water
12 flour tortillas (6 inches), warmed
3/4 cup fat-free sour cream
3/4 cup salsa

Thinly slice steak across the grain into strips; place in a 5-qt. slow cooker. Add tomatoes, jalapeno, garlic, coriander, cumin, chili powder and salt. Cover and cook on low for 7 hours. Add onion, peppers and cilantro. Cover and cook 1-2 hours longer or until meat is tender.

Combine cornstarch and water until smooth; gradually stir into slow cooker. Cover and cook on high for 30 minutes or until slightly thickened. Using a slotted spoon, spoon about 1/2 cup meat mixture down the center of each tortilla. Add 1 tablespoon each sour cream and salsa. Fold bottom of tortilla over filling and roll up. **Yield:** 12 servings.

*Editor's Note: When cutting or seeding hot peppers, use rubber or plastic gloves to protect your hands. Avoid touching your face.

Nutritional Analysis: One fajita equals 273 calories, 11 g fat (3 g saturated fat), 23 mg cholesterol, 494 mg sodium, 35 g carbohydrate, 2 g fiber, 21 g protein.
Diabetic Exchanges: 2 lean meat, 2 starch, 1 vegetable.

Bavarian Pot Roast

I grew up eating pot roast but disliked it until I got this recipe at a church social and changed a few ingredients. My 7-year-old especially enjoys the seasoned "apple gravy".
—*Patricia Gasmund, Rockford, Illinois*

1 boneless beef top round roast (about 4 pounds), halved
1-1/2 cups apple juice
1 can (8 ounces) tomato sauce
1 small onion, chopped
2 tablespoons white vinegar
1 tablespoon salt
3/4 teaspoon ground ginger *or* 1 tablespoon minced fresh gingerroot
2 to 3 teaspoons ground cinnamon
1/4 cup cornstarch
1/2 cup water

In a Dutch oven coated with nonstick cooking spray, brown roast on all sides over medium-high heat; drain. Transfer to a 5-qt. slow cooker. In a bowl, combine the juice, tomato sauce, onion, vinegar, salt, ginger and cinnamon; pour over roast. Cover and cook on high for 5-7 hours.

In a small bowl, combine cornstarch and water until smooth; stir into cooking juices until well combined. Cover and cook 1 hour longer or until the meat is tender and gravy begins to thicken. **Yield:** 12 servings.

Nutritional Analysis: One serving (4 ounces cooked beef with 1/2 cup gravy) equals 230 calories, 7 g fat (2 g saturated fat), 96 mg cholesterol, 753 mg sodium, 8 g carbohydrate, 1 g fiber, 32 g protein.
Diabetic Exchanges: 4 lean meat, 1/2 fruit.

Savory Meat Loaf

(Pictured below)

Everyone loves this tender meat loaf, which is seasoned with a hint of sage. It's good for family get-togethers, picnics and Super Bowl parties. You're sure to get rave reviews whenever you serve it.
—*Edie DeSpain, Logan, Utah*

1 egg
1 cup fat-free milk
3/4 cup quick-cooking oats
2 slices bread, crumbled
1/2 cup finely chopped onion
1 teaspoon rubbed sage
1 teaspoon salt
1/4 teaspoon pepper
1 pound lean ground beef
3/4 cup ketchup
1/2 cup water
2 tablespoons brown sugar
2 tablespoons cider vinegar
1 tablespoon Worcestershire sauce

In a bowl, combine the first eight ingredients. Crumble beef over mixture and mix well. Shape into a loaf; place in an 11-in. x 7-in. x 2-in. baking dish. In a bowl, combine the ketchup, water, brown sugar, vinegar and Worcestershire sauce; pour over meat loaf. Bake at 325° for 1 to 1-1/4 hours or until meat is no longer pink and a meat thermometer reads 160°. Let stand for 10 minutes before slicing. **Yield:** 6 servings.

Nutritional Analysis: One serving equals 267 calories, 9 g fat (3 g saturated fat), 64 mg cholesterol, 910 mg sodium, 26 g carbohydrate, 2 g fiber, 21 g protein.
Diabetic Exchanges: 3 lean meat, 1-1/2 starch.

Low-Sodium Spaghetti Sauce

There are just 57 milligrams of sodium in each cup of this thick fresh-tasting spaghetti sauce created by our Test Kitchen staff. Compare that to commercially prepared spaghetti sauces, which can contain as much as 900 milligrams per cup!

1/2 pound lean ground beef
  1 pound fresh mushrooms, sliced
  3 medium sweet red peppers, chopped
  1 medium green pepper, chopped
  1 large onion, chopped
  3 garlic cloves, minced
  1 tablespoon olive *or* canola oil
  2 cans (28 ounces *each*) tomato puree
  2 cups water
1/2 cup red wine *or* additional water
  2 bay leaves
  2 tablespoons dried oregano
  2 tablespoons dried basil
1/2 teaspoon dried rosemary, crushed
1/4 to 1/2 teaspoon crushed red pepper flakes
1/4 teaspoon dried mint
1/2 cup chopped fresh parsley
  3 tablespoons sugar

In a large nonstick skillet, cook beef over medium heat until no longer pink; drain and set aside. In the same skillet, saute mushrooms, peppers, onion and garlic in oil until softened. In a large Dutch oven, combine the next nine ingredients. Add beef and sauteed vegetables. Bring to a boil. Reduce heat; simmer, uncovered, for 2-3 hours. Stir in parsley and sugar. Discard bay leaves before serving. **Yield:** 10 servings (2-1/2 quarts).

Nutritional Analysis: One serving (1 cup) equals 143 calories, 3 g fat (1 g saturated fat), 12 mg cholesterol, 57 mg sodium, 22 g carbohydrate, 4 g fiber, 9 g protein.
Diabetic Exchanges: 4 vegetable, 1/2 fat.

Old-World Sauerbraten

(Pictured above)

I serve this popular German entree with potato pancakes and vegetables. Crushed gingersnaps, lemon and vinegar give the marinated slow-cooked beef and gravy their appetizing sweet-sour flavor.
—Susan Garoutte, Georgetown, Texas

1-1/2 cups water, *divided*
1-1/4 cups cider vinegar, *divided*
  2 large onions, sliced, *divided*
  1 medium lemon, sliced
 15 whole cloves, *divided*
  6 bay leaves, *divided*
  6 whole peppercorns
  2 tablespoons sugar
  2 teaspoons salt
  1 beef sirloin tip roast (3 pounds), cut in half
1/4 teaspoon pepper
 12 gingersnap cookies, crumbled

In a large resealable plastic bag, combine 1 cup water, 1 cup vinegar, half of the onions, lemon, 10 cloves, four bay leaves, peppercorns, sugar and salt; mix well. Add roast. Seal bag and turn to coat; refrigerate overnight, turning occasionally.

Drain and discard marinade. Place roast in a slow cooker; add pepper and remaining water, vinegar, onions, cloves and bay leaves. Cover and cook on low for 6-8 hours or until meat is tender. Remove roast and keep warm. Discard bay leaves. Stir in gingersnaps. Cover and cook on high for 10-15 minutes or until gravy is thickened. Slice roast; serve with gravy. **Yield:** 12 servings.

Nutritional Analysis: One serving (3 ounces cooked beef with 1/4 cup gravy) equals 214 calories, 7 g fat (2 g saturated fat), 71 mg cholesterol, 495 mg sodium, 12 g carbohydrate, 1 g fiber, 26 g protein.
Diabetic Exchanges: 3 lean meat, 1/2 starch.

🍎 The Story on Sauerbraten

THE GERMAN specialty called sauerbraten ("sour roast" in German) dates back to the Middle Ages. Supposedly, the legendary European ruler Charlemagne invented the recipe in order to use up leftover roasted meat.

Some 400 years later, Albert of Cologne, a 13th-century German scientist and theologian, gave the recipe a new twist by making it with fresh meat.

Today, some cooks still prefer using leftover roast to make the tender, marinated meat dish. Whichever way it's prepared, sauerbraten is traditionally accompanied by dumplings, boiled potatoes or noodles.

Chicken & Turkey Entrees

You don't have to eat like a bird—or forego flavor—in order to trim down on fat and calories. A simple solution is to choose chicken and turkey. Your family will flock to the table for these enticing entrees.

Turkey Stir-Fry (page 128)

Chicken with Homemade Noodles

(Pictured above)

When my mother-in-law created this recipe 50 years ago, money was tight. I add more meat than she did, but the homemade noodles are still the star of the show in this comforting down-home dish.
—Carla Roberts, Norcross, Georgia

    1 broiler/fryer chicken (3 to 4 pounds), cut up
    3 cups water
    1 medium onion, chopped
1/2 cup chopped green pepper
    1 celery rib, sliced
    3 garlic cloves, minced
    1 teaspoon chicken bouillon granules
1/2 teaspoon salt
1/4 teaspoon pepper
NOODLES:
    1 cup all-purpose flour
1/2 teaspoon salt
1/4 cup egg substitute
    2 tablespoons fat-free milk
    1 tablespoon snipped chives, optional
    1 teaspoon minced fresh parsley, optional

Place the first nine ingredients in a Dutch oven; slowly bring to a boil. Reduce heat; skim foam. Cover and simmer for 1 hour or until chicken is tender. Refrigerate broth and chicken for several hours or overnight.

For noodles, combine flour and salt in a small bowl. Combine egg substitute and milk; stir into flour mixture. Mix until well blended. Shape into a ball; knead on a lightly floured surface for 4-5 minutes. Roll out into a paper-thin rectangle. Dust top of dough with flour. Roll up jelly-roll style. Using a sharp knife, cut into 1/4-in. slices. Unroll noodles;

allow to dry for at least 1 hour.

Skim fat from the broth. Strain broth and return to pan, discarding vegetables. Discard chicken skin. Bone and cube chicken; discard bones and set chicken aside. Bring broth to a boil. Add noodles slowly; cook for 2-5 minutes or until tender. Add chicken; heat through. Garnish with chives and parsley if desired. **Yield:** 4 servings.

Nutritional Analysis: *One serving (1-1/2 cups) equals 393 calories, 14 g fat (4 g saturated fat), 92 mg cholesterol, 994 mg sodium, 25 g carbohydrate, 1 g fiber, 39 g protein.*
Diabetic Exchanges: *5 lean meat, 1-1/2 starch.*

Sausage Pepper Calzones

(Pictured below)

These tasty Italian sandwiches are chock-full of savory turkey sausage, sweet peppers and herbs, enhanced by zesty pizza sauce. Made from convenient frozen bread dough, the baked calzones should be cooled before they are packed in lunches or stored in the freezer.
—Marion Lowery, Medford, Oregon

    1 pound turkey Italian sausage links
    1 cup chopped onion
3/4 cup *each* chopped green, sweet red and yellow peppers
    2 garlic cloves, minced
    5 teaspoons olive *or* canola oil, *divided*
    2 tablespoons sherry *or* chicken broth
    1 teaspoon balsamic vinegar
    1 teaspoon salt
1/2 teaspoon pepper
    3 teaspoons minced fresh oregano, *divided*
    3 teaspoons minced fresh rosemary, *divided*
    2 loaves (1 pound *each*) frozen bread dough, thawed
    1 can (15 ounces) pizza sauce, *divided*
    3 teaspoons cornmeal

Remove and discard sausage casings; crumble the sausage. In a large nonstick skillet, cook sausage, onion, peppers and garlic in 2 teaspoons oil over medium heat until meat is no longer pink; drain. Stir in sherry or broth, vinegar, salt, pepper and 1 teaspoon each oregano and rosemary; heat through.

Divide each loaf of dough into six portions. On a floured surface, roll each portion into a 6-in. circle. Brush with remaining oil; sprinkle with remaining oregano and rosemary. Spread 1 tablespoon pizza sauce over each circle. Spoon about 1/4 cup pepper filling on half of each circle to within 1/2 in. of edges; fold dough over filling and seal edges. Cut a small slit in top.

Coat baking sheets with nonstick cooking spray and sprinkle with cornmeal. Place the calzones on baking sheets. Cover and let rise in a warm place for 30 minutes. Bake at 400° for 12-15 minutes or until golden brown. Warm the remaining pizza sauce; serve with calzones. **Yield:** 12 servings.

Nutritional Analysis: *One serving (1 calzone with 4-1/2 teaspoons sauce) equals 330 calories, 9 g fat (1 g saturated fat), 20 mg cholesterol, 1,043 mg sodium, 48 g carbohydrate, 4 g fiber, 15 g protein.*
Diabetic Exchanges: *3 starch, 1 vegetable, 1 lean meat, 1/2 fat.*

Chili-Spiced Chicken Breasts

Spicing up dinnertime is a snap when I bake this zippy chicken dish. The mix of chili powder, jalapeno and cayenne pepper perks up the poultry perfectly. I serve it over couscous. But you could also use rice, other pasta or potatoes.
—Stacey Nutt, Lockney, Texas

3/4 teaspoon chili powder
1/2 teaspoon salt
1/2 teaspoon ground cumin
1/4 teaspoon garlic powder
1/8 to 1/4 teaspoon cayenne pepper
4 boneless skinless chicken breast halves
 (4 ounces *each*)
1 teaspoon canola oil
1/4 cup chopped green onions
1 jalapeno pepper, seeded and finely chopped*
1 garlic clove, minced
1 can (14-1/2 ounces) diced tomatoes, undrained
1 teaspoon cornstarch
2 teaspoons water

Combine the first five ingredients; rub over chicken. In a nonstick skillet, brown chicken in oil on both sides. Add onions, jalapeno and garlic; saute for 1 minute. Add tomatoes; bring to a boil. Reduce heat; cover and simmer for 15-20 minutes or until chicken juices run clear. Remove chicken and keep warm. In a small bowl, combine cornstarch and water until smooth; stir into tomato mixture. Bring to a boil; cook and stir for 1 minute or until slightly thickened. Serve over chicken. **Yield:** 4 servings.

*Editor's Note: When cutting or seeding hot peppers, use rubber or plastic gloves to protect your hands. Avoid touching your face.

Nutritional Analysis: *One serving (1 chicken breast half with 1/3 cup sauce) equals 166 calories, 3 g fat (trace saturated fat), 66 mg cholesterol, 526 mg sodium, 7 g carbohydrate, 2 g fiber, 27 g protein.*
Diabetic Exchanges: *3 lean meat, 1 vegetable.*

Turkey-Tomato Pasta Sauce

(Pictured below)

This savory spaghetti sauce is a favorite at our house. The chunky mixture is good over any pasta.
—Sherry Hulsman, Louisville, Kentucky

1 pound turkey Italian sausage links, casings removed
1/2 cup chopped green onions
2 garlic cloves, minced
2 teaspoons olive *or* canola oil
2 cans (14-1/2 ounces *each*) diced tomatoes, undrained
1/2 cup white wine *or* chicken broth
1 cup loosely packed fresh basil, minced
1 teaspoon dried oregano
Hot cooked spaghetti
1/2 cup shredded Parmesan cheese

In a large nonstick skillet, cook the sausage, onions and garlic in oil over medium heat until sausage is no longer pink; drain. Add the tomatoes, wine or broth, basil and oregano; bring to a boil. Reduce heat; simmer, uncovered, for 10 minutes or until heated through. Serve over spaghetti; sprinkle with Parmesan. **Yield:** 8 servings.

Nutritional Analysis: *One serving (1/2 cup sauce with 1 tablespoon Parmesan, calculated without spaghetti) equals 156 calories, 8 g fat (3 g saturated fat), 34 mg cholesterol, 576 mg sodium, 7 g carbohydrate, 2 g fiber, 13 g protein.*
Diabetic Exchanges: *2 lean meat, 1 vegetable, 1/2 fat.*

Pepperoni Pizza Supreme

(Pictured below)

Here's my in-a-hurry homemade alternative to typical restaurant pizza. Our family loves the crispy combination of vegetables and the lighter cheeses and turkey pepperoni. The only thing missing is the guilt!
—Sandy Schnack, Blue Springs, Missouri

1 prebaked thin Italian bread shell crust (10 ounces)
1 can (8 ounces) pizza sauce
1 tablespoon grated Parmesan cheese
1 teaspoon Italian seasoning
1/2 teaspoon garlic powder
1/2 cup sliced fresh mushrooms
1/2 cup chopped broccoli florets
1/4 cup chopped green pepper
1/4 cup chopped sweet red pepper
1/2 cup shredded reduced-fat cheddar cheese
38 slices turkey pepperoni
1 cup (4 ounces) shredded part-skim mozzarella cheese

Place crust on a baking sheet. Spread with pizza sauce; sprinkle with Parmesan cheese, Italian seasoning and garlic powder. Top with the mushrooms, broccoli and peppers. Sprinkle with cheddar cheese. Top with pepperoni and mozzarella cheese. Bake at 400° for 14-18 minutes or until vegetables are crisp-tender and cheese is melted. **Yield:** 6 slices.

Nutritional Analysis: One slice equals 244 calories, 9 g fat (3 g saturated fat), 28 mg cholesterol, 698 mg sodium, 26 g carbohydrate, 1 g fiber, 17 g protein.
Diabetic Exchanges: 1-1/2 starch, 1-1/2 lean meat, 1 fat.

Turkey Stir-Fry

(Pictured above and on page 125)

Try this skillet dish after the holidays when you have a lot of leftover turkey to use up. The vegetables add fun color and crunch. I know your family will love it as much as mine does.
—Kylene Konosky, Jermyn, Pennsylvania

1-1/2 cups sliced fresh mushrooms
1 cup sliced celery
1/2 cup sliced onion
2 tablespoons canola oil
2 tablespoons cornstarch
1 can (10-1/2 ounces) condensed chicken broth, undiluted
1 tablespoon reduced-sodium soy sauce
2 cups cubed cooked turkey breast
2 cups fresh snow peas
1/2 cup sliced water chestnuts
Hot cooked rice, optional

In a nonstick skillet, saute the mushrooms, celery and onion in oil until tender. Combine the cornstarch, broth and soy sauce until smooth; stir into vegetable mixture. Bring to a boil; cook and stir for 1-2 minutes or until thickened.

Reduce heat to medium-low. Add turkey, peas and water chestnuts; cook until turkey is heated through and peas are tender. Serve over rice if desired. **Yield:** 4 servings.

Nutritional Analysis: One serving (1 cup turkey mixture, calculated without rice) equals 242 calories, 9 g fat (1 g saturated fat), 61 mg cholesterol, 687 mg sodium, 13 g carbohydrate, 2 g fiber, 27 g protein.
Diabetic Exchanges: 3 lean meat, 1 vegetable, 1/2 starch.

Chicken Biscuit Stew

*A hint of curry gives this stew its special
flavor. Topped with tasty moist
biscuits, it's a favorite with my family.*
—Elmeda Johnson, Williston, North Dakota

1 cup julienned carrots
1 cup thinly sliced onion
2 garlic cloves, minced
2 teaspoons olive *or* canola oil
**1 pound boneless skinless chicken breasts,
    cut into 1-inch cubes**
1 tablespoon all-purpose flour
1/4 cup water
3 tablespoons white wine *or* chicken broth
1 cup (8 ounces) fat-free plain yogurt
1 cup fresh *or* frozen peas
**1/4 teaspoon *each* curry powder, salt, pepper,
    ground cumin and ginger**
BISCUITS:
1 cup all-purpose flour
1 teaspoon baking powder
1/4 teaspoon baking soda
1/4 teaspoon salt
4-1/2 teaspoons cold butter *or* stick margarine
1/2 cup fat-free plain yogurt
1-1/2 teaspoons dried parsley flakes

In a large nonstick skillet, saute the carrots, onion and
garlic in oil until tender. Add chicken; cook and stir for 5 minutes. Combine the flour, water and wine or broth until
smooth; add to the skillet. Bring to a boil; cook and stir for
2 minutes or until thickened. Reduce heat; stir in yogurt,
peas and seasonings. Transfer to a shallow 1-1/2-qt. baking
dish coated with nonstick cooking spray; keep warm.

For biscuits, combine flour, baking powder, baking soda and salt in a bowl. Cut in butter until crumbly. Stir in yogurt and parsley. Drop eight mounds over warm chicken
mixture. Bake, uncovered, at 350° for 25-35 minutes or until biscuits are golden brown and stew bubbles around the
edges. **Yield:** 4 servings.

*Nutritional Analysis: One serving (1 cup stew with 2 bis-
cuits) equals 413 calories, 0 g fat (1 g saturated fat), 80 mg cholesterol, 895 mg sodium, 47 g carbohydrate, 5 g fiber, 37 g protein.*
*Diabetic Exchanges: 3 lean meat, 2 starch, 2 vegetable, 1/2
fat-free milk.*

Raspberry Thyme Chicken

(Pictured above)

*Here's an easy way to dress up chicken. I guarantee
you won't miss the fat and calories when you
taste this tender poultry with berry sauce.*
—Lenita Schafer, Princeton, Massachusetts

1/2 cup chopped red onion
2 teaspoons canola oil
**1-1/2 teaspoons minced fresh thyme *or* 1/2 teaspoon
    dried thyme**
1/2 teaspoon salt, *divided*
**4 boneless skinless chicken breast halves
    (1 pound)**
1/3 cup seedless raspberry preserves
2 tablespoons balsamic vinegar
1/8 teaspoon pepper

In a nonstick skillet, saute onion in oil until tender. Sprinkle
thyme and 1/4 teaspoon salt over chicken; add to skillet.
Cook for 5 minutes on each side or until juices run clear. Remove chicken and keep warm.

Add the preserves, vinegar, pepper and remaining salt
to skillet. Cook and stir over medium-low heat until preserves are melted and sauce is heated through. Spoon
onto a serving platter; top with chicken. **Yield:** 4 servings.

*Nutritional Analysis: One serving (1 chicken breast half with
2 tablespoons sauce) equals 227 calories, 4 g fat (1 g saturated
fat), 66 mg cholesterol, 383 mg sodium, 21 g carbohydrate, trace
fiber, 27 g protein.*
Diabetic Exchanges: 3 lean meat, 1 starch.

Orange-Ginger Chicken and Veggies

(Pictured at right)

This colorful stir-fry is chock-full of tasty veggies, tender chicken chunks and a light, zippy sauce. Tangy oranges and crunchy cashews add extra pizzazz.
—Nancy Johnson, Turah, Montana

  1 medium navel orange
  4 teaspoons cornstarch
1/4 teaspoon ground ginger *or* 1 teaspoon grated fresh gingerroot
  1 cup reduced-sodium chicken broth
  2 tablespoons reduced-sodium soy sauce
  2 tablespoons chili sauce
1/4 teaspoon hot pepper sauce
  1 pound boneless skinless chicken breasts, cut into 1-inch pieces
  2 garlic cloves, minced
  1 tablespoon canola oil
  2 cups broccoli florets
  1 medium sweet red pepper, julienned
  1 medium sweet yellow pepper, julienned
1/2 cup shredded carrot
1/3 cup unsalted cashews
  3 cups hot cooked rice

Grate orange peel, reserving 1-1/2 teaspoons. Peel and section orange; set orange sections aside. In a small bowl, combine the cornstarch and ginger. Stir in the broth, soy sauce, chili sauce, hot pepper sauce and reserved grated orange peel until blended; set aside.

In a large nonstick skillet or wok, stir-fry the chicken and garlic in oil for 2-3 minutes or until lightly browned. Add the broccoli, peppers and carrot; stir-fry for 5 minutes or until the vegetables are crisp-tender. Stir broth mixture and add to the pan. Bring to a boil; cook and stir for 2 minutes or until thickened. Remove from the heat; stir in cashews and reserved orange sections. Serve with rice. **Yield:** 4 servings.

Nutritional Analysis: One serving (1-1/2 cups stir-fry mixture with 3/4 cup rice) equals 467 calories, 12 g fat (2 g saturated fat), 67 mg cholesterol, 853 mg sodium, 56 g carbohydrate, 4 g fiber, 34 g protein.
Diabetic Exchanges: 3 starch, 3 lean meat, 2 vegetable, 1/2 fat.

Nostalgic Chicken and Dumplings

Enjoy old-fashioned goodness without all the fuss when you fix this supper. It features tender chicken, wonderfully light dumplings and a full-flavored sauce.
—Brenda Edwards, Hereford, Arizona

  6 bone-in chicken breast halves (10 ounces *each*), skin removed
  2 whole cloves
12 frozen pearl *or* small whole onions, thawed
  1 bay leaf
  1 garlic clove, minced

1/2 teaspoon *each* salt, dried thyme and dried marjoram
1/4 teaspoon pepper
1/2 cup reduced-sodium chicken broth
1/2 cup white wine *or* additional chicken broth
  3 tablespoons cornstarch
1/4 cup cold water
1/2 teaspoon browning sauce, optional
  1 cup reduced-fat biscuit/baking mix
  6 tablespoons fat-free milk
  1 tablespoon minced fresh parsley

Place the chicken in a slow cooker. Insert cloves into an onion; add to slow cooker. Add bay leaf and remaining onions. Sprinkle chicken with garlic, salt, thyme, marjoram and pepper. Pour broth and wine or additional broth over chicken mixture. Cover and cook on low for 4-1/2 to 5 hours or until chicken juices run clear and a meat thermometer reads 170°.

Remove chicken and keep warm. Discard cloves and bay leaf. Increase temperature to high. In a small bowl, combine cornstarch, water and browning sauce if desired until smooth. Stir into slow cooker.

In another bowl, combine biscuit mix, milk and parsley. Drop by tablespoonfuls onto simmering liquid. Cover and simmer for 20-25 minutes or until a toothpick inserted into dumplings comes out clean (do not lift cover while simmering). Serve dumplings and gravy over chicken. **Yield:** 6 servings.

Nutritional Analysis: One serving equals 295 calories, 5 g fat (1 g saturated fat), 89 mg cholesterol, 561 mg sodium, 24 g carbohydrate, 2 g fiber, 36 g protein.
Diabetic Exchanges: 4 lean meat, 1 starch, 1 vegetable.

Sausage Vegetable Skillet

Sausage lends smoky flavor to this crisp and colorful meal-in-one dish.
—Carmen Hoffman, Hanna City, Illinois

1-1/2 cups chopped onions
1-1/2 cups sliced fresh mushrooms
1/2 cup thinly sliced carrot
1/2 cup thinly sliced celery
  2 teaspoons butter *or* stick margarine
  3 cups chopped cabbage
  9 ounces reduced-fat smoked turkey sausage, cut into slices
1/4 cup chopped green pepper
  1 garlic clove, minced
1/4 teaspoon salt
Dash pepper
  1 cup cooked rice

In a large nonstick skillet, saute the onions, mushrooms, carrot and celery in butter for 5 minutes. Add the cabbage, sausage, green pepper, garlic, salt and pepper; saute for 8-10 minutes or until vegetables are tender. Add rice and heat through. **Yield:** 3 servings.

Nutritional Analysis: One serving (1-2/3 cups) equals 283 calories, 7 g fat (3 g saturated fat), 45 mg cholesterol, 1,003 mg sodium, 39 g carbohydrate, 5 g fiber, 16 g protein.
Diabetic Exchanges: 3 vegetable, 2 lean meat, 1-1/2 starch.

Nutritional Analysis: *One serving (2 kabobs with 1/4 cup sauce) equals 400 calories, 13 g fat (5 g saturated fat), 58 mg cholesterol, 1,208 mg sodium, 42 g carbohydrate, 4 g fiber, 28 g protein.*
Diabetic Exchanges: *3 lean meat, 2 starch, 2 vegetable, 1 fat.*

Chicken Noodle Casserole

(Pictured below)

I work at home while caring for our two children, so I have to be creative at mealtimes to fix something quick and nutritious that everyone enjoys. This homey casserole fits all the requirements.
—*Lori Gleason, Minneapolis, Minnesota*

 2/3 **cup chopped onion**
  1 **garlic clove, minced**
  1 **tablespoon olive *or* canola oil**
1-1/2 **pounds boneless skinless chicken breasts,**
   cut into 3/4-inch cubes
  1 **can (14-1/2 ounces) chicken broth**
1-1/2 **cups chopped carrots**
  3 **celery ribs, chopped**
 1/2 **teaspoon dried savory**
  3 **tablespoons butter *or* stick margarine**
  3 **tablespoons all-purpose flour**
 3/4 **teaspoon salt**
 1/8 **teaspoon white pepper**
1-1/2 **cups 2% milk**
1-1/4 **cups shredded reduced-fat cheddar cheese**
  8 **ounces wide egg noodles, cooked and drained**

In a large nonstick skillet, saute onion and garlic in oil until tender. Add chicken; cook and stir until no longer pink. Add the broth, carrots, celery and savory. Bring to a boil. Reduce heat; cover and simmer for 10-15 minutes or until vegetables are tender.

Pizza on a Stick

(Pictured above)

My daughter and her friends had fun turning sausage, pepperoni, veggies and pizza dough into these cute kabobs. Give our version a try or make your own using your favorite light pizza toppings.
—*Charlene Woods, Norfolk, Virginia*

  8 **ounces turkey Italian sausage links**
  2 **cups whole fresh mushrooms**
  2 **cups cherry tomatoes**
  1 **medium onion, cut into 1-inch pieces**
  1 **large green pepper, cut into 1-inch pieces**
 30 **slices turkey pepperoni (2 ounces)**
  1 **tube (10 ounces) refrigerated pizza crust**
1-1/2 **cups (6 ounces) shredded part-skim mozzarella**
   cheese
1-1/4 **cups pizza sauce, warmed**

In a large nonstick skillet, brown the sausage over medium heat until no longer pink; drain. When cool enough to handle, cut sausage into 20 pieces. On 10 metal or soaked wooden skewers, alternately thread the sausage, vegetables and pepperoni.

 Unroll the pizza dough onto a lightly floured surface; cut widthwise into 1-in.-wide strips. Starting at the pointed end of a prepared skewer, pierce skewer through one end of dough strip and press dough against last ingredient on the skewer. Spiral-wrap dough strip around skewer, allowing vegetables and meats to peek through. Wrap the remaining end of dough strip around skewer above the first ingredient. Repeat with remaining dough strips and prepared skewers.

 Arrange the kabobs on a baking sheet coated with nonstick cooking spray. Bake at 400° for 10-12 minutes or until the vegetables are tender and pizza crust is golden. Immediately sprinkle with cheese. Serve with pizza sauce.
Yield: 5 servings.

Meanwhile, in a saucepan, melt butter. Stir in the flour, salt and pepper until smooth. Gradually add milk. Bring to a boil; cook and stir for 2 minutes or until thickened. Remove from the heat; stir in cheese until melted. Pour over chicken mixture. Add noodles; mix well.

Transfer to a 3-qt. baking dish coated with nonstick cooking spray. Bake, uncovered, at 350° for 15-20 minutes or until bubbly. **Yield:** 8 servings.

Nutritional Analysis: *One serving (1 cup) equals 343 calories, 11 g fat (5 g saturated fat), 95 mg cholesterol, 681 mg sodium, 30 g carbohydrate, 2 g fiber, 31 g protein.*
Diabetic Exchanges: *3 lean meat, 2 starch, 1 fat.*

Sausage Corn Supper

This recipe has evolved over the years from frequent use. It was given to me by my sister almost 30 years ago. It was the first meal I cooked when my husband and I moved into our house. Our son was 6 months old then…he's 22 now and still likes this hearty skillet supper. It's easy, flavorful and quick.
—Trudy Coleman, Avoca, Pennsylvania

1-1/4 **pounds turkey Italian sausage links, casings removed**
   1 **medium onion, chopped**
   1 **medium green** *or* **sweet red pepper, diced**
   3 **tablespoons all-purpose flour**
   2 **bay leaves**
   1 **teaspoon dried thyme**
1/4 **teaspoon salt**
1/8 **teaspoon pepper**
   2 **cans (14-1/2 ounces** *each***) stewed tomatoes, cut up**
   1 **can (14-3/4 ounces) cream-style corn**
   3 **cups hot cooked rice**

In a large skillet, cook the sausage, onion and green pepper over medium heat until meat is no longer pink; drain. Stir in the flour, bay leaves, thyme, salt and pepper. Add the tomatoes and corn. Bring to a boil. Reduce heat; cover and simmer for 20 minutes. Discard bay leaves. Serve over rice. **Yield:** 6 servings.

Nutritional Analysis: *One serving (1 cup sausage mixture with 1/2 cup rice) equals 386 calories, 10 g fat (3 g saturated fat), 51 mg cholesterol, 1,172 mg sodium, 54 g carbohydrate, 3 g fiber, 21 g protein.*
Diabetic Exchanges: *2-1/2 starch, 2 lean meat, 2 vegetable, 1 fat.*

Apple Thyme Chicken

(Pictured at right)

Apples and chicken may seem like an unusual combination, but they make a wonderful meal when grilled to perfection. The thyme marinade gives a boost of flavor and tenderizes the chicken nicely.
—Peter Halferty, Corpus Christi, Texas

   6 **tablespoons apple juice**
   6 **tablespoons lemon juice**
4-1/2 **teaspoons cider vinegar**
4-1/2 **teaspoons canola oil**
1-1/2 **teaspoons dried thyme**
   4 **boneless skinless chicken breast halves (4 ounces** *each***)**
   2 **medium Golden Delicious** *or* **other all-purpose apples, peeled and quartered**
   1 **tablespoon honey**
SAUCE:
   2 **teaspoons cornstarch**
1/4 **teaspoon dried thyme**
3/4 **cup apple juice**

In a bowl, combine the first five ingredients; mix well. Pour half of the marinade into a large resealable plastic bag; add chicken. Seal bag and turn to coat; refrigerate for at least 2 hours. Cover and refrigerate remaining marinade.

Coat grill rack with nonstick cooking spray before starting the grill. Drain and discard marinade from chicken. Dip apples in reserved marinade; set aside. Combine the honey with the remaining marinade. Grill chicken, covered, over medium heat for 4-6 minutes on each side or until juices run clear, basting frequently with the honey marinade. Grill apples, uncovered, for 3-5 minutes, basting and turning frequently or until lightly browned.

In a saucepan, combine the cornstarch, thyme and apple juice until blended. Bring to a boil; cook and stir for 2 minutes or until thickened. Slice the grilled apples; stir into sauce. Serve with chicken. **Yield:** 4 servings.

Nutritional Analysis: *One serving (1 chicken breast half with 1/4 cup sauce) equals 226 calories, 3 g fat (1 g saturated fat), 66 mg cholesterol, 76 mg sodium, 22 g carbohydrate, 1 g fiber, 26 g protein.*
Diabetic Exchanges: *3 lean meat, 1-1/2 fruit.*

Turkey Sausage with Root Vegetables

(Pictured above)

I had a delicious stew recipe but rarely prepared it because sausage can be high in fat and sodium, so I substituted low-fat turkey sausage. Now it not only tastes good, it's hearty and healthy!
—Lisa Zeigler-Day, Forest Park, Illinois

- 1 package (14 ounces) reduced-fat smoked turkey Polish sausage, cut into 1/2-inch pieces
- 1 medium onion, chopped
- 1 cup cubed peeled rutabaga
- 1 cup sliced carrots
- 1 teaspoon canola oil
- 4 cups cubed peeled potatoes
- 1 can (14-3/4 ounces) reduced-sodium chicken broth
- 1 teaspoon dried thyme
- 1/4 teaspoon rubbed sage
- 1/4 teaspoon pepper
- 1 bay leaf
- 1/2 medium head cabbage, cut into 6 wedges
- 1 teaspoon all-purpose flour
- 1 tablespoon water
- 1 tablespoon minced fresh parsley
- 2 teaspoons cider vinegar

In a Dutch oven, cook the sausage, onion, rutabaga and carrots in oil for 5 minutes or until onion is tender. Add the potatoes, broth, thyme, sage, pepper and bay leaf. Bring to a boil. Place cabbage wedges on top. Reduce heat; cover and simmer for 20-25 minutes or until potatoes and cabbage are tender.

Carefully remove cabbage to a shallow serving bowl; keep warm. Discard bay leaf. Combine the flour and water until smooth; stir into sausage mixture. Bring to a boil; cook and stir for 2 minutes or until thickened. Stir in parsley and vinegar. Spoon over cabbage. **Yield:** 6 servings.

Nutritional Analysis: One serving (1-1/2 cups) equals 231 calories, 3 g fat (1 g saturated fat), 23 mg cholesterol, 781 mg sodium, 39 g carbohydrate, 6 g fiber, 13 g protein.
Diabetic Exchanges: 2 starch, 1 lean meat, 1 vegetable.

Breaded Turkey Rolls

(Pictured below)

You can enjoy these tender turkey rolls and not feel the least bit guilty. Although stuffed with ham and cheese, they're still lower in fat. Their special taste and appearance make them nice for company.
—Rita Pearl, Norwalk, Iowa

- 8 uncooked turkey breast slices (1 pound)
- 8 thin slices deli turkey ham (1/4 ounce *each*)
- 8 slices reduced-fat Swiss cheese (1/2 ounce *each*)
- 1 tablespoon Dijon mustard
- 7 tablespoons dry bread crumbs
- 3/4 teaspoon salt
- 1/4 teaspoon pepper
- 1/8 teaspoon paprika
- 3 tablespoons reduced-fat mayonnaise

Flatten turkey slices to 1/8-in. thickness. Top each with a slice of ham and cheese; spread with mustard. Roll up tightly and secure with toothpicks. In a shallow bowl, combine the bread crumbs, salt, pepper and paprika. Brush turkey roll-ups with mayonnaise, then coat with crumb mixture.

Place in an 11-in. x 7-in. x 2-in. baking dish coated with nonstick cooking spray. Bake, uncovered, at 425° for 20-25 minutes or until meat juices run clear. **Yield:** 4 servings.

Mediterranean Chicken Sandwiches

I copied this delightful recipe when I was in Italy visiting my Aunt Elsa. The refreshing sandwich filling is nicely flavored with oregano and mint. I like it tucked into chewy pita bread.
—Marcia Fuller, Sheridan, Montana

1-1/4 **pounds boneless skinless chicken breasts, cut into 1-inch strips**
   2 **medium tomatoes, seeded and chopped**
1/2 **cup sliced quartered seeded cucumber**
1/2 **cup sliced sweet onion**
   2 **tablespoons cider vinegar**
   1 **tablespoon olive** *or* **canola oil**
   1 **tablespoon minced fresh oregano**
     or 1 **teaspoon dried oregano**
   1 **to** 2 **teaspoons minced fresh mint**
     or 1/2 **teaspoon dried mint**
1/4 **teaspoon salt**
   3 **whole wheat pita breads, halved, warmed**
   6 **lettuce leaves**

In a large nonstick skillet coated with nonstick cooking spray, cook chicken for 5 minutes or until no longer pink. Remove from the skillet; cool slightly.

In a bowl, combine the chicken, tomatoes, cucumber and onion. In a jar with a tight-fitting lid, combine the vinegar, oil, oregano, mint and salt; shake well. Pour over chicken mixture; toss gently. Cover and refrigerate for at least 1 hour. Line pita halves with lettuce; fill with chicken mixture, using a slotted spoon. **Yield:** 6 servings.

Nutritional Analysis: One serving (1 filled pita half) equals 227 calories, 4 g fat (1 g saturated fat), 55 mg cholesterol, 335 mg sodium, 22 g carbohydrate, 3 g fiber, 26 g protein.
Diabetic Exchanges: 3 lean meat, 1 starch, 1 vegetable.

Sausage Cheese Manicotti

(Pictured at right)

This marvelous manicotti, created by our Test Kitchen staff, is cheesy, saucy and savory.

 10 **uncooked manicotti shells**
  8 **ounces turkey Italian sausage links, casings removed**
  1 **cup finely chopped sweet red pepper**
1/4 **cup chopped onion**
  2 **egg whites**
  3 **cups fat-free cottage cheese**

  1 **cup (4 ounces) shredded part-skim mozzarella cheese**
1/2 **cup shredded Parmesan cheese,** *divided*
  3 **tablespoons minced fresh parsley**
1/2 **teaspoon dried basil**
1/2 **teaspoon fennel seed**
1/4 **teaspoon white pepper**
  2 **cups meatless spaghetti sauce**
1/2 **cup water**

Cook manicotti according to package directions. Meanwhile, crumble sausage into a nonstick skillet; add the red pepper and onion. Cook over medium heat until meat is no longer pink and vegetables are tender; drain. Drain manicotti; set aside.

In a bowl, combine the sausage mixture, egg whites, cottage cheese, mozzarella cheese, 1/4 cup Parmesan cheese, parsley, basil, fennel and pepper. Stuff into manicotti shells. Combine spaghetti sauce and water; spread 1/2 cup in an ungreased 13-in. x 9-in. x 2-in. baking dish. Arrange shells over sauce; top with remaining sauce.

Cover and bake at 350° for 35-40 minutes. Uncover; sprinkle with remaining Parmesan cheese. Bake 10-15 minutes longer or until cheese is melted. Let stand for 10 minutes before serving. **Yield:** 5 servings.

Nutritional Analysis: One serving (2 stuffed shells) equals 462 calories, 13 g fat (5 g saturated fat), 51 mg cholesterol, 1,418 mg sodium, 48 g carbohydrate, 4 g fiber, 39 g protein.
Diabetic Exchanges: 4 lean meat, 2 starch, 2 vegetable, 1/2 fat-free milk.

Stir-Fried Chicken and Noodles

(Pictured at right)

*I live in a university town that draws students from
many different cultures...and I frequently come across
a tasty native dish like this Chinese one.*
—Stacey Nutt, Ames, Iowa

1/2 cup chicken broth
1/3 cup reduced-sodium soy sauce
1/4 cup white wine *or* additional chicken broth
2 garlic cloves, minced
1/4 teaspoon ground ginger
1/4 teaspoon pepper
1/8 teaspoon crushed red pepper flakes
3/4 **pound boneless skinless chicken breasts, cut
into strips**
4 teaspoons canola oil, *divided*
2 cups broccoli florets
2 cups julienned carrots
2 cups shredded Chinese *or* napa cabbage
1 cup fresh *or* frozen snow peas, cut into 1-inch
pieces
6 ounces spaghetti, broken
2 teaspoons cornstarch

In a bowl, combine the first seven ingredients; set aside
3/4 cup. Place chicken in a large resealable plastic bag; add
remaining marinade. Seal bag and turn to coat; refrigerate
for 30 minutes.

Drain and discard marinade. In a large nonstick skillet
or wok, stir-fry chicken in 2 teaspoons oil for 3-5 minutes
or until no longer pink. Remove and keep warm. Stir-fry
broccoli and carrots in remaining oil for 6 minutes. Add cabbage and peas; stir-fry 3 minutes longer or until vegetables are crisp-tender. Meanwhile, cook pasta according to
package directions.

Combine cornstarch and reserved marinade until
smooth; add to vegetable mixture. Bring to a boil; cook
and stir for 2 minutes or until thickened. Drain pasta; stir
into vegetable mixture. Return chicken to the pan; cook and
stir until heated through. **Yield:** 6 servings.

*Nutritional Analysis: One serving (1-1/3 cups) equals 258
calories, 5 g fat (1 g saturated fat), 33 mg cholesterol, 672 mg sodium, 32 g carbohydrate, 4 g fiber, 20 g protein.*
*Diabetic Exchanges: 2 vegetable, 2 very lean meat, 1-1/2
starch, 1/2 fat.*

Hawaiian Baked Chicken

*Pineapple and brown mustard pair perfectly for
marinating the poultry, which comes
out of the oven moist and tender.*
—Leona Callen, Anna Maria, Florida

12 skinless chicken thighs (3 pounds)
2 cans (8 ounces *each*) unsweetened crushed
pineapple, undrained
1/4 cup sherry *or* chicken broth
1/4 cup spicy brown mustard
1/4 cup honey
2 tablespoons butter *or* stick margarine, melted
1/2 teaspoon paprika

Arrange chicken in a shallow baking dish coated with nonstick cooking spray. In a bowl, combine the pineapple, sherry or broth, mustard, honey and butter; mix well. Spoon over
chicken; sprinkle with paprika. Bake, uncovered, at 400°
for 35-45 minutes or until a meat thermometer reads 180°.
Yield: 6 servings.

*Nutritional Analysis: One serving (2 chicken thighs with 1/3
cup sauce) equals 285 calories, 10 g fat (4 g saturated fat), 118
mg cholesterol, 288 mg sodium, 22 g carbohydrate, 1 g fiber, 26
g protein.*
Diabetic Exchanges: 3 lean meat, 1-1/2 fruit, 1 fat.

Sausage Pasta Stew

*I rely on my slow cooker to prepare this
chili-like specialty. It's packed with
turkey sausage, pasta and vegetables.*
—Sara Bowen, Upland, California

1 **pound turkey Italian sausage links, casings
removed**
4 cups water
1 jar (26 ounces) meatless spaghetti sauce
1 can (16 ounces) kidney beans, rinsed and
drained
1 medium yellow summer squash, halved
lengthwise and cut into 1-inch pieces
2 medium carrots, cut into 1/4-inch slices
1 medium sweet red *or* green pepper, diced
1/3 cup chopped onion
1-1/2 cups uncooked spiral pasta
1 cup frozen peas
1 teaspoon sugar
1/2 teaspoon salt
1/4 teaspoon pepper

In a nonstick skillet, cook sausage over medium heat until
no longer pink; drain and place in a 5-qt. slow cooker. Add
water, spaghetti sauce, beans, summer squash, carrots, red
pepper and onion; mix well. Cover and cook on low for 7-9
hours or until vegetables are tender.

Stir in the pasta, peas, sugar, salt and pepper; mix well.
Cover and cook on high for 15-20 minutes or until pasta is
tender. **Yield:** 8 servings.

*Nutritional Analysis: One serving (1-1/3 cups) equals 276
calories, 6 g fat (2 g saturated fat), 30 mg cholesterol, 1,111 mg
sodium, 38 g carbohydrate, 6 g fiber, 18 g protein.*
Diabetic Exchanges: 2 lean meat, 2 vegetable, 1-1/2 starch.

medium heat or broil 4-6 in. from the heat for 3-4 minutes on each side or until chicken is no longer pink and vegetables are tender, turning three times and basting frequently with reserved marinade. **Yield:** 4 servings.

Nutritional Analysis: *One serving (2 kabobs) equals 231 calories, 7 g fat (1 g saturated fat), 63 mg cholesterol, 275 mg sodium, 15 g carbohydrate, 3 g fiber, 26 g protein.*
Diabetic Exchanges: *3 lean meat, 2 vegetable, 1 fat.*

Asparagus Chicken Sandwiches

(Pictured below)

No one will be able to resist these lovely open-faced sandwiches that definitely say "spring". Served on toasted English muffins, slices of chicken and tomato are topped with fresh asparagus spears, then draped with a creamy lemon sauce. This is a great way to use up leftover chicken or turkey.
—Anca Cretan, Hagerstown, Maryland

　1 **pound fresh asparagus, trimmed and cut into 3-inch pieces**
1-1/2 **cups reduced-fat sour cream**
　2 **teaspoons lemon juice**
1-1/2 **teaspoons prepared mustard**
　1/2 **teaspoon salt**
　8 **ounces sliced cooked chicken breast**
　4 **English muffins, split and toasted**
　2 **medium tomatoes, sliced**
Paprika, optional

Place asparagus in a saucepan and cover with water; bring to a boil. Cover and cook for 2 minutes or until crisp-tender. Drain and set aside. In the same pan, combine the sour cream, lemon juice, mustard and salt; cook on low until

Southwestern Skewers

(Pictured above)

Juicy chicken, cherry tomatoes, whole mushrooms and sweet peppers make these skewers filling. But it's the fresh garlic, chili powder, cumin and cayenne pepper that give them their zesty kick.
—Larry Smith, Youngstown, Ohio

　1 **bottle (8 ounces) reduced-fat Italian salad dressing**
10 **garlic cloves, minced**
　1 **teaspoon white pepper**
　1 **teaspoon chili powder**
　1 **teaspoon ground cumin**
　1 **teaspoon paprika**
1/2 **teaspoon cayenne pepper**
　1 **medium green pepper, cut into 1-inch pieces**
　1 **medium sweet red pepper, cut into 1-inch pieces**
　1 **medium onion, cut into 1-inch pieces**
　8 **large fresh mushrooms**
　8 **cherry tomatoes**
　1 **pound boneless skinless chicken breasts, cut into 1-inch cubes**

In a bowl, combine the first seven ingredients; mix well. Pour half into a large resealable plastic bag; add the vegetables. Seal bag and turn to coat. Pour remaining marinade into another large resealable plastic bag; add the chicken. Seal bag and turn to coat. Refrigerate vegetables and chicken for at least 2-3 hours.

If grilling the kabobs, coat grill rack with nonstick cooking spray before starting the grill. Drain chicken, discarding marinade. Drain vegetables, reserving marinade for basting. On eight metal or soaked wooden skewers, alternately thread chicken and vegetables. Grill, covered, over heated through. Remove from the heat.

Place chicken on a microwave-safe plate; microwave on high for 45-60 seconds or until warmed. Place two English muffin halves on each serving plate. Top with chicken, tomatoes, asparagus and sauce. Sprinkle with paprika if desired. **Yield:** 4 servings.

Nutritional Analysis: One serving (2 topped muffin halves) equals 385 calories, 11 g fat (7 g saturated fat), 78 mg cholesterol, 645 mg sodium, 40 g carbohydrate, 2 g fiber, 32 g protein.

Diabetic Exchanges: 2 starch, 2 lean meat, 1 vegetable, 1 fat, 1/2 reduced-fat milk.

Gingered Chicken Stir-Fry

Ginger and soy sauce give eye-opening flavor to this colorful stir-fry.
—Donna Sauvageau, Detroit Lakes, Minnesota

1 tablespoon ketchup
1 teaspoon ground ginger *or* 1 tablespoon minced fresh gingerroot
2 tablespoons reduced-sodium soy sauce
2 garlic cloves, minced
3/4 pound boneless skinless chicken breasts, cut into thin strips
1 large green pepper, sliced
1 large sweet red pepper, sliced
6 green onions, sliced
2 teaspoons canola oil, *divided*
2 teaspoons sesame *or* additional canola oil, *divided*
Hot cooked rice, optional

In a large resealable plastic bag, combine the ketchup, ginger, soy sauce and garlic; add chicken. Seal bag and turn to coat; refrigerate for 15 minutes.

In a large nonstick skillet or wok, stir-fry peppers and onions in 1 teaspoon canola oil and 1 teaspoon sesame oil until crisp-tender. Remove vegetables with a slotted spoon; keep warm. In the same skillet, stir-fry chicken and marinade in remaining oil for 3-4 minutes or until no longer pink. Return vegetables to the pan; heat through. Serve with rice if desired. **Yield:** 3 servings.

Nutritional Analysis: One serving (1 cup chicken mixture, calculated without rice) equals 234 calories, 8 g fat (1 g saturated fat), 66 mg cholesterol, 496 mg sodium, 12 g carbohydrate, 3 g fiber, 28 g protein.

Diabetic Exchanges: 3 lean meat, 2 vegetable, 1/2 fat.

Fettuccine Italiana

(Pictured below)

I perk up a platter of fettuccine with spicy sausage and delicately flavored asparagus and mushrooms. The satisfying entree is easy enough for an everyday meal and colorful enough for company.
—Janet Quigley, Galveston, Texas

8 ounces uncooked fettuccine
1 package (14 ounces) reduced-fat smoked turkey sausage, thinly sliced
2 cups cut fresh asparagus (1-1/2-inch pieces)
1 cup sliced fresh mushrooms
1/4 cup chopped onion
1 garlic clove, minced
1/2 teaspoon dried thyme
1 tablespoon olive *or* canola oil
1 tablespoon cornstarch
1 cup reduced-sodium chicken broth
1/4 cup shredded Parmesan *or* Romano cheese

Cook fettuccine according to package directions. Meanwhile, in a large saucepan, saute sausage, asparagus, mushrooms, onion, garlic and thyme in oil until vegetables are tender. Combine cornstarch and broth until smooth; stir into sausage mixture. Bring to a boil; cook and stir for 1-2 minutes or until thickened. Drain pasta. Add to sausage mixture; toss to coat. Sprinkle with Parmesan cheese. **Yield:** 4 servings.

Nutritional Analysis: One serving equals 285 calories, 8 g fat (2 g saturated fat), 39 mg cholesterol, 908 mg sodium, 34 g carbohydrate, 3 g fiber, 19 g protein.

Diabetic Exchanges: 2 vegetable, 2 lean meat, 1-1/2 starch.

Wild Rice Chicken Bake

(Pictured above)

*This homey combination is one of my most
requested chicken recipes. It's a snap to assemble
using a boxed rice mix. Plus, it's low in calories.*
—Joyce Unruh, Shipshewana, Indiana

 1 package (6 ounces) long grain and wild rice mix
 2 medium carrots, shredded
 3/4 cup frozen peas
 1 can (8 ounces) sliced water chestnuts, drained
 1-1/4 cups water
 1 can (10-3/4 ounces) reduced-fat reduced-
   sodium condensed cream of mushroom soup,
   undiluted
 6 boneless skinless chicken breast halves
   (4 ounces *each*)
 1/8 teaspoon paprika
 1/8 teaspoon pepper
 1 garlic clove, minced
 1 tablespoon olive *or* canola oil

In a bowl, combine rice mix with contents of seasoning
packet, carrots, peas and water chestnuts. Combine water
and soup; pour over rice mixture and mix well. Transfer to
a shallow 3-qt. baking dish coated with nonstick cooking
spray. Cover and bake at 350° for 25 minutes.

Meanwhile, sprinkle chicken with paprika and pepper.
In a large nonstick skillet, cook chicken and garlic in oil for
5-6 minutes on each side or until lightly browned. Arrange
chicken over rice mixture. Cover and bake 10-15 minutes
longer or until chicken juices run clear and rice is tender.
Yield: 6 servings.

 Nutritional Analysis: One serving equals 314 calories, 5 g
fat (1 g saturated fat), 68 mg cholesterol, 762 mg sodium, 34 g carbohydrate, 4 g fiber, 31 g protein.
 Diabetic Exchanges: 3 lean meat, 2 starch, 1 vegetable.

Turkey Dumpling Stew

(Pictured below)

*My mom made this stew when I was young, and
it was always a hit. Since it's not time-consuming to
make, I can fix it on a weeknight for our children,
who love the tender dumplings.*
—Becky Mohr, Appleton, Wisconsin

 4 bacon strips, diced
 1-1/2 pounds turkey tenderloin, cut into 1-inch pieces
 4 medium carrots, cut into 1-inch pieces
 2 cups water, *divided*
 1 can (14-1/2 ounces) reduced-sodium chicken
   broth
 2 small onions, quartered
 2 celery ribs, cut into 1/2-inch pieces
 1/4 teaspoon dried rosemary, crushed
 1 bay leaf
 3 tablespoons all-purpose flour
 1/2 teaspoon salt
 1/8 to 1/4 teaspoon pepper
 1 cup reduced-fat biscuit/baking mix
 1/3 cup plus 1 tablespoon fat-free milk

In a Dutch oven or large saucepan, cook the bacon over
medium heat until crisp. Remove to paper towels; drain,
reserving 2 teaspoons drippings. Cook turkey in the drippings until no longer pink. Add the carrots, 1-3/4 cups of water, broth, onions, celery, rosemary and bay leaf. Bring to a
boil. Reduce heat; cover and simmer for 20-30 minutes or
until vegetables are tender.

Combine flour and remaining water until smooth; stir into turkey mixture. Bring to a boil; cook and stir for 2 minutes or until thickened. Discard bay leaf. Stir in the salt, pepper and reserved bacon.

In a bowl, combine biscuit mix and milk. Drop batter in
six mounds onto simmering stew. Cover and simmer for
15 minutes or until a toothpick inserted in a dumpling comes

out clean (do not lift the cover while simmering). **Yield:** 6 servings.

Nutritional Analysis: One serving (1 cup stew with 1 dumpling) equals 299 calories, 6 g fat (2 g saturated fat), 76 mg cholesterol, 787 mg sodium, 26 g carbohydrate, 2 g fiber, 34 g protein.
Diabetic Exchanges: 4 very lean meat, 2 vegetable, 1 starch, 1 fat.

Ginger Peach Chicken

My family is always glad to see this hearty skillet dinner on busy nights. It goes together quickly with ingredients that I keep on hand. I often serve it with a side of rice or pasta.
—Patty Gale, Pepperell, Massachusetts

 1 can (16 ounces) reduced-sugar sliced peaches
 4 boneless skinless chicken breast halves
  (4 ounces *each*)
 1 tablespoon butter *or* stick margarine
 1 tablespoon cornstarch
 1/2 teaspoon salt
 1/4 teaspoon ground ginger *or* 1 teaspoon minced
  fresh gingerroot
 1 can (8 ounces) sliced water chestnuts, drained

Drain peaches, reserving juice; set peaches aside. Add water to juice to measure 3/4 cup. Flatten chicken breasts to 1/2-in. thickness. In a nonstick skillet, cook chicken in butter over medium heat for 5-6 minutes on each side or until juices run clear. Remove and keep warm.

In a bowl, combine cornstarch, peach liquid, salt and ginger until smooth; stir into skillet. Bring to a boil; cook and stir for 2 minutes or until thickened. Add peaches and water chestnuts; heat through. Spoon over chicken. **Yield:** 4 servings.

Nutritional Analysis: One serving equals 226 calories, 4 g fat (2 g saturated fat), 74 mg cholesterol, 404 mg sodium, 19 g carbohydrate, 2 g fiber, 27 g protein.
Diabetic Exchanges: 3 lean meat, 1 fruit.

🍎 Stew-pendous Side Dishes

FAMILY COOKS appreciate the convenience of stews because they're a satisfying meal-in-one dish. However, when you'd like to serve a little something on the side, consider one of the following healthy add-ons:

● No matter how you slice it, bread is a perfect complement to stew. Pick up a loaf of whole wheat or multigrain bread from your grocer's bakery. Or consider serving lightened-up corn bread or low-fat tortillas.

● Salads go with everything, but they're a natural with steaming bowls of stew. Throw together a simple salad with your favorite reduced-calorie dressing.

● Reduced-fat shredded cheese, chives, chopped celery and fat-free sour cream are great garnishes for most stews.

Raisin Bagel Stackers

(Pictured above)

This stacked sandwich began by accident when I ran out of bread and replaced it with a bagel. You can easily change the fixings to meet your personal tastes. My husband prefers it with less meat, a slice of Vidalia onion and no cream cheese. We both think the raisin bagel adds the perfect touch of sweetness.
Cynthia DeKett, Lyndonville, Vermont

 2 cinnamon raisin bagels (3-1/2 inches), split
 4 teaspoons reduced-fat cream cheese
 4 lettuce leaves
 1/4 pound shaved deli smoked turkey breast
 2 fresh dill sprigs
 2 green onions, sliced
 2 slices (1/2 ounce *each*) reduced-fat Swiss
  cheese
 4 thin tomato slices
 1/8 teaspoon salt
 1/8 teaspoon pepper
 2 teaspoons reduced-fat mayonnaise

Lightly toast the bagels; spread cream cheese on bottom halves. Layer with the lettuce, turkey, dill, onions, cheese and tomato. Sprinkle with salt and pepper. Spread mayonnaise on the top halves of bagels; place over tomato. **Yield:** 2 servings.

Nutritional Analysis: One serving equals 321 calories, 5 g fat (2 g saturated fat), 32 mg cholesterol, 1,029 mg sodium, 46 g carbohydrate, 3 g fiber, 22 g protein.
Diabetic Exchanges: 3 starch, 2 lean meat.

Ultimate Chicken Sandwiches

(Pictured below)

After making these sandwiches, you'll never order the fast-food kind again. Marinating the chicken overnight in buttermilk gives it a wonderful taste and tenderness. The zippy breading is golden and crispy.
—Gregg Voss, Emerson, Nebraska

- 6 boneless skinless chicken breast halves (4 ounces *each*)
- 1 cup 1% buttermilk
- 1/2 cup reduced-fat biscuit/ baking mix
- 1/2 cup cornmeal
- 1-1/2 teaspoons paprika
- 3/4 teaspoon salt
- 3/4 teaspoon poultry seasoning
- 1/2 teaspoon garlic powder
- 1/2 teaspoon pepper
- 1/4 teaspoon cayenne pepper
- 6 onion or kaiser rolls, split
- 6 lettuce leaves
- 12 tomato slices

Pound chicken to 1/2-in. thickness. Pour buttermilk into a large resealable plastic bag; add chicken. Seal bag and turn to coat; refrigerate for 8 hours or overnight.

In a shallow bowl, combine the biscuit mix, cornmeal, paprika, salt, poultry seasoning, garlic powder, pepper and cayenne. Remove chicken one piece at a time, allowing excess buttermilk to drain off. Discard buttermilk. Coat chicken with the cornmeal mixture; place in a 13-in. x 9-in. x 2-in. baking dish coated with nonstick cooking spray.

Bake, uncovered, at 400° for 12 minutes. Turn chicken. Bake 8-12 minutes longer or until juices run clear and coating is lightly browned. Serve on rolls with lettuce and tomato. **Yield:** 6 servings.

Nutritional Analysis: One sandwich equals 372 calories, 7 g fat (3 g saturated fat), 63 mg cholesterol, 759 mg sodium, 46 g carbohydrate, 3 g fiber, 31 g protein.
Diabetic Exchanges: 3 lean meat, 3 starch.

Tomato Sausage Stew

(Pictured above)

My husband and I host a soup luncheon at his office every Christmas. When trying out new recipes for it, I modified one to make this hearty stew. It combines my favorite sausage with fennel and garlic.
—Jeanette Jones, Muncie, Indiana

- 1/2 pound turkey Italian sausage links, casings removed
- 1 large onion, chopped
- 2 garlic cloves, minced
- 3/4 cup chopped carrots
- 1 fennel bulb, chopped
- 1/3 cup chopped celery
- 1 can (14-1/2 ounces) reduced-sodium chicken broth
- 3 medium tomatoes, peeled, seeded and chopped
- 1 teaspoon dried basil
- 1 teaspoon dried oregano
- 1/4 teaspoon salt
- 1 cup uncooked small pasta shells
- 1 can (15 ounces) navy beans, rinsed and drained
- 1/2 cup shredded Parmesan cheese

In a Dutch oven, cook the sausage, onion and garlic over medium heat until meat is no longer pink; drain. Add the carrots, fennel and celery; cook until vegetables are softened. Stir in the broth to loosen any browned bits from pan. Add tomatoes, basil, oregano and salt. Bring to a boil. Reduce heat; cover and simmer for 10 minutes or until vegetables are tender.

Stir in pasta and beans. Add enough water to cover. Bring to a boil. Reduce heat; cover and simmer for 15 minutes or until pasta is tender. Sprinkle with Parmesan cheese. **Yield:** 6 servings.

Nutritional Analysis: One serving (1-1/2 cups) equals 247 calories, 6 g fat (2 g saturated fat), 24 mg cholesterol, 900 mg sodium, 36 g carbohydrate, 7 g fiber, 17 g protein.
Diabetic Exchanges: 2 lean meat, 2 vegetable, 1-1/2 starch.

Barbecued Turkey Pizza

(Pictured at right)

My bread machine makes the crust for this mouth-watering pizza. Barbecue sauce, turkey, vegetables and cheese deliver so much flavor even your biggest pizza fans won't believe it's light.
—Krista Frank, Rhododendron, Oregon

1 cup water (70° to 80°)
2 tablespoons olive *or* canola oil
1 tablespoon sugar
1 teaspoon salt
3 cups all-purpose flour
2 teaspoons active dry yeast
3/4 cup barbecue sauce
1-1/2 cups cubed cooked turkey breast
1/2 cup fresh *or* frozen corn, thawed
1 small red onion, julienned
1 small green pepper, julienned
1 garlic clove, minced
1 cup (4 ounces) shredded part-skim mozzarella cheese
1/2 cup shredded reduced-fat cheddar cheese
1/4 cup grated Parmesan cheese

In bread machine pan, place the first six ingredients in order suggested by manufacturer. Select dough setting (check dough after 5 minutes of mixing; add 1 to 2 tablespoons of water or flour if needed). When cycle is completed, turn dough onto a lightly floured surface. Punch down; cover and let stand for 10 minutes.

Roll dough into a 14-in. circle. Transfer to a 14-in. pizza pan coated with nonstick cooking spray; build up edges slightly. Spread barbecue sauce over crust. Layer with half of the turkey, corn, onion, green pepper, garlic and cheeses. Repeat layers. Bake at 400° for 25-30 minutes or until the crust is golden brown. **Yield:** 8 servings.

Nutritional Analysis: One serving equals 366 calories, 9 g fat (4 g saturated fat), 38 mg cholesterol, 663 mg sodium, 52 g carbohydrate, 2 g fiber, 20 g protein.
Diabetic Exchanges: 3 starch, 2 lean meat, 1/2 fat.

🍎 Tortilla Tips

• To lighten up Mexican dishes, substitute corn tortillas when flour tortillas are called for in the recipes.
—*L. Patricia Campbell
San Antonio, Texas*

• Many recipes recommend frying corn tortillas in hot fat so they will not break when folded or rolled for enchiladas or other Mexican specialties. I found a healthier way to accomplish this. I spray the tortillas with butter-flavored nonstick cooking spray, then fry in a hot dry skillet for about 30 seconds on each side.

They don't end up greasy, and can be folded and rolled without breaking. To make your own taco shells, fry them a bit longer and fold while hot.
—*Bruce Watson, Canon City, Colorado*

Glazed Chicken and Carrots

Apple juice lends subtle sweetness to chicken that's nicely coated with dill and tossed with carrots and celery in this pretty stir-fry. I've served it on busy nights when time is short and at family buffets, too. Everyone is sure I've spent hours in the kitchen.
—Helen Bekert, Sprakers, New York

1 teaspoon dill weed
1/2 teaspoon salt
1/4 teaspoon pepper
1 pound boneless skinless chicken breasts, cut into 1/2-inch strips
3 celery ribs, thinly sliced
2 medium carrots, thinly sliced
1 tablespoon canola oil
4 teaspoons cornstarch
1 teaspoon chicken bouillon granules
1 cup apple juice
Hot cooked rice, optional

In a bowl, combine the dill, salt and pepper; add chicken and toss to coat. In a large nonstick skillet or wok, stir-fry the chicken, celery and carrots in oil until chicken is no longer pink and vegetables are tender. In a small bowl, combine the cornstarch, bouillon and apple juice until smooth. Stir into chicken mixture. Bring to a boil; cook and stir for 2 minutes or until thickened. Serve over rice if desired. **Yield:** 4 servings.

Nutritional Analysis: One serving (1 cup chicken mixture, calculated without rice) equals 228 calories, 6 g fat (1 g saturated fat), 67 mg cholesterol, 685 mg sodium, 15 g carbohydrate, 2 g fiber, 26 g protein.
Diabetic Exchanges: 3 lean meat, 1 vegetable, 1/2 fruit.

Honey-Nut Chicken Stir-Fry

(Pictured at right)

I combine honey, ginger and orange juice in a delightful sauce for sliced carrots, celery and strips of tender chicken. Then I top off this delicious stir-fry with chopped peanuts for a fun crunch.
—Tammi McDonald, Roswell, Georgia

        1 tablespoon cornstarch
    3/4 cup orange juice
    1/4 cup honey
        3 tablespoons reduced-sodium soy sauce
    1/4 teaspoon ground ginger
        2 cups sliced celery
1-1/2 cups sliced carrots
        4 teaspoons canola oil, *divided*
        1 pound boneless skinless chicken breasts,
            cut into 1/2-inch strips
    1/4 cup coarsely chopped peanuts
Hot cooked rice, optional

In a small bowl, combine the first five ingredients until smooth; set aside. In a nonstick skillet or wok, stir-fry celery and carrots in 2 teaspoons oil until crisp-tender. Remove and keep warm. In the same skillet, stir-fry chicken in remaining oil until no longer pink.

Return vegetables to the pan. Stir orange juice mixture and add to the pan. Bring to a boil; cook and stir for 2 minutes or until thickened. Sprinkle with nuts. Serve over rice if desired. **Yield:** 4 servings.

Nutritional Analysis: *One serving (1 cup chicken mixture, calculated without rice) equals 348 calories, 11 g fat (1 g saturated fat), 66 mg cholesterol, 636 mg sodium, 34 g carbohydrate, 3 g fiber, 30 g protein.*
Diabetic Exchanges*: 3 lean meat, 1 starch, 1 fruit, 1 vegetable, 1/2 fat.*

Cranberry Salsa Chicken

I made this dish for my fiance once…and he absolutely loved it. Now that we're married, I prepare it for our dinner guests. Everyone likes it, and no one guesses they're eating "healthy".
—Amy VanGuilder Dik, Minneapolis, Minnesota

        4 boneless skinless chicken breast halves
            (4 ounces *each*)
        1 tablespoon olive *or* canola oil
        1 jar (16 ounces) chunky salsa
        1 cup dried cranberries
    1/4 cup water
        1 tablespoon honey
        2 garlic cloves, minced
    3/4 teaspoon ground cinnamon
    1/2 teaspoon ground cumin
        2 cups hot cooked couscous
    1/4 cup slivered almonds, toasted

In a large nonstick skillet, saute chicken in oil until browned on both sides. In a small bowl, combine the salsa, cranberries, water, honey, garlic, cinnamon and cumin; mix well.

Pour over chicken. Cover and cook over medium-low heat for 10-15 minutes or until chicken juices run clear. Serve over couscous. Sprinkle with almonds. **Yield:** 4 servings.

Nutritional Analysis: *One serving (1 chicken breast half and 1/2 cup cranberry salsa with 1/2 cup of couscous) equals 441 calories, 9 g fat (1 g saturated fat), 66 mg cholesterol, 859 mg sodium, 57 g carbohydrate, 5 g fiber, 31 g protein.*
Diabetic Exchanges: *3 lean meat, 2 vegetable, 1-1/2 starch, 1-1/2 fruit.*

Cajun Sausage Pasta

If you can stand a little "heat", stay in the kitchen and cook up this zesty Cajun entree. This dish has a nice "kick", and the peppers perk up its flavor. For variety, substitute chicken for the sausage.
—Crystal Leach, Columbia, South Carolina

        1 large onion, chopped
        3 garlic cloves, minced
        2 tablespoons olive *or* canola oil
        1 cup reduced-sodium chicken broth
        2 cups dry white wine *or* additional reduced-
            sodium chicken broth
        1 can (14-1/2 ounces) diced tomatoes, undrained
        1 can (6 ounces) tomato paste
        2 tablespoons sugar
        1 teaspoon ground cumin
    1/4 teaspoon cayenne pepper
    1/4 teaspoon pepper
        1 pound turkey Italian sausage links, sliced
        1 medium green pepper, julienned
        1 medium sweet red pepper, julienned
        5 cups hot cooked penne pasta

In a large saucepan, saute onion and garlic in oil until tender. Add broth and wine or additional broth. Bring to a boil; cook, uncovered, until liquid is reduced to 1 cup. Reduce heat. Stir in tomatoes, tomato paste, sugar, cumin, cayenne and pepper. Cover and simmer for 15-20 minutes.

Meanwhile, in a nonstick skillet, cook sausage and peppers over medium heat until sausage is no longer pink and peppers are tender. Stir into the tomato mixture. Serve over pasta. **Yield:** 5 servings.

Nutritional Analysis: *One serving (3/4 cup sausage mixture with 1 cup pasta) equals 555 calories, 11 g fat (3 g saturated fat), 41 mg cholesterol, 987 mg sodium, 65 g carbohydrate, 6 g fiber, 26 g protein.*

Kielbasa Cabbage Stew

(Pictured below)

If you like German potato salad, you'll love this sweet-and-sour stew. Caraway seeds, smoky kielbasa, tender potatoes and shredded cabbage make it a filling change of pace at dinnertime.
—Valrie Burrows, Shelby, Michigan

  1/2 **pound smoked turkey kielbasa *or* Polish sausage, sliced**
    1 **pound potatoes, peeled and cubed**
    2 **cups shredded cabbage**
    1 **large onion, chopped**
    1 **can (14-1/2 ounces) reduced-sodium chicken broth**
  3/4 **cup water, *divided***
    2 **tablespoons sugar**
    1 **teaspoon caraway seeds**
  1/4 **teaspoon pepper**
    1 **can (16 ounces) kidney beans, rinsed and drained**
    3 **tablespoons cider vinegar**
    2 **tablespoons all-purpose flour**

In a large saucepan or nonstick skillet, brown sausage over medium heat. Add the potatoes, cabbage, onion, broth, 1/2 cup water, sugar, caraway and pepper. Bring to a boil. Reduce heat; cover and simmer for 15-18 minutes or until potatoes are tender, stirring occasionally.

Add beans and vinegar; cover and simmer 5-10 minutes longer. Combine flour and remaining water until smooth; stir

Hawaiian Turkey Burgers

(Pictured above)

My husband and I love to grill, so hamburgers are often on the menu. This recipe uses ground turkey instead of beef. Topped with pineapple slices, the burgers are moist and juicy.
—Babette Watterson, Atglen, Pennsylvania

    1 **can (8 ounces) sliced pineapple**
  1/2 **cup dry bread crumbs**
  1/2 **cup sliced green onions**
  1/2 **cup chopped sweet red pepper**
    1 **tablespoon reduced-sodium soy sauce**
  1/4 **teaspoon salt**
    1 **pound lean ground turkey**
  1/4 **cup reduced-sodium teriyaki sauce**
    4 **sesame hamburger buns**

Coat grill rack with nonstick cooking spray before starting the grill. Drain pineapple, reserving 1/4 cup juice (discard remaining juice or save for another use); set pineapple aside. In a bowl, combine bread crumbs, onions, red pepper, soy sauce, salt and reserved pineapple juice. Crumble turkey over mixture, mix well. Shape into four patties.

Grill, covered, over medium heat for 3 minutes on each side. Brush with teriyaki sauce. Grill 4-6 minutes longer on each side or until meat is no longer pink and a meat thermometer reads 165°. Grill pineapple slices for 2 minutes on each side, basting occasionally with teriyaki sauce. Warm buns on grill; top each with a burger and pineapple slice. **Yield:** 4 servings.

Nutritional Analysis: One burger equals 391 calories, 13 g fat (3 g saturated fat), 90 mg cholesterol, 1,041 mg sodium, 42 g carbohydrate, 3 g fiber, 27 g protein.
Diabetic Exchanges: 3 lean meat, 2 starch, 1 fruit.

into stew. Bring to a boil; cook and stir for 2 minutes or until thickened. **Yield:** 4 servings.

Nutritional Analysis: One serving (1-3/4 cups) equals 322 calories, 3 g fat (1 g saturated fat), 25 mg cholesterol, 1,143 mg sodium, 57 g carbohydrate, 7 g fiber, 17 g protein.
Diabetic Exchanges: 3 starch, 2 lean meat, 1 vegetable.

Chicken Cacciatore

(Pictured on front cover)

For an entree with Italian flair, our Test Kitchen suggests these tender chicken breasts simmered in a nicely seasoned tomato sauce. The sauce has chunks of green pepper and mushrooms, and gets a little zip from balsamic vinegar and red pepper flakes.

    6 boneless skinless chicken breast halves
       (4 ounces *each*)
    1 teaspoon salt, *divided*
1/8 teaspoon pepper
    2 tablespoons olive *or* canola oil, *divided*
    1 medium green pepper, chopped
1/2 pound fresh mushrooms, sliced
    4 garlic cloves, minced
    1 can (15 ounces) tomato puree
    1 can (14-1/2 ounces) stewed tomatoes, cut up
    1 tablespoon balsamic vinegar
    2 teaspoons sugar
1-1/2 teaspoons dried basil
1-1/2 teaspoons dried oregano
1/4 teaspoon crushed red pepper flakes
1/4 cup minced fresh parsley
Hot cooked spaghetti, optional

Sprinkle chicken with 1/4 teaspoon salt and pepper. In a large nonstick skillet, brown chicken in 1 tablespoon oil. Remove and set aside. In the same skillet, saute the green pepper, mushrooms and garlic in remaining oil until vegetables are tender.

Add the tomato puree, stewed tomatoes, vinegar, sugar, basil, oregano, red pepper flakes, remaining salt and reserved chicken. Bring to a boil. Reduce heat; cover and simmer for 30 minutes. Stir in parsley. Simmer, uncovered, 15 minutes longer or until sauce is thickened. Serve over spaghetti if desired. Yield: 6 servings.

Nutritional Analysis: One serving (1 chicken breast half with 1/2 cup sauce, calculated without spaghetti) equals 248 calories, 8 g fat (1 g saturated fat), 67 mg cholesterol, 857 mg sodium, 18 g carbohydrate, 3 g fiber, 29 g protein.
Diabetic Exchanges: 3 lean meat, 3 vegetable.

Rotini Chicken Casserole

(Pictured at right)

Pasta dishes are a favorite in our family. I changed the original recipe to suit our tastes...and we all think this comforting casserole is delicious. I like to accompany it with a tossed green salad.
—Ruth Lee, Troy, Ontario

2-3/4 cups uncooked tricolor rotini *or* spiral pasta
3/4 cup chopped onion
1/2 cup chopped celery
    2 garlic cloves, minced
    1 tablespoon olive *or* canola oil
    3 cups cubed cooked chicken breast
    1 can (10-3/4 ounces) reduced-fat reduced-sodium condensed cream of chicken soup, undiluted
1-1/2 cups fat-free milk
    1 package (16 ounces) frozen Italian-blend vegetables
    1 cup (4 ounces) shredded reduced-fat cheddar cheese
    2 tablespoons minced fresh parsley
1-1/4 teaspoons dried thyme
    1 teaspoon salt
2/3 cup crushed cornflakes

Cook pasta according to package directions. Meanwhile, in a nonstick skillet, saute onion, celery and garlic in oil until tender. Drain pasta; place in a bowl. Add the onion mixture, chicken, soup, milk, frozen vegetables, cheese, parsley, thyme and salt.

Pour into a shallow 3-qt. baking dish coated with nonstick cooking spray. Cover and bake at 350° for 25 minutes. Sprinkle with cornflakes; spritz with nonstick cooking spray. Bake, uncovered, 10-15 minutes longer or until heated through. **Yield:** 8 servings.

Nutritional Analysis: One serving (1-1/3 cups) equals 341 calories, 7 g fat (3 g saturated fat), 56 mg cholesterol, 698 mg sodium, 40 g carbohydrate, 3 g fiber, 28 g protein.
Diabetic Exchanges: 3 lean meat, 2 starch, 1 vegetable.

Turkey Biscuit Potpie

(Pictured below)

My family enjoys this comforting dish that is loaded with chunks of turkey, potatoes, carrots and green beans. Topped with easy-to-make biscuits, it has wonderful down-home flavor.
—Shirley Francey, St. Catharines, Ontario

- 1 large onion, chopped
- 1 garlic clove, minced
- 1-1/2 cups cubed peeled potatoes
- 1-1/2 cups sliced carrots
- 1 cup frozen cut green beans, thawed
- 1 cup reduced-sodium chicken broth
- 4-1/2 teaspoons all-purpose flour
- 1 can (10-3/4 ounces) reduced-fat condensed cream of mushroom soup, undiluted
- 2 cups cubed cooked turkey
- 2 tablespoons minced fresh parsley
- 1/2 teaspoon dried basil
- 1/2 teaspoon dried thyme
- 1/4 teaspoon pepper

BISCUITS:
- 1 cup all-purpose flour
- 2 teaspoons baking powder
- 1/2 teaspoon dried oregano
- 2 tablespoons cold butter *or* stick margarine
- 7 tablespoons 1% milk

In a large saucepan coated with nonstick cooking spray, cook onion and garlic over medium heat until tender. Add the potatoes, carrots, beans and broth; bring to a boil. Reduce heat; cover and simmer for 15-20 minutes or until potatoes are tender.

Remove from the heat. Combine the flour and mushroom soup; stir into vegetable mixture. Add the turkey and seasonings. Transfer to a 2-qt. baking dish coated with nonstick cooking spray.

In a bowl, combine the flour, baking powder and oreg-
ano. Cut in butter until evenly distributed. Stir in milk. Drop batter in six mounds onto hot turkey mixture. Bake, uncovered, at 400° for 20-25 minutes or until a toothpick inserted in center of biscuits comes out clean and biscuits are golden brown. **Yield:** 6 servings.

Nutritional Analysis: One serving equals 301 calories, 8 g fat (4 g saturated fat), 47 mg cholesterol, 616 mg sodium, 37 g carbohydrate, 3 g fiber, 19 g protein.
Diabetic Exchanges: 2 starch, 2 very lean meat, 1 vegetable, 1 fat.

Turkey Pepper Kabobs

(Pictured above)

This is a summertime favorite at our house. While the turkey is a nice change of pace and goes great with the sweet basting sauce and pineapple, the recipe also works well with chunks of chicken.
—Traci Goodman, Paducah, Kentucky

- 1 can (8 ounces) unsweetened pineapple chunks
- 1/4 cup packed brown sugar
- 2 tablespoons canola oil
- 2 tablespoons Worcestershire sauce
- 1 garlic clove, minced
- 1 teaspoon prepared mustard
- 1 pound turkey tenderloin, cut into 1-inch cubes
- 1 large sweet onion, cut into 3/4-inch pieces
- 1 large green pepper, cut into 1-inch pieces
- 1 large sweet red pepper, cut into 1-inch pieces

Drain pineapple, reserving 1/4 cup juice (discard remaining juice or save for another use). In a bowl, combine the reserved pineapple juice, brown sugar, oil, Worcestershire sauce, garlic and mustard; mix well. Pour 1/3 cup into a large resealable plastic bag; add the turkey. Seal bag and turn to coat; refrigerate for 2-3 hours. Cover and refrigerate remaining marinade.

If grilling the kabobs, coat grill rack with nonstick cook-

ing spray before starting the grill. Drain and discard marinade from turkey. On eight metal or soaked wooden skewers, alternately thread vegetables, turkey and pineapple. Grill, uncovered, over medium heat or broil 4-6 in. from the heat for 4-5 minutes on each side or until meat is no longer pink, turning three times and basting frequently with reserved marinade. **Yield:** 4 servings.

Nutritional Analysis: One serving (2 kabobs) equals 262 calories, 4 g fat (1 g saturated fat), 82 mg cholesterol, 110 mg sodium, 24 g carbohydrate, 3 g fiber, 31 g protein.
Diabetic Exchanges: 4 very lean meat, 2 vegetable, 1 fruit.

Garlic Ginger Chicken Strips

Whether you serve these moist and tender chicken strips as an appetizer or main dish, they're sure to satisfy your hungry bunch. The five-spice powder and red pepper flakes add a bit of zip.
—Candy Snyder, Salem, Oregon

1/4 cup sherry *or* chicken broth
1/4 cup reduced-sodium soy sauce
  3 garlic cloves, minced
  1 tablespoon honey
  1 tablespoon minced fresh basil *or* 1 teaspoon dried basil
1/2 teaspoon ground ginger *or* 2 teaspoons minced fresh gingerroot
1/2 teaspoon Chinese five-spice powder
1/4 teaspoon crushed red pepper flakes, optional
1/4 teaspoon pepper
  1 pound boneless skinless chicken breasts, cut into 1-inch strips

In a bowl, combine the first nine ingredients. Remove 3 tablespoons for basting; cover and refrigerate. Place chicken in a large resealable plastic bag; add the remaining marinade. Seal bag and turn to coat. Refrigerate for at least 4 hours.

Drain and discard marinade. Broil chicken 3-4 in. from the heat for 3 minutes; turn strips over. Baste with reserved marinade. Broil 4-5 minutes longer or until chicken juices run clear, turning occasionally. **Yield:** 4 servings.

Nutritional Analysis: One serving equals 166 calories, 1 g fat (trace saturated fat), 66 mg cholesterol, 681 mg sodium, 7 g carbohydrate, trace fiber, 27 g protein.
Diabetic Exchange: 3 lean meat.

Multigrain Stuffed Pepper Cups

(Pictured at right)

This recipe is one of my family's favorites. With its mix of healthy grains, this variation on stuffed peppers is high in fiber, low in fat and delicious!
—Judy Charbonneau, Bethlehem, Connecticut

  4 large sweet red *or* green peppers
  1 pound lean ground turkey
  3 green onions, sliced
  2 garlic cloves, minced

  1 jar (26 ounces) meatless spaghetti sauce, *divided*
1/2 cup frozen corn, thawed
1/2 cup dried currants
1/2 cup white wine *or* chicken broth
1/4 cup cooked medium pearl barley
1/4 cup cooked bulgur*
1/4 cup cooked lentils
  2 tablespoons brown sugar
1/4 to 1/2 teaspoon crushed red pepper flakes
1/2 teaspoon salt
1/4 teaspoon pepper
1/4 cup shredded Parmesan cheese

Cut peppers in half lengthwise; remove stems and seeds. In a large kettle, cook peppers in boiling water for 3-5 minutes. Rinse in cold water and drain; set aside.

In a saucepan, cook turkey, onions and garlic over medium heat until meat is no longer pink; drain. Stir in 2 cups spaghetti sauce, corn, currants, wine or broth, barley, bulgur, lentils, brown sugar and seasonings. Bring to a boil. Reduce heat; simmer, uncovered, for 10-15 minutes or until heated through. Spoon a heaping 1/2 cupful into each pepper cup.

Place in a 13-in. x 9-in. x 2-in. baking dish coated with nonstick cooking spray. Top each pepper with remaining spaghetti sauce; sprinkle with Parmesan cheese. Cover and bake at 375° for 30-35 minutes or until peppers are tender and filling is heated through. **Yield:** 8 servings.

*Editor's Note: Look for bulgur in the cereal, rice or organic food aisle of your grocery store.

Nutritional Analysis: One serving (1 stuffed pepper half) equals 282 calories, 8 g fat (2 g saturated fat), 51 mg cholesterol, 649 mg sodium, 37 g carbohydrate, 6 g fiber, 16 g protein.
Diabetic Exchanges: 2 starch, 2 lean meat, 1 vegetable.

Nutritional Analysis: One serving (5 ounces cooked turkey with 1/4 cup sauce) equals 258 calories, 5 g fat (1 g saturated fat), 116 mg cholesterol, 476 mg sodium, 4 g carbohydrate, trace fiber, 41 g protein.
Diabetic Exchanges: 6 very lean meat, 1 fat.

Yogurt-Marinated Chicken

(Pictured below)

This tender marinated chicken gets its zing from chili powder and cumin. For variety, I sometimes add a tablespoon of tomato paste to the marinade or replace the chili powder with chopped green chilies.
—Naheed Saleem, Stamford, Connecticut

  1/2 **cup fat-free yogurt**
    3 **garlic cloves, minced**
    2 **tablespoons lemon juice**
    1 **tablespoon canola oil**
    1 **teaspoon sugar**
    1 **teaspoon chili powder**
  3/4 **teaspoon ground ginger *or* 1 tablespoon minced fresh gingerroot**
  1/2 **teaspoon salt**
  1/2 **teaspoon ground cumin**
    6 **bone-in skinless chicken breast halves (6 ounces *each*)**

In a large resealable plastic bag, combine the first nine ingredients; add the chicken. Seal bag and turn to coat; refrigerate for at least 8 hours or overnight.

Coat grill rack with nonstick cooking spray before starting the grill for indirect heat. Drain and discard marinade. Grill chicken, covered, bone side down over indirect medium heat for 20 minutes. Turn; grill 20-30 minutes longer or until juices run clear. **Yield:** 6 servings.

Nutritional Analysis: One serving (1 chicken breast half) equals 149 calories, 4 g fat (1 g saturated fat), 68 mg cholesterol, 163 mg sodium, 2 g carbohydrate, trace fiber, 25 g protein.
Diabetic Exchange: 3 lean meat.

Peppery Herbed Turkey Tenderloin

(Pictured above)

I won the North Carolina Turkey Cook-Off one year with these full-flavored tenderloins and rich sauce. Marinating the turkey in wine, garlic, rosemary and thyme gives it a fantastic taste.
—Virginia Anthony, Blowing Rock, North Carolina

    3 **turkey tenderloins (12 ounces *each*)**
    1 **cup dry white wine *or* 1 cup apple juice***
    3 **green onions, chopped**
    3 **tablespoons minced fresh parsley**
    6 **teaspoons olive *or* canola oil, *divided***
    1 **tablespoon finely chopped garlic**
  3/4 **teaspoon dried rosemary, crushed**
  3/4 **teaspoon dried thyme**
    1 **teaspoon coarsely ground pepper**
  3/4 **teaspoon salt, *divided***
    4 **teaspoons cornstarch**
    1 **cup reduced-sodium chicken broth**

Pat tenderloins dry; flatten to 3/4-in. thickness. In a bowl, combine the wine or juice, onions, parsley, 4 teaspoons oil, garlic, rosemary and thyme; mix well. Pour 3/4 cup marinade into a large resealable plastic bag; add turkey. Seal and turn to coat; refrigerate for at least 4 hours, turning occasionally. Cover and refrigerate remaining marinade.

Drain and discard marinade from turkey. Sprinkle turkey with pepper and 1/2 teaspoon salt. In a large nonstick skillet, cook turkey in remaining oil for 10-12 minutes or until no longer pink, turning once. Remove and keep warm. Combine cornstarch, broth, reserved marinade and remaining salt until smooth; add to skillet. Bring to a boil; cook and stir for 1-2 minutes or until thickened. Slice turkey; serve with sauce. **Yield:** 6 servings.

*Editor's Note: If using apple juice in place of wine, add 3 tablespoons cider vinegar to the marinade.

Sausage Pepper Skillet

We try to eat healthy, but that can be difficult with our busy schedules. To save time, I freeze chopped onions and peppers to use in entrees like this one. And to cut back on calories and fat, I saute foods in fat-free Italian salad dressing.
—Margaret Kruse, Virginia Beach, Virginia

1 large green pepper, julienned
1 large sweet red pepper, julienned
1 cup sliced red onion
1 garlic clove, minced
1/2 cup fat-free Italian salad dressing, *divided*
1 pound reduced-fat turkey kielbasa, sliced
1 tablespoon reduced-sodium soy sauce

In a nonstick skillet or wok, stir-fry the peppers, onion and garlic in 1/4 cup salad dressing for 5 minutes. Add sausage and remaining dressing; stir-fry for 8-10 minutes or until sausage is heated through and vegetables are crisp-tender. Sprinkle with soy sauce. **Yield:** 4 servings.

Tex-Mex Turkey Tacos

(Pictured above)

I normally don't care for ground turkey, but I love the Southwestern flair of this well-seasoned taco meat mixed with peppers, onions and black beans. It's sure to be a hit at your house, too.
—Jodi Fleury, West Gardiner, Maine

1 pound lean ground turkey
2 medium green peppers, chopped
1 medium sweet red pepper, chopped
1 medium onion, chopped
2 medium carrots, halved lengthwise and sliced
2 garlic cloves, minced
1 tablespoon olive *or* canola oil
2 cans (15 ounces *each*) black beans, rinsed and drained
1 jar (16 ounces) salsa
2 tablespoons chili powder
1 tablespoon ground cumin
24 taco shells, warmed
3 cups shredded lettuce
1-1/2 cups diced fresh tomato
1/2 cup minced fresh cilantro *or* parsley

In a large nonstick skillet coated with nonstick cooking spray, cook turkey over medium heat until no longer pink; remove and set aside. In the same skillet, saute the peppers, onion, carrots and garlic in oil for 8-10 minutes or until vegetables are tender.

Add the turkey, beans, salsa, chili powder and cumin; bring to a boil. Reduce heat; simmer, uncovered, for 10-15 minutes or until thickened. Fill each taco shell with 1/3 cup turkey mixture. Serve with lettuce, tomato and cilantro. **Yield:** 12 servings.

Using Up Leftover Turkey

SOME FOLKS look forward to leftover turkey as much as they enjoy the main meal. The next time you have a bit of the bird left, consider the following:

• The majority of turkey's fat can be found in its skin. Be sure to remove the skin from leftover turkey before adding the meat to the dish you're preparing.

• Think beyond sandwiches. Slice cooked turkey breast into strips and reheat it with some salsa. Wrap the mixture in a tortilla with reduced-fat cheese. Or, cube last night's turkey, stir-fry it with veggies in low-sodium soy sauce and serve over rice.

• Make homemade turkey stock. Put the turkey carcass in a kettle with cold water and seasonings. Bring to a boil. Reduce heat and simmer, skimming the foam off the top. When the stock is done, strain it and refrigerate. Remove fat from the surface before using.

Basil Turkey Burgers

(Pictured above)

These delicious sandwiches are a superb substitute for traditional beef burgers. My husband actually prefers these turkey burgers, topped with seasoned mayonnaise.
—*Carolyn Bixenmann, Grand Island, Nebraska*

1/4 cup fat-free mayonnaise
2 tablespoons minced fresh basil, *divided*
1/4 cup fat-free milk
2 tablespoons finely chopped onion
1 tablespoon dry bread crumbs
1/8 teaspoon salt
1/8 teaspoon pepper
12 ounces lean ground turkey
4 hamburger buns, split
4 lettuce leaves
1 large tomato, sliced

In a small bowl, combine mayonnaise and 1 tablespoon basil. Cover and refrigerate until serving. Coat grill rack with nonstick cooking spray before starting the grill. In a bowl, combine the milk, onion, bread crumbs, salt, pepper and remaining basil. Crumble turkey over mixture and mix well. Shape into four patties.

Grill, covered, over indirect medium heat for 5-6 minutes on each side or until meat is no longer pink and a thermometer reads 165°. Serve on buns with lettuce, tomato and basil mayonnaise. **Yield:** 4 servings.

Nutritional Analysis: One serving (1 burger with 1 tablespoon basil mayonnaise) equals 305 calories, 11 g fat (4 g saturated fat), 69 mg cholesterol, 567 mg sodium, 31 g carbohydrate, 2 g fiber, 21 g protein.
Diabetic Exchanges: 3 lean meat, 2 starch.

Sausage Squash Kabobs

Expect a crowd to gather around the grill when these flavorful kabobs are cooking! The recipe takes a healthy turn with turkey kielbasa, potatoes, squash and zucchini on the skewer. The zesty honey-mustard glaze gives a lovely sheen to the sausage and veggies.
—*Lisa Malynn Kent, North Richland Hills, Texas*

1 pound small red potatoes
1 tablespoon water
1/2 cup honey
1/4 cup Dijon mustard
1/2 teaspoon grated orange peel
1 pound reduced-fat turkey kielbasa, sliced 1/2 inch thick
2 small yellow summer squash, sliced 1/2 inch thick
2 small zucchini, sliced 1/2 inch thick

In a large microwave-safe bowl, combine potatoes and water. Cover and microwave on high for 6-8 minutes or until tender; drain and set aside. For glaze, combine the honey, mustard and orange peel in a small bowl.

If grilling kabobs, coat the grill rack with nonstick cooking spray before starting the grill. On eight metal or soaked wooden skewers, alternately thread the sausage, potatoes, yellow squash and zucchini; brush with half of the glaze. Grill kabobs, uncovered, over medium heat or broil 4 in. from the heat for 5-8 minutes on each side or until vegetables are tender and sausage is heated through, basting frequently with glaze and turning once. **Yield:** 4 servings.

Nutritional Analysis: One serving (2 kabobs) equals 379 calories, 7 g fat (2 g saturated fat), 51 mg cholesterol, 1,361 mg sodium, 63 g carbohydrate, 7 g fiber, 19 g protein.

Pork & Ham Favorites

Today's pork is leaner and more delicious than ever before. So it's ideal for people who are eating a little lighter. Plus, pork's pure versatility and quick cooking time make it a mealtime mainstay.

Glazed Pork Tenderloin (page 161)

Mexican Pork Stew

(Pictured below)

I heat up cold nights by serving this thick and zesty stew with corn bread. I also like to spoon leftovers into corn tortillas with a little salsa and reduced-fat sour cream for a satisfying snack.
—Mickey Terry, Del Valle, Texas

1 pound boneless pork loin roast, cut into 3/4-inch cubes
3 teaspoons olive *or* canola oil, *divided*
1 large onion, chopped
2 celery ribs, chopped
1 jalapeno pepper, seeded and chopped*
1 garlic clove, minced
1-1/2 cups water
1 tablespoon chili powder
2 teaspoons brown sugar
1 teaspoon ground cumin
1/2 teaspoon salt
1/4 teaspoon pepper
1 can (6 ounces) tomato paste
1 can (16 ounces) kidney beans, rinsed and drained
1 can (15 ounces) pinto beans, rinsed and drained
1 can (14-1/2 ounces) diced tomatoes, undrained
2 teaspoons minced fresh cilantro *or* parsley

In a Dutch oven or large saucepan over medium-high heat, brown meat on all sides in 1 teaspoon oil; drain. Remove meat and keep warm. In the same pan, saute the onion, celery, jalapeno and garlic in remaining oil until tender. Stir in the water, chili powder, brown sugar, cumin, salt and pepper. Return meat to pan. Bring to a boil. Reduce heat; cover and simmer for 30 minutes.

Stir in the tomato paste, beans and tomatoes. Return to

a boil. Reduce heat; cover and simmer 20 minutes longer or until meat is tender and beans are heated through. Garnish with cilantro. **Yield:** 5 servings.

*Editor's Note: When cutting or seeding hot peppers, use rubber or plastic gloves to protect your hands. Avoid touching your face.

Nutritional Analysis: One serving (1-1/2 cups) equals 377 calories, 9 g fat (2 g saturated fat), 50 mg cholesterol, 991 mg sodium, 43 g carbohydrate, 13 g fiber, 32 g protein.
Diabetic Exchanges: 4 lean meat, 2 starch, 1 vegetable.

Cuban Pork Roast

A citrus and spice marinade seasons this moist, tender roast. The pork is flavorful but mild, so everyone likes it. You can serve it Cuban-style with black beans and rice, or make a traditional Cuban sandwich of pork, ham, Swiss cheese, tomatoes, lettuce, mustard, mayonnaise and dill pickle.
—Virginia Cronk, Little Torch Key, Florida

1 cup lime juice
1 cup orange juice
10 garlic cloves, minced
4 teaspoons ground cumin
2 tablespoons minced fresh thyme *or* 2 teaspoons dried thyme
2 tablespoons minced fresh cilantro *or* parsley
4 bay leaves
1 boneless pork top loin roast (3 pounds)
1/2 teaspoon salt
1/4 teaspoon pepper

In a bowl, combine the first seven ingredients; mix well. Pour half of the marinade into a large resealable plastic bag; add the pork roast. Seal bag and turn to coat; refrigerate for 2 hours. Refrigerate remaining marinade.

Drain and discard marinade from pork. Place roast in an ungreased 13-in. x 9-in. x 2-in. baking dish. Pour reserved marinade over the roast. Sprinkle with salt and pepper. Cover and bake at 350° for 1 hour. Uncover; baste with pan drippings. Bake 15 minutes longer or until a meat thermometer reads 160°. Discard bay leaves. Let roast stand for 15 minutes before slicing. **Yield:** 12 servings.

Nutritional Analysis: One serving (3 ounces cooked pork) equals 168 calories, 6 g fat (2 g saturated fat), 66 mg cholesterol, 88 mg sodium, 1 g carbohydrate, trace fiber, 26 g protein.
Diabetic Exchange: 3 lean meat.

Polish-Style Sausage 'n' Potatoes

I share a bit of my heritage in this hearty layering of sliced potatoes, cabbage, onion, Polish sausage and white sauce. I love any dish with cabbage and kielbasa.
—Victoria Zmarzley-Hahn, Northampton, Pennsylvania

14 ounces reduced-fat smoked Polish sausage *or* turkey kielbasa, sliced
1 tablespoon butter *or* stick margarine
3 tablespoons all-purpose flour

1/2 teaspoon salt
1/4 teaspoon pepper
1/4 teaspoon garlic powder
1/4 teaspoon paprika
2 cups fat-free milk
2 cups sliced potatoes
2 cups shredded cabbage
1 medium onion, chopped

In a nonstick skillet, brown sausage over medium heat; set aside. For white sauce, melt butter in a saucepan. Stir in flour and seasonings until smooth. Gradually add milk. Bring to a boil; cook and stir for 2 minutes or until thickened. Remove from the heat.

In a 3 qt. baking dish coated with nonstick cooking spray, layer a third of the potatoes, cabbage, onion, sausage and white sauce. Repeat layers twice. Cover and bake at 350° for 1 to 1-1/2 hours or until the vegetables are tender. **Yield:** 4 servings.

Nutritional Analysis: One serving (1-1/4 cups) equals 298 calories, 6 g fat (3 g saturated fat), 46 mg cholesterol, 1,249 mg sodium, 41 g carbohydrate, 3 g fiber, 20 g protein.
Diabetic Exchanges: 2 starch, 2 lean meat, 1/2 fat-free milk.

Pork Loin with Raspberry Sauce

(Pictured above)

Raspberries add ruby red color and fruity sweetness to the sauce that enhances this savory pork roast. It transforms everyday pork into a special dish.
—Florence Nurczyk, Toronto, Ohio

1 boneless whole pork loin roast (3 pounds)
1 teaspoon salt, *divided*
1 teaspoon rubbed sage
1/2 teaspoon pepper
1 package (12 ounces) frozen unsweetened raspberries, thawed, *divided*
3/4 cup sugar
1 tablespoon cornstarch
1/4 teaspoon *each* ground ginger, nutmeg and cloves
1/4 cup white vinegar
1 tablespoon lemon juice
1 tablespoon butter *or* stick margarine

Place the roast on a rack in a shallow roasting pan. Rub with 3/4 teaspoon salt, sage and pepper. Bake, uncovered, at 350° for 1-1/2 hours or until a meat thermometer reads 160°.

Drain raspberries, reserving juice. Set aside 1/3 cup berries. In a sieve, mash remaining berries with the back of a spoon; reserve pulp and discard seeds. In a saucepan, combine sugar, cornstarch, ginger, nutmeg, cloves and remaining salt. Stir in vinegar, reserved raspberry juice and reserved pulp until blended. Add remaining raspberries. Bring to a boil; cook and stir for 2 minutes or until thickened. Remove from the heat; add lemon juice and butter. Stir until butter is melted.

Let roast stand for 10 minutes before slicing. Serve with the raspberry sauce. **Yield:** 8 servings.

Nutritional Analysis: One serving (3 ounces cooked pork with 2 tablespoons sauce) equals 237 calories, 7 g fat (3 g saturated fat), 69 mg cholesterol, 244 mg sodium, 16 g carbohydrate, trace fiber, 26 g protein.
Diabetic Exchanges: 3 lean meat, 1 starch.

Pork with Garlic Cream Sauce

This quick-cooking dish is a garlic lover's delight. The tender pork medallions are dressed in a creamy garlic sauce and sprinkled with sesame seeds. It's a family favorite that's oh so good!
—*Elisa Lochridge, Aloha, Oregon*

    1 pound pork tenderloin
    2 teaspoons canola oil
    2 teaspoons sesame seeds, toasted, *divided*
    1 to 2 garlic cloves, minced
    1 tablespoon butter *or* stick margarine
  1/3 cup 1% milk
    3 ounces reduced-fat cream cheese, cubed
    1 tablespoon minced chives

Cut pork into 1-in. slices; flatten to 1/2-in. thickness. Place in a 15-in. x 10-in. x 1-in. baking pan coated with nonstick cooking spray. Brush oil over all sides of pork; sprinkle with half of the sesame seeds. Broil 4-6 in. from the heat for 3-5 minutes; turn and sprinkle with remaining sesame seeds. Broil 3-5 minutes longer or until meat juices run clear.

Meanwhile, in a saucepan, saute garlic in butter for 1 minute. Stir in milk and cream cheese. Reduce heat; cook and stir until blended and smooth. Stir in chives. Serve with pork. **Yield:** 4 servings.

Nutritional Analysis: One serving (3 ounces cooked pork with 2 tablespoons sauce) equals 255 calories, 14 g fat (6 g saturated fat), 88 mg cholesterol, 151 mg sodium, 3 g carbohydrate, trace fiber, 27 g protein.
Diabetic Exchanges: 4 lean meat, 1 fat.

Braised Pork Chops

(Pictured above)

An easy herb rub gives sensational taste to these boneless pork chops that can be cooked on the stovetop in minutes. The meat turns out tender and delicious.
—*Marilyn Larsen, Port Orange, Florida*

    1 teaspoon rubbed sage
    1 teaspoon dried rosemary, crushed
    1 garlic clove, minced
  1/2 teaspoon salt
  1/8 teaspoon pepper
    4 boneless pork loin chops (4 ounces *each*)
    1 tablespoon butter *or* stick margarine
    1 tablespoon olive *or* canola oil
  3/4 cup dry white wine *or* apple juice, *divided*
    1 tablespoon minced fresh parsley

Combine the sage, rosemary, garlic, salt and pepper; rub over both sides of pork chops. In a large nonstick skillet, brown chops on both sides in butter and oil. Remove and keep warm.

Add 1/2 cup wine or juice to the skillet; bring to a boil. Return chops to pan. Reduce heat; cover and simmer for 8-10 minutes or until meat juices run clear, basting occasionally. Remove chops to a serving platter and keep warm.

Add the remaining wine or juice to the skillet. Bring to a boil, loosening any browned bits from the pan. Cook, uncovered, until liquid is reduced to 1/2 cup. Pour over pork chops; sprinkle with parsley. **Yield:** 4 servings.

Nutritional Analysis: One serving equals 232 calories, 11 g fat (4 g saturated fat), 79 mg cholesterol, 383 mg sodium, 1 g carbohydrate, trace fiber, 24 g protein.
Diabetic Exchanges: 3 lean meat, 1-1/2 fat.

Curried Pork and Fruit

Tender pork, tropical fruit and a spicy curry sauce combine in this tongue-tingling recipe. It never fails to win compliments.
—*Nancy Becker, Franklin, Illinois*

  3/4 pound pork tenderloin, thinly sliced
    1 medium onion, chopped
    2 tablespoons all-purpose flour
    1 to 2 teaspoons curry powder
  1/4 teaspoon salt
  1/8 to 1/4 teaspoon cayenne pepper
Dash ground ginger *or* 1/2 teaspoon minced fresh gingerroot
    1 cup chicken broth
    1 can (15-1/4 ounces) unsweetened tropical mixed fruit, drained
Hot cooked rice, optional

In a large skillet or wok coated with nonstick cooking spray, stir-fry pork and onion for 2-3 minutes or until pork is browned and onion is tender. Sprinkle with the flour, curry, salt, cayenne and ginger; toss to coat. Stir in the broth; bring to a boil. Add fruit; cook and stir for 2 minutes. Serve over rice if desired. **Yield:** 4 servings.

Nutritional Analysis: One serving (3/4 cup pork mixture, calculated without rice) equals 190 calories, 3 g fat (1 g saturated fat), 55 mg cholesterol, 437 mg sodium, 21 g carbohydrate, 2 g fiber, 19 g protein.
Diabetic Exchanges: 2 lean meat, 1 fruit, 1 vegetable.

LOOKING for easy ways to make a stir-fry seem special? Try these:
- While rice is the most popular accompaniment to stir-fries, you can substitute pasta instead. Try linguine, fettuccine, angel hair or couscous (located in the rice aisle of most grocery stores).
- For a little crunch, add water chestnuts, sliced celery or a handful of chopped nuts.
- Round out your meal with a fortune cookie. The sweet treats are low in fat, and they're sure to add a bit of fun to any dinner.

Microwave Potato Ham Dinner

I've had this recipe for 15 years. From the first time I made it, my family couldn't get enough. Now that our three daughters are grown and married, they fix it for their families, too.
—Sharon Price, Caldwell, Idaho

2 cups cubed peeled potatoes
1 cup sliced carrots
1 cup chopped celery
1/2 cup water
2 tablespoons chopped green pepper
2 tablespoons chopped onion
2 tablespoons reduced-fat margarine
3 tablespoons all-purpose flour
1/4 teaspoon salt
1/8 teaspoon pepper
1-1/2 cups 2% milk
1/2 cup reduced-fat shredded cheddar cheese
2 cups cubed fully cooked lean ham

In a large microwave-safe bowl, combine the potatoes, carrots, celery and water. Cover and microwave on high for 7 minutes, stirring once. Add green pepper and onion; cover and microwave on high for 4-5 minutes or until crisp-tender, stirring once. Pour into a 2-qt. microwave-safe baking dish coated with nonstick cooking spray; set aside.

In a microwave-safe bowl, heat the margarine, covered, on high for 40-50 seconds or until melted. Stir in the flour, salt and pepper until smooth. Gradually add milk. Cook, uncovered, on high for 2-3 minutes or until thickened and bubbly, stirring after each minute. Stir in the cheese until melted. Pour over the vegetables. Stir in ham. Cover and microwave on high for 4-5 minutes or until heated through. **Yield:** 4 servings.

Editor's Note: This recipe was tested with Parkay Light stick margarine in an 850-watt microwave.

Nutritional Analysis: One serving (1-1/4 cups) equals 251 calories, 9 g fat (4 g saturated fat), 39 mg cholesterol, 1,115 mg sodium, 25 g carbohydrate, 3 g fiber, 18 g protein.
Diabetic Exchanges: 2 lean meat, 1-1/2 starch, 1 vegetable, 1/2 fat.

Pork 'n' Slaw Sandwiches

(Pictured below)

Choose your favorite bottled barbecue sauce to jazz up the tender shredded pork in these satisfying sandwiches suggested by our Test Kitchen. A topping of tangy homemade coleslaw gives them a tasty twist.

3 tablespoons cider vinegar
4 teaspoons sugar
2 teaspoons canola oil
1 teaspoon Dijon mustard
1/4 teaspoon celery seed
1/4 teaspoon mustard seed
1/4 teaspoon salt
1/8 teaspoon pepper
1 cup shredded green cabbage
1 cup shredded red cabbage
1 large carrot, shredded
1-1/2 pounds pork tenderloin
1 cup barbecue sauce
6 kaiser rolls, split

For coleslaw, in a bowl, whisk together the first eight ingredients. Add cabbage and carrot; toss to coat. Set aside.

Broil pork 4-6 in. from the heat for 6-7 minutes on each side or until a meat thermometer reads 160°. Let stand for 5 minutes. Cut into strips or shred with two forks; place in a bowl. Add barbecue sauce and toss to coat. Serve 1/2 cup pork mixture and 1/3 cup coleslaw on each roll. **Yield:** 6 servings.

Nutritional Analysis: One sandwich equals 377 calories, 9 g fat (2 g saturated fat), 67 mg cholesterol, 828 mg sodium, 41 g carbohydrate, 1 g fiber, 31 g protein.
Diabetic Exchanges: 3 lean meat, 2-1/2 starch, 1 vegetable.

Pork Lo Mein

(Pictured at right)

This full-flavored stir-fry is sure to bring rave reviews from your family. Snappy snow peas, sweet pepper and pork are spiced up with ginger, sesame oil, red pepper flakes and soy sauce. Consider rice as an alternative to the pasta.
—Linda Trainor, Phoenix, Arizona

1 pork tenderloin (1 pound)
1/4 cup reduced-sodium soy sauce
3 garlic cloves, minced
1/4 teaspoon ground ginger *or* 1 teaspoon minced fresh gingerroot
1/4 teaspoon crushed red pepper flakes
2 cups fresh snow peas
1 medium sweet red pepper, julienned
3 cups cooked thin spaghetti
1/3 cup reduced-sodium chicken broth
2 teaspoons sesame oil

Cut the tenderloin in half lengthwise. Cut each half widthwise into 1/4-in. slices; set aside. In a large resealable plastic bag, combine the soy sauce, garlic, ginger and pepper flakes; add the pork. Seal bag and turn to coat; refrigerate for 20 minutes.

In a large nonstick skillet or wok coated with nonstick cooking spray, stir-fry pork and marinade for 4-5 minutes or until meat is no longer pink. Add peas and red pepper; stir-fry for 1 minute. Stir in spaghetti and broth; cook 1 minute longer. Remove from the heat; stir in sesame oil. **Yield:** 4 servings.

Nutritional Analysis: One serving (1-1/2 cups) equals 343 calories, 7 g fat (2 g saturated fat), 74 mg cholesterol, 716 mg sodium, 37 g carbohydrate, 3 g fiber, 31 g protein.
Diabetic Exchanges: 3 lean meat, 2 starch, 1 vegetable.

Hot Dog Stew

Everyone, especially kids, will be thrilled with this hearty stew, chock-full of hot dog bites and baked beans with a dash of liquid smoke. It's great at a summer cookout or on a cool fall evening.
—Dorothy Erickson, Blue Eye, Missouri

1 package (14 ounces) reduced-fat hot dogs, cut into 1/2-inch slices
1 can (11-1/2 ounces) condensed bean and bacon soup, undiluted
1 can (10-3/4 ounces) reduced-fat reduced-sodium condensed tomato soup, undiluted
1 can (15 ounces) pork and beans
1 teaspoon chili powder
1 teaspoon dried minced onion
1/4 teaspoon pepper
1/4 teaspoon liquid smoke
2/3 cup fat-free evaporated milk

In a large nonstick skillet, brown hot dogs over medium heat. Add the next seven ingredients. Cover and cook over low heat until heated through. Stir in milk; heat through. **Yield:** 6 servings.

Nutritional Analysis: One serving (1 cup) equals 275 calories, 6 g fat (2 g saturated fat), 36 mg cholesterol, 1,605 mg sodium, 37 g carbohydrate, 7 g fiber, 20 g protein.
Diabetic Exchanges: 2-1/2 starch, 2 lean meat.

Cranberry Pork Skillet

Looking for something new to do with pork, I decided to give it an international flavor. My love of Mexican and Chinese cuisines influenced this dish.
—Brenda Webb, Corpus Christi, Texas

1 tablespoon lime juice
2 medium apples, peeled and cut into 1/2-inch cubes
1-1/2 pounds pork tenderloin, cut into 1-inch pieces
2 tablespoons canola oil, *divided*
2 to 3 jalapeno peppers, seeded and chopped*
1 small onion, chopped
1 garlic clove, minced
1 cup chopped fresh *or* frozen cranberries
1 can (8 ounces) sliced water chestnuts, drained
1/2 cup unsweetened apple juice
1/4 cup packed brown sugar
1 teaspoon ground cumin
1 teaspoon grated lime peel
1/2 teaspoon salt
1/8 teaspoon pepper
2 tablespoons chopped green onion

In a bowl, toss lime juice with apples; set aside. In a large nonstick skillet, brown pork in 1 tablespoon oil. Remove and keep warm. Saute jalapenos, onion and garlic in remaining oil until tender. Add the cranberries, water chestnuts, apple juice, brown sugar, cumin, lime peel, salt, pepper and apples. Cook and stir over medium heat for 5-7 minutes.

Return pork to the pan. Reduce heat; cover and cook until fruit is tender and meat juices run clear. Garnish with green onion. **Yield:** 6 servings.

***Editor's Note:** When cutting or seeding hot peppers, use rubber or plastic gloves to protect your hands. Avoid touching your face.*

Nutritional Analysis: One serving (1 cup) equals 303 calories, 11 g fat (2 g saturated fat), 75 mg cholesterol, 262 mg sodium, 27 g carbohydrate, 4 g fiber, 24 g protein.
Diabetic Exchanges: 2-1/2 lean meat, 1-1/2 starch, 1 fat.

Italian Pork Chops

(Pictured below)

Skillet-browned chops are simmered with tomatoes, mushrooms and green pepper in this tasty treatment for pork. It's easy to prepare, especially if you buy the mushrooms already sliced.
—*Adeline Piscitelli, Sayreville, New Jersey*

- 6 bone-in pork loin chops (6 ounces *each* and 3/4 inch thick)
- 2 teaspoons olive *or* canola oil
- 1 large onion, chopped
- 1/2 pound fresh mushrooms, sliced
- 1 garlic clove, minced
- 1 can (14-1/2 ounces) Italian diced tomatoes, drained
- 1 teaspoon salt
- 1/2 teaspoon dried oregano
- 1/2 teaspoon dried basil
- 1/8 teaspoon pepper
- 1 large green pepper, julienned

In a large nonstick skillet, brown pork chops in batches on both sides in oil; remove from skillet. Add the onion, mushrooms and garlic; saute for 5 minutes or until tender. Add the tomatoes, salt, oregano, basil and pepper; mix well.

Return pork chops to skillet; arrange green pepper between the chops. Reduce heat; cover and simmer for 30 minutes or until meat is tender. **Yield:** 6 servings.

Nutritional Analysis: *One serving (1 pork chop with 1/2 cup of vegetables) equals 237 calories, 9 g fat (3 g saturated fat), 75 mg cholesterol, 573 mg sodium, 10 g carbohydrate, 2 g fiber, 29 g protein.*
Diabetic Exchanges: *3 lean meat, 2 vegetable.*

Boiled Ham Dinner

(Pictured above)

I made this often for my children when they were growing up. Now, I fix it for my grandkids.
—*Janet Tucker, Bellevue, Ohio*

- 1 chunk unsliced deli ham (1 pound)
- 6 medium carrots, halved lengthwise and cut into thirds
- 4 medium red potatoes, quartered
- 2 medium onions, cut into wedges
- 1 bay leaf
- 1 teaspoon dried thyme
- 1 teaspoon peppercorns
- 1 garlic clove, halved
- 1/2 teaspoon whole allspice
- 1/2 medium head cabbage, cut into wedges

Place the ham, carrots, potatoes and onions in a Dutch oven. Place the bay leaf, thyme, peppercorns, garlic and allspice on a double thickness of cheesecloth; bring up corners of cloth and tie with kitchen string. Add to pan. Add water just to cover the ham and vegetables; bring to a boil. Reduce heat; cover and simmer for 10 minutes. Add cabbage; cover and simmer 15-20 minutes longer or until vegetables are tender. Discard spice bag and cooking liquid. **Yield:** 4 servings.

Nutritional Analysis: *One serving equals 312 calories, 4 g fat (1 g saturated fat), 58 mg cholesterol, 1,300 mg sodium, 46 g carbohydrate, 8 g fiber, 26 g protein.*
Diabetic Exchanges: *4 vegetable, 3 lean meat, 1 starch.*

Pork Grapefruit Stir-Fry

For a refreshing change of pace, try this easy sweet-and-sour stir-fry.
—*Edie DeSpain, Logan, Utah*

3 tablespoons cornstarch
3/4 cup grapefruit juice concentrate
3/4 cup water
3 tablespoons reduced-sodium soy sauce
1 tablespoon honey
1/2 teaspoon ground ginger
3 cups sliced zucchini
1 medium sweet red *or* green pepper, julienned
1 tablespoon canola oil
1-1/2 pounds pork tenderloin, cut into thin strips
3 medium grapefruit, peeled and sectioned
1 tablespoon sesame seeds, toasted
Hot cooked rice, optional

In a small bowl, combine the cornstarch, grapefruit juice concentrate, water, soy sauce, honey and ginger; set aside. In a skillet or wok, stir-fry zucchini and red pepper in oil over medium-high heat for 3-4 minutes or until crisp-tender. Remove and keep warm. Add half of the pork; stir-fry for 4 minutes or until no longer pink. Remove and keep warm. Repeat with remaining pork. Remove and keep warm.

Add sauce to skillet; bring to a boil. Cook and stir for 2 minutes or until thickened. Return pork and vegetables to pan; stir until coated. Gently stir in grapefruit. Sprinkle with sesame seeds. Serve over rice if desired. **Yield:** 6 servings.

Nutritional Analysis: One serving (1-1/4 cups pork mixture, calculated without rice) equals 320 calories, 7 g fat (2 g saturated fat), 74 mg cholesterol, 364 mg sodium, 39 g carbohydrate, 7 g fiber, 27 g protein.
Diabetic Exchanges: *3 lean meat, 2 fruit, 1 vegetable.*

Glazed Pork Tenderloin

(Pictured on page 153)

Pork gets a tasty treatment from a simple sauce of pineapple preserves and horseradish in this recipe. The brand of horseradish you use will determine the "heat" level of the sauce.
—Bernice Dean, Garland, Texas

1/4 teaspoon salt
1/4 teaspoon pepper
1 pork tenderloin (1 pound)
2 sprigs fresh rosemary
1/2 cup pineapple preserves
1 tablespoon prepared horseradish

Combine salt and pepper; rub over pork. Place in a 13-in. x 9-in. x 2-in. baking pan coated with nonstick cooking spray. Place one sprig of rosemary under the pork and one on top. Bake, uncovered, at 425° for 10 minutes.

Meanwhile, in a saucepan, heat preserves and horseradish until preserves are melted; stir until blended. Remove top rosemary sprig. Brush pork with 1/4 cup pineapple sauce. Bake 10-20 minutes longer or until a meat thermometer reads 160°. Let stand for 5 minutes before slicing. Serve with the remaining sauce. **Yield:** 4 servings.

Nutritional Analysis: One serving (3 ounces cooked pork with 2 tablespoons sauce) equals 242 calories, 4 g fat (1 g saturated fat), 67 mg cholesterol, 226 mg sodium, 29 g carbohydrate, trace fiber, 24 g protein.
Diabetic Exchanges: *3 lean meat, 2 fruit.*

Pork with Apples and Sweet Potatoes

(Pictured below)

Here's a meal-in-one that is quick, delicious and nutritious. The tenderloin is rubbed with a few simple seasonings...and baked apples and sweet potatoes round out the dinner perfectly.
—Linda Lacek, Winter Park, Florida

1 teaspoon salt
1/2 teaspoon ground cinnamon
1/2 teaspoon ground cardamom
1/4 teaspoon pepper
4-1/2 cups cubed peeled sweet potatoes (about 1-1/2 pounds)
4 teaspoons olive *or* canola oil, *divided*
2 pork tenderloins (3/4 pound *each*)
4 large Granny Smith *or* other tart apples, peeled and cored

In a small bowl, combine the salt, cinnamon, cardamom and pepper. Place sweet potatoes in a large bowl. Sprinkle with 1 teaspoon spice mixture and 3 teaspoons oil; toss to coat. Spread in a single layer in a 15-in. x 10-in. x 1-in. baking pan coated with nonstick cooking spray. Bake, uncovered, at 425° for 10 minutes.

Rub the remaining oil over pork; rub with remaining spice mixture. Place over the sweet potatoes. Bake for 15 minutes. Cut each apple into eight wedges. Turn pork; arrange apples around meat. Bake 15 minutes longer or until a meat thermometer reads 160°. **Yield:** 6 servings.

Nutritional Analysis: One serving equals 321 calories, 8 g fat (2 g saturated fat), 67 mg cholesterol, 452 mg sodium, 37 g carbohydrate, 5 g fiber, 26 g protein.
Diabetic Exchanges: *3 lean meat, 1-1/2 starch, 1 fruit.*

Spiced Pineapple Ham

A friend wanted a recipe for spiced pineapple but couldn't find one. So the two of us combined several recipes to come up with this sweet sauce.
—Betty Claycomb, Alverton, Pennsylvania

   1 cup unsweetened pineapple juice
1/2 teaspoon whole cloves
   1 cinnamon stick (3 inches)
   3 tablespoons brown sugar
   1 tablespoon cornstarch
   2 tablespoons cider vinegar
   1 cup unsweetened pineapple tidbits, drained
   6 boneless fully cooked lean ham steaks (4 ounces *each*)

In a saucepan, bring pineapple juice, cloves and cinnamon stick to a boil. Reduce heat; cook, uncovered, for 5 minutes. Strain juice, discarding cloves and cinnamon. Return juice to the pan. In a bowl, combine brown sugar and cornstarch; stir in vinegar until smooth. Stir into pineapple juice. Bring to a boil; cook and stir for 2 minutes or until thickened. Stir in pineapple; heat through.

In a large nonstick skillet, cook ham steaks until browned and heated through. Serve with the pineapple sauce. **Yield:** 6 servings.

Nutritional Analysis: *One serving (1 ham steak with 1/4 cup sauce) equals 185 calories, 4 g fat (1 g saturated fat), 58 mg cholesterol, 1,180 mg sodium, 17 g carbohydrate, trace fiber, 21 g protein.*
Diabetic Exchanges: *3 lean meat, 1 fruit.*

Pork Fried Rice for Two

My husband and I often make a meal of this appealing stir-fry. It's nicely seasoned and chock-full of vegetables.
—Laura Kittleson, Casselberry, Florida

1/8 teaspoon Chinese five-spice powder
   6 ounces boneless pork loin, cut into 1/4-inch cubes
1/2 teaspoon fennel seed, crushed
1-1/2 teaspoons canola oil, *divided*
   2 cups broccoli florets
   1 celery rib with leaves, sliced
1/2 cup shredded carrot
1/4 cup chopped green onions
1-1/2 cups cold cooked brown rice
   1 tablespoon reduced-sodium soy sauce
1/8 teaspoon pepper

Sprinkle five-spice powder over pork; toss to coat. In a large nonstick skillet or wok coated with nonstick cooking spray, stir-fry pork for 3 minutes or until browned. Remove and keep warm. Stir-fry fennel seed in 3/4 teaspoon oil for 30 seconds. Add broccoli, celery, carrot and onions; stir-fry for 3 minutes or until crisp-tender. Remove; keep warm.

Stir-fry the rice in remaining oil for 2 minutes. Stir in soy sauce and pepper. Return pork and vegetables to the pan; cook and stir until heated through. **Yield:** 2 servings.

Nutritional Analysis: *One serving (1-3/4 cups) equals 367 calories, 10 g fat (2 g saturated fat), 50 mg cholesterol, 417 mg sodium, 44 g carbohydrate, 5 g fiber, 26 g protein.*
Diabetic Exchanges: *2 lean meat, 2 starch, 2 vegetable, 1/2 fat.*

Apple-Topped Pork Chops

(Pictured above)

This tasty entree features pork, apples and honey. Everyone likes it, and I've given the recipe out many times. Sometimes I slice the apples into rings and place one on each chop when serving them.
—Helen Koehler, Marshalltown, Iowa

   4 boneless pork loin chops (4 ounces *each*)
   1 teaspoon canola oil
1/4 cup white wine *or* chicken broth
   2 medium tart apples, peeled and sliced
   1 tablespoon butter *or* stick margarine
1/2 cup plus 2 tablespoons unsweetened apple juice, *divided*
1/4 cup honey
   2 teaspoons cornstarch

In a nonstick skillet, brown pork chops on both sides in oil. Place in an 11-in. x 7-in. x 2-in. baking dish coated with nonstick cooking spray. Add wine or broth to the skillet, stirring to loosen browned bits. Pour over chops. Cover and bake at 350° for 20 minutes.

Meanwhile, in the same skillet, saute apples in butter for 3-4 minutes. Add 1/2 cup apple juice and honey; cook for 1-2 minutes. Spoon over chops. Bake, uncovered, for 5-10 minutes or until heated through. Remove chops and apples to a serving platter and keep warm, reserving pan juices.

In a saucepan, combine cornstarch and remaining apple juice until smooth; add reserved pan juices. Bring to a boil; cook and stir for 2 minutes or until thickened. Serve over pork and apples. **Yield:** 4 servings.

Nutritional Analysis: *One serving equals 338 calories, 11 g fat (5 g saturated fat), 71 mg cholesterol, 69 mg sodium, 32 g carbohydrate, 1 g fiber, 25 g protein.*
Diabetic Exchanges: *3 lean meat, 2 fruit, 1 fat.*

Fish & Seafood Fare

Fabulous fish dinners and sensational seafood entrees can add appetizing variety to any cook's healthy menu planning. You'll quickly get hooked on these from-the-sea favorites swimming in fantastic flavor!

Apple Halibut Kabobs (page 176)

Teriyaki Tuna Steaks

(Pictured at right)

After sampling some wonderful tuna at a Japanese restaurant, I decided to try my hand at coming up with the recipe. I was pleased with the results.
—Michelle Dennis, Clarks Hill, Indiana

  1/4 cup reduced-sodium soy sauce
    3 tablespoons brown sugar
    3 tablespoons olive *or* canola oil
    2 tablespoons white wine vinegar *or* cider vinegar
    2 tablespoons sherry *or* chicken broth
    2 tablespoons unsweetened pineapple juice
    2 garlic cloves, minced
1-1/2 teaspoons ground ginger *or* 2 tablespoons minced fresh gingerroot
    4 tuna steaks (6 ounces *each*)

In a bowl, combine the first eight ingredients; mix well. Remove 1/3 cup to a small bowl for basting; cover and refrigerate. Pour remaining marinade into a large resealable plastic bag; add tuna. Seal bag and turn to coat; refrigerate for up to 1 hour.

Coat grill rack with nonstick cooking spray before starting the grill. Drain and discard marinade. Grill tuna, uncovered, over medium heat for 5-6 minutes on each side or until fish flakes easily with a fork, basting frequently with reserved marinade. **Yield:** 4 servings.

Nutritional Analysis: One serving equals 338 calories, 9 g fat (1 g saturated fat), 99 mg cholesterol, 484 mg sodium, 9 g carbohydrate, trace fiber, 52 g protein.
Diabetic Exchanges: 5 lean meat, 1/2 starch.

Feta Tomato-Basil Fish

(Pictured at right)

I rely on my husband for the main ingredient in this fuss-free dish. He fills our freezer after his summer fishing trip.
—Alicia Szeszol, Lindenhurst, Illinois

  1/3 cup chopped onion
    1 garlic clove, minced
    2 teaspoons olive *or* canola oil
    1 can (14-1/2 ounces) Italian diced tomatoes, drained
1-1/2 teaspoons minced fresh basil *or* 1/2 teaspoon dried basil
    1 pound walleye, bass *or* other whitefish fillets
    4 ounces crumbled feta cheese

In a saucepan, saute onion and garlic in oil until tender. Add tomatoes and basil. Bring to a boil. Reduce heat; simmer, uncovered, for 5 minutes. Meanwhile, broil fish 4-6 in. from the heat for 5-6 minutes. Top each fillet with tomato mixture and cheese. Broil 5-7 minutes longer or until fish flakes easily with a fork. **Yield:** 4 servings.

Nutritional Analysis: One serving equals 295 calories, 10 g fat (5 g saturated fat), 172 mg cholesterol, 799 mg sodium, 11 g carbohydrate, 1 g fiber, 38 g protein.
Diabetic Exchanges: 5 very lean meat, 2 vegetable, 1 fat.

Salmon-Wrapped Asparagus

My inspiration for this deliciously different salmon dish came from a variety of Saturday morning cooking shows. Dinner guests always admire how pretty each fish bundle looks.
—Amy Clark, Chesapeake, Virginia

    2 pounds fresh asparagus, trimmed
1-1/2 pounds salmon fillets
1-1/2 cups water
  1/2 cup dry white wine *or* chicken broth
    1 tablespoon minced green onion
    1 tablespoon minced chives
    1 teaspoon salt
  1/2 teaspoon whole black peppercorns
MUSHROOM SAUCE:
  1/2 pound fresh mushrooms, sliced
  1/2 cup sliced green onions
    2 tablespoons butter *or* stick margarine
    1 teaspoon olive *or* canola oil
    2 tablespoons all-purpose flour
  1/2 teaspoon salt
  1/8 teaspoon pepper
    1 cup 2% milk
    1 tablespoon minced chives

In a large skillet, bring 1/2 in. of water to a boil; add asparagus spears. Reduce heat; cover and simmer for 2 minutes. Drain and immediately place asparagus in ice water; drain and pat dry. Cut salmon widthwise into 1/4-in.-thick slices. To form one bundle, place three to four slices cut side down, overlapping edges slightly; wrap around five to six asparagus spears. Secure with toothpicks. Repeat for remaining bundles.

In a large skillet, bring 1-1/2 cups water, wine or broth, onion, chives, salt and peppercorns to a boil. Using a spatula, carefully add bundles. Reduce heat; cover and simmer for 7-8 minutes or until fish flakes easily with a fork.

Meanwhile, for sauce, in a skillet, saute mushrooms and green onions in butter and oil until tender. Stir in flour, salt and pepper until blended. Gradually add milk. Bring to a boil; cook and stir for 2 minutes or until thickened. Add chives. Serve over bundles. **Yield:** 6 servings.

Nutritional Analysis: One serving (1 bundle with 1/3 cup sauce) equals 277 calories, 10 g fat (4 g saturated fat), 97 mg cholesterol, 710 mg sodium, 14 g carbohydrate, 4 g fiber, 29 g protein.
Diabetic Exchanges: 3-1/2 lean meat, 2 vegetable, 1 fat.

🍎 A Serving of Feta Facts

AMERICANS might tag it the "other white cheese", but in Greek cooking it is *the* white cheese.

While most people associate feta cheese with Greece, it originated in the Balkan countries. Feta was traditionally made with sheep or goat's milk, but is now also made with cow's milk.

Because it is soaked in brine, feta is often referred to as "pickled cheese".

Feta can be used in many recipes that require cheese. Add crumbled feta to pasta, rice, salads or omelets. Or serve feta with olives and salami on bread.

Mediterranean Seafood Stew

(Pictured above)

*Even though this dish is loaded with orange roughy,
shrimp and scallops, guests who say they
don't like seafood ask for the recipe.*
—*Virginia Anthony, Blowing Rock, North Carolina*

    1 medium onion, finely chopped
1-1/2 teaspoons minced garlic, *divided*
    1 tablespoon olive *or* canola oil
  1/2 pound plum tomatoes, seeded and diced
    1 teaspoon grated lemon peel
  1/4 teaspoon crushed red pepper flakes
    1 cup clam juice
  1/3 cup white wine *or* additional clam juice
    1 tablespoon tomato paste
  1/2 teaspoon salt
    1 pound orange roughy *or* red snapper fillets, cut
      into 1-inch cubes
    1 pound uncooked large shrimp, peeled and
      deveined
  1/2 pound sea scallops
  1/3 cup minced fresh parsley
  1/3 cup reduced-fat mayonnaise

In a Dutch oven or large saucepan, saute onion and 1/2 teaspoon garlic in oil until tender. Add the tomatoes, lemon peel
and pepper flakes; cook and stir for 2 minutes. Add the clam
juice, wine or additional clam juice, tomato paste and salt.
Bring to a boil. Reduce heat; cover and simmer for 10 minutes or until heated through.

Add the fish, shrimp, scallops and parsley. Cover and
cook for 8-10 minutes or until fish flakes easily with a fork,
the shrimp turn pink and scallops are opaque. Combine
mayonnaise and remaining garlic; dollop onto each serving.
Yield: 6 servings.

*Nutritional Analysis: One serving (1 cup stew with 2 tea-
spoons mayonnaise topping) equals 221 calories, 8 g fat (1 g saturated fat), 123 mg cholesterol, 607 mg sodium, 7 g carbohydrate,
1 g fiber, 28 g protein.*
Diabetic Exchanges: 4 very lean meat, 1 vegetable, 1 fat.

Italian Fish Fillets

*My husband and I resolved to eat healthier, so I was
pleased to find this quick recipe for fish fillets. I tried
it with cod and added a few twists of my own.
Italian salad dressing, diced tomatoes and
green pepper give the fish delicious flavor.*
—*Mindy Holliday, Westfield, Indiana*

    1 medium green *or* sweet yellow pepper,
      julienned
    1 small onion, julienned
  1/2 cup fat-free Italian salad dressing
  1/2 teaspoon Italian seasoning
    2 cans (14-1/2 ounces *each*) diced tomatoes,
      drained
1-1/2 pounds fresh *or* frozen cod fillets, thawed

In a large nonstick skillet, cook green pepper, onion, salad
dressing and Italian seasoning for 5 minutes or until vegetables are tender. Stir in the tomatoes; add fillets. Bring to
a boil. Reduce heat; cover and simmer for 10 minutes or until fish flakes easily with a fork. Serve with a slotted spoon.
Yield: 4 servings.

*Nutritional Analysis: One serving equals 216 calories, 2 g
fat (trace saturated fat), 74 mg cholesterol, 784 mg sodium, 17 g
carbohydrate, 4 g fiber, 33 g protein.*
Diabetic Exchanges: 4 lean meat, 3 vegetable.

Grilled Spiced Fish

*These moist flaky fillets provide a welcome change of
pace at summer cookouts. I pepper a savory herb rub
with cayenne, then work it into the fish. Even steak
lovers will be smacking their lips.*
—*Chris McBee, Xenia, Ohio*

4 red snapper *or* orange roughy fillets (6 ounces
   each)
1 tablespoon olive *or* canola oil
2 teaspoons paprika
1 teaspoon salt
1 teaspoon onion powder
1 teaspoon garlic powder
1/2 teaspoon cayenne pepper
1/4 teaspoon white pepper
1/4 teaspoon *each* dried oregano, basil and thyme

Brush fish with oil. In a small bowl, combine the seasonings;
sprinkle over fish and press into both sides. Cover and refrigerate for 30-60 minutes. Coat grill rack with nonstick
cooking spray before starting the grill. Grill fillets uncovered,
over medium heat for 3-4 minutes on each side or until
fish flakes easily with a fork. **Yield:** 4 servings.

*Nutritional Analysis: One serving (1 fillet) equals 154 calo-
ries, 5 g fat (1 g saturated fat), 34 mg cholesterol, 694 mg sodium, 1 g carbohydrate, trace fiber, 25 g protein.*
Diabetic Exchanges: 4 very lean meat, 1/2 fat.

Favorite Recipe Made Lighter

REELING in compliments is easy when you serve a rich mouth-watering entree like Creamy Halibut Enchiladas from Jennifer Rohde of Yuma, Arizona.

If your head is swimming with the idea of setting this savory main dish in front of your hungry bunch, but you'd like a lighter version, check out our Test Kitchen's Makeover Creamy Halibut Enchiladas.

Creamy Halibut Enchiladas

- 4 cups water
- 2 pounds halibut, cut into 1-inch cubes
- 2 packages (3 ounces *each*) cream cheese, softened
- 2/3 cup sour cream
- 3 tablespoons mayonnaise
- 2 cans (4 ounces *each*) chopped green chilies
- 1 can (4-1/4 ounces) chopped ripe olives, drained
- 4 green onions, chopped
- 1-1/2 teaspoons ground cumin
- 1/2 teaspoon salt
- 1/4 teaspoon pepper
- 8 flour tortillas (8 inches)
- 1-1/2 cups (6 ounces) shredded pepper Jack *or* Monterey Jack cheese
- 1/3 cup shredded Parmesan cheese
- 1-1/2 cups whipping cream
- 1/2 cup salsa

In a large saucepan, bring water to a boil. Carefully add fish; reduce heat. Cover and simmer for 5 minutes or until fish flakes easily with a fork; drain well. In a mixing bowl, combine the cream cheese, sour cream, mayonnaise, chilies, olives, onions, cumin, salt and pepper. Fold in fish.

Place 1/2 cup down the center of each tortilla; roll up. Place enchiladas in a greased 13-in. x 9-in. x 2-in. baking dish. Sprinkle with cheeses; drizzle with cream. Bake, uncovered, at 350° for 30-35 minutes or until bubbly. Serve with salsa. **Yield:** 8 servings.

Nutritional Analysis: One serving (1 enchilada with 1 tablespoon salsa) equals 720 calories, 49 g fat (25 g saturated fat), 159 mg cholesterol, 1,144 mg sodium, 33 g carbohydrate, 1 g fiber, 38 g protein.

Makeover Creamy Halibut Enchiladas

(Pictured at right)

- 4 cups water
- 2 pounds halibut, cut into 1-inch cubes
- 6 ounces reduced-fat cream cheese
- 2/3 cup fat-free sour cream
- 4 green onions, chopped
- 2 cans (4 ounces *each*) chopped green chilies
- 1 can (4-1/4 ounces) chopped ripe olives, drained
- 2 jalapeno peppers, seeded and chopped*
- 1-1/2 teaspoons ground cumin
- 8 flour tortillas (8 inches)
- 4-1/2 teaspoons all-purpose flour
- 1-1/2 cups fat-free half-and-half cream
- 1-1/4 cups (5 ounces) shredded reduced-fat Monterey Jack *or* part-skim mozzarella cheese
- 1/3 cup shredded Parmesan cheese
- 1/2 cup salsa

In a large saucepan, bring water to a boil. Carefully add fish; reduce heat. Cover and simmer for 5 minutes or until fish flakes easily with a fork; drain well. In a mixing bowl, combine the cream cheese, sour cream, onions, chilies, olives, jalapenos and cumin. Fold in fish.

Place generous 1/2 cup down center of each tortilla; roll up. Place enchiladas in a 13-in. x 9-in. x 2-in. baking dish coated with nonstick cooking spray. Combine flour and cream until smooth; pour over enchiladas. Cover and bake at 350° for 20-25 minutes or until heated through. Uncover; sprinkle with cheeses. Broil 4 in. from heat for 2 minutes or until lightly browned. Serve with salsa. **Yield:** 8 servings.

*Editor's Note: When cutting or seeding hot peppers, use rubber or plastic gloves to protect your hands. Avoid touching your face.

Nutritional Analysis: One serving (1 enchilada with 1 tablespoon salsa) equals 464 calories, 16 g fat (6 g saturated fat), 66 mg cholesterol, 948 mg sodium, 40 g carbohydrate, 1 g fiber, 39 g protein.

Diabetic Exchanges: 3 lean meat, 2 starch, 1 fat, 1/2 fat-free milk.

Island Spiced Salmon

(Pictured at right)

Try this tasty treatment for salmon. The mildly sweet and spicy rub is delicious on the moist fish and is a nice switch from traditional butter and lemon.
—Kathryn Samodell, Bullhead City, Arizona

2 tablespoons brown sugar
2 tablespoons chili powder
2 teaspoons ground cumin
1 teaspoon salt
1/2 teaspoon ground cinnamon
1 salmon fillet (2 pounds)

In a small bowl, combine the first five ingredients; mix well. Rub over flesh side of fillet; refrigerate for 30 minutes. Place skin side down in a 13-in. x 9-in. x 2-in. baking dish coated with nonstick cooking spray. Bake at 375° for 20-25 minutes or until fish flakes easily with a fork. **Yield:** 8 servings.

Nutritional Analysis: One serving (4 ounces cooked salmon) equals 229 calories, 13 g fat (3 g saturated fat), 67 mg cholesterol, 382 mg sodium, 5 g carbohydrate, 1 g fiber, 23 g protein.
Diabetic Exchanges: 3 lean meat, 1 fat.

Grilled Sole with Nectarines

(Pictured at right)

I found this recipe years ago and adapted it to suit my family's tastes. We enjoy the delicate herb flavor of this grilled fish.
—Mary Rhoden, Waldport, Oregon

4 sole fillets (6 ounces *each*)
2 medium nectarines *or* peaches, peeled and sliced
1/2 cup sliced green onions
1-1/2 teaspoons chopped fresh tarragon *or* 1/2 teaspoon dried tarragon
1/4 teaspoon salt
1/8 teaspoon pepper
1 teaspoon butter *or* stick margarine, melted

Place each fillet on a double thickness of heavy-duty foil (about 18 in. x 12 in.). Arrange nectarines around the fillets. Sprinkle with green onions, tarragon, salt, pepper and butter. Fold foil around fish and seal tightly. Grill, covered, over medium heat for 7-8 minutes or until fish flakes easily with a fork. **Yield:** 4 servings.

Nutritional Analysis: One serving equals 201 calories, 3 g fat (1 g saturated fat), 84 mg cholesterol, 296 mg sodium, 9 g carbohydrate, 1 g fiber, 33 g protein.
Diabetic Exchanges: 4 lean meat, 1/2 fruit.

Homemade Fish Fingers

Once you've tried these mouth-watering morsels, you'll never buy fish sticks again! Our Test Kitchen staff coated pieces of cod in a tasty Parmesan,
herb and bread crumb mixture that is sure to have folks asking for seconds.

1 pound frozen cod fillets, partially thawed
1/2 cup seasoned bread crumbs
2 tablespoons grated Parmesan cheese
1 tablespoon minced fresh parsley
1 teaspoon grated lemon peel
1/2 teaspoon paprika
1/2 teaspoon dried thyme
1/4 teaspoon garlic salt
1/2 cup 1% buttermilk
1/4 cup plus 2 tablespoons all-purpose flour

Cut fillets into 3/4-in. strips; set aside. In a shallow bowl, combine the bread crumbs, Parmesan cheese, parsley, lemon peel, paprika, thyme and garlic salt. Place buttermilk in another shallow bowl and flour in a third bowl. Coat fish strips with flour; dip into buttermilk, then coat with crumb mixture. Place on a baking sheet coated with nonstick cooking spray. Refrigerate for 20 minutes.
Bake at 425° for 15-20 minutes or until fish flakes easily with a fork. Let stand for 2 minutes before removing from baking sheets. **Yield:** 4 servings.

Nutritional Analysis: One serving equals 217 calories, 3 g fat (1 g saturated fat), 52 mg cholesterol, 382 mg sodium, 21 g carbohydrate, 1 g fiber, 25 g protein.
Diabetic Exchanges: 3 very lean meat, 1-1/2 starch.

Seafood Pasta Sauce

Something's fishy around my kitchen, and my husband isn't a bit suspicious! When I make low-fat, high-taste recipes like this one featuring two kinds of salsa, he's none the wiser.
—Michelle Van Aller, Bedford, Texas

3/4 cup chopped green onions
2 garlic cloves, minced
1 tablespoon butter *or* stick margarine
1/2 cup white wine *or* chicken broth
1-1/2 cups medium chunky salsa
1/2 cup mild salsa
1 can (4 ounces) chopped green chilies, drained
1 tablespoon lime juice
1 pound uncooked medium shrimp, peeled and deveined
1 pound bay scallops
Hot cooked pasta
5 tablespoons grated Parmesan cheese

In a large nonstick skillet, saute onions and garlic in butter until tender. Add wine or broth; simmer, uncovered, for 3 minutes. Stir in both types of salsa, chilies and lime juice; cook and stir until heated through. Add shrimp and scallops; cook for 4-5 minutes or until shrimp turn pink and scallops are opaque. Serve over pasta. Sprinkle with Parmesan cheese. **Yield:** 8 servings.

Nutritional Analysis: One serving (3/4 cup seafood sauce, calculated without pasta) equals 140 calories, 3 g fat (2 g saturated fat), 92 mg cholesterol, 728 mg sodium, 9 g carbohydrate, 1 g fiber, 18 g protein.
Diabetic Exchanges: 2 very lean meat, 2 vegetable, 1/2 fat.

Spicy Shrimp Wraps

(Pictured at right)

Here's a quick and easy recipe that's deliciously big on seafood flavor and the sunny sweetness of mango. Coated with tasty taco seasoning, the cooked shrimp are tucked inside a tortilla wrap, along with coleslaw and dressed-up bottled salsa.
—*Frankie Allen Mann, Warrior, Alabama*

  1 cup salsa
  1 medium ripe mango, peeled, pitted and diced
    or 2 medium ripe peaches, peeled and chopped
  1 tablespoon ketchup
  1 envelope reduced-sodium taco seasoning
  1 tablespoon olive *or* canola oil
  1 pound uncooked medium shrimp, peeled and
    deveined
  6 flour tortillas (8 inches), warmed
1-1/2 cups coleslaw mix
  6 tablespoons reduced-fat sour cream

In a small bowl, combine the salsa, mango and ketchup; set aside. In a large resealable plastic bag, combine taco seasoning and oil; add shrimp. Seal bag and shake to coat. In a nonstick skillet or wok, cook shrimp over medium-high heat for 2-3 minutes or until pink. Top tortillas with coleslaw mix, salsa mixture and shrimp. Fold bottom third of tortilla up over filling; fold sides over. Serve with sour cream. **Yield:** 6 servings.

Nutritional Analysis: One serving (1 wrap with 1 tablespoon sour cream) equals 292 calories, 8 g fat (2 g saturated fat), 97 mg cholesterol, 907 mg sodium, 40 g carbohydrate, 2 g fiber, 16 g protein.
Diabetic Exchanges: 2 starch, 2 very lean meat, 1 fat, 1/2 fruit.

Hearty Tuna Casserole

Here's a jazzed-up version of Mom's tuna casserole that's sure to be comfort food for the whole family!
—*Jan Heshelman, Bloomfield, Indiana*

  3 cups uncooked yolk-free wide noodles
  2 cans (6 ounces *each*) light water-packed tuna,
    drained and flaked
  1 cup shredded zucchini
3/4 cup reduced-fat sour cream
  1 celery rib with leaves, thinly sliced
1/4 cup chopped onion
1/4 cup reduced-fat mayonnaise
  2 teaspoons prepared mustard
1/2 teaspoon dried thyme
1/4 teaspoon salt
  1 cup (4 ounces) shredded part-skim mozzarella
    cheese
  1 medium tomato, chopped

Cook noodles according to package directions; drain. In a bowl, combine the noodles, tuna, zucchini, sour cream, celery, onion, mayonnaise, mustard, thyme and salt; mix well. Spoon half into a 2-qt. baking dish coated with nonstick cooking spray. Sprinkle with half of the cheese. Repeat layers. Top with tomato. Cover and bake at 350° for 30-35 minutes. Uncover; bake 5 minutes longer. **Yield:** 6 servings.

Nutritional Analysis: One serving (3/4 cup) equals 279 calories, 10 g fat (5 g saturated fat), 41 mg cholesterol, 516 mg sodium, 22 g carbohydrate, 2 g fiber, 25 g protein.
Diabetic Exchanges: 3 lean meat, 1 starch, 1 vegetable.

Stuffed Flounder

Everyone likes the flavorful mushroom and onion stuffing wrapped inside these tender fillets.
—*Joanne Matt, Howell, New Jersey*

  2 cups chopped fresh mushrooms
  1 cup chopped green onions
  2 garlic cloves, minced
1/2 teaspoon salt
1/4 teaspoon ground thyme
1/4 teaspoon pepper
  4 teaspoons olive *or* canola oil, *divided*
  3 tablespoons dry bread crumbs
  4 flounder *or* sole fillets (6 ounces *each*)
  2 teaspoons lemon juice
  2 teaspoons chopped fresh parsley

In a nonstick skillet, saute the mushrooms, onions, garlic, salt, thyme and pepper in 2 teaspoons oil until vegetables are tender. Stir in bread crumbs. Remove from the heat.

Sprinkle fillets with lemon juice; spread evenly with vegetable mixture and roll up. Place seam side down in an 11-in. x 7-in. x 2-in. baking dish coated with nonstick cooking spray. Brush with remaining oil. Bake at 400° for 20-25 minutes or until fish flakes easily with a fork. Sprinkle with parsley. **Yield:** 4 servings.

Nutritional Analysis: One fillet equals 235 calories, 7 g fat (1 g saturated fat), 82 mg cholesterol, 481 mg sodium, 8 g carbohydrate, 1 g fiber, 34 g protein.
Diabetic Exchanges: 5 very lean meat, 1 vegetable, 1 fat.

Shrimp-ly Delicious

SUCCULENT SHRIMP is one of America's favorite seafoods. Here are a few facts on the flavorful crustaceans:

- A serving of 3 ounces of cooked shrimp has about 80 calories, 1 gram of fat and 166 milligrams of cholesterol (higher than most seafood).
- Shrimp, raw or cooked, should feel firm and smell mildly sweet. Avoid any with spots or an ammonia odor.
- Cook shrimp quickly until the flesh turns opaque; whole shrimp should begin to curl. If shells are left on, they should turn pink. Shrimp cooked in the shell usually have more flavor than shrimp peeled before cooking. Overcooking makes shrimp dry and rubbery.
- Shrimp are graded by size and number per pound: colossal shrimp—10 or less per pound; jumbo—11-15; extra-large—16-20; large—21-30; medium—31-35; small—36-45; and miniature —about 100 per pound.

Oven-Fried Catfish

(Pictured at right)

This moist baked catfish gets its crisp golden coating from cornflake crumbs.
—Phyllis Early, Holland, Michigan

    4 catfish fillets (6 ounces *each*)
    1 cup cornflake crumbs
    1 teaspoon celery salt
    1/2 teaspoon onion powder
    1/4 teaspoon paprika
    1/8 teaspoon pepper
    1 egg white
    2 tablespoons fat-free milk

Pat fish dry with paper towels. In a shallow bowl, combine the next five ingredients. In another bowl, beat the egg white and milk. Dip fillets into egg white mixture, then coat with crumb mixture. Place in a 13-in. x 9-in. x 2-in. baking dish coated with nonstick cooking spray. Bake, uncovered, at 350° for 25-30 minutes or until fish flakes easily with a fork. **Yield:** 4 servings.

Nutritional Analysis: One fillet equals 319 calories, 13 g fat (3 g saturated fat), 80 mg cholesterol, 719 mg sodium, 19 g carbohydrate, trace fiber, 30 g protein.
***Diabetic Exchanges:** 4 lean meat, 1 starch.*

Halibut with Zesty Peach Salsa

(Pictured at right)

Our Test Kitchen came up with a fun way to serve halibut by marinating it in juices and brown sugar.

    1/3 cup orange juice
    2 tablespoons canola oil
    2 tablespoons lime juice
    1 tablespoon brown sugar
    2 teaspoons grated lime peel
    1 garlic clove, minced
    1/2 teaspoon salt
    4 halibut steaks (6 ounces *each*)
SALSA:
    2 cups chopped fresh *or* frozen peaches
    1/4 cup chopped sweet red pepper
    1/4 cup chopped red onion
    1 jalapeno pepper, seeded and chopped*
    2 tablespoons orange juice
    1 tablespoon minced fresh cilantro *or* parsley
    2 teaspoons lime juice
    1/4 teaspoon salt

In a bowl, combine the first seven ingredients; mix well. Remove 1/4 cup for basting; cover and refrigerate. Pour remaining marinade into a large resealable plastic bag; add the halibut. Seal bag and turn to coat; refrigerate for 2 hours. In a bowl, combine salsa ingredients; cover and refrigerate until serving.

If grilling the fish, coat grill rack with nonstick cooking spray before starting the grill. Drain and discard marinade from fish. Grill, uncovered, over medium heat or broil 4-6 in. from the heat for 4-6 minutes on each side or until fish flakes easily with a fork, basting occasionally with reserved marinade. Serve with peach salsa. **Yield:** 4 servings.

Editor's Note: When cutting or seeding hot peppers, use rubber or plastic gloves to protect your hands. Avoid touching your face.

Nutritional Analysis: One serving (1 halibut steak with 1/2 cup salsa) equals 269 calories, 6 g fat (1 g saturated fat), 54 mg cholesterol, 338 mg sodium, 15 g carbohydrate, 2 g fiber, 36 g protein.
***Diabetic Exchanges:** 5 very lean meat, 1 fruit, 1/2 fat.*

Cod Fillets in Spicy Tomato Sauce

A dash of cayenne pepper adds zip to this flaky fish dish that will have cod lovers hooked after just one bite.
—Joy Beck, Cincinnati, Ohio

    1 pound fresh *or* frozen cod fillets, thawed, cut into 4 pieces
    1 can (8 ounces) tomato sauce
    1 celery rib, sliced
    1/2 cup sliced fresh mushrooms
    3 tablespoons water
  4-1/2 teaspoons dried minced onion
    1/2 teaspoon chicken bouillon granules
    1/8 teaspoon pepper
Dash cayenne pepper

Arrange fish in a 1-1/2-qt. microwave-safe dish coated with nonstick cooking spray. In a bowl, combine the remaining ingredients; pour over fish. Cover and microwave on high for 10-12 minutes or until fish flakes easily with a fork, turning once. **Yield:** 4 servings.

Nutritional Analysis: One serving (1 piece of fish with 1/3 cup sauce) equals 120 calories, 1 g fat (trace saturated fat), 49 mg cholesterol, 558 mg sodium, 6 g carbohydrate, 1 g fiber, 21g protein.
***Diabetic Exchanges:** 3 very lean meat, 1 vegetable.*

Cajun Shrimp

I stir up a batch of these zippy shrimp to bring pizzazz to my table.
—Donna Thomason, El Paso, Texas

    2 teaspoons paprika
    1 teaspoon dried thyme
    1/2 teaspoon salt
    1/4 teaspoon ground nutmeg
    1/4 teaspoon garlic powder
    1/8 to 1/4 teaspoon cayenne pepper
    1 tablespoon olive *or* canola oil
    1 pound uncooked medium shrimp, peeled and deveined

In a large nonstick skillet, saute the paprika, thyme, salt, nutmeg, garlic powder and cayenne in oil for 30 seconds, stirring constantly. Add shrimp; saute for 2-3 minutes or until shrimp turn pink, stirring occasionally. **Yield:** 4 servings.

Nutritional Analysis: One serving equals 117 calories, 4 g fat (1 g saturated fat), 161 mg cholesterol, 479 mg sodium, 1 g carbohydrate, trace fiber, 18 g protein.
***Diabetic Exchanges:** 3 very lean meat, 1/2 fat.*

Jambalaya

(Pictured at right)

I'm happy to share the recipe for this quick-to-cook jambalaya. Unlike some versions, this one doesn't have to simmer for hours. Folks who like their food a bit spicy are sure to enjoy it. Jalapeno and cayenne pepper add some zip.
—Betty May, Topeka, Kansas,

1/2 pound boneless skinless chicken breasts, cut into 1-inch pieces
1 large onion, chopped
3/4 cup chopped green pepper
1 celery rib, chopped
2 jalapeno peppers, seeded and finely chopped*
2 garlic cloves, minced
1 tablespoon canola oil
2 cans (14-1/2 ounces *each*) diced tomatoes, undrained
1/2 cup water
1 teaspoon dried thyme
1/2 teaspoon salt
1/4 teaspoon pepper
1/8 to 1/4 teaspoon cayenne pepper
1 pound uncooked medium shrimp, peeled and deveined
2 cups cooked long grain rice

In a large Dutch oven or saucepan, saute the chicken, onion, green pepper, celery, jalapenos and garlic in oil until chicken is no longer pink. Add the tomatoes, water, thyme, salt, pepper and cayenne; bring to a boil. Reduce heat; cover and simmer for 15 minutes. Add shrimp; simmer 6-8 minutes longer or until shrimp turn pink. Stir in rice. **Yield:** 6 servings.

*Editor's Note: When cutting or seeding hot peppers, use rubber or plastic gloves to protect your hands. Avoid touching your face.

Nutritional Analysis: One serving (1-1/2 cups) equals 229 calories, 4 g fat (1 g saturated fat), 112 mg cholesterol, 502 mg sodium, 27 g carbohydrate, 4 g fiber, 21 g protein.
Diabetic Exchanges: 3 very lean meat, 2 vegetable, 1 starch, 1/2 fat.

Tropical Fish Fillets

(Pictured at right)

A hint of lime, cilantro, coriander and cumin seasons these fish fillets. My husband and I have four children and we all like fish. Sometimes you have to do a little something exotic with it to add some spice to life. This recipe does just that.
—Adrene Schmidt, Waldersee, Manitoba

4 fresh *or* frozen orange roughy *or* red snapper fillets (6 ounces *each*), thawed
3 tablespoons all-purpose flour
1 tablespoon butter *or* stick margarine
1/2 cup reduced-sodium chicken broth
2 tablespoons lime juice
1 tablespoon minced fresh cilantro *or* parsley
1 teaspoon grated lime peel

1/2 teaspoon ground coriander
1/4 teaspoon ground cumin

Coat fish fillets with flour. In a large nonstick skillet, melt butter. Add fillets; cook over medium-high heat for 3 minutes on each side or until fish flakes easily with a fork. Remove and keep warm. In the same skillet, add the remaining ingredients; cook for 2-3 minutes or until heated through, stirring constantly. Serve over fillets. **Yield:** 4 servings.

Nutritional Analysis: One serving (1 fillet with 2 tablespoons sauce) equals 170 calories, 4 g fat (2 g saturated fat), 42 mg cholesterol, 215 mg sodium, 6 g carbohydrate, trace fiber, 26 g protein.
Diabetic Exchanges: 4 very lean meat, 1/2 starch.

Scallops and Asparagus Stir-Fry

Savory scallops, crisp-tender asparagus and juicy cherry tomatoes blend together beautifully in this fresh-tasting stir-fry. Sesame oil and soy sauce delicately accent the colorful combo that's festive enough to serve when company comes.
—Lisa Lancaster, Tracy, California

3/4 pound fresh asparagus, trimmed and cut into 2-inch pieces
1 tablespoon cornstarch
3/4 cup chicken broth
1 teaspoon reduced-sodium soy sauce
3/4 pound sea scallops, halved
1 cup sliced fresh mushrooms
1 garlic clove, minced
2 teaspoons canola oil
1 cup halved cherry tomatoes
2 green onions, sliced
1 teaspoon sesame oil
1/8 teaspoon pepper
2 cups hot cooked rice

Place asparagus in a saucepan and cover with water; bring to a boil. Cook, uncovered, for 3-5 minutes or until crisp-tender; drain and set aside. In a small bowl, combine the cornstarch, broth and soy sauce until smooth; set aside.

In a large nonstick skillet or wok, stir-fry scallops, mushrooms and garlic in canola oil until scallops are opaque and mushrooms are tender. Stir cornstarch mixture; add to skillet. Bring to a boil; cook and stir until sauce is thickened. Add the tomatoes, onions, sesame oil, pepper and reserved asparagus; heat through. Serve over rice. **Yield:** 4 servings.

Nutritional Analysis: One serving (1 cup stir-fry mixture with 1/2 cup rice) equals 215 calories, 5 g fat (1 g saturated fat), 14 mg cholesterol, 314 mg sodium, 30 g carbohydrate, 2 g fiber, 11 g protein.
Diabetic Exchanges: 1-1/2 starch, 1 vegetable, 1 lean meat, 1/2 fat.

Spicy Shrimp Fettuccine

This dressed-up seafood entree makes a tasty impression on family and friends. Nicely spiced shrimp, tomatoes and spinach top off the saucy fettuccine.
—*Judy Farrar, Richmond, Virginia*

    8 ounces uncooked fettuccine
    1 medium onion, chopped
    1 garlic clove, minced
    1 tablespoon olive *or* canola oil
    4 plum tomatoes, chopped
    1 cup chicken broth
    2 cups coarsely chopped fresh spinach
  3/4 pound cooked medium shrimp, peeled and deveined
    2 tablespoons minced fresh parsley
    1 tablespoon balsamic vinegar
    1 tablespoon butter *or* stick margarine
  1/2 teaspoon salt
  1/4 teaspoon pepper
  1/8 teaspoon cayenne pepper
    2 ounces feta cheese, crumbled

Cook fettuccine according to package directions. Meanwhile, in a large nonstick skillet, saute onion and garlic in oil until tender. Add tomatoes and broth. Bring to a boil. Reduce heat; simmer, uncovered, for 3 minutes. Add the spinach, shrimp, parsley and vinegar. Simmer, uncovered, for 2 minutes or until shrimp is heated through. Stir in the butter, salt, pepper and cayenne. Drain fettuccine; top with shrimp mixture and feta cheese. **Yield:** 4 servings.

Nutritional Analysis: One serving (1 cup shrimp mixture with 1 cup fettuccine) equals 419 calories, 12 g fat (5 g saturated fat), 150 mg cholesterol, 861 mg sodium, 49 g carbohydrate, 4 g fiber, 28 g protein.
Diabetic Exchanges: 3 lean meat, 2-1/2 starch, 1 vegetable, 1 fat.

Skillet Sole

My fish stories have a delicious ending when I have these fillets simmering in the skillet. The mild-tasting fish is perfectly seasoned by the tomato juice, green pepper, onion and herbs.
—*Marceil Conley, Warsaw, Indiana*

    1 cup chopped onion
  1/3 cup chopped green pepper
    1 cup tomato juice
    1 tablespoon dried parsley flakes
    1 teaspoon salt
    1 teaspoon dried oregano
    1 pound sole *or* flounder fillets

In a large nonstick skillet coated with nonstick cooking spray, saute onion and green pepper until tender. Stir in the tomato juice, parsley, salt and oregano. Cook for 5 minutes or until heated through. Add fillets. Cover and cook over medium heat for 12-15 minutes or until fish flakes easily with a fork. **Yield:** 4 servings.

Nutritional Analysis: One serving equals 136 calories, 1 g fat (trace saturated fat), 54 mg cholesterol, 896 mg sodium, 7 g carbohydrate, 1 g fiber, 23 g protein.
Diabetic Exchanges: 3 very lean meat, 1 vegetable.

Apple Halibut Kabobs

(Pictured on page 163)

I'm very glad I tried this recipe. The apple and halibut flavors complement one another so well.
—*Marilyn Rodriguez, Fairbanks, Alaska*

  1/2 cup dry white wine *or* unsweetened apple juice
    2 tablespoons lime juice
    2 tablespoons olive *or* canola oil
    2 tablespoons diced onion
    1 teaspoon salt
  1/2 teaspoon dried thyme
  1/4 teaspoon pepper
 1-1/2 pounds halibut, cut into 1-inch cubes
    1 small red onion, cut into 1-inch pieces
    1 medium Golden Delicious apple, cut into 1-inch pieces
    1 medium sweet red pepper, cut into 1-inch pieces

In a bowl, combine the first seven ingredients; mix well. Pour half into a large resealable plastic bag; add halibut. Seal bag and turn to coat. Pour remaining marinade into another large resealable plastic bag; add the onion, apple and red pepper. Seal bag and turn to coat. Refrigerate fish and apple mixture for 4-6 hours, turning occasionally.

If grilling the kabobs, coat grill rack with nonstick cooking spray before starting the grill. Drain fish, discarding marinade. Drain fruit and vegetables, reserving marinade for basting. On eight metal or soaked wooden skewers, alternately thread fish, onion, apple and red pepper. Grill, covered, over medium heat or broil 4-6 in. from the heat for 2-3 minutes on each side or until fish flakes easily with a fork, and fruit and vegetables are tender, turning once. Baste frequently with reserved marinade. **Yield:** 4 servings.

Nutritional Analysis: One serving (2 kabobs) equals 241 calories, 6 g fat (1 g saturated fat), 54 mg cholesterol, 240 mg sodium, 9 g carbohydrate, 1 g fiber, 36 g protein.
Diabetic Exchanges: 5 very lean meat, 1 vegetable.

Seared Salmon with Balsamic Sauce

A friend gave me this simple and delicious recipe, which I've passed on to other fish fans.
—*Trish Horton, Colorado Springs, Colorado*

    4 salmon fillets (4 ounces *each*)
  1/2 teaspoon salt

1/4 teaspoon pepper
　2 teaspoons canola oil
　1/4 cup water
　1/4 cup balsamic vinegar
4-1/2 teaspoons lemon juice
　4 teaspoons brown sugar

Sprinkle both sides of fillets with salt and pepper. In a large nonstick skillet, cook salmon in oil over medium heat for 10-15 minutes or until fish flakes easily with a fork, turning once. Remove and keep warm. Combine the water, vinegar, lemon juice and brown sugar; pour into skillet. Bring to a boil; cook until liquid is reduced to about 1/3 cup. Serve over salmon. **Yield:** 4 servings.

Nutritional Analysis: One serving (one fillet with 2 table-spoons sauce) equals 257 calories, 15 g fat (3 g saturated fat), 67 mg cholesterol, 366 mg sodium, 7 g carbohydrate, trace fiber, 23 g protein.
　Diabetic Exchanges: 3 lean meat, 1 fat, 1/2 starch.

Shrimp with Snow Peas

(Pictured below)

This medley of shrimp, crisp snow peas and other fresh veggies is mildly seasoned with lemon and dill.
—Ruth Andrewson, Peck, Idaho

　2 tablespoons cornstarch
　1 teaspoon sugar

　1 teaspoon chicken bouillon granules
　1 teaspoon dill weed
　1/2 teaspoon salt
　1/2 teaspoon grated lemon peel
　1/8 teaspoon pepper
　1 cup water
　3 tablespoons lemon juice
　1 pound uncooked medium shrimp, peeled and deveined
　2 cups sliced fresh mushrooms
1-1/2 cups sliced celery
　1 medium sweet yellow *or* red pepper, julienned
　1/4 cup thinly sliced green onions
　1 tablespoon olive *or* canola oil
　6 ounces fresh *or* frozen snow peas, thawed
　2 cups cooked rice

In a small bowl, combine the cornstarch, sugar, bouillon, dill, salt, lemon peel and pepper. Stir in water and lemon juice until blended; set aside.
　In a large nonstick skillet or wok, stir-fry the shrimp, mushrooms, celery, yellow pepper and onions in oil for 5 minutes. Add the peas; stir-fry 1-2 minutes longer or until crisp-tender. Stir bouillon mixture; add to skillet. Bring to a boil; cook and stir for 2 minutes or until thickened. Serve with rice. **Yield:** 4 servings.

Nutritional Analysis: One serving (1-3/4 cups stir-fry mixture with 1/2 cup rice) equals 322 calories, 6 g fat (1 g saturated fat), 173 mg cholesterol, 797 mg sodium, 38 g carbohydrate, 4 g fiber, 28 g protein.
　Diabetic Exchanges: 3 very lean meat, 2 starch, 2 vegetable, 1/2 fat.

Tuna Noodle Casserole

Families are sure to love the creamy texture and comforting taste of this traditional tuna casserole. Plus, it goes together in a jiffy.
—*Ruby Wells, Cynthiana, Kentucky*

1 can (10-3/4 ounces) reduced-fat reduced-sodium condensed cream of celery soup, undiluted
1/2 cup fat-free milk
2 cups cooked yolk-free wide noodles
1 cup frozen peas, thawed
1 can (6 ounces) light water-packed tuna, drained and flaked
1 jar (2 ounces) diced pimientos, drained
2 tablespoons dry bread crumbs
1 tablespoon butter *or* stick margarine, melted

In a large bowl, combine soup and milk until smooth. Add the noodles, peas, tuna and pimientos; mix well. Pour into a 1-1/2-qt. baking dish coated with nonstick cooking spray. Bake, uncovered, at 400° for 25 minutes. Toss bread crumbs and butter; sprinkle over the top. Bake 5 minutes longer or until golden brown. **Yield:** 4 servings.

Nutritional Analysis: One serving (1 cup) equals 255 calories, 6 g fat (3 g saturated fat), 29 mg cholesterol, 582 mg sodium, 31 g carbohydrate, 4 g fiber, 18 g protein.
Diabetic Exchanges: 2 starch, 2 lean meat.

Firecracker Salmon Steaks

(Pictured below)

Red pepper flakes and cayenne provide the fiery flavor that gives these salmon steaks their name. Basting the fish with the zippy sauce while grilling creates a glossy glaze.
—*Phyllis Schmalz, Kansas City, Kansas*

1/4 cup balsamic vinegar
1/4 cup chili sauce
1/4 cup packed brown sugar
3 garlic cloves, minced
2 teaspoons minced fresh parsley
1/4 teaspoon ground ginger *or* 1 teaspoon minced fresh gingerroot
1/4 to 1/2 teaspoon cayenne pepper
1/4 to 1/2 teaspoon crushed red pepper flakes, optional
4 salmon steaks (6 ounces *each*)

In a small bowl, combine the first eight ingredients. If grilling the salmon, coat grill rack with nonstick cooking spray before starting the grill. Grill salmon, uncovered, over medium heat or broil 4-6 in. from the heat for 4-5 minutes on each side or until fish flakes easily with a fork, brushing occasionally with sauce. **Yield:** 4 servings.

Nutritional Analysis: One serving equals 373 calories, 17 g fat (4 g saturated fat), 106 mg cholesterol, 565 mg sodium, 22 g carbohydrate, trace fiber, 32 g protein.
Diabetic Exchanges: 5 lean meat, 1-1/2 starch.

Peppery Shrimp and Rice

This recipe has evolved over the years to satisfy my husband's yearning for shrimp over rice, which he enjoyed while growing up in Louisiana. Chili sauce and red pepper flakes give a Cajun kick to this pretty, palatable dish.
—*Cynthia Schaible Boyll, Loveland, Ohio*

2 celery ribs, finely chopped
1 medium onion, chopped
1 garlic clove, minced
1 tablespoon olive *or* canola oil
1 small green pepper, chopped
1 small sweet red pepper, chopped
1 can (15 ounces) tomato sauce
1/2 cup sherry *or* chicken broth
1 tablespoon chili sauce
2 teaspoons sugar
2 teaspoons dried basil
1 teaspoon dried oregano
1/2 teaspoon crushed red pepper flakes, optional
3/4 pound cooked medium shrimp, peeled and deveined
4 cups hot cooked rice

In a large nonstick skillet, saute the celery, onion and garlic in oil for 3 minutes. Add peppers; cook 3 minutes longer. Stir in tomato sauce, sherry or broth, chili sauce, sugar, basil, oregano and pepper flakes if desired. Bring to a boil. Reduce heat; simmer, uncovered, for 15-20 minutes or until vegetables are tender. Add shrimp; heat through. Serve over rice. **Yield:** 4 servings.

Nutritional Analysis: One serving (1-1/4 cups shrimp mixture with 1 cup rice) equals 428 calories, 6 g fat (1 g saturated fat), 129 mg cholesterol, 913 mg sodium, 65 g carbohydrate, 5 g fiber, 24 g protein.
Diabetic Exchanges: 3 starch, 3 lean meat, 1 vegetable.

Meatless Main Dishes

You won't find any meat in these main dishes
...but you won't miss it either. This hearty
vegetarian fare is so delightfully satisfying,
even your most ardent meat-and-potatoes
lovers will give it rave reviews.

Sweet Pepper Burritos (page 182)

Great Grain Burgers

(Pictured above)

I've experimented with many combinations of ingredients to make a good meatless burger...and this is our favorite. These patties cook up golden brown and crispy and make delicious sandwiches.
—*Pat Whitaker, Lebanon, Oregon*

1/2 cup uncooked brown rice
1/2 cup uncooked bulgur*
 1 tablespoon salt-free seasoning blend
1/4 teaspoon poultry seasoning
 2 cups water
 2 cups finely chopped fresh mushrooms
3/4 cup old-fashioned oats
 1 cup (4 ounces) shredded part-skim mozzarella cheese
1/4 cup shredded reduced-fat cheddar cheese
1/3 cup finely chopped onion
1/2 cup fat-free cottage cheese
1/4 cup egg substitute
 2 tablespoons minced fresh parsley
 1 teaspoon salt
1/2 teaspoon dried basil
1/8 teaspoon celery seed
 3 teaspoons canola oil, *divided*
 12 sandwich rolls, optional
Lettuce leaves and tomato slices, optional

In a saucepan, combine the first five ingredients; bring to a boil. Reduce heat; cover and simmer for 30 minutes or until rice is tender. Remove from the heat; cool completely. Refrigerate.

In a large bowl, combine the mushrooms, oats, mozzarella cheese, cheddar cheese and onion. In a blender or food processor, process cottage cheese and egg substitute until smooth. Add to the mushroom mixture. Stir in the parsley, salt, basil, celery seed and chilled rice mixture. Shape 1/2 cupfuls into patties. In a nonstick skillet, cook four patties in 1 teaspoon of oil for 5 minutes on each side or until lightly browned and crisp. Repeat with remaining patties and oil. Serve on rolls with lettuce and tomato if desired. **Yield:** 12 servings.

*Editor's Note: Look for bulgur in the cereal, rice or organic food aisle of your grocery store.

Nutritional Analysis: One cooked patty equals 126 calories, 4 g fat (2 g saturated fat), 8 mg cholesterol, 296 mg sodium, 15 g carbohydrate, 2 g fiber, 7 g protein.
Diabetic Exchanges: 1 starch, 1 lean meat.

Roasted Veggie Wraps

Give roasted veggies an Italian accent with salad dressing mix and shredded mozzarella, then fold them into flour tortillas. My husband and I really enjoy the assortment of vegetables in these handheld sandwiches. They make a great light lunch.
—*Jeanette Simec, Ottawa, Illinois*

 1 envelope Parmesan Italian salad dressing mix
1/4 cup water
1/4 cup red wine vinegar *or* cider vinegar
 2 tablespoons olive *or* canola oil
 1 medium sweet red pepper, sliced
 1 cup julienned carrots
 1 cup quartered fresh mushrooms
 1 cup broccoli florets
 1 medium onion, sliced and separated into rings
 1 medium yellow summer squash, sliced
 6 flour tortillas (8 inches)
1-1/2 cups (6 ounces) shredded part-skim mozzarella cheese
Salsa, optional

In a jar with a tight-fitting lid, combine the dressing mix, water, vinegar and oil; shake well. Place vegetables in a bowl; drizzle with dressing and toss to coat. Spread vegetables in two 15-in. x 10-in. x 1-in. baking pans coated with nonstick spray. Bake, uncovered, at 425° for 20-25 minutes or until tender, stirring occasionally.

Spoon about 3/4 cup roasted vegetables off center on each tortilla; sprinkle each with 1/4 cup cheese. Place on a baking sheet. Broil 4-6 in. from the heat for 2 minutes or until the cheese is melted. Fold the sides and one end of tortilla over filling and roll up. Serve with salsa if desired. **Yield:** 6 servings.

Nutritional Analysis: One serving equals 299 calories, 12 g fat (4 g saturated fat), 16 mg cholesterol, 849 mg sodium, 35 g carbohydrate, 2 g fiber, 13 g protein.
Diabetic Exchanges: 2 vegetable, 1-1/2 starch, 1-1/2 fat, 1 lean meat.

Barley Vegetable Stew

This hearty barley stew is sure to take the edge off cool-weather days. Sometimes I substitute millet for the barley. I pre-toast it in a skillet over medium heat, just until it starts to pop. It adds a nice nutty flavor.
—*Barbara Lane, Waupaca, Wisconsin*

 1 large onion, chopped
 2 garlic cloves, minced
 4 teaspoons olive *or* canola oil
 1 large carrot, chopped

1 small butternut squash, peeled and cubed
  (about 3 cups)
1 medium sweet potato, peeled and cubed
1/2 cup chopped sweet red pepper
5 cups chicken *or* vegetable broth
1/2 cup quick-cooking barley
1/2 teaspoon dried thyme
1/4 teaspoon pepper
1 large tomato, seeded and chopped

In a Dutch oven, saute onion and garlic in oil. Add the carrot, squash, sweet potato and red pepper. Saute 5 minutes longer. Stir in the broth, barley, thyme and pepper. Bring to a boil. Reduce heat; cover and simmer for 10 minutes or until barley is tender. Add the tomato; heat through. **Yield:** 9 servings.

Nutritional Analysis: One serving (1 cup) equals 121 calories, 3 g fat (trace saturated fat), 0 cholesterol, 532 mg sodium, 23 g carbohydrate, 5 g fiber, 4 g protein.
Diabetic Exchanges: 1 starch, 1 vegetable, 1/2 fat.

Fettuccine with Blue Cheese

This fabulous fettuccine is extra cheesy and nicely seasoned with herbs. No one would guess it's lower in fat than the traditionally rich and creamy Italian restaurant specialty.
—Phyllis Ciardo, Albany, California

2 eggs
4 cups (32 ounces) fat-free cottage cheese
1/2 cup egg substitute
6 ounces blue cheese, crumbled
1/4 cup all-purpose flour
1 tablespoon minced fresh parsley
2 garlic cloves, minced
2 teaspoons dried thyme
1/4 teaspoon salt
1/8 teaspoon cayenne pepper
8 ounces fettuccine, cooked and drained
Paprika

In a large mixing bowl, beat the first 10 ingredients on low speed for 2 minutes or until blended. Fold in fettuccine. Transfer to a 13-in. x 9-in. x 2-in. baking dish coated with nonstick cooking spray; sprinkle with paprika. Bake, uncovered, at 325° for 40-45 minutes or until a knife inserted near the center comes out clean. Let stand for 10 minutes before serving. **Yield:** 8 servings.

🍎 Eggplant Pointers

THE NEXT TIME you prepare a pan of lasagna, try substituting eggplant slices for the lasagna noodles. (I slice the eggplant lengthwise.) If it's tender, there's no need to peel it.

And instead of adding meat to my spaghetti sauce, I've found cubed eggplant is a tasty twist.
—Buddy Samuels, Concordia, Missouri

Nutritional Analysis: One serving equals 298 calories, 8 g fat (5 g saturated fat), 79 mg cholesterol, 789 mg sodium, 29 g carbohydrate, 1 g fiber, 27 g protein.
Diabetic Exchanges: 3 lean meat, 2 starch.

Zippy Bean Stew

(Pictured below)

This bean stew is a staple for my co-workers and me once the weather turns cool. Although this is a low-fat dish, it definitely doesn't taste like it!
—Debbie Matthews, Bluefield, West Virginia

1 can (14-1/2 ounces) reduced-sodium vegetable
  or chicken broth
1 can (16 ounces) kidney beans, rinsed and
  drained
1 can (15 ounces) pinto beans, rinsed and
  drained
1 can (14-1/2 ounces) diced tomatoes and green
  chilies
1 can (4 ounces) chopped green chilies,
  undrained
1 package (10 ounces) frozen corn, thawed
3 cups water
1 large onion, chopped
2 medium carrots, sliced
2 garlic cloves, minced
2 teaspoons chili powder

Combine all ingredients in a slow cooker. Cover and cook on high for 4-5 hours or until heated through and flavors are blended. **Yield:** 6 servings.

Nutritional Analysis: One serving (1-1/2 cups) equals 218 calories, 1 g fat (trace saturated fat), 0 cholesterol, 964 mg sodium, 44 g carbohydrate, 10 g fiber, 11 g protein.
Diabetic Exchanges: 2 starch, 2 vegetable, 1 very lean meat.

Sweet Pepper Burritos

(Pictured below and on page 179)

Diners meet up with plenty of flavor when they dig into this meatless mainstay that's bursting with cheese, rice, onion and peppers. These burritos are a fun change of pace from traditional sandwiches.
—Marian Platt, Sequim, Washington

  1 medium onion, chopped
  1 tablespoon canola oil
  2 medium sweet red peppers, diced
  1 medium sweet yellow pepper, diced
  1 medium green pepper, diced
  2 teaspoons ground cumin
  2 cups cooked brown rice
1-1/2 cups (6 ounces) shredded reduced-fat cheddar
    cheese
  3 ounces fat-free cream cheese, cubed
  1/2 teaspoon salt
  1/2 teaspoon pepper
  6 flour tortillas (10 inches)
Salsa, optional

In a large nonstick skillet, saute onion in oil for 2 minutes. Add the peppers; saute for 5 minutes or until crisp-tender. Sprinkle with cumin; saute 1 minute longer. Stir in the rice, cheeses, salt and pepper; mix well.

Spoon about 2/3 cup of filling off center on each tortilla; fold sides and ends over filling and roll up. Place seam side down in a 13-in. x 9-in. x 2-in. baking dish coated with nonstick cooking spray. Cover and bake at 425° for 10-15 minutes or until heated through. Let stand for 5 minutes; serve with salsa if desired. **Yield:** 6 servings.

Nutritional Analysis: One serving (1 burrito, calculated without salsa) equals 429 calories, 13 g fat (5 g saturated fat), 21 mg cholesterol, 671 mg sodium, 54 g carbohydrate, 9 g fiber, 18 g protein.
Diabetic Exchanges: 3 starch, 2 vegetable, 2 fat, 1 lean meat.

Three-Cheese Rice Lasagna

Fans of traditional lasagna are sure to be intrigued by this tasty twist—a rice-based version. I discovered this recipe in a weight-loss class, and my family loves it. It has all the flavor of classic lasagna made with noodles with only a fraction of the fat.
—Gwen Cantwell, Sharon, Wisconsin

1 jar (14 ounces) meatless spaghetti sauce
1 jar (4-1/2 ounces) sliced mushrooms, drained
1 cup (8 ounces) 1% cottage cheese
1 cup (4 ounces) shredded part-skim mozzarella
    cheese
1 egg white
3 cups cooked long grain rice
2 tablespoons grated Parmesan cheese

In a small bowl, combine spaghetti sauce and mushrooms; set aside. In another bowl, combine the cottage cheese, mozzarella cheese and egg white; mix well.

In a microwave-safe 8-in. square baking dish coated with nonstick cooking spray, layer a third of the sauce, half of the rice and half of the cottage cheese mixture; repeat layers. Top with the remaining sauce. Microwave, uncovered, on high for 5 minutes. Microwave at 50% power for 10-15 minutes or until heated through. Sprinkle with Parmesan cheese. Let stand for 5 minutes before serving. **Yield:** 6 servings.

Editor's Note: This recipe was tested in an 850-watt microwave.

Nutritional Analysis: One serving (1 cup) equals 238 calories, 6 g fat (3 g saturated fat), 14 mg cholesterol, 664 mg sodium, 31 g carbohydrate, 2 g fiber, 15 g protein.
Diabetic Exchanges: 2 starch, 1 lean meat, 1/2 fat.

Egg Foo Yong with Sauce

I'm trying to cut back on meat and have to watch my cholesterol, so I eliminated the meat in this recipe and used egg substitute.
—Rochelle Higgins, Fredericksburg, Virginia

    4 teaspoons cornstarch
    1 tablespoon sugar
  1/2 teaspoon ground ginger *or* 2 teaspoons grated
      fresh gingerroot
    1 cup reduced-sodium chicken *or* vegetable
      broth
    2 tablespoons reduced-sodium soy sauce
    2 tablespoons sherry *or* apple juice
EGG FOO YONG:
1-1/2 cups egg substitute
  1/4 cup chopped green onions
    2 cups canned bean sprouts, rinsed and drained
    1 can (8 ounces) water chestnuts, drained and
      chopped
    1 can (4 ounces) mushroom stems and pieces,
      drained
  1/4 teaspoon salt
  1/8 teaspoon Chinese five spice
    2 tablespoons canola oil

In a small saucepan, combine the cornstarch, sugar and ginger. Stir in broth until smooth. Add soy sauce and sherry or apple juice. Bring to a boil; cook and stir for 2-3 minutes or until thickened. Remove from the heat; set aside.

In a bowl, combine egg substitute and onions; let stand for 10 minutes. Add bean sprouts, water chestnuts, mushrooms, salt and Chinese five spice; mix well. In a nonstick skillet, heat the oil. Drop batter by 1/4 cupfuls into oil. Cook until golden brown, about 2 to 2-1/2 minutes on each side. Serve with sauce. **Yield:** 4 servings.

Nutritional Analysis: One serving (3 patties and 1/4 cup sauce) equals 209 calories, 10 g fat (1 g saturated fat), 1 mg cholesterol, 955 mg sodium, 14 g carbohydrate, 3 g fiber, 14 g protein.
Diabetic Exchanges: 2 lean meat, 1 vegetable, 1 fat, 1/2 starch.

Ziti Alfredo with Vegetables

A creamy dressing, lots of flavor and an unexpected hint of nutmeg make this hearty pasta dish so delicious I can't resist fixing it often.
—Emma Magielda, Amsterdam, New York

   1 **medium onion, chopped**
   2 **garlic cloves, minced**
   2 **teaspoons olive** *or* **canola oil**
   8 **ounces uncooked ziti** *or* **other small tube pasta**
   2 **tablespoons butter** *or* **stick margarine**
   3 **tablespoons all-purpose flour**
   1 **cup fat-free milk**
1-1/2 **cups fat-free half-and-half cream**
   1 **cup shredded Parmesan cheese**
   2 **teaspoons Italian seasoning**
1/4 **teaspoon salt**
Dash white pepper
Dash ground nutmeg
   1 **can (14-1/2 ounces) Italian diced tomatoes, drained**
   1 **package (10 ounces) frozen chopped spinach, thawed and squeezed dry**

In a small saucepan, saute onion and garlic in oil until tender; set aside. Cook pasta according to package directions. Meanwhile, in a large saucepan, melt butter; stir in flour until smooth. Reduce heat; slowly add milk. Stir in cream; bring to a boil over medium-low heat. Cook and stir for 2 minutes or until thickened.

Reduce heat; add the Parmesan, Italian seasoning, salt, pepper and nutmeg. Stir until cheese is melted. Add the tomatoes, spinach and onion mixture; heat through. Drain pasta; toss with vegetable mixture. **Yield:** 8 servings.

Nutritional Analysis: One serving (1 cup) equals 264 calories, 8 g fat (4 g saturated fat), 16 mg cholesterol, 488 mg sodium, 35 g carbohydrate, 3 g fiber, 13 g protein.
Diabetic Exchanges: 1-1/2 starch, 1-1/2 fat, 1 vegetable, 1/2 fat-free milk.

Tomato-Mushroom Bow Tie Pasta

(Pictured above)

With fresh mushrooms, plum tomatoes and herbs to spice up its flavor, this dish tastes like summertime to me. Chock-full of garden goodness, the chunky sauce cooks up quickly, too.
—Jacqueline Graves, Lawrenceville, Georgia

   8 **ounces uncooked bow tie pasta**
1/2 **pound fresh mushrooms, sliced**
1/2 **cup sliced green onions**
   2 **garlic cloves, minced**
   1 **tablespoon butter** *or* **stick margarine**
   1 **tablespoon olive** *or* **canola oil**
   2 **pounds plum tomatoes, peeled, seeded and chopped**
1/4 **cup minced fresh basil** *or* **4 teaspoons dried basil**
   2 **tablespoons minced fresh parsley**
1/2 **teaspoon salt**
1/2 **teaspoon pepper**
1/4 **cup shredded Parmesan cheese**

Cook pasta according to package directions. Meanwhile, in a large nonstick skillet, saute the mushrooms, onions and garlic in butter and oil for 5 minutes or until tender. Add tomatoes; cook, uncovered, over medium heat for 10 minutes or until tender, stirring occasionally. Stir in the basil, parsley, salt and pepper; cook 2-3 minutes longer. Drain pasta; top with tomato mixture and Parmesan cheese. **Yield:** 4 servings.

Nutritional Analysis: One serving (1 cup pasta with 3/4 cup sauce and 1 tablespoon cheese) equals 358 calories, 10 g fat (4 g saturated fat), 13 mg cholesterol, 469 mg sodium, 56 g carbohydrate, 6 g fiber, 14 g protein.
Diabetic Exchanges: 3 vegetable, 2-1/2 starch, 1 lean meat, 1 fat.

Red Beans and Rice

I'm originally from Honduras, where beans are served in different variations for breakfast, lunch and dinner. This bean and rice dish has been enjoyed by my family for generations. It's not spicy but gets nice flavor from the cilantro and cumin.
—Carin Perkins, Waukesha, Wisconsin

> 1 medium onion, chopped
> 1/2 cup chopped green pepper
> 2 garlic cloves, minced
> 2 tablespoons olive *or* canola oil
> 1/3 cup minced fresh cilantro *or* parsley
> 3 cans (16 ounces *each*) red beans, rinsed and drained
> 1/2 teaspoon salt
> 1/2 teaspoon ground cumin
> 1/8 teaspoon pepper
> 3 cups hot cooked rice

In a large nonstick skillet, saute the onion, green pepper and garlic in oil until tender. Add cilantro; cook and stir until wilted, about 1 minute. Stir in the beans, salt, cumin and pepper. Cover and simmer for 10-15 minutes. Serve over rice. **Yield:** 6 servings.

Nutritional Analysis: *One serving (3/4 cup bean mixture with 1/2 cup rice) equals 345 calories, 6 g fat (1 g saturated fat), 0 cholesterol, 1,001 mg sodium, 58 g carbohydrate, 11 g fiber, 13 g protein.*
Diabetic Exchanges: *3-1/2 starch, 1 very lean meat, 1 fat.*

Veggie Black Bean Stew

(Pictured above)

Cilantro, honey and garlic are an ideal match for black beans and fresh vegetables in this stew.
—Marilyn Waters, Outing, Minnesota

> 2 large onions, chopped
> 1/2 cup *each* chopped celery, carrot and sweet red pepper
> 2 tablespoons minced garlic
> 1/4 cup dry sherry *or* reduced-sodium chicken broth
> 1 tablespoon olive *or* canola oil
> 3 cans (15 ounces *each*) black beans, rinsed and drained
> 1 can (14-1/2 ounces) reduced-sodium chicken *or* vegetable broth
> 1 can (14-1/2 ounces) diced tomatoes, undrained
> 2 tablespoons tomato paste
> 2 tablespoons honey
> 4 teaspoons chili powder
> 2 teaspoons ground cumin
> 1/2 teaspoon dried oregano
> 1/4 cup minced fresh cilantro *or* parsley
> 5 tablespoons shredded Monterey Jack cheese
> 5 tablespoons reduced-fat sour cream
> 2 tablespoons chopped green onion

In a Dutch oven or large saucepan, saute the onions, celery, carrot, red pepper and garlic in sherry or broth and oil until tender. Add the beans, can of broth, tomatoes, tomato paste, honey, chili power, cumin and oregano. Bring to a boil. Reduce heat; cover and simmer for 40 minutes.

Stir in the cilantro; simmer 5-15 minutes longer or until stew is thickened. Garnish with cheese, sour cream and green onion. **Yield:** 5 servings.

Nutritional Analysis: *One serving (1-1/2 cups) equals 335 calories, 8 g fat (3 g saturated fat), 14 mg cholesterol, 1,482 mg sodium, 62 g carbohydrate, 17 g fiber, 17 g protein.*
Diabetic Exchanges: *3 vegetable, 2-1/2 starch, 2 very lean meat, 1 fat.*

Carrot Lentil Casserole

My husband loves this hearty meatless casserole, especially on a chilly winter evening. It's wonderful served with crusty bread and a green salad.
—Stacey Krawczyk, Champaign, Illinois

> 1 large onion, chopped
> 1 cup finely chopped carrots
> 3/4 cup lentils, rinsed
> 3/4 cup uncooked brown rice
> 3/4 cup shredded reduced-fat cheddar cheese
> 1/2 cup chopped green pepper
> 1/2 teaspoon *each* dried thyme, basil and oregano
> 1/4 teaspoon salt
> 1/4 teaspoon rubbed sage
> 1/4 teaspoon garlic powder
> 1 can (14-1/2 ounces) chicken *or* vegetable broth
> 1 can (14-1/2 ounces) diced tomatoes, undrained

In a 1-1/2-qt. baking dish coated with nonstick cooking spray, combine the onion, carrots, lentils, rice, cheese, green pepper and seasonings. Stir in broth and tomatoes. Cover and bake at 350° for 1 to 1-1/2 hours or until the liquid is absorbed and lentils and rice are tender. **Yield:** 6 servings.

Nutritional Analysis: *One serving (1 cup) equals 239 calories, 4 g fat (2 g saturated fat), 8 mg cholesterol, 557 mg sodium, 41 g carbohydrate, 8 g fiber, 14 g protein.*
Diabetic Exchanges: *2 starch, 1 lean meat, 1 vegetable.*

Favorite Lasagna Recipe Made Lighter

ON A COOL DAY, nothing hits the spot more than a comforting casserole such as Creamy Broccoli Lasagna. The recipe comes from Launa Shoemaker of Hendersonville, North Carolina. "People can't resist the combination of a rich homemade white sauce, broccoli, mushrooms and Swiss cheese," she notes.

If this dish sounds tempting to you, but you'd like a lighter version, check out Makeover Creamy Broccoli Lasagna created by our Test Kitchen home economists.

They prepared the casserole using less butter, fat-free milk instead of whole milk and lighter cottage cheese and Swiss cheese.

Their trimmed-down version has a third fewer calories, two-thirds less cholesterol and just a quarter of the fat and saturated fat. Yet it's still creamy and delightfully satisfying.

Creamy Broccoli Lasagna

    9 uncooked lasagna noodles
1/4 cup chopped onion
1/4 cup butter *or* margarine
1/4 cup all-purpose flour
    2 teaspoons chicken *or* vegetable bouillon
        granules
3/4 teaspoon garlic salt
1/4 teaspoon pepper
1/4 teaspoon dried thyme
2-1/2 cups milk
    6 cups broccoli florets
1-1/2 cups small-curd cottage cheese
    2 jars (4-1/2 ounces *each*) sliced mushrooms,
        drained
    2 packages (6 ounces *each*) sliced Swiss cheese

Makeover Creamy Broccoli Lasagna

(Pictured below left)

    9 uncooked lasagna noodles
    1 pound fresh mushrooms, sliced
1/4 cup chopped onion
    2 tablespoons butter *or* stick margarine
1/3 cup all-purpose flour
    1 teaspoon chicken *or* vegetable bouillon
        granules
3/4 teaspoon garlic salt
1/4 teaspoon pepper
1/4 teaspoon dried thyme
2-1/2 cups fat-free milk
    6 cups broccoli florets
1-1/2 cups 1% small-curd cottage cheese
    10 ounces reduced-fat Swiss cheese, shredded,
        divided

Cook noodles according to package directions. Meanwhile, in a large saucepan, saute onion in butter until tender. Add the flour, bouillon, garlic salt, pepper and thyme; stir until smooth. Gradually add milk. Bring to a boil; cook and stir for 2 minutes or until thickened. Add broccoli; cook for 3-5 minutes. Stir in cottage cheese and mushrooms. Drain noodles.

In a greased 13-in. x 9-in. x 2-in. baking dish, layer three noodles, a third of the sauce and a third of the Swiss cheese. Repeat layers twice. Bake, uncovered, at 350° for 35-40 minutes or until bubbly and broccoli is tender. Let stand for 10 minutes before cutting. **Yield:** 12 servings.

Nutritional Analysis: One serving equals 291 calories, 15 g fat (9 g saturated fat), 49 mg cholesterol, 542 mg sodium, 23 g carbohydrate, 2 g fiber, 17 g protein.

Cook noodles according to package directions. Meanwhile, in a large saucepan, saute mushrooms and onion in butter until tender. Add the flour, bouillon, garlic salt, pepper and thyme; stir until blended. Gradually add milk. Bring to a boil; cook and stir for 2 minutes or until thickened. Add broccoli; cook for 3-5 minutes. Stir in cottage cheese and three-fourths of the Swiss cheese. Drain noodles.

In a 13-in. x 9-in. x 2-in. baking dish coated with nonstick cooking spray, layer three noodles and a third of the sauce. Repeat layers twice. Cover and bake at 350° for 35-40 minutes or until bubbly and broccoli is tender. Sprinkle with remaining Swiss cheese. Bake, uncovered, 5 minutes longer or until cheese is melted. Let stand for 10 minutes before cutting. **Yield:** 12 servings.

Nutritional Analysis: One serving equals 190 calories, 4 g fat (2 g saturated fat), 16 mg cholesterol, 443 mg sodium, 22 g carbohydrate, 2 g fiber, 17 g protein.
Diabetic Exchanges: 2 lean meat, 1 starch, 1 vegetable.

Black Bean Soft Tacos

Spiced just right, these bean-based tacos have plenty of south-of-the-border appeal. I liven up my black bean filling with diced tomatoes, green chilies and a variety of seasonings, then garnish each taco with a slice of avocado.
—Lynn Hamilton, Naperville, Illinois

1 medium onion, chopped
2 garlic cloves, minced
1 tablespoon canola oil
2 cans (15 ounces *each*) black beans, rinsed and drained
1 can (14-1/2 ounces) diced tomatoes
1 can (4 ounces) chopped green chilies
1 tablespoon chili powder
1 teaspoon ground cumin
1 teaspoon dried oregano
1/2 teaspoon salt
1/4 teaspoon garlic powder
1/4 teaspoon pepper
8 flour tortillas (6 inches), warmed
1/2 cup shredded reduced-fat cheddar cheese
1 ripe avocado, peeled and sliced

In a nonstick skillet, saute onion and garlic in oil until tender. Stir in the beans, tomatoes, chilies and seasonings. Bring to a boil. Reduce heat; simmer, uncovered, for 3-5 minutes or until mixture begins to thicken. Spoon about 1/2 cup off center on each tortilla; sprinkle with cheese. Fold one side of tortilla over filling. Garnish with avocado. **Yield:** 8 servings.

Nutritional Analysis: One taco equals 279 calories, 8 g fat (2 g saturated fat), 5 mg cholesterol, 828 mg sodium, 40 g carbohydrate, 11 g fiber, 12 g protein.
Diabetic Exchanges: 2 starch, 1 lean meat, 1 vegetable, 1 fat.

Cheesy Beans and Rice

(Pictured above)

After my dad had heart trouble years ago, my mom adapted an old recipe to come up with this colorful all-in-one dish. It has been a favorite for a long time. Even our kids like it, and they can be quite picky!
—Linda Rindels, Littleton, Colorado

1 cup uncooked brown rice
1 can (16 ounces) kidney beans, rinsed and drained
1 large onion, chopped
1 tablespoon canola oil
1 can (14-1/2 ounces) diced tomatoes and green chilies, undrained
2 teaspoons chili powder
1/4 teaspoon salt
1-1/4 cups shredded reduced-fat cheddar cheese, *divided*

Cook rice according to package directions. Transfer to a bowl; add the beans. In a nonstick skillet, saute onion in oil for 4-5 minutes. Stir in the tomatoes, chili powder and salt. Bring to a boil; remove from the heat.

In a 2-qt. baking dish coated with nonstick cooking spray, layer a third of the rice mixture, cheese and tomato mixture. Repeat layers. Top with remaining rice mixture and tomato mixture.

Cover and bake at 350° for 30 minutes or until heated through. Uncover; sprinkle with remaining cheese. Bake 5-10 minutes longer or until cheese melts. **Yield:** 6 servings.

Nutritional Analysis: One serving (1 cup) equals 306 calories, 7 g fat (3 g saturated fat), 13 mg cholesterol, 470 mg sodium, 47 g carbohydrate, 9 g fiber, 15 g protein.
Diabetic Exchanges: 2-1/2 starch, 2 lean meat, 1 vegetable.

Counting on Beans?

A BOUNTY OF BEANS means there are lots of little legumes to choose from when you're preparing protein-rich fare for your family. Keep these clues on colors, sizes and uses in mind...

Pinto beans—Medium-size ovals, mottled beige-and-brown color. Use in chili and dips.

Navy beans—Small white ovals. Great in baked beans, soups and casseroles.

Lima beans—Kidney shapes, creamy white or pale green color. Wonderful addition to soups and casseroles.

Black beans—Medium-size black-skinned ovals. Often star in Southwest dishes, soups and refried beans.

Kidney beans—Large kidney shapes, pale or dark reddish-brown in color. Use in soups, salads or chili, or serve over rice.

Great northern beans—Medium white ovals. Use in soups and baked beans.

Pasta and Veggies in Garlic Sauce

Big garlic flavor and a little heat from red pepper flakes help perk up this fresh-tasting pasta dish.
—Doris Heath, Franklin, North Carolina

12 ounces uncooked penne *or* medium tube pasta
6 garlic cloves, minced
1/4 teaspoon crushed red pepper flakes, optional
2 tablespoons olive *or* canola oil
1 can (15 ounces) garbanzo beans *or* chickpeas, rinsed and drained
2 medium tomatoes, seeded and cut into 1/2-inch pieces
1 package (10 ounces) fresh spinach, torn
1/4 teaspoon salt
1/4 cup grated Parmesan cheese

Cook pasta according to package directions. In a skillet, saute garlic and pepper flakes in oil for 1 minute. Add garbanzo beans and tomatoes; cook and stir for 2 minutes. Add spinach and salt; cook and stir until spinach is wilted. Drain pasta; add to vegetable mixture. Sprinkle with Parmesan cheese; toss to coat. **Yield:** 6 servings.

Nutritional Analysis: *One serving (1-1/2 cups) equals 370 calories, 8 g fat (2 g saturated fat), 3 mg cholesterol, 432 mg sodium, 62 g carbohydrate, 6 g fiber, 15 g protein.*
Diabetic Exchanges: *3-1/2 starch, 1 vegetable, 1 very lean meat, 1 fat.*

Moroccan Stew

Fragrant cinnamon, cumin and coriander give this hearty meatless medley its exotic Moroccan flavor.
—Rita Reinke, Wauwatosa, Wisconsin

2 cups cauliflowerets
3 medium carrots, cut into 2-inch julienned strips
1 medium onion, quartered and thinly sliced
2 teaspoons olive *or* canola oil
1 cup sliced zucchini
1/2 cup water
1 teaspoon ground cumin
1/2 teaspoon salt
1/2 teaspoon ground coriander
1/4 teaspoon ground cinnamon
1/8 teaspoon cayenne pepper
1/8 teaspoon pepper
1 can (15 ounces) garbanzo beans *or* chickpeas, rinsed and drained
1 can (14-1/2 ounces) diced tomatoes, undrained
Hot cooked rice, optional

In a large nonstick skillet, saute the cauliflower, carrots and onion in oil for 10 minutes. Add the zucchini, water, cumin, salt, coriander, cinnamon, cayenne and pepper. Bring to a boil. Reduce heat; cover and simmer for 5 minutes. Stir in garbanzo beans and tomatoes; simmer 5 minutes longer. Serve over rice if desired. **Yield:** 5 servings.

Nutritional Analysis: *One serving (1 cup stew, calculated without rice) equals 138 calories, 3 g fat (trace saturated fat), 0 cholesterol, 512 mg sodium, 25 g carbohydrate, 6 g fiber, 5 g protein.*
Diabetic Exchanges: *3 vegetable, 1/2 starch, 1/2 fat.*

Garden Primavera

(Pictured below)

I made several changes to the original recipe for this pasta and vegetable toss to better suit our family's tastes. With its pretty color and fresh flavor, the meatless main dish is a favorite at our house.
—Anne Heinonen, Howell, Michigan

8 ounces uncooked fettuccine
1 cup broccoli florets
1 medium sweet red pepper, julienned
1/2 cup sliced carrot
1/2 cup sliced mushrooms
1/4 cup sliced celery
1 garlic clove, minced
1 tablespoon olive *or* canola oil
3/4 cup V8 juice
1/4 cup chopped fresh basil
1 cup frozen peas, thawed
1/2 teaspoon salt
1/8 teaspoon pepper
2 tablespoons shredded Parmesan cheese

Cook fettuccine according to package directions. Meanwhile, in a large nonstick skillet, saute the broccoli, red pepper, carrot, mushrooms, celery and garlic in oil for 3 minutes. Add V8 juice and basil. Reduce heat; simmer, uncovered, for 3 minutes. Stir in the peas, salt and pepper; simmer 2 minutes longer or until peas are tender. Drain the fettuccine; add to vegetable mixture and toss to coat. Sprinkle with Parmesan cheese. **Yield:** 4 servings.

Nutritional Analysis: *One serving (1-1/2 cups) equals 310 calories, 6 g fat (1 g saturated fat), 2 mg cholesterol, 529 mg sodium, 54 g carbohydrate, 6 g fiber, 12 g protein.*
Diabetic Exchanges: *3 starch, 2 vegetable, 1 fat.*

Black Bean Tortilla Casserole

(Pictured below)

*A cousin gave me this recipe since she knows
my family loves Southwestern fare.*
—Sue Briski, Appleton, Wisconsin

 2 large onions, chopped
1-1/2 cups chopped green peppers
 1 can (14-1/2 ounces) diced tomatoes, drained
 3/4 cup picante sauce
 2 garlic cloves, minced
 2 teaspoons ground cumin
 2 cans (15 ounces *each*) black beans, rinsed and
 drained
 8 corn tortillas (6 inches)
 2 cups (8 ounces) shredded reduced-fat
 Monterey Jack cheese, *divided*
TOPPINGS:
1-1/2 cups shredded lettuce
 1 cup chopped fresh tomatoes
 1/2 cup thinly sliced green onions
 1/2 cup sliced ripe olives

In a saucepan, combine the onions, peppers, tomatoes, picante sauce, garlic and cumin. Bring to a boil. Reduce heat; simmer, uncovered, for 10-12 minutes. Stir in the beans. Spread a third of the mixture in a 13-in. x 9-in. x 2-in. baking dish coated with nonstick cooking spray. Layer with four tortillas and 2/3 cup cheese. Repeat layers; top with remaining beans.

Cover and bake at 350° for 30-35 minutes or until heated through. Sprinkle with remaining cheese. Let stand for 5 minutes or until cheese is melted. Serve with toppings. **Yield:** 9 servings.

Nutritional Analysis: *One serving (1 piece with toppings) equals 246 calories, 7 g fat (3 g saturated fat), 18 mg cholesterol, 746 mg sodium, 31 g carbohydrate, 8 g fiber, 16 g protein.*
Diabetic Exchanges: *2 lean meat, 1-1/2 starch, 1 vegetable.*

Vegetable Spaghetti Bake

*This fresh-tasting main dish is loaded with
vegetables, cheese, noodles and spaghetti sauce.
It makes excellent use of garden produce, but
my family enjoys it any time of year.*
—Laurie Messer, Bonifay, Florida

 8 ounces uncooked spaghetti
 1 jar (28 ounces) meatless spaghetti sauce,
 divided
1-1/2 cups cut zucchini (1/2-inch pieces)
 1 cup sliced celery
 1 cup thinly sliced carrots
 1 cup sliced fresh mushrooms
 1 medium onion, chopped
 1 tablespoon olive *or* canola oil
 2 cups (16 ounces) fat-free cottage cheese
 2 cups (8 ounces) shredded part-skim mozzarella
 cheese
 2 tablespoons grated Parmesan cheese

Cook spaghetti according to package directions; drain and place in a large bowl. Add 1-1/2 cups spaghetti sauce; set aside. In a large nonstick skillet, saute the zucchini, celery, carrots, mushrooms and onion in oil until tender.

Spread 1/2 cup spaghetti sauce in a 13-in. x 9-in. x 2-in. baking dish coated with nonstick cooking spray. Layer with half each of the spaghetti mixture, cottage cheese, vegetables and mozzarella cheese. Repeat layers. Cover with remaining sauce; sprinkle with Parmesan cheese. Cover and bake at 350° for 30 minutes. Uncover; bake 10-15 minutes longer or until bubbly. Let stand for 10 minutes before serving. **Yield:** 9 servings.

Nutritional Analysis: *One serving (3/4 cup) equals 290 calories, 7 g fat (3 g saturated fat), 20 mg cholesterol, 645 mg sodium, 36 g carbohydrate, 4 g fiber, 18 g protein.*
Diabetic Exchanges: *2-1/2 starch, 2 lean meat.*

Lentil Loaf

*This lentil loaf is so flavorful, you won't miss the meat.
And it's packed with fiber and nutrients.*
—Tracy Fleming, Phoenix, Arizona

 1 can (14-1/2 ounces) vegetable broth
 3/4 cup lentils, rinsed
1-3/4 cups shredded carrots
 1 cup finely chopped onion
 1 cup chopped fresh mushrooms
 1 tablespoon olive *or* canola oil
 2 tablespoons minced fresh basil *or* 2 teaspoons
 dried basil
 1 tablespoon minced fresh parsley
 1 cup (4 ounces) shredded part-skim mozzarella
 cheese
 1/2 cup cooked brown rice
 1 egg
 1 egg white
 1/2 teaspoon garlic powder
 1/2 teaspoon salt
 1/4 teaspoon pepper
 2 tablespoons tomato paste
 2 tablespoons water

In a saucepan, bring broth and lentils to a boil. Reduce heat; cover and simmer for 30 minutes or until tender. In a non-stick skillet, saute the carrots, onion and mushrooms in oil for 10 minutes or until tender. Add basil and parsley; saute 5 minutes longer. In a large bowl, combine the carrot mixture, cooked lentils, cheese, rice, egg, egg white, garlic powder, salt and pepper; mix well.

Transfer to a 9-in. x 5-in. x 3-in. loaf pan coated with nonstick cooking spray. Combine tomato paste and water until smooth; spread over top of loaf. Bake at 350° for 45-50 minutes or until a meat thermometer inserted into the center reads 160°. Let stand for 10 minutes before cutting. **Yield:** 6 servings.

Nutritional Analysis: One serving equals 218 calories, 7 g fat (3 g saturated fat), 46 mg cholesterol, 613 mg sodium, 26 g carbohydrate, 9 g fiber, 15 g protein.
Diabetic Exchanges: 2 lean meat, 1 starch, 1 vegetable.

Broccoli Bean Pasta

(Pictured above)

I enjoy creating new recipes out of old ones—this is a variation on macaroni and cheese. My mother gets the credit for all my cooking successes. She started me out at age 5.
—John Aramanda, Beaufort, North Carolina

    10 cups water
     6 ounces uncooked small pasta shells
     3 cups broccoli florets
     3 garlic cloves, minced
     2 tablespoons olive *or* canola oil
     1 can (15 ounces) garbanzo beans *or* chickpeas,
       rinsed and drained
   2/3 cup dry white wine *or* vegetable broth
   1/8 teaspoon crushed red pepper flakes
     2 teaspoons cornstarch
   1/2 teaspoon salt
   1/2 cup fat-free evaporated milk
   1/2 cup shredded Parmesan cheese, *divided*

In a large saucepan, bring water to a boil. Add pasta; cook for 7 minutes. Add broccoli; cook 4-5 minutes longer or until pasta and broccoli are tender. Meanwhile, in a large nonstick skillet, saute garlic in oil for 1 minute. Add the beans, wine or broth and pepper flakes. Bring to a boil. Reduce heat; simmer, uncovered, for 7-8 minutes or until slightly reduced.

Drain pasta and broccoli; keep warm. Combine cornstarch, salt and milk until smooth; stir into bean mixture. Bring to a boil; cook and stir for 2 minutes or until thickened. Reduce heat; stir in 1/4 cup Parmesan cheese. Add pasta mixture; toss to coat. Sprinkle with remaining cheese. **Yield:** 5 servings.

Nutritional Analysis: One serving (1 cup) equals 361 calories, 12 g fat (3 g saturated fat), 6 mg cholesterol, 461 mg sodium, 48 g carbohydrate, 6 g fiber, 16 g protein.
Diabetic Exchanges: 3 starch, 1-1/2 fat, 1 lean meat.

Garden Paella

One bite of the delicious rice recipe our Test Kitchen concocted and you're bound to have a passion for paella. Colorful and filling, it makes a good hearty side dish or meatless entree. Paella is ideal potluck and party food, too.

     1 large onion, chopped
     2 tablespoons olive *or* canola oil
 1-1/2 cups uncooked long grain rice
     3 garlic cloves, minced
 2-1/2 cups vegetable broth
 1-1/2 cups sliced carrots
 1-1/2 cups frozen cut green beans, thawed
     1 medium sweet red pepper, julienned
     1 medium zucchini, quartered lengthwise and cut
       into 1/2-inch slices
     1 teaspoon salt
   1/2 teaspoon dried thyme
   1/4 teaspoon ground turmeric
   1/8 teaspoon paprika
     1 can (14 ounces) water-packed artichoke hearts,
       drained and quartered
     2 plum tomatoes, seeded and chopped
     1 cup frozen peas, thawed
     1 cup frozen corn, thawed

In a large nonstick skillet, saute onion in oil for 2 minutes. Add rice and garlic; saute 1 minute longer. Add the next nine ingredients; mix well. Bring to a boil. Reduce heat; cover and simmer for 25-30 minutes or until liquid is absorbed and rice is tender. Stir in the artichoke hearts, tomatoes, peas and corn; heat through. **Yield:** 6 servings.

Nutritional Analysis: One serving (1-2/3 cups) equals 359 calories, 6 g fat (1 g saturated fat), 0 cholesterol, 1,254 mg sodium, 68 g carbohydrate, 8 g fiber, 11 g protein.
Diabetic Exchanges: 3 starch, 3 vegetable, 1 fat.

ed, about 5 minutes. Pour over pasta; toss gently to coat. Sprinkle with pecans and remaining blue cheese. **Yield:** 6 servings.

Nutritional Analysis: One serving (1 cup) equals 368 calories, 13 g fat (4 g saturated fat), 14 mg cholesterol, 689 mg sodium, 53 g carbohydrate, 3 g fiber, 13 g protein.

Lentil Barley Stew

You can have your comfort food and nutrition, too, when you stir up this scrumptious stew. We love this dish! Filled with wholesome barley, it's hearty and satisfying and tastes even better the next day.
—*Sandy Starks, Amherst, New York*

  1/2 cup chopped celery
  1/3 cup chopped onion
    1 tablespoon butter *or* stick margarine
    3 cups V8 juice
2-1/2 cups chopped seeded plum tomatoes (about 8)
1-1/2 cups water
  3/4 cup lentils, rinsed
  1/2 cup medium pearl barley
  1/2 teaspoon salt
  1/2 teaspoon pepper
  1/2 teaspoon dried rosemary, crushed
  1/2 cup shredded carrot
  3/4 cup shredded reduced-fat cheddar cheese

In a large saucepan, saute celery and onion in butter until tender. Add V8 juice, tomatoes, water, lentils, barley and seasonings. Bring to a boil. Reduce heat; cover and simmer for 45 minutes. Add carrot; cook 10 minutes longer or until barley and lentils are tender. If desired, stir in additional water for a thinner stew. Sprinkle with cheese. **Yield:** 6 servings.

Nutritional Analysis: One serving (1 cup stew with 2 tablespoons cheese) equals 231 calories, 4 g fat (2 g saturated fat), 8 mg cholesterol, 631 mg sodium, 38 g carbohydrate, 6 g fiber, 13 g protein.
Diabetic Exchanges: 2 starch, 1 very lean meat, 1 vegetable, 1/2 fat.

Creamy Spinach Pasta

(Pictured above)

Our Test Kitchen tossed tender tube pasta with fresh spinach, onion, blue cheese and chicken broth to create this aromatic entree. A sprinkling of toasted honey pecans tops it all with a touch of sweetness.

  1/4 cup chopped pecans
    2 tablespoons honey
    1 tablespoon sugar
    1 tablespoon olive *or* canola oil
    1 tablespoon balsamic vinegar
    1 large onion, sliced and separated into rings
  12 ounces uncooked penne *or* medium tube pasta
    3 cups torn fresh spinach
  3/4 cup chicken *or* vegetable broth, *divided*
  3/4 teaspoon salt
  1/4 teaspoon pepper
  1/8 teaspoon crushed red pepper flakes
    1 cup (4 ounces) crumbled blue cheese, *divided*

Line a baking sheet with foil; coat well with nonstick cooking spray. In a small bowl, combine pecans and honey; spread over prepared pan. Bake at 300° for 15 minutes. Meanwhile, in a nonstick skillet, combine the sugar, oil and vinegar; add onion. Cook over medium heat for 15-20 minutes or until onion begins to caramelize.

In a saucepan, cook pasta according to package directions. Remove pecans from the oven; set aside and keep warm. Add the spinach, 1/4 cup broth, salt, pepper and red pepper flakes to the onion mixture; cook 5 minutes longer. Drain pasta; add onion mixture and toss.

In the same skillet, combine 2/3 cup blue cheese and remaining broth. Cook over medium heat until cheese is melt-

From the Bread Basket

Is your family getting enough grains?
It's easy to ingrain the goodness of wheat,
oats, rye and more into your meal plans
when you present an incredible assortment
of breads, rolls and muffins.

Sweet Potato Yeast Rolls (page 198)

German Rye Bread

We like this homemade rye so much that I seldom buy bread anymore. For the past 10 years, I've made this bread for our church bake sales and it always goes quickly.
—Mary Ann Bonk, New Berlin, Wisconsin

1 package (1/4 ounce) active dry yeast
4 cups warm water (110° to 115°), *divided*
2 cups rye flour
6 tablespoons sugar
2 tablespoons caraway seeds
2 teaspoons salt
7 to 8 cups all-purpose flour
2 teaspoons cornmeal
TOPPING:
  1 egg, lightly beaten
  4 teaspoons caraway seeds

In a 4-qt. glass bowl, dissolve yeast in 2 cups warm water; whisk in rye flour until smooth. Cover loosely with a clean kitchen towel. Let stand in a warm place for about 4 hours or until batter falls about 1 in. and surface bubble activity is reduced. Stir in the sugar, caraway seeds, salt, 5 cups all-purpose flour and remaining water; mix well. Stir in enough remaining flour to form a firm dough. Turn onto a floured surface; knead until smooth and elastic, about 8 minutes. Cover and let rest for 15 minutes.

Divide dough into four portions. Cover and let rest for 15 minutes. Shape into four round loaves, about 6 in. each. Coat two baking sheets with nonstick cooking spray; sprinkle each with 1 teaspoon cornmeal. Place loaves on pans. Cover and let rise until doubled, about 45 minutes.

With a sharp knife, make several slashes across the top of each loaf. Brush with egg. Sprinkle each loaf with 1 teaspoon caraway seeds. Bake at 400° for 30-35 minutes, rotating pans after 15 minutes, or until browned. Cool on wire racks. **Yield:** 4 loaves (8 slices each).

Nutritional Analysis: One slice equals 136 calories, 1 g fat (trace saturated fat), 7 mg cholesterol, 150 mg sodium, 29 g carbohydrate, 2 g fiber, 4 g protein.
Diabetic Exchange: 2 starch.

Cheddar-Topped English Muffin Bread

(Pictured above)

Slices of this firm bread have that great English muffin texture your family is sure to love. A sprinkling of shredded cheddar cheese gives a pretty golden-brown color to the top of the loaves.
—Anne Smithson, Cary, North Carolina

2 tablespoons cornmeal
5 cups all-purpose flour
2 packages (1/4 ounce *each***) quick-rise yeast**
1 tablespoon sugar
2 teaspoons salt
1/4 teaspoon baking soda
2 cups warm fat-free milk (120° to 130°)
1/2 cup warm water (120° to 130°)
1/2 cup shredded reduced-fat cheddar cheese

Coat two 8-in. x 4-in. x 2-in. loaf pans with nonstick cooking spray; sprinkle with the cornmeal and set aside. In a mixing bowl, combine the 3 cups flour, yeast, sugar, salt and baking soda. Add milk and water; beat until smooth. Stir in the remaining flour (dough will be very sticky). Transfer to prepared pans. Cover and let rise in a warm place for 30 minutes.

Sprinkle with cheese. Bake at 400° for 25-30 minutes or until golden brown. Remove from pans and cool on wire racks. **Yield:** 2 loaves (12 slices each).

Nutritional Analysis: One slice equals 112 calories, trace fat (trace saturated fat), 2 mg cholesterol, 235 mg sodium, 22 g carbohydrate, 1 g fiber, 4 g protein.
Diabetic Exchange: 1-1/2 starch.

🍎 Muffin Morsels

- Do not overmix batter. If you stir out all lumps, your muffins could have tunnels, peaks and a tough texture.
- If your muffin recipe does not fill all the cups in your pan, fill the empty cups with water. The muffins will bake more evenly.
- Unless directed otherwise, muffins should go directly into the oven as soon as the batter is mixed.
- Check muffins for doneness 5-7 minutes before the end of recommended baking time to avoid overbaking. Muffins are done if a toothpick inserted near the center comes out clean.
- Muffins are best served warm. To prevent sogginess, don't let them cool in the pan longer than the recipe says.

Apple Wheat Muffins

(Pictured above)

To perk up your mornings or snack times, try these moist munchable muffins. Apples and raisins lend natural sweetness to the whole grain flavor. These muffins impressed judges enough to earn a prize in a healthy recipe contest I entered.
—Mina Dyck, Boissevain, Manitoba

  1 cup whole wheat flour
3/4 cup wheat bran
1/2 cup sugar
1-1/2 teaspoons ground cinnamon
  1 teaspoon baking powder
  1 teaspoon baking soda
  1 egg
1/2 cup reduced-fat vanilla yogurt
1/2 cup unsweetened applesauce
1/4 cup canola oil
1/2 cup grated apple
1/2 cup raisins
  1 teaspoon grated orange peel

In a bowl, combine the first six ingredients. In another bowl, whisk the egg, yogurt, applesauce and oil. Stir into dry ingredients until just moistened. Fold in the apple, raisins and orange peel.

Coat muffin cups with nonstick cooking spray or use paper liners; fill three-fourths full with batter. Bake at 400° for 18-22 minutes or until a toothpick comes out clean. Cool for 5 minutes before removing from pan to a wire rack. **Yield:** 1 dozen.

Nutritional Analysis: One muffin equals 159 calories, 6 g fat (1 g saturated fat), 18 mg cholesterol, 138 mg sodium, 26 g carbohydrate, 3 g fiber, 3 g protein.
Diabetic Exchanges: 1 starch, 1 fat, 1/2 fruit.

Maple Oat Bread

(Pictured below)

The first time I made this old-fashioned oat bread, my husband, two daughters and I ate the entire loaf! It's the best bread we've ever tasted. Sweetened with a hint of maple syrup, the golden brown yeast bread will rise to any mealtime occasion.
—Michele Odstrcilek, Lemont, Illinois

  1 cup old-fashioned oats
  1 cup boiling water
  1 package (1/4 ounce) active dry yeast
1/3 cup warm water (110° to 115°)
1/2 cup maple syrup
  2 teaspoons canola oil
1-1/2 teaspoons salt
3-1/2 to 4 cups all-purpose flour
TOPPING:
  1 egg white, lightly beaten
  2 tablespoons old-fashioned oats

In a blender or food processor, cover and process oats for 6-7 seconds or until coarsely chopped. Transfer to a small bowl; add boiling water. Let stand until mixture cools to 110°-115°. In a mixing bowl, dissolve yeast in 1/3 cup warm water; add syrup, oil, salt, oat mixture and 2 cups flour; beat until smooth. Stir in enough remaining flour to form a soft dough. Turn onto a lightly floured surface; knead until smooth and elastic, about 6-8 minutes. Place in a greased bowl, turning once to grease top. Cover and let rise in a warm place until doubled, about 1 hour.

Punch dough down. Turn onto a lightly floured surface. Shape into a flattened 9-in. round loaf. Place in a greased 9-in. round baking dish. Cover and let rise until doubled, about 45 minutes. Brush with egg white; sprinkle with oats. Bake at 350° for 30-35 minutes or until golden brown. Remove from pan to a wire rack to cool. **Yield:** 1 loaf (16 slices).

Nutritional Analysis: One slice equals 169 calories, 1 g fat (trace saturated fat), 0 cholesterol, 225 mg sodium, 35 g carbohydrate, 2 g fiber, 5 g protein.
Diabetic Exchange: 2 starch

Herbed Vegetable Spiral Bread

(Pictured above)

This wonderful swirled bread is easy to put together...and while it's rising and baking, I make the rest of the meal. Pretty and flavorful, it's great for company or a special holiday. Everyone thinks I bought this special golden loaf at a gourmet bakery!
—Denielle Duncan, Markham, Ontario

1/2 cup shredded part-skim mozzarella cheese
1/2 cup canned Mexicorn, drained
1/4 cup grated Parmesan cheese
1/4 cup minced fresh parsley
  2 garlic cloves, minced
  1 teaspoon dried oregano
1/2 teaspoon dried basil
1/2 teaspoon ground cumin
1/4 teaspoon salt
1/8 to 1/4 teaspoon crushed red pepper flakes, optional
  1 loaf (1 pound) frozen bread dough, thawed
  1 tablespoon cornmeal
  1 egg, lightly beaten

In a bowl, combine the mozzarella, corn, Parmesan, parsley, garlic and seasonings; set aside. On a lightly floured surface, roll dough into a 16-in. x 12-in. rectangle. Spread cheese mixture over dough to within 3/4 in. of edges. Roll up jelly-roll style, starting with a long side; pinch seams and ends to seal. Sprinkle a large baking sheet with cornmeal. Place dough seam side down on baking sheet; tuck ends under. Cover and let rise in a warm place until doubled, about 35 minutes.

Brush with egg. Bake at 350° for 35-40 minutes or until golden brown and bread sounds hollow when tapped. Cool for 20 minutes before slicing. Store leftovers in the refrigerator. **Yield:** 16 slices.

Nutritional Analysis: One slice equals 107 calories, 3 g fat (1 g saturated fat), 16 mg cholesterol, 280 mg sodium, 17 g carbohydrate, 1 g fiber, 5 g protein.
Diabetic Exchanges: 1 starch, 1/2 fat.

Cranberry-Apple Bread

Don't wait until the Christmas season to bake these lovely little loaves. This quick bread is wonderful anytime, with its sweet-tart mix of cranberries and apples. The loaves freeze well, too.
—Patty Kile, Greentown, Pennsylvania

2-1/3 cups reduced-fat biscuit/baking mix
3/4 cup sugar
  5 egg whites
1/2 cup reduced-fat sour cream
1/4 cup fat-free milk
1/4 cup canola oil
  1 teaspoon grated orange peel
  1 cup chopped peeled apple
3/4 cup fresh *or* frozen cranberries, chopped
1/2 cup confectioners' sugar
  2 to 3 teaspoons orange juice

In a bowl, combine biscuit mix and sugar. In another bowl, beat egg whites, sour cream, milk, oil and orange peel. Stir into dry ingredients just until moistened. Fold in apple and cranberries. Pour into three 5-3/4-in. x 3-in. x 2-in. loaf pans coated with nonstick cooking spray. Bake at 375° for 35-40 minutes or until a toothpick comes out clean. Cool for 10 minutes before removing from pans to wire racks.

In a bowl, combine confectioners' sugar and enough orange juice to achieve a drizzling consistency; drizzle over cooled loaves. **Yield:** 3 loaves (8 slices each).

Nutritional Analysis: One slice equals 113 calories, 4 g fat (1 g saturated fat), 2 mg cholesterol, 156 mg sodium, 18 g carbohydrate, trace fiber, 2 g protein.
Diabetic Exchanges: 1 starch, 1/2 fat.

Favorite Quick Bread Recipe Made Lighter

EVER GET a hankering for a slice of old-fashioned banana bread? Who doesn't? Carlene Jolley of Fulton, Kentucky makes a Banana Nut Bread that smells heavenly in the oven and comes out moist and chock-full of banana flavor and crunchy nuts.

Maybe you'd like to head to the kitchen right now and mix up a loaf, but you're worried about the fat and calories. Then check out the Makeover Banana Nut Bread recipe created by our Test Kitchen home economists!

This slimmed-down version replaces 75% of the butter with unsweetened applesauce. The amount of sugar was decreased, too, by adding a little honey and using more banana. The revised recipe calls for 1/2 cup fewer nuts. Plus, some of the all-purpose flour was replaced with whole wheat flour to add even more nutritional value.

Our panel of taste testers went wild over this lighter version! The texture was moist and tender—not gummy as some lighter quick breads can be. And the lovely loaf had big banana flavor. "No one will ever guess this bread is low in fat," said one tester.

But it is! Our lighter version has about two-thirds less fat, a third fewer calories, less than half the cholesterol and 20% less sodium than the original.

Banana Nut Bread

1/2 cup butter *or* margarine, softened
1-1/2 cups sugar
2 eggs
1 cup mashed ripe bananas (about 2 medium)
2 tablespoons milk
1 teaspoon vanilla *or* rum extract
2 cups all-purpose flour
1 teaspoon baking soda
1/2 teaspoon salt
3/4 cup chopped pecans

In a mixing bowl, cream the butter and sugar. Add eggs, one at a time, beating well after each addition. Stir in the bananas, milk and extract. Combine the flour, baking soda and salt; stir into the banana mixture just until moistened. Fold in nuts.

Pour into a greased 9-in. x 5-in. x 3-in. loaf pan. Bake at 325° for 65-75 minutes or until a toothpick inserted near the center comes out clean. Cool for 10 minutes before removing from pan to a wire rack. **Yield:** 1 loaf (10 slices).

Nutritional Analysis: One slice equals 387 calories, 17 g fat (7 g saturated fat), 68 mg cholesterol, 352 mg sodium, 55 g carbohydrate, 2 g fiber, 5 g protein.

Makeover Banana Nut Bread

(Pictured below)

2 tablespoons butter *or* stick margarine, softened
3/4 cup sugar
1 egg
1 egg white
2 cups mashed ripe bananas (about 4 medium)
1/4 cup unsweetened applesauce
1/4 cup honey
1 teaspoon vanilla *or* rum extract
1-1/3 cups all-purpose flour
2/3 cup whole wheat flour
1 teaspoon baking soda
1/2 teaspoon salt
1/4 cup chopped pecans

In a mixing bowl, beat butter and sugar for 2 minutes or until crumbly. Add egg, then egg white, beating well after each addition. Beat on high speed until light and fluffy. Stir in the bananas, applesauce, honey and extract. Combine the flours, baking soda and salt; stir into banana mixture just until moistened.

Pour into a 9-in. x 5-in. x 3-in. loaf pan coated with non-stick cooking spray. Sprinkle with nuts. Bake at 325° for 60-65 minutes or until a toothpick inserted near the center comes out clean. Cool for 10 minutes before removing from pan to a wire rack. **Yield:** 1 loaf (10 slices).

Nutritional Analysis: One slice equals 266 calories, 6 g fat (2 g saturated fat), 27 mg cholesterol, 280 mg sodium, 52 g carbohydrate, 3 g fiber, 4 g protein.
Diabetic Exchanges: 2-1/2 starch, 1 fruit, 1 fat.

Cinnamon Pecan Ring

(Pictured above)

Yogurt tenderizes the golden yeast dough in this tasty recipe developed by our Test Kitchen.

2-3/4 to 3-1/2 cups all-purpose flour
  1/2 cup sugar, *divided*
    1 package (1/4 ounce) active dry yeast
    1 teaspoon salt
  1/8 teaspoon baking soda
  1/2 cup fat-free plain yogurt
  1/2 cup fat-free milk
  1/4 cup water
    3 tablespoons butter *or* stick margarine, *divided*
  3/4 cup chopped pecans, toasted
  1/4 cup packed brown sugar
    1 tablespoon ground cinnamon
    1 egg white, lightly beaten
ICING:
  1/2 cup confectioners' sugar
    2 teaspoons fat-free milk
  1/4 teaspoon vanilla extract

In a mixing bowl, combine 1 cup flour, 1/4 cup sugar, yeast, salt and baking soda. In a saucepan, heat the yogurt, milk, water and 2 tablespoons butter to 120°-130°. Add to dry ingredients; beat on medium speed for 2 minutes. Stir in enough remaining flour to form a soft dough. Turn onto a floured surface; knead until smooth and elastic, about 6-8 minutes. Transfer to a bowl coated with nonstick cooking spray; turn once to grease top. Cover and let rise in a warm place until doubled, about 1 hour.

Punch dough down. Roll into a 14-in. x 10-in. rectangle. Melt remaining butter; brush over dough. Combine pecans, brown sugar, cinnamon and remaining sugar; sprinkle evenly over dough to within 1/2 in. of edges. Roll up jelly-roll style, starting with a long side; pinch seam.

Line a baking sheet with foil; coat well with nonstick cooking spray. Place dough seam side down on prepared pan; pinch ends together to form a ring. With scissors, cut from the outside edge two-thirds of the way toward center of ring

at 1-in. intervals. Separate strips slightly and twist. Cover and let rise until doubled, about 45 minutes.

Brush with egg white. Bake at 350° for 20-25 minutes or until golden brown. Immediately remove from pan to a wire rack. Combine icing ingredients; drizzle over warm ring. **Yield:** 14 servings.

Nutritional Analysis: *One piece equals 229 calories, 7 g fat (2 g saturated fat), 7 mg cholesterol, 216 mg sodium, 37 g carbohydrate, 2 g fiber, 4 g protein.*
Diabetic Exchanges: *2-1/2 starch, 1-1/2 fat.*

Apple Pockets

(Pictured below)

This is a great way to enjoy the taste of apple pie without the guilt. The cute golden bundles are shaped from a homemade yeast dough, but it's their old-fashioned flavor that really appeals.
—Sharon Martin, Terre Hill, Pennsylvania

2-1/4 cups all-purpose flour, *divided*
    1 package (1/4 ounce) quick-rise yeast
    1 tablespoon sugar
  1/2 teaspoon salt
  2/3 cup water
  1/4 cup butter *or* stick margarine
FILLING:
    4 cups thinly sliced peeled Rome Beauty *or* other
      baking apples (2 to 3 medium)
  1/3 cup sugar
    2 tablespoons all-purpose flour
  1/2 teaspoon ground cinnamon
TOPPING:
  1/4 cup milk
    4 teaspoons sugar

In a mixing bowl, combine 1 cup flour, yeast, sugar and salt. In a saucepan, heat the water and butter to 120°-130°. Add to the dry ingredients; beat just until moistened. Stir in enough remaining flour to form a soft dough. Turn onto a floured surface; knead until smooth and elastic, about 6-8 minutes. Cover and let rest for 10 minutes.

Divide the dough into four portions. Roll each portion into an 8-in. square. Cut into four 4-in. squares. Cut apple

slices into thirds; toss with the sugar, flour and cinnamon. Place 1/4 cup filling on each square; bring the corners up over the filling and pinch to seal. Secure with a toothpick if needed. Place 3 in. apart on baking sheets coated with non-stick cooking spray. Cover and let rise in a warm place for 30 minutes.

Brush with milk; sprinkle with sugar. Bake at 375° for 12-14 minutes or until golden brown. Remove to wire racks. Discard toothpicks before serving. **Yield:** 16 servings.

Nutritional Analysis: *One pocket equals 136 calories, 3 g fat (2 g saturated fat), 8 mg cholesterol, 105 mg sodium, 25 g carbohydrate, 1 g fiber, 2 g protein.*
Diabetic Exchanges: *1 starch, 1/2 fruit, 1/2 fat.*

Honey Granola Bread

After years of making whole-grain loaves, I discovered a bread recipe that I think rises above all the rest. This hearty bread tastes great toasted, too. Granola adds to the nutty texture.
—Erika Pimper, Brigham City, Utah

     3-1/2 cups all-purpose flour
        2 packages (1/4 ounce *each*) active dry yeast
        1 teaspoon salt
     1-3/4 cups fat-free milk
        1/2 cup plus 2 tablespoons honey
        1/3 cup butter *or* stick margarine
        2 eggs
        2 cups whole wheat flour
        1 cup reduced-fat granola without raisins
        1 cup rye flour
        1/2 cup cornmeal
        1/2 cup quick-cooking oats
        1/4 cup slivered almonds, toasted and chopped

In a large mixing bowl, combine 2 cups all-purpose flour, yeast and salt. In a saucepan, heat the milk, honey and butter to 120°-130°. Add to dry ingredients; beat just until moistened. Add eggs; beat until smooth. Stir in whole wheat flour and enough remaining all-purpose flour to form a soft dough (dough will be sticky). Stir in the granola, rye flour, cornmeal, oats and almonds.

Turn dough onto a floured surface; knead until smooth and elastic, about 6-8 minutes. Place in a greased bowl, turning once to grease top. Cover and let rise in a warm place until doubled, about 1 hour.

Punch dough down. Turn onto a floured surface. Divide in half; cover and let rest for 10 minutes. Shape each portion into a ball. Place on a greased baking sheet; flatten into 5-in. circles. Cover and let rise in a warm place until doubled, about 30 minutes. Bake at 375° for 20 minutes; cover with foil. Bake 10 minutes longer or until bread sounds hollow when tapped. Remove to wire racks. **Yield:** 2 loaves (16 slices each).

Nutritional Analysis: *One serving (1 slice) equals 165 calories, 3 g fat (1 g saturated fat), 19 mg cholesterol, 113 mg sodium, 30 g carbohydrate, 2 g fiber, 5 g protein.*
Diabetic Exchanges: *2 starch, 1/2 fat.*

Hearty Oat Loaf

(Pictured above)

I like to serve wedges of this bread with stew or bean soup. My husband thinks it's a big treat—little does he know how easy it is to make. My children eat it for breakfast the next day with butter and strawberry jam.
—Judi Havens, Denton, Texas

        2 cups all-purpose flour
        1 cup whole wheat flour
        1/2 cup plus 2 tablespoons quick-cooking oats, *divided*
        1/4 cup sugar
        3 teaspoons baking powder
        3/4 teaspoon salt
        1 egg
     1-1/2 cups fat-free milk
        3 tablespoons canola oil

In a large bowl, combine the flours, 1/2 cup oats, sugar, baking powder and salt. In another bowl, combine the egg, milk and oil; stir into dry ingredients just until moistened. Spread batter into an 8- or 9-in. round baking pan coated with nonstick cooking spray. Sprinkle with remaining oats.

Bake at 350° for 40-50 minutes or until a toothpick inserted near the center comes out clean. Cool for 5 minutes before removing from pan to a wire rack. Serve warm. **Yield:** 1 loaf (10 wedges).

Nutritional Analysis: *One wedge equals 229 calories, 6 g fat (1 g saturated fat), 22 mg cholesterol, 272 mg sodium, 38 g carbohydrate, 3 g fiber, 7 g protein.*
Diabetic Exchanges: *2-1/2 starch, 1 fat.*

Parmesan Basil Biscuits

(Pictured below)

Rise to the occasion and serve these light flavorful biscuits the next time you invite guests to dinner. The olive oil, Parmesan cheese and basil make the golden gems so tasty, they don't even need butter! The recipe comes from our Test Kitchen.

2-1/4 cups all-purpose flour
1/4 cup shredded Parmesan cheese
2 tablespoons minced fresh basil *or* 2 teaspoons dried basil
2-1/2 teaspoons baking powder
1/2 teaspoon baking soda
1/2 teaspoon salt
1/4 teaspoon pepper
1 cup 1% buttermilk
3 tablespoons olive *or* canola oil

In a large bowl, combine the flour, cheese, basil, baking powder, baking soda, salt and pepper; mix well. Add the buttermilk and oil; stir just until combined. Turn onto a floured surface; gently knead three times. Roll dough to 1/2-in. thickness; cut with a floured 2-1/2-in. biscuit cutter. Place 1 in. apart on an ungreased baking sheet. Bake at 400° for 16-18 minutes or until lightly browned. Serve warm. **Yield:** 1 dozen.

Nutritional Analysis: One biscuit equals 129 calories, 4 g fat (1 g saturated fat), 2 mg cholesterol, 301 mg sodium, 19 g carbohydrate, 1 g fiber, 4 g protein.
Diabetic Exchanges: 1 starch, 1 fat.

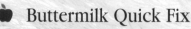

Buttermilk Quick Fix

YOU'RE halfway through the recipe and, oh no, you're out of buttermilk. No problem—just mix your own! Here are two easy methods:
- Place 1 tablespoon of distilled white vinegar in a glass measuring cup and add 1% milk to equal 1 cup. Stir, then let stand for 5 minutes until the milk thickens and curdles.
- Or combine 2/3 cup of plain nonfat or low-fat yogurt with 1/2 cup 1% milk to yield 1 cup buttermilk.

Sweet Potato Yeast Rolls

(Pictured on page 191)

Mashed sweet potatoes add a hint of color and flavor to these home-baked dinner rolls suggested by our Test Kitchen. The tempting golden knots have a tender texture as well as a lovely look from a sprinkling of sesame seeds.

1 package (1/4 ounce) active dry yeast
1 cup warm fat-free milk (110° to 115°)
1 teaspoon plus 1/3 cup sugar, *divided*
1/3 cup cold mashed sweet potatoes
2 eggs, *separated*
2 tablespoons butter *or* stick margarine, softened
3/4 teaspoon salt
3-1/2 to 4 cups all-purpose flour
4 teaspoons cold water
1 tablespoon sesame seeds

In a large mixing bowl, dissolve yeast in warm milk. Add 1 teaspoon sugar; let stand for 5 minutes. Add the sweet potatoes, egg yolks, butter, salt, remaining sugar and 2 cups flour. Beat until smooth. Stir in enough remaining flour to form a soft dough. Turn onto a floured surface; knead until smooth and elastic, about 6-8 minutes. Place in a bowl coated with nonstick cooking spray, turning once to coat top. Cover and let rise in a warm place until doubled, about 1-1/2 hours.

Punch dough down. Turn onto a lightly floured surface; divide into 30 balls. Roll each ball into a 10-in. rope; tie each rope into a loose knot. Place 2 in. apart on baking sheets coated with nonstick cooking spray. Cover and let rise until doubled, about 30 minutes.

In a small bowl, beat egg whites and cold water; brush over rolls. Sprinkle with sesame seeds. Bake at 350° for 15-17 minutes or until lightly browned. Remove from pans to cool on wire racks. **Yield:** 2-1/2 dozen.

Nutritional Analysis: One roll equals 92 calories, 1 g fat (1 g saturated fat), 16 mg cholesterol, 76 mg sodium, 16 g carbohydrate, 1 g fiber, 3 g protein.
Diabetic Exchange: 1 starch.

Herb-Crusted Bread

(Pictured below)

Minced onion and garlic plus a sprinkling of dill help perk up the flavor in this wholesome rustic-looking loaf. The dough mixes up easily in a bread machine. I like to serve this crusty bread alongside soup, pasta and saucy tomato dishes.
—Becky Steinberger, Denmark, Wisconsin

>   5 tablespoons old-fashioned oats
>   1 cup water (70° to 80°)
> 4-1/2 teaspoons sugar
> 4-1/2 teaspoons olive *or* canola oil
>   1 teaspoon salt
>   2 cups bread flour
>   1/4 cup rye flour
>   1/4 cup whole wheat flour
> 2-1/2 teaspoons active dry yeast
>   1/2 teaspoon *each* dried minced onion, dried
>   minced garlic, dill weed and poppy seeds
> **TOPPING:**
>   1 egg, lightly beaten
>   1/2 teaspoon *each* coarse salt, dried minced onion,
>   dried minced garlic, dill weed and poppy seeds

In a blender, process oats until finely ground. In bread machine pan, place the oats, water, sugar, oil, salt, flours, yeast and seasonings in order suggested by manufacturer. Select dough setting (check dough after 5 minutes of mixing; add 1 to 2 tablespoons of water or flour if needed).

When the cycle is completed, turn dough onto a lightly floured surface. Shape into a loaf, about 15 in. long. Transfer to a baking sheet coated with nonstick cooking spray. Cover and let rise in a warm place until doubled, about 45 minutes.

Carefully brush dough with egg; sprinkle with salt, onion, garlic, dill and poppy seeds. Bake at 350° for 25-30 minutes or until golden brown. **Yield:** 1 loaf (16 slices).

Nutritional Analysis: One slice equals 98 calories, 2 g fat (trace saturated fat), 13 mg cholesterol, 225 mg sodium, 17 g carbohydrate, 1 g fiber, 3 g protein.
Diabetic Exchange: 1 starch.

Oatmeal Molasses Bread

(Pictured above)

This Norwegian bread was popular in Spring Grove, Minnesota, where I grew up. My mother used to make eight loaves at a time in a wood-burning stove. It's delicious toasted.
—Lyla Franklin, Phoenix, Arizona

>   2 cups boiling water
>   1 cup quick-cooking oats
>   1 package (1/4 ounce) active dry yeast
>   1/2 cup warm water (110° to 115°)
>   1/2 cup molasses
>   1 tablespoon canola oil
>   1 teaspoon salt
>   6 to 6-1/2 cups all-purpose flour
>   1 teaspoon butter *or* stick margarine, melted

In a bowl, pour boiling water over oats. Let stand until mixture cools to 110°-115°, stirring occasionally. In a mixing bowl, dissolve yeast in warm water. Add the molasses, oil, salt, oat mixture and 3 cups flour; beat until smooth. Stir in enough remaining flour to form a soft dough. Turn onto a floured surface; knead until smooth and elastic, about 6-8 minutes. Place in a bowl coated with nonstick cooking spray, turning once to coat top. Cover and let rise in a warm place until doubled, about 1-1/2 hours.

Punch dough down. Turn onto a lightly floured surface; divide in half. Shape into loaves. Place in two 9-in. x 5-in. x 3-in. loaf pans coated with nonstick cooking spray. Cover and let rise until doubled, about 1 hour.

Bake at 350° for 40-45 minutes or until golden brown. Remove from pans to cool on wire racks. Brush with melted butter. **Yield:** 2 loaves (16 slices each).

Nutritional Analysis: One slice equals 114 calories, 1 g fat (trace saturated fat), trace cholesterol, 77 mg sodium, 23 g carbohydrate, 1 g fiber, 3 g protein.
Diabetic Exchange: 1-1/2 starch.

Nutritional Analysis: *One biscuit equals 133 calories, 4 g fat (2 g saturated fat), 8 mg cholesterol, 355 mg sodium, 20 g carbohydrate, trace fiber, 4 g protein.*
Diabetic Exchanges: *1-1/2 starch, 1/2 fat.*

Hearty Brown Quick Bread

Not only is this bread high in fiber and low in fat, but it's moist, rich, delicious and filling. Sweet plump raisins and crunchy pecans make this whole wheat loaf an instant favorite.
—Susan Lane, Waukesha, Wisconsin

4 cups whole wheat flour
2 cups all-purpose flour
2 cups packed brown sugar
1/2 cup sugar
2 teaspoons baking soda
1 teaspoon salt
3 cups 1% buttermilk
2 eggs, lightly beaten
1 cup raisins
1/2 cup chopped pecans

In a large bowl, stir together the first six ingredients. Stir in buttermilk and eggs just until moistened. Fold in raisins and nuts. Pour into two 9-in. x 5-in. x 3-in. loaf pans coated with nonstick cooking spray. Bake at 350° for 50-60 minutes or until a toothpick inserted near the center comes out clean. Cool for 10 minutes before removing from pans to wire racks. **Yield:** 2 loaves (12 slices each).

Nutritional Analysis: *One slice equals 246 calories, 3 g fat (1 g saturated fat), 20 mg cholesterol, 250 mg sodium, 51 g carbohydrate, 3 g fiber, 6 g protein.*
Diabetic Exchange: *3 starch.*

Rosemary Biscuits

Seasoned with rosemary, these light and tender biscuits are extra special. And with just four ingredients, they're a snap to make.
—Jacqueline Graves, Lawrenceville, Georgia

3 ounces reduced-fat cream cheese, cubed
1-3/4 cups reduced-fat biscuit/baking mix
1/2 cup fat-free milk
2 teaspoons minced fresh rosemary *or* 3/4 teaspoon dried rosemary, crushed

In a large bowl, cut cream cheese into biscuit mix until crumbly. Stir in milk and rosemary just until moistened. Turn dough onto a lightly floured surface; knead 10 times. Roll out into a 6-in. square. Cut into four 3-in. squares; cut each square diagonally in half. Place on a baking sheet coated with nonstick cooking spray. Bake at 400° for 10-12 minutes or until golden brown. Serve warm. **Yield:** 8 servings.

Orange Blossom Muffins

(Pictured below)

My husband and I tasted a muffin similar to these at a bed-and-breakfast when we celebrated our first anniversary. When I told a friend about them, she shared the recipe for these moist and tender muffins. They are fun to serve full-size or as mini muffins.
—Rhonda Lyons, Marshall, Texas

2 tablespoons plus 1/4 cup sugar, *divided*
4-1/2 teaspoons all-purpose flour
1/2 teaspoon ground cinnamon
1/4 teaspoon ground nutmeg
1 tablespoon cold butter *or* stick margarine
2 cups reduced-fat biscuit/baking mix
1 egg
1/2 cup orange juice
1/2 cup orange marmalade
2 tablespoons canola oil
1/4 cup chopped pecans

In a small bowl, combine 2 tablespoons sugar, flour, cinnamon and nutmeg; cut in butter until crumbly. Set aside for topping. Place the biscuit mix in a bowl. Combine the egg, orange juice, marmalade, oil and remaining sugar; stir into biscuit mix just until moistened. Fold in pecans.

Coat muffin cups with nonstick cooking spray or use paper liners; fill two-thirds full with batter. Sprinkle with reserved crumb mixture. Bake at 400° for 18-20 minutes or until a toothpick comes out clean. Cool for 5 minutes before removing from pan to a wire rack. Serve warm. **Yield:** 1 dozen.

Nutritional Analysis: *One muffin equals 194 calories, 7 g fat (1 g saturated fat), 20 mg cholesterol, 255 mg sodium, 32 g carbohydrate, 1 g fiber, 2 g protein.*
Diabetic Exchanges: *1 starch, 1 fruit, 1 fat.*

Dazzling Desserts

It used to be the words "rich", "creamy" and "yummy" were never spoken in the same sentence as "low fat", especially when the conversation turned to desserts. But now you can have your cake and eat it too!

Cranberry Meringue Pie and Lemon Cheese Pie (page 222)

Delightful Brownies

Create a moist fudgy brownie with less fat. My secret is using baby food as a fat substitute. Even your most devoted brownie fan will have a hard time telling that this is a trimmed-down version.
—Pamela Raybon, Edna, Texas

    3 tablespoons butter *or* stick margarine, softened
    2 egg whites
    1 jar (4 ounces) prune baby food
    1 teaspoon vanilla extract
  2/3 cup sugar
  1/2 cup all-purpose flour
    1 package (1.4 ounces) sugar-free instant chocolate pudding mix
  1/2 teaspoon baking powder
  1/4 teaspoon salt
  3/4 cup miniature semisweet chocolate chips

In a mixing bowl, beat butter and egg whites until blended. Beat in baby food and vanilla. Combine the sugar, flour, pudding mix, baking powder and salt; add to the egg mixture. Stir in chocolate chips. Spread into an 8-in. square baking pan coated with nonstick cooking spray. Bake at 350° for 30-35 minutes or until a toothpick inserted near the center comes out clean. Cool on a wire rack. **Yield:** 1 dozen.

Nutritional Analysis: *One brownie equals 176 calories, 6 g fat (4 g saturated fat), 8 mg cholesterol, 338 mg sodium, 30 g carbohydrate, 2 g fiber, 2 g protein.*
Diabetic Exchanges: *2 starch, 1 fat.*

Chewy Date Cookies

Brown sugar, cinnamon, lemon peel and dates make a flavorful combination in this old-fashioned favorite, which comes straight from our Test Kitchen.

  1/3 cup butter (no substitutes), softened
  2/3 cup packed brown sugar
    1 egg
  3/4 cup all-purpose flour
  2/3 cup whole wheat flour
    2 teaspoons grated lemon peel
1-1/2 teaspoons baking powder
  1/2 teaspoon ground cinnamon
  1/2 teaspoon ground nutmeg
  1/4 teaspoon salt
  1/4 cup fat-free milk
    1 cup chopped dates

In a mixing bowl, cream butter and sugar. Add egg; mix well. Combine flours, lemon peel, baking powder, cinnamon, nutmeg and salt; add to creamed mixture alternately with milk, beating well after each addition. Stir in dates.

Drop by rounded tablespoonfuls 2 in. apart onto ungreased baking sheets. Bake at 325° for 13-15 minutes or until golden brown. Remove to wire racks to cool. Store in an airtight container. **Yield:** about 2-1/2 dozen.

Nutritional Analysis: *One cookie equals 77 calories, 2 g fat (1 g saturated fat), 13 mg cholesterol, 57 mg sodium, 14 g carbohydrate, 1 g fiber, 1 g protein.*
Diabetic Exchanges: *1 fruit, 1/2 fat.*

Tutti-Frutti Angel Food Cake

(Pictured at right)

Each heavenly slice of this made-from-scratch cake is feather-light.
—Jill Kinder, Richlands, Virginia

1-1/2 cups egg whites (about 11)
1-1/4 teaspoons cream of tartar
  1/2 teaspoon salt
    1 teaspoon vanilla extract
  1/2 teaspoon almond extract
    1 to 2 drops red food coloring, optional
1-1/2 cups sugar
1-1/4 cups cake flour
    1 cup finely chopped mixed candied fruit

In a large mixing bowl, beat the egg whites until foamy. Add cream of tartar and salt; beat until soft peaks form. Add extracts and food coloring if desired. Add sugar, 1 tablespoon at a time, beating well after each addition; beat until stiff glossy peaks form. Gradually fold in flour, 1/4 cup at a time. Fold in candied fruit. Gently spoon into an ungreased 10-in. tube pan. Bake at 375° for 35-40 minutes or until cake springs back when lightly touched. Immediately invert pan; cool completely. Run a knife around sides of cake and remove. **Yield:** 12 servings.

Nutritional Analysis: *One piece equals 226 calories, trace fat (trace saturated fat), 0 cholesterol, 169 mg sodium, 53 g carbohydrate, 2 g fiber, 4 g protein.*

Cherry Meringue Dessert

(Pictured at right)

It's hard to resist this elegant treat with its sweet cherry flavor and fun crunchy crust.
—Bernardine Adamson, Sarcoxie, Missouri

    6 egg whites
  3/4 teaspoon cream of tartar
    2 teaspoons vanilla extract
    2 cups sugar
    2 cups crushed saltines (about 60 crackers)
  1/2 cup chopped pecans
    1 carton (8 ounces) frozen reduced-fat whipped topping, thawed
    1 can (20 ounces) reduced-sugar cherry pie filling

In a large mixing bowl, beat the egg whites until foamy. Add cream of tartar and vanilla; beat until soft peaks form. Gradually beat in sugar, 1 tablespoon at a time, until stiff glossy peaks form. Fold in saltines and pecans.

Transfer to a 13-in. x 9-in. x 2-in. baking dish coated with nonstick cooking spray. Bake at 350° for 20-25 minutes or until lightly browned and edges begin to crack. Cool on a wire rack. Spread whipped topping over crust. Carefully spoon pie filling over top. **Yield:** 15 servings.

Nutritional Analysis: *One piece equals 241 calories, 6 g fat (2 g saturated fat), 0 cholesterol, 129 mg sodium, 45 g carbohydrate, 1 g fiber, 3 g protein.*
Diabetic Exchanges: *2 fruit, 1 starch, 1 fat.*

Hot Fudge Sundae Cake

I hope you'll enjoy this fudgy cake as much as our family does. It's a snap to make in the microwave. My husband has to watch his cholesterol, but he doesn't feel deprived when I serve this.
—*Florence Beer, Houlton, Wisconsin*

1 cup all-purpose flour
3/4 cup sugar
2 tablespoons plus 1/4 cup baking cocoa, *divided*
2 teaspoons baking powder
1/4 teaspoon salt
1/2 cup fat-free milk
2 tablespoons canola oil
1 teaspoon vanilla extract
1/2 cup chopped pecans
1 cup packed brown sugar
1-3/4 cups boiling water
10 tablespoons reduced-fat whipped topping

In an ungreased 2-1/2-qt. microwave-safe dish, combine the flour, sugar, 2 tablespoons cocoa, baking powder and salt. Stir in milk, oil and vanilla until combined. Fold in nuts. Combine brown sugar and remaining cocoa; sprinkle over batter. Pour boiling water over batter (do not stir). Microwave, uncovered, on high for 9-10 minutes, rotating a quarter turn every 3 minutes, or until top of cake springs back when lightly touched. Serve with whipped topping. **Yield:** 10 servings.

Editor's Note: This recipe was tested in an 850-watt microwave.

Nutritional Analysis: *One serving equals 274 calories, 8 g fat (1 g saturated fat), trace cholesterol, 121 mg sodium, 50 g carbohydrate, 2 g fiber, 3 g protein.*
Diabetic Exchanges: *2-1/2 starch, 1-1/2 fat.*

Lemon Chiffon Dessert

(Pictured above)

This light fluffy treat was a hit when I shared it at a club meeting I hosted. My diabetic sister-in-law gave me the recipe.
—*Darlene Inman, Waynoka, Oklahoma*

2 envelopes unflavored gelatin
1-1/4 cups cold water, *divided*
1-1/3 cups fat-free milk
2-1/2 teaspoons unsweetened lemon soft drink mix*
3 to 4 drops yellow food coloring, optional
1/8 teaspoon salt
3/4 cup reduced-fat cottage cheese
1 cup reduced-fat whipped topping
1 tablespoon graham cracker crumbs

In a small saucepan, sprinkle gelatin over 1/2 cup cold water; let stand for 1 minute. Cook and stir over low heat until gelatin is completely dissolved; set aside.

In a mixing bowl, combine the milk, drink mix, food coloring if desired, salt and remaining water; beat on high speed until blended. Place the cottage cheese in a blender or food processor; cover and process until smooth. Add milk mixture and gelatin; cover and process until thickened.

Spoon into six 6-oz. custard cups. Cover and refrigerate for 1 hour. Spread with whipped topping; sprinkle with cracker crumbs. **Yield:** 6 servings.

*Editor's Note: This recipe was tested with Crystal Light lemon flavor drink mix.

Nutritional Analysis: *One serving equals 81 calories, 2 g fat (2 g saturated fat), 2 mg cholesterol, 202 mg sodium, 7 g carbohydrate, trace fiber, 7 g protein.*
Diabetic Exchanges: *1 very lean meat, 1/2 starch.*

Peanut Butter Bread Pudding

Traditional bread pudding gets a new twist in this deliciously different dessert. With both chocolate chips and peanut butter, this bread pudding does not taste light. And it's so comforting!
—*Sharon Paddock, Wauchula, Florida*

3 cups fat-free milk
1 package (.8 ounce) sugar-free cook-and-serve vanilla pudding mix
1 teaspoon vanilla extract
2 tablespoons reduced-fat peanut butter
4 cups cubed French bread
1/4 cup chopped dry roasted peanuts
2 tablespoons miniature semisweet chocolate chips

In a large bowl, whisk the milk, pudding mix and vanilla for 2 minutes or until smooth. Add peanut butter; mix well. Add the remaining ingredients; mix gently to combine. Pour into an 8-in. square baking dish coated with nonstick cooking spray. Bake at 350° for 40-45 minutes or until set. Cool for 5 minutes on a wire rack before cutting. **Yield:** 6 servings.

Nutritional Analysis: *One serving equals 255 calories, 7 g fat (2 g saturated fat), 3 mg cholesterol, 567 mg sodium, 39 g carbohydrate, 2 g fiber, 10 g protein.*
Diabetic Exchanges: *2 starch, 1 fat, 1/2 fat-free milk.*

Favorite Brownie Recipe Made Lighter

ROCKY ROAD FUDGE BROWNIES from Nanette Swinson would make a delicious addition to any cookie tray. But if you're watching what you eat, like Nanette is, you might prefer a lighter version.

"I hope you enjoy a good challenge!" writes the Hope, Michigan cook. "These rich gooey brownies are one of our favorites. But I find it hard to believe that your staff will be able to pare them down much."

The home economists in our Test Kitchen were up to the challenge. First, they started with a reduced-fat brownie mix that requires only water to prepare, instead of the standard box mix, which calls for oil and eggs.

Then they cut the amount of pecans in half and the amount of marshmallows by a third.

To lighten up the icing, they used fat-free milk instead of whole milk, replaced some of the chocolate with baking cocoa, and substituted marshmallow creme for some of the sugar and butter.

Makeover Rocky Road Fudge Brownies remain sweetly satisfying, but have about 40% fewer calories and less than half the fat and saturated fat of the original.

Rocky Road Fudge Brownies

1 package fudge brownie mix (13-inch x 9-inch pan size)
1 cup chopped pecans
3 cups miniature marshmallows
1/2 cup milk
1/2 cup butter *or* margarine
2 squares (1 ounce *each*) unsweetened chocolate
3-3/4 cups confectioners' sugar
1/2 teaspoon vanilla extract

Prepare brownie mix according to package directions for fudge-like brownies; stir in pecans. Spread batter into a greased 13-in. x 9-in. x 2-in. baking pan. Bake at 350° for 25-30 minutes or until a toothpick inserted near the center comes out clean. Sprinkle with marshmallows. Cool on a wire rack.

In a saucepan, combine the milk, butter and chocolate. Cook and stir over low heat until smooth. Transfer to a mixing bowl; beat in confectioners' sugar and vanilla until smooth. Spread over marshmallows. **Yield:** 2 dozen.

Nutritional Analysis: One brownie equals 306 calories, 14 g fat (4 g saturated fat), 29 mg cholesterol, 126 mg sodium, 46 g carbohydrate, 2 g fiber, 3 g protein.

Makeover Rocky Road Fudge Brownies

(Pictured below)

1 package reduced-fat fudge brownie mix (13-inch x 9-inch pan size)
1/2 cup chopped pecans
2 cups miniature marshmallows
1 cup marshmallow creme
1/4 cup fat-free milk
3 tablespoons butter *or* stick margarine
3 tablespoons baking cocoa
1 square (1 ounce) unsweetened chocolate
1 cup confectioners' sugar
1/2 teaspoon vanilla extract

Prepare brownie mix according to package directions; stir in pecans. Spread batter into a 13-in. x 9-in. x 2-in. baking pan coated with nonstick cooking spray. Bake at 350° for 25-30 minutes or until a toothpick inserted near the center comes out clean. Sprinkle with marshmallows. Cool on a wire rack.

In a saucepan, combine marshmallow creme, milk, butter, cocoa and chocolate. Cook and stir over low heat until melted and smooth. Transfer to a mixing bowl; beat in confectioners' sugar and vanilla until smooth. Drizzle over marshmallows. **Yield:** 2 dozen.

Nutritional Analysis: One brownie equals 180 calories, 6 g fat (2 g saturated fat), 4 mg cholesterol, 109 mg sodium, 32 g carbohydrate, 1 g fiber, 2 g protein.
Diabetic Exchanges: 2 starch, 1 fat.

Moist Apple Cake

This appetizing apple cinnamon cake, draped with a warm brown sugar sauce, is a crowd-pleaser at parties or at the office. I adapted a friend's recipe by decreasing the oil and substituting applesauce. I also switched to fat-free milk...but no one will ever guess this treat is light.
—Lisa Miller, West Chester, Ohio

  2-1/2 cups all-purpose flour
    2 cups sugar
    2 teaspoons baking powder
    1 teaspoon baking soda
    1 teaspoon salt
    1 teaspoon ground cinnamon
    2 eggs
    3/4 cup unsweetened applesauce
    1/4 cup canola oil
    1 teaspoon vanilla extract
    3 cups chopped peeled tart apples (about 3 medium)
    1/2 cup chopped pecans
SAUCE:
    3 tablespoons butter *or* stick margarine
    1 cup packed brown sugar
    1/3 cup fat-free milk
    1 teaspoon vanilla extract

In a large mixing bowl, combine the flour, sugar, baking powder, baking soda, salt and cinnamon. In another mixing bowl, beat eggs until frothy. Add applesauce, oil and vanilla; beat until blended. Stir into flour mixture; mix well. Fold in apples and pecans.

Pour into a 13-in. x 9-in. x 2-in. baking pan coated with nonstick cooking spray. Bake at 350° for 40-45 minutes or until a toothpick inserted near the center comes out clean. In a small saucepan, melt butter. Add the brown sugar, milk and vanilla. Bring to a boil, stirring constantly. Pour over warm cake. Serve warm. **Yield:** 15 servings.

Nutritional Analysis: One serving (1 piece) equals 341 calories, 10 g fat (2 g saturated fat), 35 mg cholesterol, 346 mg sodium, 62 g carbohydrate, 2 g fiber, 3 g protein.

Creamy Chocolate Almond Pie

(Pictured at right and on back cover)

Folks will be lining up for seconds after one bite of this dreamy dessert. Crunchy almonds and a hint of coconut add a special touch to the pretty pudding pie.
—Mary Jones, St. Louis, Missouri

  1-1/4 cups reduced-fat chocolate wafer crumbs (about 40 wafers)
    2 tablespoons sugar
    2 tablespoons butter *or* stick margarine, melted
    1 egg white
FILLING:
    2/3 cup nonfat dry milk powder
  1-1/3 cups cold water
    1 package (1.4 ounces) sugar-free instant chocolate pudding mix
    1 cup reduced-fat whipped topping, *divided*

    1/4 cup chopped almonds
    3/4 teaspoon coconut extract, *divided*
    2 tablespoons flaked coconut, toasted
    1 tablespoon miniature semisweet chocolate chips

In a food processor, combine wafer crumbs, sugar and butter; pulse until blended. Add egg white; pulse until moistened. Press mixture onto the bottom and up the sides of a 9-in. pie plate. Bake at 375° for 8-10 minutes or until lightly browned. Cool completely before filling.

In a bowl, whisk milk powder and water until blended. Add pudding mix; whisk for 2 minutes or until slightly thickened. Fold in 1/4 cup whipped topping, almonds and 1/2 teaspoon extract. Pour into prepared crust; refrigerate for 15 minutes. Combine remaining whipped topping and extract; spread over filling. Sprinkle with coconut and chocolate chips; refrigerate until serving. **Yield:** 8 servings.

Nutritional Analysis: One piece equals 218 calories, 9 g fat (4 g saturated fat), 9 mg cholesterol, 206 mg sodium, 31 g carbohydrate, 2 g fiber, 6 g protein.
Diabetic Exchanges: 2 starch, 1-1/2 fat.

Orange Dream Cups

(Pictured at right and on back cover)

Hollowed-out orange "cups" make this recipe unique and fun...and the light fluffy filling is so refreshing. These cute dessert cups are always a hit with kids and company.
—Elizabeth Alvarez, Bedford, Texas

    4 large navel oranges
    1 package (3 ounces) orange gelatin
    1 cup boiling water
  1-1/2 cups fat-free frozen vanilla yogurt

Cut each orange in half widthwise; carefully remove fruit from both halves, leaving shells intact. Set shells aside. Section orange pulp, then dice (discard orange juice or save for another use). In a bowl, dissolve gelatin in boiling water. Add frozen yogurt; stir until melted. Fold in orange pulp. Refrigerate until thickened. Spoon into reserved orange shells. Cover and freeze for 3 hours. **Yield:** 8 servings.

Nutritional Analysis: One serving (1 filled orange half) equals 119 calories, trace fat (trace saturated fat), 0 cholesterol, 50 mg sodium, 28 g carbohydrate, 2 g fiber, 3 g protein.
Diabetic Exchanges: 1-1/2 fruit, 1/2 fat-free milk.

Carrot Chocolate Chip Cookies

The recipe for these scrumptious cookies was handwritten in a cookbook I received from my husband's grandmother. She told my husband when he was young that these treats were a good way to get his carrots. He loved them anyway!
—Karin Woodbury, Ocala, Florida

    2 eggs
    1 cup packed brown sugar
  1/3 cup fat-free milk
  1/3 cup canola oil
    2 cups all-purpose flour
    1 teaspoon baking powder
  1/2 teaspoon salt
  1/2 teaspoon ground cinnamon
  1/4 teaspoon baking soda
  1/4 teaspoon ground nutmeg
    1 cup (6 ounces) semisweet chocolate chips
    1 cup quick-cooking oats
    1 cup grated carrots
    1 cup raisins

In a large mixing bowl, beat eggs, brown sugar, milk and oil. Combine the flour, baking powder, salt, cinnamon, baking soda and nutmeg; add to egg mixture and mix well. Stir in the chips, oats, carrots and raisins. Drop by heaping teaspoonfuls onto baking sheets coated with nonstick cooking spray; flatten slightly. Bake at 350° for 10-13 minutes or until golden brown. Remove to wire racks to cool. **Yield:** about 7 dozen.

Nutritional Analysis: One serving (4 cookies) equals 197 calories, 7 g fat (2 g saturated fat), 20 mg cholesterol, 99 mg sodium, 33 g carbohydrate, 2 g fiber, 3 g protein.
Diabetic Exchanges: 2 starch, 1 fat.

Strawberries with Crisp Wontons

Five-spice powder and crisp sugar-dusted wontons lend an Oriental flair to this dessert from our Test Kitchen staff. The sweet juicy berries paired with a spicy topping bring an elegant ending to any meal.

    4 wonton wrappers
    1 tablespoon butter *or* stick margarine, melted
    2 tablespoons plus 1 teaspoon sugar, *divided*
    2 pints fresh strawberries, sliced
    2 cups reduced-fat whipped topping
  1/8 teaspoon Chinese five-spice powder

Brush both sides of wonton wrappers with melted butter. Place 2 tablespoons sugar in a shallow dish; press wontons into sugar to coat both sides. Cut each wonton in half diagonally. Place on a baking sheet coated with nonstick cooking spray. Bake at 425° for 4-5 minutes or until golden brown. Turn and bake 2 minutes longer or until golden brown. Remove to wire racks to cool.

Toss strawberries with remaining sugar. Combine the whipped topping and five-spice powder. Divide the strawberries among four plates. Top each with whipped topping and two wonton pieces. **Yield:** 4 servings.

Nutritional Analysis: One serving equals 200 calories, 8 g fat (6 g saturated fat), 8 mg cholesterol, 77 mg sodium, 30 g carbohydrate, 3 g fiber, 2 g protein.
Diabetic Exchanges: 1-1/2 fat, 1 starch, 1 fruit.

Cake-Topped Apple Cobbler

(Pictured below)

I was born and raised in the Midwest, and this sweet dessert reminds me of home. The kitchen smells wonderful while it's baking. It's done when you tap on the crunchy topping and it sounds hollow.
—Dawn Ace, Berkeley, California

    6 cups sliced peeled Granny Smith apples
1-1/2 cups sugar, *divided*
  1/2 teaspoon ground cinnamon
    2 tablespoons butter *or* stick margarine, softened
    1 egg
  1/4 cup egg substitute
    1 cup all-purpose flour
    1 teaspoon baking powder
4-1/2 cups fat-free frozen vanilla yogurt

Arrange apple slices in an 8-in. square baking dish coated with nonstick cooking spray. Combine 1/2 cup sugar and cinnamon; sprinkle over apples.

In a small mixing bowl, beat butter and remaining sugar until crumbly, about 2 minutes. Add egg and egg substitute; mix well. Combine flour and baking powder; add to egg mixture and beat until blended. Drop by spoonfuls over the apples and spread evenly. Bake at 350° for 40-45 minutes or until golden brown. Serve warm with frozen yogurt. **Yield:** 9 servings.

Nutritional Analysis: One serving (1 piece with 1/2 cup frozen yogurt) equals 352 calories, 6 g fat (3 g saturated fat), 40 mg cholesterol, 137 mg sodium, 72 g carbohydrate, 2 g fiber, 7 g protein.

Nutritional Analysis: One cookie equals 109 calories, 3 g fat (2 g saturated fat), 13 mg cholesterol, 154 mg sodium, 19 g carbohydrate, 1 g fiber, 2 g protein.
Diabetic Exchanges: 1 starch, 1/2 fat.

Strawberry Mousse

(Pictured below)

To cut calories from a strawberry pie recipe, I lightened up the filling and served it in dessert dishes instead of a pie crust. With its pretty color and fruity flavor, it's an elegant dessert without much fuss.
—Waydella Hart, Parsons, Kansas

4 cups quartered fresh strawberries *or* frozen unsweetened strawberries
1/2 cup sugar
1 package (1 ounce) sugar-free instant vanilla pudding mix
1 carton (8 ounces) frozen reduced-fat whipped topping, thawed

In a food processor or blender, combine strawberries and sugar; cover and process until smooth. Strain and discard seeds. Return strawberry mixture to the food processor. Add pudding mix; cover and process until smooth. Transfer to a large bowl; fold in whipped topping. Spoon into dessert dishes. Refrigerate until serving. **Yield:** 8 servings.

Nutritional Analysis: One serving (1/2 cup) equals 145 calories, 3 g fat (3 g saturated fat), 0 cholesterol, 148 mg sodium, 27 g carbohydrate, 2 g fiber, trace protein.
Diabetic Exchanges: 1 starch, 1 fruit, 1/2 fat.

Cranberry Oat Yummies

(Pictured above)

I like to think these oatmeal treats are better for you than the standard chocolate chip cookie. Our three sons just can't get enough of them. And they have no idea I've made the cookies healthier.
—Carol Birkemeier, Nashville, Indiana

1/2 cup butter *or* stick margarine, melted
1/2 cup sugar
1 cup packed brown sugar
1 egg
1/4 cup egg substitute
2 tablespoons corn syrup
1-1/2 teaspoons vanilla extract
3 cups quick-cooking oats
1 cup all-purpose flour
1 teaspoon baking soda
1 teaspoon ground cinnamon
1/2 teaspoon baking powder
1/2 teaspoon salt
1/8 teaspoon ground nutmeg
1 cup dried cranberries

In a mixing bowl, beat butter and sugars. Add egg, egg substitute, corn syrup and vanilla; mix well. Combine the oats, flour, baking soda, cinnamon, baking powder, salt and nutmeg; gradually add to egg mixture. Stir in cranberries.

Drop by heaping tablespoonfuls 2 in. apart onto ungreased baking sheets. Bake at 375° for 8-10 minutes or until golden brown. Cool for 2 minutes before removing from pans to wire racks. **Yield:** 3 dozen.

In a bowl, whisk milk and pudding mix for 2 minutes or until slightly thickened. Add vanilla; mix well. Stir in rice. Serve immediately or cover and refrigerate. **Yield:** 6 servings.

Nutritional Analysis: One serving (1/2 cup) equals 115 calories, 2 g fat (1 g saturated fat), 7 mg cholesterol, 241 mg sodium, 20 g carbohydrate, trace fiber, 4 g protein.
Diabetic Exchange: 1-1/2 starch.

Peanut Butter Oatmeal Cookies

(Pictured below)

These cookies are soft and chewy with the tasty combination of oatmeal and peanut butter. I take them to work and on camping trips since they travel very well.
—Rollin Barkeim, Trempealeau, Wisconsin

> 3 egg whites
> 1 cup packed brown sugar
> 1 cup reduced-fat peanut butter
> 1/2 cup unsweetened applesauce
> 1/4 cup honey
> 2 teaspoons vanilla extract
> 3 cups quick-cooking oats
> 1 cup all-purpose flour
> 1 cup nonfat dry milk powder
> 2 teaspoons baking soda

In a mixing bowl, beat egg whites and brown sugar. Beat in peanut butter, applesauce, honey and vanilla. Combine the oats, flour, milk powder and baking soda; gradually add to peanut butter mixture, beating until combined. Drop by tablespoonfuls 2 in. apart onto baking sheets coated with nonstick cooking spray. Bake at 350° for 8-10 minutes or until golden brown. Remove to wire racks to cool. **Yield:** 5 dozen.

Nutritional Analysis: One serving (2 cookies) equals 137 calories, 3 g fat (1 g saturated fat), trace cholesterol, 153 mg sodium, 22 g carbohydrate, 1 g fiber, 5 g protein.
Diabetic Exchanges: 1 starch, 1/2 fat.

Caramel Brownie Pizza

(Pictured above)

This moist fudgy pizza topped with caramel, chips and nuts is sure to satisfy your family's sweet tooth. To prevent the tips of wedges from breaking when serving, I keep the toppings thinner in the center.
—Amy Branson, Bristol, Virginia

> 1 package reduced-fat brownie mix (13-inch x 9-inch pan size)
> 1/2 cup fat-free caramel apple dip
> 1/2 cup miniature chocolate chips
> 1/4 cup chopped pecans

Prepare brownie batter according to package directions. Coat a 12-in. pizza pan with nonstick cooking spray. Spread batter over pan to within 1 in. of the edge. Bake at 350° for 25-30 minutes or until a toothpick inserted 2 in. from edge comes out clean. Cool completely on a wire rack. Spread caramel apple dip over the top; sprinkle with chocolate chips and pecans. **Yield:** 12 servings.

Nutritional Analysis: One serving equals 330 calories, 8 g fat (3 g saturated fat), 2 mg cholesterol, 260 mg sodium, 63 g carbohydrate, 2 g fiber, 4 g protein.

Sugarless Rice Pudding

I can whip up a batch of this rice pudding in no time. It has plenty of old-fashioned goodness without the sugar.
—Ruth Hannan, Harrisburg, Pennsylvania

> 2 cups cold 2% milk
> 1 package (1 ounce) sugar-free instant vanilla pudding mix
> 1/4 teaspoon vanilla extract
> 2 cups cold cooked rice

Favorite Upside-Down Cake Recipe Made Lighter

FOLKS have been flipping over upside-down cake for generations. One scrumptious version—Peach Upside-Down Cake—is suggested by Terri Kirschner of Carlisle, Indiana. "This dessert is very popular with my family and guests," Terri says.

If you'd like to serve a similar treat but would prefer one that's been slimmed down, try our Test Kitchen's Makeover Peach Upside-Down Cake. Our kitchen crew used a little less sugar, brown sugar and butter, then added buttermilk to replace some of the moisture.

Peach Upside-Down Cake

- 3/4 cup butter *or* margarine, softened, *divided*
- 1/2 cup packed brown sugar
- 2 cups sliced peeled fresh peaches
- 3/4 cup sugar
- 1 egg
- 1 teaspoon vanilla extract
- 1-1/4 cups all-purpose flour
- 1-1/4 teaspoons baking powder
- 1/4 teaspoon salt
- 1/2 cup milk

Melt 1/4 cup butter; pour into an ungreased 9-in. round baking pan. Sprinkle with brown sugar. Arrange peach slices in a single layer over sugar. In a mixing bowl, cream sugar and remaining butter. Add egg and vanilla; mix well. Combine flour, baking powder and salt; add to creamed mixture alternately with milk. Spoon over peaches.

Bake at 350° for 45-50 minutes or until a toothpick inserted near the center comes out clean. Cool for 10 minutes before inverting onto a serving plate. Serve warm. **Yield:** 8 servings.

Nutritional Analysis: One piece equals 386 calories, 19 g fat (11 g saturated fat), 75 mg cholesterol, 347 mg sodium, 53 g carbohydrate, 1 g fiber, 4 g protein.

Makeover Peach Upside-Down Cake

(Pictured at right)

- 1 can (15 ounces) reduced-sugar sliced peaches
- 1/3 cup packed brown sugar
- 4 tablespoons butter *or* stick margarine, melted, *divided*
- 1/4 teaspoon ground cinnamon
- 1/8 teaspoon ground nutmeg
- 1-1/2 cups all-purpose flour
- 2/3 cup sugar
- 3/4 teaspoon baking powder
- 1/4 teaspoon baking soda
- 1/4 teaspoon salt
- 1 cup 1% buttermilk
- 1 egg
- 1 teaspoon vanilla extract

Drain peaches, reserving 2 tablespoons juice. Pat peaches dry. In a small bowl, combine the brown sugar, 1 tablespoon butter, cinnamon, nutmeg and reserved peach juice. Spread into a 9-in. round baking pan coated with nonstick cooking spray. Cut peach slices in half lengthwise; arrange in a single layer over brown sugar mixture.

In a large bowl, combine the flour, sugar, baking powder, baking soda and salt. In another bowl, combine the buttermilk, egg, vanilla and remaining butter. Add to dry ingredients and stir until blended. Spoon over peaches. Bake at 350° for 30-35 minutes or until a toothpick inserted near the center comes out clean. Cool for 10 minutes before inverting onto a serving plate. Serve warm. **Yield:** 8 servings.

Nutritional Analysis: One piece equals 273 calories, 7 g fat (4 g saturated fat), 43 mg cholesterol, 240 mg sodium, 49 g carbohydrate, 1 g fiber, 4 g protein.
Diabetic Exchanges: 3 starch, 1 fat.

Double-Chocolate Cream Roll

(Pictured above)

Guests will never guess that this cake roll is low in fat!
An update of an old recipe, this version
replaces the original whipped cream filling
with pudding and nondairy topping.
—Rose Monfort, Sparta, Tennessee

1-1/2 teaspoons shortening
   5 eggs, *separated*
   1 teaspoon vanilla extract
   1 cup plus 2 teaspoons confectioners' sugar,
    divided
   3 tablespoons baking cocoa
1/8 teaspoon salt
1-1/2 cups cold fat-free milk
   2 packages (3.3 ounces *each*) instant white
    chocolate pudding mix *or* 2 packages
    (3.4 ounces *each*) instant vanilla pudding mix
   1 carton (8 ounces) frozen reduced-fat whipped
    topping, thawed
   3 tablespoons fat-free caramel ice cream topping,
    divided
1/2 cup chopped walnuts, *divided*
   1 tablespoon fat-free hot fudge ice cream
    topping, warmed

Coat a 15-in. x 10-in. x 1-in. baking pan with nonstick cooking spray; line with parchment paper. Grease the paper with shortening; set aside. In a mixing bowl, beat egg yolks on high speed until thick and lemon-colored. Add vanilla. Combine 1 cup confectioners' sugar, cocoa and salt; gradually add to egg yolks. In another mixing bowl, beat egg whites until stiff peaks form. Fold into egg yolk mixture. Spread into prepared pan.

Bake at 350° for 14-16 minutes or until cake springs back when lightly touched. Immediately invert the cake onto a kitchen towel dusted with remaining confectioners' sugar. Gently but quickly peel off parchment paper. Roll up cake in the towel jelly-roll style, starting with a short side. Cool completely on a wire rack.

In a mixing bowl, beat milk and pudding mix on low speed for 2 minutes. Fold in whipped topping. Set aside 1 cup. Unroll cake; spread remaining filling evenly over cake to within 1/2 in. of edges. Drizzle with 2 tablespoons of caramel topping; sprinkle with 6 tablespoons of walnuts. Roll up again. Spread reserved filling over cake roll. Drizzle with hot fudge sauce and remaining caramel topping. Sprinkle with remaining walnuts. Cover and chill for 1 hour before serving. Refrigerate leftovers. **Yield:** 12 servings.

Nutritional Analysis: One slice equals 227 calories, 8 g fat (3 g saturated fat), 89 mg cholesterol, 301 mg sodium, 33 g carbohydrate, 1 g fiber, 5 g protein.
Diabetic Exchanges: 2 starch, 1-1/2 fat.

Strawberry Italian Ice

(Pictured at left)

We discovered Italian ice about a year ago, and it has become a family favorite. The recipes I found, however, required quite a bit of sugar, so I developed my own version using fresh strawberries, fruit juice concentrate and a hint of lemon.
—Jaye Hansen, Winter Haven, Florida

2 pints fresh strawberries, hulled and halved
3/4 cup unsweetened apple juice concentrate
1 to 3 tablespoons lemon juice
Fresh mint, optional

Place first three ingredients in a blender or food processor; cover and process until smooth. Pour into an ungreased 8-in. square dish. Cover and freeze for 1-1/2 to 2 hours or until partially set. Spoon into a mixing bowl; beat on medium speed for 1-1/2 minutes. Return to dish; freeze for 2-3 hours or until firm. Remove from freezer 10 minutes before serving. Garnish with mint if desired. **Yield:** 5 servings.

Nutritional Analysis: One serving (3/4 cup) equals 109 calories, 1 g fat (trace saturated fat), 0 cholesterol, 12 mg sodium, 27 g carbohydrate, 3 g fiber, 1 g protein.
Diabetic Exchange: 2 fruit.

Cherry Chocolate Pie

Packaged pudding mix, canned cherries and a frozen crust simplify preparation of this dessert. Friends often request it when they come to our house. Sometimes I'll sprinkle toasted pecans on top for crunch.
—Pearl Lenz, Wichita, Kansas

1 can (14-1/2 ounces) pitted tart cherries in water
2 tablespoons sugar
2 cups 2% milk
2 packages (1.3 ounces *each*) sugar-free cook-and-serve chocolate pudding mix
1 frozen pastry shell (9 inches), baked

Drain cherries, reserving the liquid. In a bowl, combine cherries and sugar; set aside. In a large saucepan, combine the milk and reserved cherry liquid. Stir in pudding mix. Cook and stir over medium heat until mixture comes to a boil; cook and stir 1-2 minutes longer or until thickened. Stir in cherries. Pour into crust. Cool on a wire rack. Refrigerate leftovers. **Yield:** 8 servings.

Nutritional Analysis: One piece equals 169 calories, 6 g fat (3 g saturated fat), 8 mg cholesterol, 194 mg sodium, 27 g carbohydrate, 1 g fiber, 4 g protein.
Diabetic Exchanges: 1-1/2 starch, 1 fat, 1/2 fruit.

Apple Pie Coffee Cake

(Pictured at right)

This moist spice cake is low in fat but full of flavor! Apple pie filling is my secret ingredient. For a fun
variation, try it with a chocolate cake mix and cherry pie filling...or yellow cake mix and peach filling.
—Sandra Castillo, Sun Prairie, Wisconsin

1 package (18-1/4 ounces) spice cake mix
1 can (21 ounces) apple pie filling
3 eggs
3/4 cup fat-free sour cream
1/4 cup water
2 tablespoons canola oil
1 teaspoon almond extract
2 tablespoons brown sugar
1-1/2 teaspoons ground cinnamon
GLAZE:
2/3 cup confectioners' sugar
2 teaspoons fat-free milk

Set aside 1 tablespoon cake mix. Set aside 1-1/2 cups pie filling. In a mixing bowl, combine eggs, sour cream, water, oil, extract and remaining cake mix and pie filling. Beat on medium speed for 2 minutes. Pour half into a 10-in. fluted tube pan coated with nonstick cooking spray.

Combine the brown sugar, cinnamon and reserved cake mix; sprinkle over batter. Spoon reserved pie filling over batter to within 3/4 in. of edges; top with remaining batter. Bake at 350° for 40-45 minutes or until a toothpick inserted near the center comes out clean. Cool for 10 minutes before removing from pan to a wire rack.

In a small bowl, combine glaze ingredients. Drizzle over cooled cake. **Yield:** 14 servings.

Nutritional Analysis: One piece equals 283 calories, 8 g fat (2 g saturated fat), 46 mg cholesterol, 296 mg sodium, 49 g carbohydrate, 2 g fiber, 5 g protein.
Diabetic Exchanges: 2 starch, 1-1/2 fat, 1 fruit.

Honey Lemon Cookies

I brought home a blue ribbon from the state fair with these delightful cookies flavored with lemon peel and rolled in a wheat germ coating.
—Pat Habiger, Spearville, Kansas

  1/3 cup butter *or* stick margarine, softened
  1/2 cup sugar
  1/2 cup honey
    1 egg
    1 teaspoon grated lemon peel
2-1/4 cups all-purpose flour
  1/2 cup wheat germ, *divided*
    1 teaspoon baking powder
  1/4 teaspoon salt

In a mixing bowl, cream the butter and sugar. Beat in the honey, egg and lemon peel. Combine the flour, 1/4 cup wheat germ, baking powder and salt; gradually add to the creamed mixture. Cover and refrigerate for 1 hour or until easy to handle.

Roll dough into 1-in. balls; roll in remaining wheat germ. Place 2 in. apart on baking sheets coated with nonstick cooking spray. Bake at 350° for 11-12 minutes or until lightly browned. Remove to wire racks to cool. Store in a resealable plastic bag. **Yield:** about 4 dozen.

Nutritional Analysis: One serving (3 cookies) equals 172 calories, 5 g fat (3 g saturated fat), 24 mg cholesterol, 95 mg sodium, 30 g carbohydrate, 1 g fiber, 3 g protein.
Diabetic Exchanges: 1 starch, 1 fruit, 1 fat.

Cool Raspberry Peach Pie

(Pictured at right)

This pretty pie combines two favorite fruits. This recipe makes the most of raspberries and peaches when they're at their peak.
—Mindee Myers, Lincoln, Nebraska

1-1/2 cups reduced-fat vanilla wafer crumbs (about 50 wafers)
    2 tablespoons sugar
    2 tablespoons butter *or* stick margarine, melted
    1 egg white
FILLING:
  1/2 cup sugar
    3 tablespoons cornstarch
  1/4 cup water
    4 cups sliced peeled fresh peaches *or* frozen unsweetened peach slices, thawed (about 1-1/2 pounds)
    3 cups unsweetened raspberries

In a food processor, combine the wafer crumbs, sugar and butter; pulse until blended. Add egg white; pulse until moistened. Press mixture onto the bottom and up the sides of a 9-in. pie plate. Bake at 375° for 8-10 minutes or until lightly browned. Cool completely on a wire rack.

In a large saucepan, combine sugar and cornstarch. Stir

in water until smooth. Add peaches; stir to coat. Bring to a boil; cook and stir for 2 minutes or until thickened. Remove from the heat; gently stir in raspberries. Spoon into prepared crust. Refrigerate until chilled. Refrigerate leftovers. **Yield:** 8 servings.

Nutritional Analysis: One piece equals 252 calories, 5 g fat (2 g saturated fat), 8 mg cholesterol, 119 mg sodium, 52 g carbohydrate, 5 g fiber, 2 g protein.

Caramel Fudge Brownies

(Pictured at right)

These brownies are so rich and yummy, you'll never guess they're lightened up.
—Priscilla Renfrow, Wilson, North Carolina

    4 squares (1 ounce *each*) unsweetened chocolate
    3 egg whites, lightly beaten
    1 cup sugar
    2 jars (2-1/2 ounces *each*) prune baby food
    1 teaspoon vanilla extract
  1/2 teaspoon salt
  1/2 cup all-purpose flour
  1/4 cup chopped walnuts
    6 tablespoons fat-free caramel ice cream topping
    9 tablespoons reduced-fat whipped topping

In a microwave or saucepan, melt chocolate; stir until smooth. In a bowl, combine the egg whites, sugar, melted chocolate, prunes, vanilla and salt; mix well. Stir in flour until just moistened.

Pour into an 8-in. square baking pan coated with nonstick cooking spray. Sprinkle with walnuts. Bake at 350° for 30-32 minutes or until the top springs back when lightly touched. Cool on a wire rack. Cut into squares; drizzle with caramel topping and dollop with whipped topping. **Yield:** 9 servings.

Nutritional Analysis: One piece equals 251 calories, 10 g fat (5 g saturated fat), 0 cholesterol, 170 mg sodium, 42 g carbohydrate, 3 g fiber, 4 g protein.
Diabetic Exchanges: 2 starch, 2 fat, 1/2 fruit.

🍎 Brownie Bites

KEEP these brownie basics in mind the next time you're serving up a batch of the mouth-watering bars:
- Refrigerate brownies in the pan to firm them up before cutting.
- Use a sharp knife when cutting brownies to prevent edges from tearing. If the brownie is especially moist, wipe the blade between cuts.
- Moist, dense brownies will keep up to a week; drier, cake-like brownies, 1-2 days.
- In warm weather, you can store brownies in the refrigerator for 3-4 days.

Blueberries 'n' Cream Pie

(Pictured below)

After taking one bite of this appealing pie, friends always ask for the recipe. It's especially good served warm. You can substitute peaches for the berries with equally fantastic results.
—*Doreen Meyers, Chambersburg, Pennsylvania*

1/2 cup plus 1 tablespoon fat-free milk, *divided*
3 tablespoons butter *or* stick margarine, melted
1 egg
3/4 cup all-purpose flour
1 package (.8 ounce) sugar-free cook-and-serve vanilla pudding mix
1 teaspoon baking powder
1/8 teaspoon salt
2 cups fresh *or* frozen blueberries, thawed
1 package (8 ounces) reduced-fat cream cheese
1/2 cup sugar
TOPPING:
2 teaspoons sugar
1/8 teaspoon ground cinnamon

In a mixing bowl, beat 1/2 cup milk, butter and egg. Combine the flour, pudding mix, baking powder and salt; stir into egg mixture just until moistened. Pour into a 9-in. pie plate coated with nonstick cooking spray. Arrange blueberries over batter to within 1/2 in. of edge of plate.

In a mixing bowl, beat cream cheese, sugar and remaining milk until smooth. Spread over blueberries to within 1 in. of berry edge. For topping, combine sugar and cinnamon; sprinkle over the cream cheese mixture. Bake at 350° for 30-35 minutes or until set. Serve warm. Refrigerate leftovers. **Yield:** 8 servings.

Nutritional Analysis: One piece equals 249 calories, 12 g fat (7 g saturated fat), 60 mg cholesterol, 302 mg sodium, 31 g carbohydrate, 1 g fiber, 6 g protein.
Diabetic Exchanges: 2 fat, 1-1/2 starch, 1/2 fruit.

Apricot Apple Compote

You won't have to skip dessert when this comforting compote is on the menu. I asked a friend of mine how she could eat dessert and still stay thin, and she handed me this recipe. A touch of cinnamon and lemon accents the fruity flavor...and the dish is a snap to make.
—*Suzan Wiener, Spring Hill, Florida*

10 dried apricots, halved and sliced
1/2 cup water
4 medium apples, peeled and sliced
1 tablespoon sugar
1 teaspoon lemon juice
1/8 teaspoon grated lemon peel
1/8 teaspoon ground cinnamon

In a bowl, soak the apricots in water for 30 minutes. Drain, reserving 3 tablespoons water. In a saucepan, combine the apricots, apples, sugar and reserved water; bring to a boil. Reduce heat; cover and simmer for 20 minutes or until apples are tender. Remove from the heat. Stir in the lemon juice, peel and cinnamon. Serve warm or cold. **Yield:** 3 servings.

Nutritional Analysis: One serving (2/3 cup) equals 142 calories, 1 g fat (trace saturated fat), 0 cholesterol, 1 mg sodium, 37 g carbohydrate, 4 g fiber, 1 g protein.
Diabetic Exchange: 2-1/2 fruit.

Peanut Butter Ice Cream

I have the scoop when it comes to dessert! With just a handful of ingredients and my ice cream maker, I churn out this creamy peanut butter concoction with a nutty crunch. You won't believe it's light.
—*Florence Vella, Linden, New Jersey*

2 cups fat-free half-and-half cream
1 can (14 ounces) fat-free sweetened condensed milk
1/2 cup reduced-fat chunky peanut butter
1 envelope whipped topping mix
1 teaspoon vanilla extract

In a bowl, combine all of the ingredients. Cover and refrigerate for 1 hour. Freeze in an ice cream freezer according to manufacturer's instructions. Allow to ripen in the ice cream freezer or firm up in your refrigerator freezer for 2-4 hours before serving. **Yield:** 8 servings.

Nutritional Analysis: One serving (1/2 cup) equals 287 calories, 6 g fat (2 g saturated fat), 3 mg cholesterol, 201 mg sodium, 45 g carbohydrate, 1 g fiber, 11 g protein.
Diabetic Exchanges: 2 starch, 1 fat-free milk, 1 fat.

Nutritional Analysis: *One piece equals 212 calories, 5 g fat (2 g saturated fat), 31 mg cholesterol, 203 mg sodium, 40 g carbohydrate, 1 g fiber, 3 g protein.*
Diabetic Exchanges: *2 starch, 1 fat, 1/2 fruit.*

Watermelon Slush

(Pictured below)

This frosty treat makes a refreshing ending to a summer meal. Simply scoop the slushy mixture into bowls or tall glasses and top with lemon-lime soda.
—*Elizabeth Montgomery, Taylorville, Illinois*

8 cups cubed seedless watermelon
1/4 cup lime juice
1/4 cup sugar
2 cups diet lemon-lime soda, chilled

In a blender or food processor, cover and process the watermelon, lime juice and sugar in batches until smooth. Pour into a freezer-proof container. Cover and freeze for 30 minutes or until edges begin to freeze. Stir and return to freezer. Repeat every 20 minutes or until slushy, about 90 minutes. Spoon 3/4 cup into bowls or glasses; add 1/4 cup soda. **Yield:** 8 servings.

Nutritional Analysis: *One serving (1 cup) equals 75 calories, 1 g fat (trace saturated fat), 0 cholesterol, 12 mg sodium, 18 g carbohydrate, 1 g fiber, 1 g protein.*
Diabetic Exchange: *1 fruit.*

Cranberry Crumb Cake

(Pictured above)

This cranberry cake is light, easy to prepare and goes great with a cup of coffee. The flavor of cranberry comes through in every sweet-tart bite...and the streusel topping looks so pretty.
—*Sue Ellen Smith, Philadelphia, Mississippi*

1 cup all-purpose flour
1/2 cup plus 1/3 cup sugar, *divided*
2 teaspoons baking powder
1/2 teaspoon salt
1 egg, lightly beaten
1/2 cup fat-free milk
1 tablespoon orange juice
1 tablespoon canola oil
1/4 teaspoon almond extract
2 cups fresh *or* frozen cranberries, chopped
TOPPING:
1/4 cup all-purpose flour
3 tablespoons sugar
2 tablespoons cold butter

In a bowl, combine the flour, 1/2 cup sugar, baking powder and salt. Combine the egg, milk, orange juice, oil and extract; stir into dry ingredients. Spoon into an 8-in. square baking dish coated with nonstick cooking spray. Combine cranberries and remaining sugar; spoon over batter.

For topping, combine flour and sugar in a small bowl; cut in the butter until crumbly. Sprinkle over cranberries. Bake at 375° for 35-45 minutes or until edges begin to pull away from sides of pan. Refrigerate leftovers. **Yield:** 9 servings.

Lime Frozen Yogurt

*Wedges of grilled pineapple complement the cool
and tangy frozen yogurt in this delightful dessert.
It's a real refresher on warm days!*
—Kelly Krauss, Little Falls, New Jersey

   4 cups fat-free plain yogurt
1-1/2 cups sugar
   2/3 cup lime juice
   2 tablespoons grated lime peel
   1/4 teaspoon salt
   1 large fresh pineapple, peeled, cored and cut
      into 3/4-inch wedges
Fresh mint, optional

In a bowl, combine the yogurt, sugar, lime juice, lime peel
and salt; stir until the sugar is dissolved. Freeze in an ice
cream freezer according to manufacturer's instructions. Allow to ripen in the ice cream freezer or firm up in your refrigerator freezer for 2-4 hours before serving.

Coat grill rack with nonstick cooking spray before starting the grill. Grill pineapple, uncovered, over medium heat
for 2 minutes. Turn and grill 1-2 minutes longer or until heated through. Serve with lime frozen yogurt. Garnish with mint
if desired. **Yield:** 6 servings.

*Nutritional Analysis: One serving (3/4 cup frozen yogurt
with 1/6 of the pineapple) equals 307 calories, trace fat (trace
saturated fat), 3 mg cholesterol, 189 mg sodium, 75 g carbohydrate, 1 g fiber, 7 g protein.*

Very Berry Parfaits

(Pictured above)

*When I asked drop-in company to stay for dinner, I
happened to have all the ingredients on hand to create
this elegant layered berry treat. Everyone thought this
low-sugar dessert was yummy and refreshing.*
—Andree Garrett, Plymouth, Michigan

   1 package (.3 ounce) sugar-free strawberry
      gelatin
   1 cup boiling water
   1 cup cold water
   2 cups fresh *or* frozen blueberries, *divided*
   2 cups sliced fresh *or* frozen unsweetened
      strawberries, *divided*
1-3/4 cups cold fat-free milk
   1 package (1 ounce) sugar-free instant vanilla
      pudding mix

In a bowl, dissolve gelatin in boiling water. Stir in cold water. Pour into eight parfait glasses; refrigerate until firm,
about 1 hour. Top with half of the blueberries and half of
the strawberries. In a bowl, whisk milk and pudding mix for
2 minutes or until slightly thickened; pour over berries. Top
with remaining berries. Cover and refrigerate 1 hour longer.
Yield: 8 servings.

*Nutritional Analysis: One parfait equals 68 calories, trace
fat (trace saturated fat), 1 mg cholesterol, 208 mg sodium, 14 g
carbohydrate, 2 g fiber, 3 g protein.*
Diabetic Exchanges: 1/2 starch, 1/2 fruit.

Butterscotch Pie

*Being diabetic and having a craving for a butterscotch
pie, I went into the kitchen and came up with this
version that suits my diet and taste buds perfectly.*
—Edward Post, Etiwanda, California

   15 reduced-fat graham cracker squares (2-1/2
      inches x 2-1/2 inches)
   2 cups cold fat-free milk
   1 package (1 ounce) sugar-free instant vanilla
      pudding mix
   1 package (1.4 ounces) sugar-free instant
      butterscotch pudding mix
   2 cups (16 ounces) reduced-fat sour cream
   1 large ripe banana, cut into 1/4-inch slices
   1 cup reduced-fat whipped topping

In a 9-in. square dish, arrange nine graham cracker
squares. Break the remaining crackers in half; stand up
around the sides of the dish. In a bowl, whisk milk and
pudding mixes for 2 minutes or until slightly thickened.
Add sour cream; mix well. Arrange banana slices over graham crackers; top with pudding mixture. Cover and refrigerate for at least 5-6 hours. Serve with whipped topping.
Yield: 9 servings.

Editor's Note: This dessert has a soft set.

*Nutritional Analysis: One piece equals 216 calories, 6 g fat
(5 g saturated fat), 20 mg cholesterol, 516 mg sodium, 31 g carbohydrate, 1 g fiber, 7 g protein.*
Diabetic Exchanges: 1-1/2 starch, 1 fat, 1/2 fat-free milk.

Favorite Cake Recipe Made Lighter

WONDERING what to do with that bounty of garden zucchini? Bake it into a luscious Chocolate Zucchini Cake!

Says Denise Leonard of Exeter, New Hampshire, "My mom made this delicious chocolaty treat for us every summer when I was growing up. Now I have a family of my own and would like to fix them a lighter version."

Our Test Kitchen was happy to help out with Denise's request. They came up with a version that replaces two-thirds of the oil with applesauce, uses two eggs and two egg whites in place of four eggs, cuts back on the nuts and adds moisture by substituting corn syrup for some of the sugar.

Makeover Chocolate Zucchini Cake has all the moistness and rich chocolate flavor of Denise's mom's cake, but with fewer calories, fat and sugar.

In a mixing bowl, beat eggs on high until thick and lemon-colored. Gradually beat in sugar. Add oil and chocolate; beat well. Combine the flour, baking powder, baking soda and salt; add to the egg mixture. Beat on low just until combined. Stir in zucchini and nuts.

Pour into a greased and floured 10-in. fluted tube pan. Bake at 350° for 65-75 minutes or until a toothpick inserted near the center comes out clean. Cool for 10 minutes before removing from the pan to a wire rack to cool completely. **Yield:** 14 servings.

Nutritional Analysis: *One piece equals 580 calories, 33 g fat (4 g saturated fat), 61 mg cholesterol, 302 mg sodium, 68 g carbohydrate, 2 g fiber, 7 g protein.*

Chocolate Zucchini Cake

4 eggs
3 cups sugar
1-1/2 cups vegetable oil
3 squares (1 ounce *each*) unsweetened chocolate, melted and cooled
3 cups all-purpose flour
1-1/2 teaspoons baking powder
1 teaspoon baking soda
1 teaspoon salt
3 cups shredded zucchini, squeezed dry
1 cup finely chopped nuts

Makeover Chocolate Zucchini Cake

(Pictured below left)

2 eggs
2 egg whites
1-1/2 cups sugar
1/2 cup packed brown sugar
1/2 cup unsweetened applesauce
1/2 cup canola oil
1/4 cup corn syrup
3 squares (1 ounce *each*) unsweetened chocolate, melted and cooled
3 cups all-purpose flour
1-1/2 teaspoons baking powder
1 teaspoon baking soda
1 teaspoon salt
3 cups shredded zucchini, squeezed dry
1/2 cup finely chopped nuts
1 teaspoon confectioners' sugar

In a mixing bowl, combine the first eight ingredients; beat until smooth. Combine the flour, baking powder, baking soda and salt; add to the egg mixture and mix just until combined. Fold in zucchini and nuts.

Pour into a 10-in. fluted tube pan coated with non-stick cooking spray and floured. Bake at 350° for 55-65 minutes or until a toothpick inserted near the center comes out clean. Cool for 10 minutes before removing from pan to a wire rack; cool completely. Dust with confectioners' sugar. **Yield:** 14 servings.

Nutritional Analysis: *One piece equals 373 calories, 14 g fat (2 g saturated fat), 30 mg cholesterol, 311 mg sodium, 59 g carbohydrate, 2 g fiber, 6 g protein.*

Nutritional Analysis: One piece equals 167 calories, 8 g fat (1 g saturated fat), 0 cholesterol, 238 mg sodium, 22 g carbohydrate, 5 g fiber, 3 g protein.
Diabetic Exchanges: 1-1/2 fat, 1 starch, 1/2 fruit.

Nectarine Blueberry Crumble

A peachy use of the season's bounty is this fruitful dessert. I bring this juicy crumble to get-togethers of all kinds. Crushed macaroons make a delightfully different topping for the blueberries and nectarines. For a special treat, serve it with low-fat frozen yogurt.
—Marilyn Schroeder, Alexandria, Minnesota

2-1/2 pounds ripe nectarines (about 8 large)
 2 cups fresh *or* frozen blueberries
 1/3 cup sugar
 1/4 teaspoon ground nutmeg
 2 tablespoons lemon juice
 1/3 cup packed brown sugar
 2 tablespoons butter *or* stick margarine, cubed
 1 egg white
 2/3 cup crushed macaroons
 1/2 cup quick-cooking oats

Peel nectarines and remove pits; cut fruit into 1/2-in. slices. Place in a bowl; add the blueberries, sugar and nutmeg. Drizzle with lemon juice; toss lightly. Transfer to a shallow 3-qt. baking dish coated with nonstick cooking spray.

In a bowl, combine the brown sugar, butter and egg white; mix well. Stir in macaroon crumbs and oats. Spoon over the fruit mixture. Bake, uncovered, at 375° for 40-45 minutes or until golden brown and bubbly around the edges. **Yield:** 10 servings.

Nutritional Analysis: One serving equals 195 calories, 5 g fat (3 g saturated fat), 6 mg cholesterol, 45 mg sodium, 38 g carbohydrate, 3 g fiber, 3 g protein.
Diabetic Exchanges: 1-1/2 fruit, 1 starch, 1 fat.

Raspberry Pie with Oat Crust

(Pictured above)

A diabetic for 30 years, I adapted this recipe to fit my needs. When I serve this pie, no one can believe it's sugarless. The oatmeal crust is so tender... and the filling is berry delicious!
—Ginny Arandas, Greensburg, Pennsylvania

3/4 cup all-purpose flour
1/2 cup quick-cooking oats
1/2 teaspoon salt
1/4 cup canola oil
 3 to 4 tablespoons cold water
FILLING:
 2 cups water
 1 package (.8 ounce) sugar-free cook-and-serve vanilla pudding mix
 1 package (.3 ounce) sugar-free raspberry gelatin
 4 cups fresh raspberries

In a food processor, combine the flour, oats and salt. While processing, slowly drizzle in oil. Gradually add water until a ball forms. Roll out dough between two sheets of waxed paper. Remove top sheet of waxed paper; invert dough onto a 9-in. pie plate. Remove remaining waxed paper. Trim, seal and flute edges. Prick bottom of crust with a fork in several places. Bake at 400° for 10-12 minutes or until golden brown. Cool completely on a wire rack.

In a saucepan, heat water over medium heat. Whisk in pudding mix. Cook and stir for 5 minutes or until thickened and bubbly. Whisk in gelatin until completely dissolved. Remove from the heat; cool slightly. Fold in raspberries. Spoon into crust. Chill for at least 3 hours or overnight. Refrigerate leftovers. **Yield:** 8 servings.

🍎 Blueberry Basics

GETTING THE BLUES can be a good thing—when it comes to blueberries, that is! Blueberries are low in calories, virtually fat-free and a good source of fiber and vitamin C.

Here are some true-blue tips provided by the North American Blueberry Council:

● Whether you are doing your "picking" at the grocery store or the berry patch, look for blueberries that are firm and dry, not mushy.
● Blueberries should have a smooth skin and appear deep purple-blue with a silvery-white bloom.
● Keep in mind that size can range anywhere from small (190-250 berries per cup) to extra large (fewer than 90 berries per cup).
● Store blueberries in the refrigerator and use them within 10 days of purchase.
● Rinse and drain berries just before using.

Cran-Apple Crisp

(Pictured below)

Cranberries, walnuts, brown sugar and orange peel help give this apple-packed crowd-pleaser its rich flavor. After the first taste, guests will be asking for the recipe...and a second helping.
—Diane Everett, Newtown, Connecticut

    8 cups sliced peeled Granny Smith *or* other tart
      apples (about 5 large)
    3/4 cup sugar
    1/2 cup dried cranberries
    1/2 cup chopped walnuts
    1/4 cup all-purpose flour
1-1/2 to 2 teaspoons grated orange peel
    1/2 cup packed brown sugar
    1/3 cup whole wheat flour
    1/3 cup nonfat dry milk powder
      1 teaspoon ground cinnamon
    1/4 to 1/2 teaspoon cloves
      5 tablespoons cold butter
    1/3 cup quick-cooking oats

In a bowl, combine the first six ingredients; toss to coat. Transfer to a 13-in. x 9-in. x 2-in. baking dish coated with nonstick cooking spray. For topping, in a bowl, combine the brown sugar, whole wheat flour, milk powder, cinnamon and cloves. Cut in butter until mixture resembles coarse crumbs. Stir in oats. Sprinkle over apples. Bake, uncovered, at 350° for 40-45 minutes or until golden brown. **Yield:** 15 servings.

Nutritional Analysis: One serving equals 202 calories, 7 g fat (3 g saturated fat), 11 mg cholesterol, 51 mg sodium, 35 g carbohydrate, 2 g fiber, 2 g protein.
Diabetic Exchanges: *1-1/2 fat, 1 starch, 1 fruit.*

Sweet Potato Pie

(Pictured above)

Take a bite of this classic Southern dessert and you'll never guess it's been lightened up by our Test Kitchen home economists. The pleasing pie gets great fall flavor from a hint of pumpkin pie spice.

    2 pounds sweet potatoes (about 3 medium)
    3/4 cup packed brown sugar
    1/4 cup all-purpose flour
      2 teaspoons grated orange peel
      1 teaspoon pumpkin pie spice
      1 teaspoon vanilla extract
    1/8 teaspoon salt
      1 cup fat-free milk
    1/2 cup egg substitute
      1 unbaked pastry shell (9 inches)
    1/2 cup reduced-fat whipped topping

Bake sweet potatoes at 350° for 1 hour or until very soft. Cool slightly. Cut potatoes in half; scoop out the pulp and discard shells. Place pulp in a food processor or blender; cover and process until smooth.

In a bowl, combine the pulp, brown sugar, flour, orange peel, pumpkin pie spice, vanilla and salt. Stir in milk and egg substitute until well blended. Pour into pastry shell.

Bake at 375° for 45-50 minutes or until a knife inserted near the center comes out clean. Cool on a wire rack for 2 hours. Garnish with whipped topping. Refrigerate leftovers. **Yield:** 8 servings.

Nutritional Analysis: One serving (1 piece with 1 tablespoon whipped topping) equals 319 calories, 8 g fat (4 g saturated fat), 6 mg cholesterol, 196 mg sodium, 56 g carbohydrate, 2 g fiber, 6 g protein.

Creamy Banana Pudding

Our family has made this comforting old-fashioned treat a tradition for holidays, birthdays and Sunday dinners.
—Kelly Shealy, Barnwell, South Carolina

> 3 cups cold fat-free milk
> 2 packages (1 ounce *each*) sugar-free instant vanilla pudding mix
> 1 cup (8 ounces) fat-free sour cream
> 1 carton (8 ounces) frozen fat-free whipped topping, thawed
> 34 vanilla wafers
> 3 large firm bananas, sliced

In a bowl, whisk milk and pudding mixes for 2 minutes or until slightly thickened. Stir in sour cream. Fold in whipped topping until well blended. Place half of the vanilla wafers in an 11-in. x 7-in. x 2-in. dish. Top with half of the pudding mixture, half of the bananas, then remaining wafers, bananas and pudding mixture. Cover and refrigerate overnight. **Yield:** 10 servings.

Nutritional Analysis: One serving equals 210 calories, 3 g fat (1 g saturated fat), 2 mg cholesterol, 358 mg sodium, 39 g carbohydrate, 1 g fiber, 5 g protein.
Diabetic Exchanges: *1-1/2 starch, 1 fruit, 1/2 reduced-fat milk.*

Cranberry Meringue Pie

(Pictured at right and on page 201)

This sweet-tart cranberry pie is simply mouth-watering and a nice change for the holidays from the typical apple and pumpkin pies.
—Tina Dierking, Skowhegan, Maine

> 1 package (12 ounces) fresh *or* frozen cranberries, thawed
> 1 cup orange juice
> 3/4 cup water
> 3/4 cup sugar
> Sugar substitute equivalent to 3/4 cup sugar*
> 1/3 cup quick-cooking tapioca
> 2 teaspoons grated orange peel
> 1/4 teaspoon salt
> MERINGUE:
> 4 egg whites
> 1/4 teaspoon cream of tartar
> 1/2 cup sugar
> 1 pastry shell (9 inches), baked

Place cranberries in a food processor; cover and pulse until coarsely chopped. In a large saucepan, combine the cranberries and next seven ingredients. Let stand for 5 minutes. Bring to a boil over medium heat, stirring constantly. Reduce heat; simmer for 10 minutes, stirring constantly. Keep warm.

In a mixing bowl, beat egg whites until foamy. Add cream of tartar; beat on medium speed until soft peaks form. Gradually beat in sugar, 1 tablespoon at a time, beating until stiff peaks form. Spoon warm filling into pastry shell. Spread meringue evenly over filling, sealing to crust. Bake at 350° for 18-22 minutes or until golden brown. Cool for 1 hour. Chill, covered, for at least 4 hours. Refrigerate leftovers.

Yield: 8 servings.
*Editor's Note: This recipe uses both sugar and sugar substitute. It was tested with Splenda No Calorie Sweetener.

Nutritional Analysis: One piece equals 329 calories, 7 g fat (3 g saturated fat), 5 mg cholesterol, 202 mg sodium, 64 g carbohydrate, 2 g fiber, 3 g protein.

Lemon Cheese Pie

(Pictured at right and on page 201)

Your guests will never dream that this scrumptious pie, created by our Test Kitchen staff, is lighter. It's the perfect make-ahead dessert for any festive occasion.

> 1 sheet refrigerated pie pastry
> 1 cup sugar
> 1/4 cup plus 2 teaspoons cornstarch
> 1/2 teaspoon salt
> 1 cup water
> 2 tablespoons butter *or* stick margarine
> 2 teaspoons grated lemon peel
> 3 to 4 drops yellow food coloring, optional
> 1/2 cup plus 1 teaspoon lemon juice, *divided*
> 1 package (8 ounces) fat-free cream cheese
> 1/2 cup confectioners' sugar
> 1 cup reduced-fat whipped topping

Lightly roll out pastry into a 12-in. circle; transfer to a 9-in. pie plate. Trim pastry to 1/2 in. beyond edge of plate, reserving scraps for garnish. Flute edges. Line unpricked pastry shell with a double thickness of heavy-duty foil. Bake at 450° for 8 minutes. Remove foil; bake 5 minutes longer. Cool on a wire rack.

Roll out pastry scraps to 1/8-in. thickness. Cut out star shapes with 1-1/2-in. cookie cutters. Place on a baking sheet. Bake at 450° for 8 minutes or until golden brown. Cool on a wire rack.

In a large saucepan, combine the sugar, cornstarch and salt. Stir in water until blended. Bring to a boil; cook and stir for 2 minutes or until very thick. Remove from the heat; stir in butter, lemon peel and food coloring if desired. Gently stir in 1/2 cup lemon juice. Cool to room temperature, about 1 hour.

In a mixing bowl, beat cream cheese and confectioners' sugar until smooth. Fold in whipped topping and remaining lemon juice. Spread into crust; top with lemon filling. Refrigerate for 6 hours or until the top is set. Garnish with pastry stars. **Yield:** 8 servings.

Nutritional Analysis: One piece equals 341 calories, 11 g fat (6 g saturated fat), 15 mg cholesterol, 431 mg sodium, 55 g carbohydrate, trace fiber, 5 g protein.

garnish with remaining whipped topping. **Yield:** 2 cakes (8 slices each).

Nutritional Analysis: One slice equals 175 calories, 2 g fat (2 g saturated fat), 0 cholesterol, 171 mg sodium, 36 g carbohydrate, trace fiber, 3 g protein.
Diabetic Exchanges: 1-1/2 starch, 1 fruit.

Slow-Cooker Berry Cobbler

I adapted my mom's yummy cobbler recipe for the slow cooker. With the hot summers here in Arizona, we can still enjoy this comforting dessert, and I don't have to turn on the oven.
—*Karen Jarocki, Yuma, Arizona*

1-1/4 cups all-purpose flour, *divided*
   2 tablespoons plus 1 cup sugar, *divided*
   1 teaspoon baking powder
1/4 teaspoon ground cinnamon
   1 egg, lightly beaten
1/4 cup fat-free milk
   2 tablespoons canola oil
1/8 teaspoon salt
   2 cups unsweetened raspberries
   2 cups unsweetened blueberries
   2 cups reduced-fat frozen vanilla yogurt, optional

In a bowl, combine 1 cup flour, 2 tablespoons sugar, baking powder and cinnamon. In another bowl, combine the egg, milk and oil; stir into dry ingredients just until moistened (batter will be thick). Spread batter evenly onto the bottom of a 5-qt. slow cooker coated with nonstick cooking spray.

In a bowl, combine salt and remaining flour and sugar; add berries and toss to coat. Spread over batter. Cover and cook on high for 2 to 2-1/2 hours or until a toothpick inserted into cobbler comes out without crumbs. Top each serving with 1/4 cup frozen yogurt if desired. **Yield:** 8 servings.

Nutritional Analysis: One serving (calculated without frozen yogurt) equals 250 calories, 4 g fat (trace saturated fat), 27 mg cholesterol, 142 mg sodium, 51 g carbohydrate, 4 g fiber, 3 g protein.

Cherry Angel Cake Roll

(Pictured above)

I keep up a fast pace at college but still like to entertain. These pretty party cakes require just a handful of ingredients, yet always seem to impress guests.
—*Lisa Ruehlow, Madison, Wisconsin*

   1 package (16 ounces) angel food cake mix
   4 tablespoons confectioners' sugar, *divided*
   1 carton (8 ounces) reduced-fat frozen whipped topping, thawed, *divided*
   1 can (20 ounces) reduced-sugar cherry pie filling
1/4 teaspoon almond extract

Line two 15-in. x 10-in. x 1-in. baking pans with ungreased parchment paper. Prepare cake batter according to package directions. Spread evenly in prepared pans. Bake at 350° for 12-16 minutes or until golden brown. Meanwhile, sprinkle 3 tablespoons confectioners' sugar over two kitchen towels. Immediately invert cakes onto prepared towels. Gently peel off parchment paper. Roll up cakes in towels jelly-roll style, starting with a short side. Cool completely on a wire rack.

Unroll cakes. Spread each with 1 cup whipped topping to within 1 in. of edges. Combine pie filling and extract; spread over whipped topping on each cake. Roll up again. Place seam side down on a serving platter. Refrigerate for 1-2 hours. Dust with remaining confectioners' sugar. Slice;

🍎 Cut Out Crust...Cut Calories!

MY FAMILY doesn't care for pie crust, so I make pie fillings without the crust, which means less fat and fewer calories!

For pumpkin pie, I double the filling recipe, pour the mixture into a 13-in. x 9-in. baking dish and bake at 350° for 50 minutes (or until a knife inserted near the center comes out clean). For other pies, I put the pie filling into a pie pan or similar sized dish that's been sprayed with nonstick cooking spray.
—*Barbara Tuttle, Beaverton, Oregon*

Pumpkin Spice Cookies

(Pictured below)

These big soft spice cookies, created by our Test Kitchen staff, have a sweet white frosting that makes them an extra special treat. Enjoy!

1 package (18-1/4 ounces) reduced-fat yellow cake mix
1/2 cup quick-cooking oats
2 to 2-1/2 teaspoons pumpkin pie spice
1 egg
1 can (15 ounces) solid-pack pumpkin
2 tablespoons canola oil
3 cups confectioners' sugar
1 teaspoon grated orange peel
3 to 4 tablespoons orange juice

In a bowl, combine the cake mix, oats and pumpkin pie spice. In another bowl, beat the egg, pumpkin and oil; stir into dry ingredients just until moistened. Drop by 2 tablespoonfuls onto baking sheets coated with nonstick cooking spray; flatten with the back of a spoon. Bake at 350° for 18-20 minutes or until the edges are golden brown. Remove to wire racks to cool.

In a bowl, combine confectioners' sugar, orange peel and enough orange juice to achieve desired spreading consistency. Frost cooled cookies. **Yield:** 32 cookies.

Nutritional Analysis: One cookie equals 123 calories, 2 g fat (trace saturated fat), 7 mg cholesterol, 102 mg sodium, 25 g carbohydrate, 1 g fiber, 1 g protein.
Diabetic Exchanges: 1-1/2 starch, 1/2 fat.

Crimson Crumble Bars

(Pictured above)

Baking is my favorite pastime. These moist cranberry bars have a refreshing sweet-tart taste and a pleasant crumble topping. They're great as a snack or anytime treat.
—Paula Eriksen, Palm Harbor, Florida

1 cup sugar
2 teaspoons cornstarch
2 cups fresh *or* frozen cranberries
1 can (8 ounces) unsweetened crushed pineapple, undrained
1 cup all-purpose flour
2/3 cup old-fashioned oats
2/3 cup packed brown sugar
1/4 teaspoon salt
1/2 cup cold butter *or* stick margarine
1/2 cup chopped pecans

In a saucepan, combine the sugar, cornstarch, cranberries and pineapple; bring to a boil, stirring often. Reduce heat; cover and simmer for 10-15 minutes or until the berries pop. Remove from the heat.

In a large bowl, combine the flour, oats, brown sugar and salt. Cut in butter until mixture resembles coarse crumbs. Stir in pecans. Set aside 1-1/2 cups for topping. Press remaining crumb mixture onto the bottom of a 13-in. x 9-in. x 2-in. baking pan coated with nonstick cooking spray. Bake at 350° for 8-10 minutes or until firm; cool for 10 minutes.

Pour fruit filling over crust. Sprinkle with reserved crumb mixture. Bake for 25-30 minutes or until golden brown. Cool on a wire rack. **Yield:** 2 dozen.

Nutritional Analysis: One bar equals 152 calories, 6 g fat (3 g saturated fat), 10 mg cholesterol, 67 mg sodium, 24 g carbohydrate, 1 g fiber, 2 g protein.
Diabetic Exchanges: 1 starch, 1 fat, 1/2 fruit.

Nutritional Analysis: One serving (3/4 cup) equals 194 calories, 6 g fat (3 g saturated fat), 13 mg cholesterol, 451 mg sodium, 31 g carbohydrate, 1 g fiber, 4 g protein.
Diabetic Exchanges: 2 starch, 1 fat.

Microwave Apple Crisp

Microwaving brings out the natural sweetness of the apples in this warm, comforting crisp.
—Anna Mae Kocher, Sunman, Indiana

   6 cups sliced peeled tart apples
   2 tablespoons sugar
3/4 teaspoon ground cinnamon, *divided*
1/4 cup water
1/2 cup all-purpose flour
1/3 cup packed brown sugar
1/8 teaspoon salt
   3 tablespoons cold butter *or* stick margarine

In a bowl, toss apples with sugar and 1/4 teaspoon cinnamon. Place in an ungreased 8-in. square microwave-safe dish. Sprinkle with water. In another bowl, combine the flour, brown sugar, salt and remaining cinnamon; cut in butter until crumbly. Sprinkle over apples. Microwave, uncovered, on high for 10-12 minutes or until apples are tender. **Yield:** 5 servings.
   Editor's Note: This recipe was tested in an 850-watt microwave.

Nutritional Analysis: One serving (3/4 cup) equals 257 calories, 7 g fat (4 g saturated fat), 19 mg cholesterol, 135 mg sodium, 49 g carbohydrate, 3 g fiber, 2 g protein.
Diabetic Exchanges: 1-1/2 starch, 1-1/2 fruit, 1 fat.

Pumpkin Trifle

(Pictured above)

There's more to pumpkin than pie with this impressive trifle. It's elegant with alternating layers of gingerbread cake and pumpkin/butterscotch pudding.
—Hyla Lehenbauer, New London, Missouri

   1 package (14-1/2 ounces) gingerbread cake mix*
1-1/4 cups water
   1 egg
   4 cups cold fat-free milk
   4 packages (1 ounce *each*) sugar-free instant butterscotch pudding mix
   1 can (15 ounces) solid-pack pumpkin
   1 teaspoon ground cinnamon
1/4 teaspoon *each* ground ginger, nutmeg and allspice
   1 carton (12 ounces) reduced-fat frozen whipped topping, thawed

In a mixing bowl, combine the cake mix, water and egg; mix well. Pour into an ungreased 8-in. square baking pan. Bake at 350° for 35-40 minutes or until a toothpick inserted near center comes out clean. Cool for 10 minutes before removing from pan to a wire rack. When completely cooled, crumble cake. Set aside 1/4 cup crumbs for garnish.
   In a bowl, whisk milk and pudding mixes for 2 minutes or until slightly thickened. Let stand for 2 minutes or until soft set. Stir in pumpkin and spices; mix well. In a trifle bowl or 3-1/2-qt. glass serving bowl, layer a fourth of the cake crumbs, half of the pumpkin mixture, a fourth of the cake crumbs and half of the whipped topping. Repeat layers. Garnish with reserved cake crumbs. Serve immediately or refrigerate. **Yield:** 18 servings.
   ***Editor's Note:** This recipe was tested with Betty Crocker gingerbread cake mix.

Guilt-Free Chocolate Cake

You won't miss the fat when you taste this moist, fudgy dessert. I substituted yogurt for the oil called for in a reduced-fat box mix to create this delicious cake.
—Brenda Ruse, Truro, Nova Scotia

   1 package (18-1/4 ounces) reduced-fat devil's food cake mix
1/2 cup baking cocoa
   2 egg whites
   1 egg
1-1/3 cups water
   1 cup reduced-fat plain yogurt
1-1/2 teaspoons confectioners' sugar

In a large mixing bowl, combine cake mix and cocoa. Combine the egg whites, egg, water and yogurt; add to dry ingredients and beat well. Pour into a 10-cup fluted tube pan coated with nonstick cooking spray.
   Bake at 350° for 35-40 minutes or until a toothpick inserted near the center comes out clean. Cool for 10 minutes before removing from pan to a wire rack to cool completely. Sprinkle with confectioners' sugar. **Yield:** 12 servings.

Nutritional Analysis: One piece equals 191 calories, 3 g fat (1 g saturated fat), 19 mg cholesterol, 399 mg sodium, 40 g carbohydrate, 2 g fiber, 5 g protein.
Diabetic Exchange: 2-1/2 starch.

Favorite Recipe Made Lighter

DOES THINKING about the fat and calories in a serving of homemade ice cream give you an ice cream headache?

"Strawberry-Banana Ice Cream is chock-full of strawberries and chopped pecans and has the most delightful flavor," says Jeanette Shropshire from Canyon Lake, Texas.

"However, we're trying to cut calories. I've made this recipe using fat-free sweetened condensed milk and light whipped topping without hurting the taste," she says. "What else can I do to lower the calorie count?"

Besides the changes Jeanette suggested, our Test Kitchen home economists came up with some additional modifications to create Makeover Strawberry-Banana Ice Cream.

Strawberry-Banana Ice Cream

- 6 eggs
- 2 cups sugar
- 4 cups half-and-half cream
- 1 can (14 ounces) sweetened condensed milk
- 1-1/2 teaspoons vanilla extract
- Red food coloring, optional
  - 1 carton (8 ounces) frozen whipped topping, thawed
  - 1 package (16 ounces) frozen unsweetened whole strawberries, coarsely chopped
  - 2 medium firm bananas, sliced
  - 1 cup chopped pecans, toasted

In a heavy saucepan, combine the eggs and sugar. Gradually add cream. Cook and stir over low heat until mixture reaches 160° and coats the back of a metal spoon. Remove from the heat. Cool quickly by placing pan in a bowl of ice water; stir for 2 minutes. Stir in milk, vanilla and food coloring if desired. Press plastic wrap onto surface of mixture. Refrigerate for several hours or overnight.

Fold whipped topping into cream mixture. Fold in strawberries, bananas and pecans. Fill cylinder of ice cream freezer two-thirds full; freeze according to manufacturer's directions. Refrigerate remaining mixture until ready to freeze. Allow to ripen in ice cream freezer or firm up in the refrigerator freezer for 2-4 hours before serving. **Yield:** about 3 quarts.

Nutritional Analysis: One serving (1/2 cup) equals 245 calories, 12 g fat (6 g saturated fat), 68 mg cholesterol, 50 mg sodium, 32 g carbohydrate, 1 g fiber, 4 g protein.

Makeover Strawberry-Banana Ice Cream

(Pictured below left)

- 4 teaspoons cornstarch
- 2 cups sugar
- 4 cups fat-free half-and-half cream
- 3 eggs, lightly beaten
- 1 can (14 ounces) fat-free sweetened condensed milk
- 1-1/2 teaspoons vanilla extract
- Red food coloring, optional
  - 1 carton (8 ounces) reduced-fat frozen whipped topping, thawed
  - 1 package (16 ounces) frozen unsweetened whole strawberries, coarsely chopped
  - 2 medium firm bananas, sliced
  - 1/2 cup chopped pecans, toasted

In a heavy saucepan, combine the cornstarch and sugar. Gradually add cream. Bring to a boil over medium heat; cook and stir for 1 minute. Remove from the heat. Stir a small amount of hot filling into eggs; return all to the pan, stirring constantly. Bring to a gentle boil; cook and stir for 2 minutes. Remove from the heat. Cool quickly by placing pan in a bowl of ice water; stir for 2 minutes. Stir in milk, vanilla and food coloring if desired. Press plastic wrap onto surface of mixture. Refrigerate for several hours or overnight.

Fold whipped topping into cream mixture. Fold in strawberries, bananas and pecans. Fill cylinder of ice cream freezer two-thirds full; freeze according to manufacturer's directions. Refrigerate remaining mixture until ready to freeze. Allow to ripen in ice cream freezer or firm up in the refrigerator freezer for 2-4 hours before serving. **Yield:** 3 quarts.

Nutritional Analysis: One serving (1/2 cup) equals 203 calories, 4 g fat (1 g saturated fat), 28 mg cholesterol, 66 mg sodium, 38 g carbohydrate, 1 g fiber, 4 g protein.
Diabetic Exchanges: 2 starch, 1-1/2 fat-free milk, 1/2 fat.

Cake-Topped Blueberry Dessert

Bountiful blueberries are the basis for this refreshing meal-ender. A yummy cake layer with delicate orange flavor crowns sweet berries. It's perfect for summer menus. And it can be made in a jiffy.
—*Ellen Carleton, Mont Vernon, New Hampshire*

    3 cups fresh *or* frozen blueberries
1/2 cup packed brown sugar
    1 tablespoon butter *or* stick margarine
    3 tablespoons shortening
1/2 cup sugar
    1 egg
    1 teaspoon grated orange peel
1-1/4 cups all-purpose flour
1-1/2 teaspoons baking powder
1/4 teaspoon salt
1/3 cup orange juice

In a saucepan, combine the blueberries, brown sugar and butter; cook for 5 minutes or until saucy. Pour into an 8-in. square baking dish coated with nonstick cooking spray. In a mixing bowl, cream shortening and sugar. Beat in egg and orange peel. Combine the flour, baking powder and salt; add to the creamed mixture alternately with orange juice, beating just until combined.

Drop batter by spoonfuls over blueberry mixture. Bake at 350° for 30-35 minutes or until a toothpick inserted near center of cake comes out clean. Serve warm. **Yield:** 9 servings.

Nutritional Analysis: *One piece equals 241 calories, 6 g fat (2 g saturated fat), 27 mg cholesterol, 132 mg sodium, 44 g carbohydrate, 2 g fiber, 3 g protien.*

Dark Chocolate Sauce

(Pictured at right)

You don't have to cross chocolate off your dessert menu, thanks to recipes like this one. It's simple to satisfy your sweet tooth by draping low-fat pound cake or fat-free ice cream with this rich glossy sauce. Use it to make hot chocolate, too...or as a dip for fresh fruit.
—*Deanne Bagley, Bath, New York*

1/2 cup packed brown sugar
1/2 cup baking cocoa
    1 tablespoon cornstarch
1/2 cup reduced-fat milk
1/4 cup strong brewed coffee
    1 teaspoon vanilla extract

In a saucepan, combine the brown sugar, cocoa and cornstarch. Stir in milk and coffee until smooth. Bring to a boil; cook and stir for 1-2 minutes or until thickened. Remove from the heat. Stir in vanilla. Store in the refrigerator. **Yield:** 8 servings.

Nutritional Analysis: *One serving (2 tablespoons) equals 77 calories, 1 g fat (1 g saturated fat), 1 mg cholesterol, 16 mg sodium, 18 g carbohydrate, 2 g fiber, 2 g protein.*
Diabetic Exchange: *1 starch.*

Fruit-Filled Orange Cake

(Pictured at right)

Be sure to leave room for a fruitful slice of this light and pretty cake. Made from a mix, it couldn't be easier—and you can get creative with the garnish. This cake is just as delicious served the next day...if there's any left.
—*Nicholette Measel, Medway, Ohio*

    1 package (18-1/4 ounces) reduced-fat yellow cake mix
3/4 cup water
1/2 cup orange juice
1/2 cup egg substitute
    1 egg, lightly beaten
    2 tablespoons canola oil
1/2 teaspoon grated orange peel
    1 carton (6 ounces) reduced-fat orange-cream yogurt
    2 cups reduced-fat whipped topping
    1 cup diced fresh strawberries, patted dry
    1 cup canned unsweetened pineapple tidbits, drained and patted dry

Coat two 9-in. round baking pans with nonstick cooking spray; line with waxed paper. Coat waxed paper with nonstick cooking spray; set aside. In a mixing bowl, combine the first six ingredients. Beat on low speed for 1 minute, scraping bowl constantly. Fold in orange peel. Pour into prepared pans. Bake at 350° for 18-24 minutes or until a toothpick inserted near the center comes out clean. Cool for 10 minutes before removing from pans to wire racks.

In a bowl, combine the yogurt and whipped topping. In another bowl, combine the strawberries and pineapple. Place one cooled cake layer on a serving plate. Spread with half of the yogurt mixture; top with half of the fruit mixture. Top with second cake layer. Spread remaining yogurt mixture over top of cake; sprinkle with remaining fruit. Store in the refrigerator. **Yield:** 12 servings.

Nutritional Analysis: *One piece equals 255 calories, 6 g fat (2 g saturated fat), 19 mg cholesterol, 312 mg sodium, 47 g carbohydrate, trace fiber, 5 g protein.*
Diabetic Exchanges: *3 starch, 1/2 fat.*

❦ Colorful Cake

PREPARING angel food cake from a boxed mix as a light dessert? Here's a suggestion for dressing it up. After stirring together the batter, I pour half into the cake pan. Then I put drops of food coloring in different areas and gently swirl them into the batter with a toothpick. I add the rest of the batter and repeat with more food coloring.

Once you've baked, cooled and cut the cake, you'll see the colorful design. It's fun to coordinate the colors for different holidays. For example, use green and red for Christmas and red and blue for the Fourth of July. —*June Brown, Graham, Alabama*

Orange Poppy Seed Cake

(Pictured below)

I used orange juice concentrate instead of oil in a poppy seed cake recipe to come up with this terrific dessert. We enjoy moist slices during the holidays and throughout the year.
—Brenda Craig, Spokane, Washington

> 1 package (18-1/4 ounces) reduced-fat yellow cake mix
> 2 tablespoons poppy seeds
> 1 cup fat-free sour cream
> 3/4 cup egg substitute
> 1 can (6 ounces) frozen orange juice concentrate, thawed
> 1/3 cup water
> 1/4 teaspoon almond extract
> 2 tablespoons sugar
> 1/2 teaspoon ground cinnamon
> GLAZE:
> 1-3/4 cups confectioners' sugar
> 2 tablespoons fat-free milk
> 1 tablespoon orange juice

In a large bowl, combine the cake mix and poppy seeds. In a small mixing bowl, combine the sour cream, egg substitute, orange juice concentrate, water and almond extract; beat until smooth. Stir into cake mix just until combined. Coat a 10-in. fluted tube pan with nonstick cooking spray.

Combine the sugar and cinnamon; sprinkle evenly in pan. Pour batter into pan.

Bake at 350° for 40-45 minutes or until a toothpick inserted near the center comes out clean. Cool for 10 minutes before removing from pan to a wire rack. Combine glaze ingredients; drizzle over cooled cake. **Yield:** 14 servings.

Nutritional Analysis: One piece equals 247 calories, 1 g fat (1 g saturated fat), trace cholesterol, 283 mg sodium, 55 g carbohydrate, trace fiber, 5 g protein.

Baked Pumpkin Pudding

Even after your favorite turkey dinner, you'll find room for this perfect pudding dessert—a treat served hot or cold. Mildly spiced, it will leave you sweetly satisfied, but not overly full.
—Gerri Saylor, Graniteville, South Carolina

> 1/2 cup egg substitute
> 2 cups cooked *or* canned pumpkin
> 3/4 cup sugar
> 1 tablespoon honey
> 1 teaspoon ground cinnamon
> 1/2 teaspoon ground ginger
> 1/4 teaspoon ground cloves
> 1-1/2 cups fat-free evaporated milk
> 5 tablespoons reduced-fat whipped topping

In a bowl, beat the egg substitute, pumpkin, sugar, honey and spices until blended. Gradually beat in milk. Pour into five 8-oz. custard cups coated with nonstick cooking spray. Place in a 15-in. x 10-in. x 1-in. baking pan.

Bake, uncovered, at 425° for 10 minutes. Reduce heat to 350°. Bake 30-35 minutes longer or until a knife inserted near the center comes out clean. Serve warm or cold. Garnish with whipped topping. Store in the refrigerator. **Yield:** 5 servings.

Nutritional Analysis: One serving equals 245 calories, 1 g fat (1 g saturated fat), 3 mg cholesterol, 143 mg sodium, 51 g carbohydrate, 4 g fiber, 10 g protein.

Pistachio Fluff

Pineapple, maraschino cherries and mandarin oranges complement the pistachio pudding in this cloud-like concoction that's perfect for a holiday buffet. This is a jazzed-up version of a recipe my mother gave me.
—Ann Sloane, Greendale, Wisconsin

> 2 cups (16 ounces) 1% cottage cheese
> 1 carton (32 ounces) fat-free reduced-sugar vanilla yogurt, *divided*
> 1 package (1 ounce) sugar-free instant pistachio pudding mix
> 1 carton (8 ounces) frozen reduced-fat whipped topping, thawed
> 1 can (20 ounces) unsweetened crushed pineapple, drained
> 1 can (11 ounces) mandarin oranges, drained
> 1/2 cup halved maraschino cherries

In a food processor, combine cottage cheese and 1 cup yogurt; cover and process until smooth. Place remaining yogurt in a large bowl. Add pudding mix; whisk for 2 minutes or until slightly thickened. Add cottage cheese mixture; mix well. Stir in remaining ingredients. Refrigerate until serving. **Yield:** 14 servings.

Nutritional Analysis: One serving (3/4 cup) equals 137 calories, 2 g fat (2 g saturated fat), 3 mg cholesterol, 249 mg sodium, 21 g carbohydrate, trace fiber, 7 g protein.
Diabetic Exchanges: 1/2 starch, 1/2 fruit, 1/2 fat-free milk, 1/2 fat.

Cherry Cheesecake Pie

(Pictured above)

Cottage cheese is the secret to this creamy slimmed-down dessert. It's festively topped with sweet cherry pie filling.
—Sandra Lee Herr, Stevens, Pennsylvania

  2 eggs, lightly beaten
  4 ounces reduced-fat cream cheese, cubed
1/2 cup fat-free cottage cheese
1/4 cup nonfat dry milk powder
Sugar substitute equivalent to 1/4 cup sugar*
    1 tablespoon lemon juice
    2 teaspoons vanilla extract
    1 reduced-fat graham cracker crust (8 inches)

  1 can (20 ounces) reduced-sugar cherry pie filling

In a food processor, combine the first seven ingredients; cover and process until smooth. Pour into pie crust. Bake at 350° for 25-30 minutes or until center is almost set. Cool for 1 hour. Cover and refrigerate overnight. Slice; top with pie filling. **Yield:** 8 servings.

***Editor's Note:** This recipe was tested with Splenda No Calorie Sweetener. Look for it in the baking aisle of your grocery store.*

Nutritional Analysis: One piece equals 225 calories, 6 g fat (2 g saturated fat), 59 mg cholesterol, 241 mg sodium, 35 g carbohydrate, trace fiber, 7 g protein.
Diabetic Exchanges: 1 fat-free milk, 1 fruit, 1 fat, 1/2 starch.

Finnish Berry Dessert

(Pictured below)

I'm from Finland and have several native recipes that I've altered over time to appeal to American tastes. This refreshing dessert gives folks a taste of my homeland.
—Sirpa Jarvis, The Plains, Ohio

- 1-1/2 cups blueberries
- 1-1/2 cups fresh strawberries, quartered
- 1 cup unsweetened raspberries
- 3 tablespoons sugar, *divided*
- 2 tablespoons cornstarch
- 1-1/2 cups apple-raspberry juice
- Frozen vanilla yogurt, optional

In a large heat-proof bowl, combine fruit and 2 tablespoons sugar. In a saucepan, combine cornstarch and juice until smooth. Bring to a boil; cook and stir for 2 minutes or until thickened. Remove from the heat; cool for 10 minutes. Pour over fruit; toss to coat. Sprinkle with remaining sugar. Cover and refrigerate until chilled. Serve in individual dessert dishes; top with frozen yogurt if desired. **Yield:** 8 servings.

Nutritional Analysis: One serving (1/2 cup fruit, calculated without frozen yogurt) equals 78 calories, trace fat (trace saturated fat), 0 mg cholesterol, 3 mg sodium, 19 g carbohydrate, 3 g fiber, trace protein.
Diabetic Exchange: 1-1/2 fruit.

Pumpkin Squares

Since I was trying to steer clear of high-calorie desserts, I created this recipe so I could still enjoy the flavors of the holidays. My family enjoys and requests this treat, which they say tastes just like pumpkin pie. They can't believe it's light.
—Jennifer Geigel, Embrun, Ontario

- 1 envelope unflavored gelatin
- 1/2 cup cold water
- 1 can (29 ounces) solid-pack pumpkin
- 1/4 cup packed brown sugar
- 1 teaspoon ground cinnamon
- 1 teaspoon vanilla extract
- 1/2 teaspoon salt
- 1/2 teaspoon ground ginger
- 1/8 teaspoon ground cloves
- Sugar substitute equivalent to 1/2 cup sugar*
- 5 whole graham crackers (about 5 inches x 2-1/2 inches)
- 1/2 cup reduced-fat whipped topping

In a saucepan, sprinkle gelatin over cold water; let stand for 2 minutes. Heat over low heat, stirring until gelatin is completely dissolved. Add the pumpkin, brown sugar, cinnamon, vanilla, salt, ginger and cloves. Bring to a boil, stirring constantly. Reduce heat; simmer, uncovered, for 5 minutes, stirring frequently. Remove from the heat; cool to room temperature. Stir in sugar substitute.

Line the bottom of an 8-in. square dish with graham crackers. Pour pumpkin mixture over crackers. Cover and refrigerate overnight. Serve with whipped topping. **Yield:** 9 servings.

*Editor's Note: This recipe was tested with Splenda No Calorie Sweetener. Look for it in the baking aisle of your grocery store.

Nutritional Analysis: One piece equals 120 calories, 2 g fat (1 g saturated fat), 0 cholesterol, 190 mg sodium, 23 g carbohydrate, 4 g fiber, 5 g protein.
Diabetic Exchange: 1-1/2 starch.

🍎 Making Graham Cracker Crusts

- When making a graham cracker crust, I eliminate the sugar altogether. The graham crackers have a light natural sweetness, plus most pie fillings are sweet enough on their own that no one notices the difference.
  —*Marilyn McNulty*
  Iowa City, Iowa
- I replace all of the butter with applesauce in my graham cracker crusts. The crust isn't as rich, but it is a bit sweeter. The amount of applesauce depends on the consistency you prefer. I think the crust sticks together quite well.
  —*Louise Wilson, Ottawa, Ontario*

Bavarian Apple Tart

(Pictured above)

*Everyone in my card club commented on this tart's
wonderful taste. No one guessed that the delicate crust,
creamy filling and sweet topping are light.
There wasn't a leftover in sight when I served this.*
—Mary Anne Engel, West Allis, Wisconsin

1/3 cup butter *or* stick margarine, softened
1/3 cup sugar
1/2 teaspoon vanilla extract
 1 cup all-purpose flour
1/8 teaspoon ground cinnamon
FILLING:
 1 package (8 ounces) reduced-fat cream cheese
1/4 cup sugar
 1 egg
1-1/2 teaspoons vanilla extract
TOPPING:
 4 cups thinly sliced peeled Granny Smith *or* other
 tart apples (about 2 medium)
1/3 cup sugar
3/4 teaspoon ground cinnamon

In a mixing bowl, cream the butter and sugar. Add the vanilla, flour and cinnamon. Press onto the bottom and 1 in. up the sides of a 9-in. springform pan coated with nonstick cooking spray.

In a mixing bowl, beat the cream cheese and sugar. Beat in the egg and vanilla just until combined. Spread over crust. In another bowl, toss the apples, sugar and cinnamon; arrange over filling. Bake at 400° for 40 minutes or until apples are tender and crust is golden brown. Cool on a wire rack. Store in the refrigerator. **Yield:** 12 servings.

Nutritional Analysis: One piece equals 213 calories, 9 g fat (5 g saturated fat), 42 mg cholesterol, 113 mg sodium, 30 g carbohydrate, 1 g fiber, 4 g protein.
Diabetic Exchanges: 2 fat, 1-1/2 starch, 1/2 fruit.

Strawberry Chiffon Pie

(Pictured below)

*This recipe was given to me by a friend many years
ago while we were attending a weight-loss class.
I always feel guilt-free when I eat this light and fluffy
strawberry pie...and my family loves it.*
—Gale Spross, Wills Point, Texas

1 package (.3 ounce) sugar-free strawberry
 gelatin
3/4 cup boiling water
1-1/4 cups cold water
 1 cup reduced-fat frozen whipped topping,
 thawed
2-1/4 cups sliced fresh strawberries, *divided*
 1 reduced-fat graham cracker crust (8 inches)

In a large bowl, dissolve gelatin in boiling water. Stir in cold water. Refrigerate until slightly thickened. Fold in the whipped topping and 2 cups of strawberries. Pour into the crust. Refrigerate for 3 hours or until set. Garnish with the remaining strawberries. **Yield:** 8 servings.

Nutritional Analysis: One piece equals 138 calories, 4 g fat (2 g saturated fat), 0 cholesterol, 117 mg sodium, 21 g carbohydrate, 1 g fiber, 2 g protein.
Diabetic Exchanges: 1 starch, 1/2 fruit, 1/2 fat.

Blackberry Cobbler

(Pictured below)

This tasty treat has helped my family stay healthy, lose weight and still be able to enjoy dessert! Other kinds of berries or even fresh peaches are just as delicious in this cobbler.
—Leslie Browning, Lebanon, Kentucky

    1/2 cup sugar
4-1/2 teaspoons quick-cooking tapioca
    1/4 teaspoon ground allspice
      5 cups fresh *or* frozen blackberries, thawed
      2 tablespoons orange juice
DOUGH:
      1 cup all-purpose flour
    1/3 cup plus 1 tablespoon sugar, *divided*
    1/4 teaspoon baking soda
    1/4 teaspoon salt
    1/3 cup reduced-fat vanilla yogurt
    1/3 cup fat-free milk
      3 tablespoons butter, melted

In a large bowl, combine the sugar, tapioca and allspice. Add blackberries and orange juice; toss to coat. Let stand for 15 minutes. Spoon into a 2-qt. baking dish coated with nonstick cooking spray.

In a mixing bowl, combine the flour, 1/3 cup sugar, baking soda and salt. Combine the yogurt, milk and butter; stir into dry ingredients until smooth. Spread over the berry mixture. Bake at 350° for 20 minutes. Sprinkle with remaining sugar. Bake 25-30 minutes longer or until golden brown. Serve warm. **Yield:** 10 servings.

Nutritional Analysis: One serving equals 199 calories, 4 g fat (2 g saturated fat), 10 mg cholesterol, 135 mg sodium, 40 g carbohydrate, 4 g fiber, 3 g protein.
Diabetic Exchanges: 1-1/2 starch, 1 fruit, 1/2 fat.

Apple Gingerbread

(Pictured above)

This nicely spiced cake, with chunks of apple and a hint of ginger, cinnamon and nutmeg, always wins raves. I like it best served warm with a dollop of whipped topping. It freezes well, too.
—Pam Blockey, Bozeman, Montana

    2/3 cup sugar
    1/3 cup unsweetened applesauce
      1 egg
      3 tablespoons molasses
      1 cup all-purpose flour
    1/2 cup whole wheat flour
      2 teaspoons ground ginger
      1 teaspoon baking powder
      1 teaspoon baking soda
      1 teaspoon ground cinnamon
    1/4 teaspoon ground nutmeg
    1/8 teaspoon ground allspice
    1/2 cup reduced-fat plain yogurt
1-1/2 cups chopped peeled Granny Smith *or* other tart apples (about 1 medium)
      1 cup plus 2 tablespoons reduced-fat whipped topping

In a mixing bowl, combine the sugar, applesauce, egg and molasses; mix well. Combine the flours, ginger, baking powder, baking soda and spices; add to the molasses mixture alternately with yogurt, beating just until combined. Fold in the apples.

Pour into an 8-in. square baking dish coated with nonstick cooking spray. Bake at 350° for 30-35 minutes or until a toothpick inserted near the center comes out clean. Cool on a wire rack. Cut into squares; dollop with whipped topping. **Yield:** 9 servings.

Nutritional Analysis: One serving (1 piece with 2 tablespoons whipped topping) equals 203 calories, 2 g fat (1 g saturated fat), 24 mg cholesterol, 186 mg sodium, 42 g carbohydrate, 2 g fiber, 4 g protein.
Diabetic Exchanges: 2 starch, 1 fruit.

Favorite Crumb Cake Recipe Made Lighter

FOR A SWEET TREAT, Carolyn Nicholas' family enjoys the old-fashioned goodness of Spice Crumb Cake. "This is my great-grandmother's recipe," says the Winter Springs, Florida cook. "Because of the streusel topping, I can't figure out how to eliminate the fat," she explains. "Can you help?"

Our Test Kitchen staff updated Great-Grandma's recipe by mixing the ingredients for the cake and topping separately.

For the cake, they replaced the shortening with a small amount of oil and some applesauce, and substituted two egg whites for one of the eggs.

Even though they used butter instead of shortening in the topping to retain the from-scratch flavor, Makeover Spice Crumb Cake has less fat, calories and cholesterol than the original.

Spice Crumb Cake

- 3 cups all-purpose flour
- 2 cups packed brown sugar
- 2 teaspoons baking soda
- 2 teaspoons *each* ground cinnamon, nutmeg and cloves
- 1 teaspoon salt
- 1 cup shortening
- 2 eggs
- 2 cups buttermilk
- 2 tablespoons molasses

In a bowl, combine the flour, brown sugar, baking soda, spices and salt; cut in shortening until mixture resembles coarse crumbs. Remove and set aside 1 cup for topping. In another bowl, beat the eggs, buttermilk and molasses. Add to the remaining flour mixture; mix well.

Pour into a greased 13-in. x 9-in. x 2-in. baking pan. Sprinkle with reserved topping. Bake at 350° for 35-40 minutes or until a toothpick inserted near center comes out clean. Cool on a wire rack. **Yield:** 18 servings.

Nutritional Analysis: One piece equals 291 calories, 12 g fat (5 g saturated fat), 26 mg cholesterol, 326 mg sodium, 43 g carbohydrate, 1 g fiber, 4 g protein.

Makeover Spice Crumb Cake

(Pictured at right)

- 1 egg
- 2 egg whites
- 2 cups 1% buttermilk
- 1/4 cup canola oil
- 1/4 cup unsweetened applesauce
- 2 tablespoons molasses
- 2-1/2 cups all-purpose flour
- 1-1/2 cups packed brown sugar
- 1-1/4 teaspoons baking soda
- 1-3/4 teaspoons *each* ground cinnamon, nutmeg and cloves
- 1/2 teaspoon baking powder
- 1/2 teaspoon salt

TOPPING:
- 1/3 cup packed brown sugar
- 3/4 cup all-purpose flour
- 1/4 teaspoon *each* ground cinnamon, nutmeg and cloves
- 1/4 cup cold butter *or* stick margarine

In a large mixing bowl, beat the egg, egg whites, buttermilk, oil, applesauce and molasses. Combine the flour, brown sugar, baking soda, spices, baking powder and salt; add to egg mixture and mix well. Pour into a 13-in. x 9-in. x 2-in. baking pan coated with nonstick cooking spray.

For topping, combine the brown sugar, flour and spices in a bowl; cut in butter until mixture resembles coarse crumbs. Sprinkle over batter. Bake at 350° for 35-40 minutes or until a toothpick inserted near the center comes out clean. Cool on a wire rack. **Yield:** 18 servings.

Nutritional Analysis: One piece equals 249 calories, 8 g fat (2 g saturated fat), 20 mg cholesterol, 241 mg sodium, 42 g carbohydrate, 1 g fiber, 4 g protein.

Gingerbread Cookies

(Pictured below)

When your friends reach into a tin of these old-fashioned cookies, they're sure to think Grandma baked them! Our Test Kitchen staff came up with this lighter recipe for crunchy gingerbread cookies with lovely icing accents.

6 tablespoons butter *or* stick margarine, softened
1 cup sugar
1 cup molasses
1 egg
2 tablespoons white vinegar
4 cups all-purpose flour
2 teaspoons ground ginger
1-1/4 teaspoons baking soda
1 teaspoon ground cinnamon
1/2 teaspoon ground cloves
1/4 teaspoon salt
5 cups confectioners' sugar
5 to 6 tablespoons fat-free milk
Assorted paste food coloring, optional

In a mixing bowl, beat butter and sugar until crumbly, about 2 minutes. Beat in the molasses, egg and vinegar. Combine the flour, ginger, baking soda, cinnamon, cloves and salt; gradually add to the creamed mixture. Cover and refrigerate for 4 hours or until easy to handle (dough will be sticky).

On a lightly floured surface, roll out dough to 1/8-in. thickness. Cut with 4-in. cookie cutters dipped in flour. Using a floured spatula, place cookies 1 in. apart on baking sheets coated with nonstick cooking spray. Bake at 375° for 5-6 minutes or until set. Remove to wire racks to cool.

For icing, combine confectioners' sugar and milk in a bowl. Spread over cooled cookies; let dry completely. If desired, combine paste food coloring and a few drops of water; using a fine brush or the blunt end of a wooden skewer, decorate cookies. **Yield:** 6-1/2 dozen.

Nutritional Analysis: *One cookie equals 81 calories, 1 g fat (1 g saturated fat), 5 mg cholesterol, 39 mg sodium, 18 g carbohydrate, trace fiber, 1 g protein.*
Diabetic Exchange: *1 starch.*

Chocolate Fudge

(Pictured below left)

No one will believe this rich, tantalizing candy is lower in fat, so you'd better include the recipe when you package this sweet treat. This yummy fudge is so quick and easy to make.
—Vickie McGuckin, Trenton, Michigan

2-1/2 cups sugar
2/3 cup fat-free evaporated milk
2 tablespoons butter (no substitutes)
2 cups (12 ounces) semisweet chocolate chips
1 jar (7 ounces) marshmallow creme
1/2 cup chopped pecans
1 jar (2-1/2 ounces) prune baby food
1 teaspoon vanilla extract

Line an 8-in. square pan with foil and coat the foil with nonstick cooking spray; set aside. In a heavy saucepan over medium heat, bring the sugar, milk and butter to a boil, stirring constantly. Cook and stir for 5 minutes. Remove from the heat; stir in chocolate chips until smooth. Stir in the marshmallow creme, pecans, baby food and vanilla. Pour into prepared pan. Refrigerate for 1 hour or until firm.

Lift fudge out of pan and remove foil; cut into 1-in. squares. Store in an airtight container in the refrigerator. **Yield:** 3 pounds (64 pieces).

Nutritional Analysis: *One piece equals 79 calories, 3 g fat (1 g saturated fat), 1 mg cholesterol, 10 mg sodium, 14 g carbohydrate, trace fiber, 1 g protein.*
Diabetic Exchanges: *1 starch, 1/2 fat.*

Tangy Citrus Gelatin Cups

Orange and grapefruit juices give these cute dessert cups their zesty flavor. They're pretty enough to serve guests but easy enough to make for an everyday snack...or even breakfast. I tried out this recipe on friends, and they loved it.
—Barb Klenk, Bridgeton, New Jersey

  3 cups orange juice, *divided*
1/2 cup unsweetened grapefruit juice
  2 packages (.3 ounce *each*) sugar-free orange gelatin
  1 can (8 ounces) unsweetened crushed pineapple
  1 envelope whipped topping mix
1/2 cup fat-free milk
1/2 teaspoon vanilla extract

Chill 2 cups orange juice. In a saucepan or microwave, bring grapefruit juice and remaining orange juice to a boil. Stir in gelatin until dissolved. Stir in chilled orange juice. Drain pineapple, reserving juice; set pineapple aside. Stir pineapple juice into gelatin mixture. Refrigerate until partially set, about 1 hour. Fold in reserved pineapple.

In a mixing bowl, beat whipped topping mix, milk and vanilla on low speed until blended. Beat on high for 4 minutes or until soft peaks form. Fold into gelatin mixture. Divide among individual serving dishes. Refrigerate until set, about 2 hours. **Yield:** 9 servings.

Nutritional Analysis: One serving (3/4 cup) equals 93 calories, 1 g fat (1 g saturated fat), trace cholesterol, 16 mg sodium, 18 g carbohydrate, trace fiber, 2 g protein.
Diabetic Exchange: *1 fruit.*

No-Bake Chocolate Cookies

This is my son's all-time favorite cookie. He will share just about anything, but these are an exception...he gobbles them up! Coconut and oats provide the chewy texture
—Carol Brandon, Uxbridge, Ontario

  2 cups sugar
1/2 cup fat-free milk
1/2 cup butter *or* stick margarine
  3 cups quick-cooking oats
  1 cup flaked coconut
  6 tablespoons baking cocoa
1/2 teaspoon vanilla extract

In a large saucepan, combine the sugar, milk and butter; bring to a boil, stirring constantly. Boil for 2 minutes. Remove from the heat. Stir in the oats, coconut, cocoa and vanilla. Working quickly, drop by rounded tablespoonfuls onto waxed paper. Let stand until set, about 1 hour. **Yield:** 3 dozen.

Nutritional Analysis: One cookie equals 108 calories, 4 g fat (3 g saturated fat), 7 mg cholesterol, 35 mg sodium, 18 g carbohydrate, 1 g fiber, 1 g protein.
Diabetic Exchanges: *1 starch, 1 fat.*

Fruit-Filled Angel Food Torte

(Pictured above)

I was so tired of eating plain angel food cake and fruit for dessert that I decided to combine the two with a little whipped topping—the result is this scrumptious and refreshing torte. It tastes as good as it looks!
—Hettie Johnson, Jacksonville, Florida

  1 carton (12 ounces) frozen reduced-fat whipped topping, thawed, *divided*
  1 can (15 ounces) reduced-sugar fruit cocktail, drained
  1 prepared angel food cake (10 inches)
  1 can (11 ounces) mandarin oranges, drained
  1 large navel orange, sliced, optional
Fresh mint, optional

Fold 1-1/2 cups whipped topping into fruit cocktail just until blended. Split cake horizontally into three layers; place one layer on a serving plate. Spread with half of the fruit mixture. Repeat layers. Top with remaining cake layer. Frost top and sides with remaining whipped topping. Arrange mandarin oranges on top. Refrigerate until serving. Garnish with orange slices and mint if desired. **Yield:** 12 servings.

Nutritional Analysis: One piece equals 177 calories, 4 g fat (4 g saturated fat), 0 cholesterol, 218 mg sodium, 32 g carbohydrate, 1 g fiber, 2 g protein.
Diabetic Exchanges: *1-1/2 starch, 1/2 fruit, 1/2 fat.*

Blackberry Trifle

*Light and luscious, this attractive trifle is an impressive
way to use blackberries. Special enough for company,
no one will guess how easy it is to put together with
instant pudding and prepared pound cake.*
—*Arlyn Kramer, Dumas, Arkansas*

1-1/2 cups cold 1% milk
**1 package (1 ounce) sugar-free instant vanilla
  pudding mix**
1/2 cup reduced-fat sour cream
**1 carton (8 ounces) frozen reduced-fat whipped
  topping, thawed**
**1 loaf (13.6 ounces) reduced-fat pound cake,
  cubed**
4 cups frozen or fresh unsweetened blackberries

In a bowl, whisk milk and pudding mix for 2 minutes or until slightly thickened. Add sour cream; mix well. Fold in whipped topping. In a 2-qt. trifle dish or deep glass bowl, layer half of the cake cubes, half of the berries and half of the pudding mixture. Repeat layers. Cover and refrigerate for 2-3 hours before serving. **Yield:** 8 servings.

*Nutritional Analysis: One serving (1 cup) equals 291 calories,
6 g fat (5 g saturated fat), 8 mg cholesterol, 402 mg sodium, 52 g
carbohydrate, 4 g fiber, 5 g protein.*
Diabetic Exchanges: 2 starch, 1-1/2 fruit, 1 fat.

Maple Honey Cheesecake

(Pictured at right and on front cover)

*Maple syrup and hazelnuts add a festive flavor to
this rich and creamy cheesecake that's sure to
win raves at your holiday table.*
—*Paula Marchesi, Lenhartsville, Pennsylvania*

**2/3 cup reduced-fat cinnamon graham cracker
  crumbs (10 squares)**
2 tablespoons sugar
1 tablespoon butter or stick margarine, melted
**3 packages (8 ounces each) reduced-fat cream
  cheese**
1 package (8 ounces) fat-free cream cheese
2 tablespoons cornstarch
1/2 cup honey
1/2 cup maple syrup
1/4 teaspoon salt
3 egg whites
**1/4 cup plus 2 tablespoons chopped hazelnuts,
  toasted, divided**
1/2 teaspoon ground cinnamon

In a bowl, combine the cracker crumbs, sugar and butter. Press onto bottom of a 9-in. springform pan coated with nonstick cooking spray. Bake at 325° for 10 minutes. Cool on a wire rack.

In a mixing bowl, beat cream cheese until smooth. Add the cornstarch, honey, syrup and salt, beating just until combined. Add egg whites; beat on low speed just until blended (batter will be very thick). Spoon half of the batter over crust; smooth top. Toss 1/4 cup hazelnuts with cinnamon; sprinkle over batter. Spoon remaining batter over nuts; smooth top. Place pan on a baking sheet.

Bake at 325° for 50-55 minutes or until the edges are set and the center is jiggly. Cool on a wire rack for 10 minutes. Carefully run a knife around edge of pan to loosen; cool 1 hour longer. Refrigerate overnight. Remove sides of pan. Sprinkle with remaining hazelnuts. Refrigerate leftovers. **Yield:** 12 servings.

*Nutritional Analysis: One piece equals 295 calories, 14 g fat
(7 g saturated fat), 36 mg cholesterol, 372 mg sodium, 33 g carbohydrate, 1 g fiber, 10 g protein.*
Diabetic Exchanges: 2 fat, 1-1/2 starch, 1 fat-free milk.

Chocolate-Filled
Raspberry Meringues

(Pictured at right)

*Whenever I serve these pretty pink meringue cups filled
with fluffy chocolate mousse, I get compliments.*
—*Millie Charles, Bloomfield Hills, Michigan*

3 egg whites
1/4 teaspoon cream of tartar
3 tablespoons raspberry gelatin powder
3/4 cup sugar
1 package (4 ounces) German sweet chocolate
3 tablespoons water
1/2 cup cold fat-free milk
1-1/2 teaspoons vanilla extract
1 envelope whipped topping mix
3/4 cup fresh raspberries

Place egg whites in a mixing bowl; let stand at room temperature for 30 minutes. Beat egg whites and cream of tartar on medium speed until soft peaks form. Gradually beat in gelatin. Add sugar, 1 tablespoon at a time, beating on high until stiff peaks form and sugar is dissolved.

Drop meringue into eight mounds on a parchment-lined baking sheet. Shape into 3-1/2-in. cups with the back of a spoon. Bake at 250° for 45 minutes. Turn oven off; leave meringues in the oven for 1 to 1-1/2 hours.

For filling, in a microwave or heavy saucepan, melt chocolate with water; stir until smooth. Cool. In a small mixing bowl, beat milk, vanilla and whipped topping mix until soft peaks form. Fold into melted chocolate. Spoon into meringue cups. Refrigerate until serving. Garnish with raspberries. **Yield:** 8 servings.

*Nutritional Analysis: One serving (1 filled meringue cup)
equals 205 calories, 5 g fat (3 g saturated fat), trace cholesterol,
41 mg sodium, 39 g carbohydrate, 1 g fiber, 4 g protein.*
Diabetic Exchanges: 2 starch, 1 fat, 1/2 fruit.

Banana Split Dessert

(Pictured above)

My father-in-law is diabetic, but this creamy pudding dessert is one treat he can eat. It has all the flavors of a true banana split.
—Ann Jansen, DePere, Wisconsin

2 cups reduced-fat graham cracker crumbs (about 32 squares)
5 tablespoons reduced-fat margarine*, melted
1 can (12 ounces) cold reduced-fat evaporated milk
1/4 cup cold fat-free milk
2 packages (1 ounce *each*) sugar-free instant vanilla pudding mix
2 medium firm bananas, sliced
1 can (20 ounces) unsweetened crushed pineapple, drained
1 carton (8 ounces) reduced-fat frozen whipped topping, thawed
3 tablespoons chopped walnuts
3 tablespoons chocolate syrup
5 maraschino cherries, quartered

Combine cracker crumbs and margarine; press onto the bottom of a 13-in. x 9-in. x 2-in. dish coated with nonstick cooking spray. In a bowl, whisk the evaporated milk, fat-free milk and pudding mixes for 2 minutes or until slightly thickened. Spread pudding evenly over crust. Layer with bananas, pineapple and whipped topping. Sprinkle with nuts; drizzle with chocolate syrup. Top with cherries. Refrigerate for at least 1 hour before cutting. **Yield:** 15 servings.
*Editor's Note: This recipe was tested with Parkay Light stick margarine.

Nutritional Analysis: One piece equals 194 calories, 6 g fat (3 g saturated fat), 4 mg cholesterol, 312 mg sodium, 33 g carbohydrate, 1 g fiber, 3 g protein.
Diabetic Exchanges: 1 starch, 1 fruit, 1 fat.

Thumbprint Cookies

Looking for a lighter alternative to traditional Christmas cookies? Try these pretty jam-filled thumbprints from our Test Kitchen staff. The melt-in-your-mouth treats have a buttery taste and get nice crunch from chopped pecans.

6 tablespoons butter *or* stick margarine, softened
1/2 cup sugar
1 egg
2 tablespoons canola oil
1 teaspoon vanilla extract
1/4 teaspoon butter flavoring *or* almond extract
1-1/2 cups all-purpose flour
1/4 cup cornstarch
1 teaspoon baking powder
1/4 teaspoon salt
1 egg white
1/3 cup chopped pecans
7-1/2 teaspoons assorted jams

In a mixing bowl, cream the butter and sugar. Beat in egg. Beat in oil, vanilla and butter flavoring. Combine the flour, cornstarch, baking powder and salt; stir into creamed mixture. Roll into 1-in. balls. In a small bowl, lightly beat egg white. Dip each ball halfway into egg white, then into pecans.

Place nut side up 2 in. apart on baking sheets coated with nonstick cooking spray. Using the end of a wooden spoon handle, make an indentation in the center of each. Bake at 350° for 8-10 minutes or until the edges are lightly browned. Remove to wire racks. Fill each cookie with 1/4 teaspoon jam; cool. **Yield:** 2-1/2 dozen.

Nutritional Analysis: One cookie equals 84 calories, 4 g fat (2 g saturated fat), 13 mg cholesterol, 64 mg sodium, 10 g carbohydrate, trace fiber, 1 g protein.
Diabetic Exchanges: 1 fat, 1/2 starch.

🍎 Bananas Have Apeel

GOING BANANAS—it's what the world is doing these days! That versatile fruit is popular everywhere.

Bananas grow in bunches in hot tropical areas on plants that range from 8 to 30 feet tall. They resemble trees, but have no woody trunks.

There are many banana varieties…and they range in size and peel color. However, most of them are too thin-skinned to be shipped successfully to far-away markets. Bananas are a good source of energy and nutritious, too. They contain phosphorus, potassium and vitamins A and C.

One medium banana has about 105 calories. One pound is equal to 3 medium or 4 small bananas.

Fine Dining Pared Down

A special occasion calls for candles, fine china and a marvelous meal. But there's no need to add to your guests' waistlines at the same time. Pamper friends and family with these elegant but light menus.

Citrus Grilled Turkey Breast, Steamed Vegetable Ribbons and Crunchy Pears (page 248)

Dinner for the Two of You

Glazed Cornish Hen With Rice Pilaf

This easy but elegant entree from our Test Kitchen makes a lovely centerpiece for a romantic Valentine's Day dinner. The peach-mustard glaze adds a sweet tang to the moist, tender poultry, which is perched on a mound of mildly seasoned pilaf.

   1 cup cooked white rice
1/2 cup cooked wild rice
1/2 cup chopped peeled tart apple
1/4 cup white wine *or* apple juice
   2 tablespoons slivered almonds
1/4 teaspoon salt
1/4 teaspoon poultry seasoning
Dash curry powder
1/4 cup peach preserves
   1 tablespoon Dijon mustard
   1 teaspoon prepared horseradish
1/4 teaspoon dried tarragon
   1 Cornish game hen (20 ounces), split
     lengthwise

In a bowl, combine the first eight ingredients; set aside. In a saucepan, combine the preserves, mustard, horseradish and tarragon. Cook and stir over medium heat until preserves are melted. Carefully loosen skin around hen breast, thighs and drumsticks. Set aside 1/4 cup glaze; spoon remaining glaze under skin.

Place the rice mixture in two mounds in an 11-in. x 7-in. x 2-in. baking dish coated with nonstick cooking spray; arrange hen halves skin side up over rice. Bake, uncovered, at 400° for 45-55 minutes or until meat juices run clear. Let stand for 10 minutes before serving. Warm reserved glaze; brush over hen halves. **Yield:** 2 servings.

Nutritional Analysis: One serving (half of hen, skin removed, with 1 cup rice mixture) equals 491 calories, 9 g fat (1 g saturated fat), 117 mg cholesterol, 590 mg sodium, 74 g carbohydrate, 3 g fiber, 31 g protein.

Sweet Carrots

Our home economists offer a flavorful way to dress up carrots without a lot of fuss. Simply steam the veggies, then season with butter, brown sugar, vinegar and chives. The carrots are colorful and good.

1-1/2 cups baby carrots
   2 teaspoons brown sugar
   1 teaspoon butter *or* stick margarine
   1 teaspoon white wine vinegar *or* cider vinegar
1/8 teaspoon salt
   1 teaspoon minced chives

Place carrots in a steamer basket. Place in a saucepan over 1 in. of water; bring to a boil. Cover and steam for 5-8 minutes or until tender. Transfer carrots to a bowl. Add the brown sugar, butter, vinegar and salt; toss until butter is melted and carrots are coated. Sprinkle with chives. **Yield:** 2 servings.

Nutritional Analysis: One serving (3/4 cup) equals 76 calories, 2 g fat (1 g saturated fat), 5 mg cholesterol, 202 mg sodium, 14 g carbohydrate, 3 g fiber, 1 g protein.
Diabetic Exchanges: 2 vegetable, 1/2 fruit.

Valentine Strawberry Shortcake

Our Test Kitchen lets succulent strawberries star in this festive finale even Cupid would crave. The juicy berries mingle with a creamy yogurt sauce that's sandwiched between heart-shaped shortcake halves. It's sweet to eat and loaded with love...not calories!

1/4 cup fat-free plain yogurt
   2 tablespoons reduced-fat sour cream
   2 tablespoons confectioners' sugar
1/4 teaspoon rum extract *or* vanilla extract
   1 pint fresh strawberries, sliced, *divided*
SHORTCAKE:
2/3 cup all-purpose flour
   2 tablespoons whole wheat flour
   2 tablespoons plus 1/2 teaspoon sugar, *divided*
3/4 teaspoon baking powder
1/4 teaspoon baking soda
1/8 teaspoon salt
   5 teaspoons cold butter *or* stick margarine
1/3 cup 1% buttermilk

In a small bowl, combine the yogurt, sour cream, confectioners' sugar and extract. In a small bowl, mash 1/2 cup strawberries; stir into yogurt mixture. Cover and refrigerate.

In a bowl, combine the flours, 2 tablespoons sugar, baking powder, baking soda and salt. Cut in the butter until mixture resembles coarse crumbs. Stir in the buttermilk until a soft dough forms (dough will be sticky). On a floured surface, gently knead dough 10 times. Gently pat or roll into a 1/2-in.-thick circle. Cut out two hearts with a 3-1/2-in. cutter.

Place on a baking sheet coated with nonstick cooking spray. Sprinkle with remaining sugar. Bake at 400° for 12-14 minutes or until golden brown. Remove to a wire rack to cool slightly. To assemble, split shortcakes in half. Place cake bottoms on dessert plates; spread with yogurt mixture. Top with remaining strawberries and shortcake tops. **Yield:** 2 servings.

Nutritional Analysis: One serving equals 445 calories, 12 g fat (7 g saturated fat), 33 mg cholesterol, 560 mg sodium, 75 g carbohydrate, 5 g fiber, 10 g protein.

Special Springtime Supper

Pepper-Crusted Pork Tenderloin

Our Test Kitchen staff developed this elegant entree that's sure to impress guests with its golden crumb coating. The meat slices up so moist and tender, you can serve it without sauce and still have a succulent taste-tempting main dish.

　　2 pork tenderloins (3/4 pound *each*)
　　3 tablespoons Dijon mustard
　　1 tablespoon 1% buttermilk
　　2 teaspoons minced fresh thyme
　　1 to 2 teaspoons coarsely ground pepper
1/4 teaspoon salt
2/3 cup soft bread crumbs

Place tenderloins side by side and tie together with kitchen string. In a bowl, combine the mustard, buttermilk, thyme, pepper and salt; spread over surface of meat. Press crumbs onto meat. Place on a rack in a shallow roasting pan. Cover and bake at 425° for 15 minutes. Uncover; bake 35-40 minutes longer or until a meat thermometer reads 160°. Let stand for 5 minutes. Remove string before slicing. **Yield:** 6 servings.

Nutritional Analysis: One serving (3 ounces cooked pork) equals 178 calories, 5 g fat (1 g saturated fat), 67 mg cholesterol, 383 mg sodium, 6 g carbohydrate, trace fiber, 25 g protein.
Diabetic Exchanges: 3 lean meat, 1/2 starch.

Garlic Twice-Baked Potatoes

You'll have to announce dinner only once when our Test Kitchen's twice-baked potatoes are on the menu! Their aroma is sure to make everyone eager to come to the table. Garlic and rosemary add herbal goodness to the mashed potato filling. A sprinkling of paprika serves as a colorful garnish.

　　6 medium baking potatoes
　　1 whole garlic bulb
　　1 teaspoon olive *or* canola oil
　　2 tablespoons butter *or* stick margarine, softened
1/2 cup fat-free milk
1/2 cup 1% buttermilk
1-1/2 teaspoons minced fresh rosemary *or* 1/2
　　　teaspoon dried rosemary, crushed
1/2 teaspoon salt
1/8 teaspoon pepper
Paprika

Bake the potatoes at 400° for 45-55 minutes or until tender. Meanwhile, remove papery outer skin from garlic (do not peel or separate cloves). Place garlic in a double thickness of heavy-duty foil. Drizzle with oil. Wrap foil around garlic. Bake at 400° for 30-35 minutes or until softened. Cool for 10 minutes. Cut top off garlic head, leaving root end intact. Squeeze softened garlic into a small bowl; set aside.

　　Cut a thin slice off the top of each potato and discard.

Scoop out the pulp, leaving a thin shell. In a bowl, mash the pulp with butter. Stir in the milk, buttermilk, rosemary, salt, pepper and roasted garlic. Pipe or spoon into potato shells. Place on an ungreased baking sheet. Bake at 425° for 20-25 minutes or until heated through. Sprinkle with paprika. **Yield:** 6 servings.

Nutritional Analysis: One serving (1 stuffed potato) equals 194 calories, 5 g fat (3 g saturated fat), 11 mg cholesterol, 277 mg sodium, 34 g carbohydrate, 3 g fiber, 5 g protein.
Diabetic Exchanges: 2 starch, 1 fat.

Patriotic Banana Split

This lip-smacking salute to summertime is a creative cross between a classic banana split and a fruit salad. Our home economists took a scoop of watermelon, fresh berries and a sweet creamy topping to produce a red, white and blue finale. And best of all, you won't have to worry about your dessert melting!

　　4 ounces reduced-fat cream cheese
1/2 cup marshmallow creme
　　1 tablespoon lemon juice
　　1 teaspoon grated lemon peel
1/2 medium seedless watermelon
　　6 large ripe bananas, quartered
1/3 cup fresh blueberries
1/3 cup reduced-fat granola cereal without raisins

In a mixing bowl, beat the cream cheese, marshmallow creme, lemon juice and peel until smooth; set aside. Using an ice cream scoop, scoop six balls from watermelon (save remaining melon for another use). In shallow dessert bowls, arrange four banana quarters; top with a watermelon ball. Spoon cream cheese topping over melon. Sprinkle with blueberries and cereal. Serve immediately. **Yield:** 6 servings.

Nutritional Analysis: One serving equals 254 calories, 6 g fat (3 g saturated fat), 14 mg cholesterol, 91 mg sodium, 50 g carbohydrate, 4 g fiber, 4 g protein.
Diabetic Exchanges: 3 fruit, 1 fat, 1/2 starch.

Enticing Easter Menu

Lamb with Mint Salsa

This flavorful entree from our Test Kitchen is well-seasoned with an herb rub of basil, garlic, rosemary and thyme. Tender slices of meat are served with a refreshing salsa.

1 tablespoon plus 2 teaspoons olive *or* canola oil
2 garlic cloves, minced
1 teaspoon *each* dried basil, thyme and rosemary, crushed
1/2 teaspoon salt
1/4 teaspoon pepper
2 racks of lamb (8 ribs *each*), trimmed
SALSA:
1 cup minced fresh mint
1 small cucumber, peeled, seeded and chopped
1/2 cup seeded chopped tomato
1/3 cup finely chopped onion
1/3 cup chopped sweet yellow pepper
1 jalapeno pepper, seeded and chopped*
3 tablespoons lemon juice
2 tablespoons sugar
2 garlic cloves, minced
3/4 teaspoon ground ginger
1/4 teaspoon salt

In a small bowl, combine the oil, garlic and seasonings. Rub over lamb. Place in a roasting pan; cover and refrigerate for 1 hour. In a bowl, combine the salsa ingredients; cover and refrigerate until serving.

Bake lamb, uncovered, at 425° for 20-30 minutes or until meat reaches desired doneness (for rare, a meat thermometer should read 140°; medium, 160°; well-done, 170°). Remove from the oven and cover loosely with foil. Let stand for 5-10 minutes before slicing. Serve with salsa. **Yield:** 8 servings.

*Editor's Note: When cutting or seeding hot peppers, use rubber gloves to protect your hands. Avoid touching your face.

Nutritional Analysis: One serving (2 ribs with 1/4 cup salsa) equals 191 calories, 9 g fat (3 g saturated fat), 60 mg cholesterol, 278 mg sodium, 7 g carbohydrate, 1 g fiber, 20 g protein.
Diabetic Exchanges: 3 lean meat, 1 vegetable.

Asparagus Tossed Salad

Asparagus takes the spotlight in this springtime salad created by our home economists.

2 medium carrots, sliced
1 pound fresh asparagus, cut into 1-inch pieces
8 cups torn Bibb lettuce
ORANGE GINGER VINAIGRETTE:
1/4 cup orange juice
4-1/2 teaspoons olive *or* canola oil
1 tablespoon white wine vinegar *or* cider vinegar
1 tablespoon honey

1/2 teaspoon Dijon mustard
1/4 teaspoon ground ginger
1/4 teaspoon grated orange peel
1/8 teaspoon salt

In a large saucepan, bring 4 cups of water to a boil. Add carrots; cover and boil for 1 minute. Add asparagus; cover and boil 3 minutes longer. Drain and immediately place vegetables in ice water; drain and pat dry. In a salad bowl, combine lettuce, carrots and asparagus. In a jar with a tight-fitting lid, combine the vinaigrette ingredients; shake well. Drizzle over salad and toss to coat. Serve immediately. **Yield:** 8 servings.

Nutritional Analysis: One serving (1-1/4 cups) equals 57 calories, 3 g fat (trace saturated fat), 0 cholesterol, 61 mg sodium, 8 g carbohydrate, 2 g fiber, 2 g protein.
Diabetic Exchanges: 1 vegetable, 1 fat.

Silky Lemon Pie

If you love lemon, our Test Kitchen knows you'll be delighted with this delicious dessert. There's a sweet-tart burst of flavor in each bite of the custard-like filling.

1 cup all-purpose flour
1 teaspoon sugar
1/4 teaspoon salt
3 tablespoons canola oil
1 tablespoon butter *or* stick margarine, melted
2 to 3 tablespoons cold water
FILLING:
1-3/4 cups sugar
1/2 cup lemon juice
1 tablespoon grated lemon peel
1/2 teaspoon salt
3 egg whites
1 package (8 ounces) reduced-fat cream cheese, cubed
2 eggs
1 teaspoon confectioners' sugar

In a bowl, combine flour, sugar and salt. Using a fork, stir in oil and butter until dough is crumbly. Gradually add enough water until dough will hold together. Roll out between plastic wrap to an 11-in. circle. Freeze for 10 minutes. Remove top sheet of plastic wrap from pastry; invert onto a 9-in. pie plate coated with nonstick cooking spray. Remove remaining plastic wrap. Trim edges and flute. Chill while preparing filling.

In a saucepan, bring sugar, lemon juice, peel and salt to a boil. Reduce heat; cook and stir until sugar is dissolved. Cool for 10-15 minutes. In a small mixing bowl, beat egg whites and cream cheese. Add eggs; beat until smooth. Gradually beat in lemon mixture. Pour into crust. Bake at 350° for 30-35 minutes or until set. Cool on a wire rack for 1 hour. Sprinkle with confectioners' sugar. Refrigerate leftovers. **Yield:** 8 servings.

Nutritional Analysis: One piece equals 356 calories, 10 g fat (3 g saturated fat), 67 mg cholesterol, 376 mg sodium, 59 g carbohydrate, 1 g fiber, 8 g protein.

Backyard Barbecue

Citrus Grilled Turkey Breast

(Also pictured on page 241)

Treat guests to a sit-down dinner featuring this delicious grilled entree with a luscious herb and citrus gravy. It comes from our Test Kitchen.

- 1 bone-in turkey breast (4 to 5 pounds)
- 1/4 cup fresh parsley sprigs
- 1/4 cup fresh basil leaves
- 3 tablespoons butter *or* stick margarine
- 4 garlic cloves, halved
- 1/2 teaspoon salt
- 1 medium lemon, thinly sliced
- 1 medium orange, thinly sliced
- 1 tablespoon cornstarch
- 2 tablespoons water
- 1 cup orange juice
- 1 teaspoon grated orange peel
- 1 teaspoon grated lemon peel
- 1/4 teaspoon pepper

Using fingers, carefully loosen the skin from both sides of turkey breast. In a food processor or blender, combine the parsley, basil, butter, garlic and salt; cover and process until smooth. Spread under turkey skin; arrange lemon and orange slices over herb mixture. Secure skin to underside of breast with toothpicks.

Coat grill rack with nonstick cooking spray before starting the grill. Prepare grill for indirect heat, using a drip pan; place turkey over drip pan. Grill, covered, over indirect medium heat for 1-3/4 to 2-1/4 hours or until a meat thermometer reads 170° and juices run clear. Cover and let stand for 10 minutes.

Meanwhile, pour pan drippings into a measuring cup; skim fat. In a saucepan, combine the cornstarch and water until smooth. Add the orange juice, orange peel, lemon peel, pepper and pan drippings. Bring to a boil; cook and stir for 2 minutes or until thickened. Discard the skin, lemon and orange slices from turkey breast. Remove herb mixture from turkey; stir into gravy. Slice turkey and serve with gravy. **Yield:** 8 servings with leftovers.

Nutritional Analysis: One serving (4 ounces cooked turkey with 3 tablespoons gravy) equals 192 calories, 2 g fat (1 g saturated fat), 101 mg cholesterol, 224 mg sodium, 5 g carbohydrate, trace fiber, 35 g protein.
Diabetic Exchanges: *5 very lean meat, 1/2 fruit.*

Steamed Vegetable Ribbons

(Also pictured on page 241)

These extra-thin slices of zucchini and carrot add a pretty touch to a dinner plate, confirms our Test Kitchen staff.

- 4 large carrots, peeled
- 8 small zucchini
- 4 teaspoons lemon juice
- 2 teaspoons olive *or* canola oil
- 1 teaspoon salt
- 1/8 to 1/4 teaspoon pepper

With a vegetable peeler or metal cheese slicer, cut very thin slices down the length of each carrot and zucchini, making long ribbons. Place carrots in a steamer basket over 1 in. of boiling water in a saucepan; cover and steam for 2 minutes. Add zucchini; cover and steam 2-3 minutes longer or until vegetables are tender. Transfer vegetables to a bowl. Add the lemon juice, oil, salt and pepper; toss to coat. **Yield:** 8 servings.

Nutritional Analysis: One serving equals 43 calories, 1 g fat (trace saturated fat), 0 cholesterol, 309 mg sodium, 7 g carbohydrate, 3 g fiber, 2 g protein.
Diabetic Exchange: *2 vegetable.*

Crunchy Pears

(Also pictured on page 241)

Crisp-tender baked pears dressed in a cookie crumb and almond coating provide an elegant ending to a special meal. My family says I serve this whenever a creative mood strikes.
—Nancy Sparrow, Baltimore, Maryland

- 8 large firm pears
- 1/2 cup orange juice
- 1/3 cup orange marmalade
- 1/3 cup reduced-fat vanilla wafer crumbs (about 14 wafers)
- 1/3 cup finely chopped almonds
- 1 cup (8 ounces) fat-free reduced-sugar orange *or* plain yogurt

Core pears from bottom, leaving stems intact. Peel pears, leaving a small amount of peel at stem end. Cut 1/4 in. from bottom to level if necessary. In a bowl, combine orange juice and marmalade; spoon over pears, letting excess drip into bowl. Set aside for sauce. Place wafer crumbs and almonds in a large shallow dish. Roll pears in crumb mixture to coat the bottom three-fourths of each pear.

Place in a 13-in. x 9-in. x 2-in. baking dish coated with nonstick cooking spray. Bake at 350° for 35-45 minutes or until tender. Meanwhile, for sauce, combine yogurt and reserved marmalade mixture; refrigerate until serving. Serve with warm pears. **Yield:** 8 servings.

Nutritional Analysis: One serving (1 pear with 1/4 cup sauce) equals 231 calories, 5 g fat (1 g saturated fat), 2 mg cholesterol, 55 mg sodium, 46 g carbohydrate, 5 g fiber, 4 g protein.
Diabetic Exchanges: *2 fruit, 1 starch, 1 fat.*

Flavorful Fare Fit for Fall

Flank Steak with Cranberry Sauce

This tasty and tender steak, served with a mild sweet-tart cranberry sauce, makes a pretty presentation.
—*Ellen De Munnik, Chesterfield, Michigan*

2 teaspoons grated orange peel
1/2 teaspoon salt
1/2 teaspoon ground cinnamon
1 beef flank steak (1-1/2 pounds)
CRANBERRY SAUCE:
1/4 cup chopped green onions
1 garlic clove, minced
3/4 cup dried cranberries
1/2 cup reduced-sodium beef broth
1/2 cup red wine *or* reduced-sodium beef broth
1/2 cup cranberry juice
2 teaspoons cornstarch
2 tablespoons cold water
1/4 teaspoon salt
1/4 teaspoon pepper

Combine the orange peel, salt and cinnamon; rub over steak. Cover and refrigerate for 1 hour. In a saucepan coated with nonstick cooking spray, saute onions and garlic until tender. Add the cranberries, broth, wine or broth and cranberry juice. Bring to a boil. Reduce heat; simmer, uncovered, for 10 minutes. Combine cornstarch and water; stir into cranberry mixture. Bring to a boil; cook and stir for 2 minutes or until thickened. Stir in salt and pepper. Reduce heat to low; keep warm.

Broil steak 3-4 in. from the heat for 7-9 minutes on each side or until meat reaches desired doneness. Slice steak across the grain; serve with cranberry sauce. **Yield:** 6 servings.

Nutritional Analysis: One serving (3 ounces cooked beef with 1/4 cup sauce) equals 253 calories, 9 g fat (4 g saturated fat), 59 mg cholesterol, 373 mg sodium, 15 g carbohydrate, 1 g fiber, 24 g protein.
Diabetic Exchanges: 3 lean meat, 1 fruit.

Couscous-Stuffed Mushrooms

Because so many people are watching their weight nowadays, I came up with these light bites.
—*Lee Bremson, Kansas City, Missouri*

18 medium fresh mushrooms
3 green onions, chopped
2 garlic cloves, minced
1 tablespoon olive *or* canola oil
1 cup dry white wine *or* chicken broth
2 tablespoons reduced-sodium soy sauce
FILLING:
1/2 cup reduced-sodium chicken broth
1/4 cup uncooked couscous
1/3 cup minced fresh parsley
2 tablespoons chopped fresh basil *or* 2 teaspoons dried basil
1/4 cup grated Romano cheese
1 egg white, lightly beaten
2 tablespoons chopped walnuts, toasted
1/4 teaspoon salt
1/8 teaspoon pepper

Remove mushroom stems; discard or save for another use. Set caps aside. In a large nonstick skillet, saute onions and garlic in oil for 1 minute. Stir in wine or broth and soy sauce; add mushroom caps. Bring to a boil. Reduce heat; cover and simmer for 5-6 minutes or until mushrooms are tender. Remove mushrooms with a slotted spoon, reserving liquid in skillet. Place mushrooms stem side down on paper towels.

In a saucepan, bring broth to a boil. Stir in couscous. Remove from the heat; cover and let stand for 5 minutes. Fluff with fork; add to reserved mushroom liquid. Cover and cook on low until liquid is absorbed, about 5 minutes. Add the next five ingredients and toss gently.

Sprinkle inside of mushroom caps with salt and pepper. Stuff with couscous mixture. Place in an 11-in. x 7-in. x 2-in. baking pan coated with nonstick cooking spray. Bake at 350° for 15-20 minutes or until stuffing is lightly browned. **Yield:** 6 servings.

Nutritional Analysis: One serving (3 stuffed mushrooms) equals 113 calories, 5 g fat (1 g saturated fat), 4 mg cholesterol, 416 mg sodium, 10 g carbohydrate, 2 g fiber, 5 g protein.
Diabetic Exchanges: 1 fat, 1 vegetable, 1/2 starch.

Chocolate Chip Mint Ice Cream

Top off any meal in style with this creamy smooth concoction.
—*Sandy Powers, Cranford, New Jersey*

2 cups fat-free half-and-half
1 can (14 ounces) fat-free sweetened condensed milk
1 envelope whipped topping mix
1/4 teaspoon peppermint extract
2 to 3 drops green food coloring
1 square (1 ounce) semisweet chocolate, coarsely chopped

In a small mixing bowl, beat the half-and-half, milk, whipped topping mix, extract and food coloring on high speed for 3 minutes. Cover and refrigerate overnight. Pour into the cylinder of an ice cream freezer. Freeze according to manufacturer's directions. Stir in chocolate. Allow to firm up in refrigerator freezer for 24 hours before serving. **Yield:** 7 servings.

Nutritional Analysis: One serving (1/2 cup) equals 255 calories, 3 g fat (2 g saturated fat), 4 mg cholesterol, 128 mg sodium, 47 g carbohydrate, trace fiber, 8 g protein.

Elegant Holiday Dinner

Spinach-Stuffed Chicken Rolls

A delightful spinach stuffing, flecked with red pepper and onion, highlights this moist and tender entree from our Test Kitchen. The chicken is drizzled with a silky mushroom sauce, making an attractive main dish for a special-occasion meal.

3/4 cup *each* chopped onion, celery and sweet red pepper
2 garlic cloves, minced
2 tablespoons butter *or* stick margarine, *divided*
2 cups chopped fresh spinach
1/2 cup egg substitute
2 cups seasoned stuffing croutons, lightly crushed
6 boneless skinless chicken breast halves (6 ounces *each*)
2 tablespoons cornstarch
1 cup chicken broth
1 teaspoon lemon juice
1/2 teaspoon browning sauce, optional
2 cups sliced fresh mushrooms
1/4 teaspoon salt-free lemon-pepper seasoning, optional

In a nonstick skillet, saute the onion, celery, red pepper and garlic in 1 tablespoon butter until tender. Add spinach; cook and stir until spinach is wilted. Cool. Add egg substitute and croutons; mix well.

Flatten chicken to 1/4-in. thickness. Top each piece with spinach stuffing; roll up and secure with toothpicks. Place in a 13-in. x 9-in. x 2-in. baking dish coated with nonstick cooking spray. Cover and bake at 350° for 40-45 minutes or until chicken juices run clear.

In a small bowl, combine the cornstarch, broth, lemon juice and browning sauce if desired until smooth. In a nonstick skillet, saute mushrooms in remaining butter until tender. Gradually stir in broth mixture. Bring to a boil; cook and stir for 1-2 minutes or until thickened.

Remove toothpicks from the roll-ups. Serve with the mushroom sauce. Sprinkle with lemon-pepper if desired. **Yield:** 6 servings.

Nutritional Analysis: One serving (1 chicken roll-up with 3 tablespoons sauce) equals 349 calories, 10 g fat (4 g saturated fat), 105 mg cholesterol, 631 mg sodium, 23 g carbohydrate, 3 g fiber, 41 g protein.
Diabetic Exchanges: 5 very lean meat, 1 starch, 1 vegetable, 1 fat.

Brussels Sprouts with Pecans

No one in our family enjoyed brussels sprouts until I served this simply delicious saute. Now it's a favorite at our holiday get-togethers. For a fun alternative, substitute chestnuts for the pecans if you can find them at your grocery store.
—Juanita Haugen, Pleasanton, California

1 pound brussels sprouts, halved
1/2 pound pecan halves
2 tablespoons butter *or* stick margarine
1/2 teaspoon salt
1/4 teaspoon pepper

In a large skillet, saute brussels sprouts and pecans in butter for 5-7 minutes or until crisp-tender. Sprinkle with salt and pepper. **Yield:** 6 servings.

Nutritional Analysis: One serving (2/3 cup) equals 128 calories, 11 g fat (3 g saturated fat), 10 mg cholesterol, 252 mg sodium, 8 g carbohydrate, 3 g fiber, 3 g protein.
Diabetic Exchanges: 2 fat, 1 vegetable.

Cranberry Ice

This slightly tangy treat tops off a big holiday meal in a refreshing way…and its dark pink color adds a festive look to any table! My grandma used to make it every year, and the grandkids would fight over who got the last of it.
—Natalie Berg, Midland, Michigan

4 cups fresh *or* frozen cranberries
3 cups water
1-1/8 teaspoons unflavored gelatin
1 cup cold water
2-1/2 cups sugar
1 cup orange juice
1/4 cup lemon juice
1/2 cup whipping cream

In a large saucepan, bring cranberries and water to a boil. Reduce heat; cook, uncovered, over medium heat until the berries pop. Remove from the heat.

In a bowl, sprinkle gelatin over cold water; let stand for 5 minutes. Meanwhile, strain cranberries through a food mill into a large bowl, discarding seeds and skin. Add the sugar, orange juice, lemon juice and softened gelatin; stir until gelatin is dissolved. Stir in cream. Pour into a 13-in. x 9-in. x 2-in. pan. Cover and freeze for 3-4 hours or until firm. **Yield:** 7 cups.

Nutritional Analysis: One serving (1/2 cup) equals 191 calories, 3 g fat (2 g saturated fat), 12 mg cholesterol, 4 mg sodium, 42 g carbohydrate, 1 g fiber, 1 g protein.

Family-Style Suppers

In this chapter, you'll "meet" cooks
who share how they prepare good-for-you
fare for their families' tables. You'll also
find a special dinner that doesn't
break your household budget.

Baked Chimichangas, Broccoli Raisin Salad and
Pinapple Orange Sherbet (pages 258 and 259)

A Meal for Just $1.43 a Plate!

Oven-Fried Chicken

Tarragon, ginger and cayenne pepper season the cornmeal coating I use on my "fried" chicken. The moist meat and crunchy coating are sure to make this homey entree a mealtime mainstay at your house, too.
—Daucia Brooks, Westmoreland, Tennessee

- 1/2 cup cornmeal
- 1/2 cup dry bread crumbs
- 1 teaspoon dried tarragon
- 1 teaspoon ground ginger
- 1/2 teaspoon salt
- 1/4 teaspoon cayenne pepper
- 1/4 teaspoon pepper
- 3 egg whites
- 2 tablespoons fat-free milk
- 1/2 cup all-purpose flour
- 6 bone-in skinless chicken breast halves (6 ounces *each*)
- Refrigerated butter-flavored spray*

In a shallow bowl, combine the first seven ingredients. In another shallow bowl, combine egg whites and milk. Place flour in a third shallow bowl. Coat chicken with flour; dip in the egg white mixture, then roll in cornmeal mixture. Place in a 15-in. x 10-in. x 1-in. baking pan coated with nonstick cooking spray. Bake, uncovered, at 350° for 40 minutes. Spritz with butter-flavored spray. Bake 10-15 minutes longer or until juices run clear. **Yield:** 6 servings.

*Editor's Note: This recipe was tested with I Can't Believe It's Not Butter Spray.

Nutritional Analysis: One serving (1 chicken breast half) equals 248 calories, 2 g fat (1 g saturated fat), 63 mg cholesterol, 375 mg sodium, 24 g carbohydrate, 1 g fiber, 30 g protein.
Diabetic Exchanges: 4 very lean meat, 1-1/2 starch.

Candied Carrots

Tender sliced carrots are draped in a maple syrup and lemon juice glaze that makes this side dish a standout.
— Ruby Williams, Bogalusa, Louisiana

- 4 cups sliced carrots
- 3 tablespoons reduced-calorie pancake syrup
- 1 tablespoon lemon juice
- 2 teaspoons minced fresh parsley
- 1 teaspoon butter *or* stick margarine
- 1/2 teaspoon salt
- Dash pepper

In a saucepan, place 1 in. of water and carrots. Bring to a boil. Reduce heat; cover and simmer until crisp-tender. Drain. Stir in the remaining ingredients. Simmer, uncovered, until most of the liquid has evaporated. **Yield:** 6 servings.

Nutritional Analysis: One serving (3/4 cup) equals 66 calories, 1 g fat (trace saturated fat), 2 mg cholesterol, 286 mg sodium, 15 g carbohydrate, 3 g fiber, 1 g protein.
Diabetic Exchange: 2 vegetable.

Chewy Fudge Drop Cookies

Chocolate lovers won't be able to eat just one of these chewy treats from our Test Kitchen ovens. The delectable fudge drops are loaded with chocolate flavor and topped with a sprinkling of powdered sugar.

- 1 cup (6 ounces) semisweet chocolate chips, *divided*
- 3 tablespoons canola oil
- 1 cup packed brown sugar
- 3 egg whites
- 2 tablespoons plus 1-1/2 teaspoons light corn syrup
- 1 tablespoon water
- 2-1/2 teaspoons vanilla extract
- 1-3/4 cups all-purpose flour
- 2/3 cup plus 1 tablespoon confectioners' sugar, *divided*
- 1/3 cup baking cocoa
- 2-1/4 teaspoons baking powder
- 1/8 teaspoon salt

In a saucepan, melt 3/4 cup chocolate chips and oil over low heat, stirring constantly. Pour into a large bowl; cool for 5 minutes. Stir in brown sugar. Add egg whites, corn syrup, water and vanilla; stir well. Combine the flour, 2/3 cup confectioners' sugar, cocoa, baking powder and salt; stir into chocolate mixture until combined. Stir in the remaining chocolate chips (dough will be very stiff).

Drop by tablespoonfuls 2 in. apart onto baking sheets coated with nonstick cooking spray. Bake at 350° for 8-10 minutes or until puffed and set. Cool for 2 minutes before removing to wire racks. Sprinkle cooled cookies with remaining confectioners' sugar. **Yield:** 4 dozen.

Nutritional Analysis: One serving (2 cookies) equals 139 calories, 4 g fat (1 g saturated fat), 0 cholesterol, 48 mg sodium, 26 g carbohydrate, 1 g fiber, 2 g protein.
Diabetic Exchanges: 1-1/2 starch, 1 fat.

Make It Italian Tonight

WHEN Sue and Mike Yaeger first met, their lives changed for the better...and the healthier.

"Before meeting my husband, I didn't concern myself with the amount of fat or the number of calories in home-made dishes," Sue shares from the couple's Boone, Iowa home. "I reduced the salt called for in recipes—a practice I learned from my mother—but that was my only attempt at healthy cooking.

"When Mike and I started dating, however, he introduced me to the benefits of a well-rounded diet," she explains. "We agreed to prepare a low-fat, reduced-calorie meal for one another each week.

"We learned about creating nutritious menus, making the most of lighter ingredients and taking advantage of different cooking methods," says Sue. "As a result, I've changed the way I cook and the things I eat."

Even though Sue and Mike have now been married for 11 years and have two sons—Nick and Kurt—nutrition remains a key ingredient at mealtime.

"Because we've been eating healthy for so long, Mike and I don't notice that fat is missing from the dishes we prepare.

"Our boys don't like greasy foods because they aren't used to them," Sue reports. "I butter their bread if they want, but they usually prefer it plain. Similarly, they like healthier versions of many foods, such as reduced-fat cheese, because it's what they're accustomed to eating."

Sue's family enjoys a variety of meats, so she is sure to select lean cuts. "I thoroughly trim whatever fat I can from the meat I buy," she adds. "I usually bake or stir-fry it, but we love to fire up the grill and barbecue outside, too."

Sue is a stay-at-home mom who squeezes aerobics into her schedule on a regular basis. Mike, a veterinary pathologist, jogs and lifts weights. As a family, they watch and play football, basketball and soccer.

"Eating healthy and exercising give Mike and me more energy to keep up with the boys," Sue relates. "And that's important to all of us."

Sue keeps meals on the lighter side by replacing some of the ingredients in family favorites. "My Zesty Turkey Spaghetti Sauce is good for you because it calls for lean cubed turkey instead of meatballs," she explains. "For extra flavor, I add turkey pepperoni to the sauce, along with green pepper, onion and mushrooms.

"This is one of the entrees I served Mike when we first met, and it's just as big of a hit now as it was then," promises Sue. "It's easy to prepare, and the seasonings can be modified to fit anyone's tastes."

As Sue's hearty spaghetti sauce simmers, she tosses together a Mock Caesar Salad. This lightened-up version of the classic is a tasty complement to the main dish that the whole family will enjoy.

Best of all, the thick creamy dressing has the flavor you'd expect with only a fraction of the fat.

How does Sue reward her family for their healthy eating efforts? With a sweet chocolate treat that Mike dreamed up.

"He made Chocolate Mousse one night using skim milk and a few lighter convenience items," Sue recalls. "The result was this fluffy rich-tasting dessert that the kids and I request time and again."

Zesty Turkey Spaghetti Sauce

1 pound uncooked turkey tenderloin, cubed
1 medium green pepper, cut into 3/4-inch pieces
1 medium onion, cut into wedges
2/3 cup sliced fresh mushrooms
1 tablespoon canola oil
1 jar (15-1/2 ounces) meatless spaghetti sauce
1 cup sliced turkey pepperoni, halved
1/2 cup dry red wine *or* chicken broth
1 tablespoon tomato paste
10 ounces uncooked vermicelli

In a Dutch oven or large kettle, saute the turkey, green pepper, onion and mushrooms in oil until vegetables are tender. Stir in the spaghetti sauce, pepperoni, wine or broth and tomato paste. Bring to a boil. Reduce heat; cover and simmer for 45 minutes. Uncover; simmer 15-20 minutes longer or until thickened. Meanwhile, cook vermicelli according to package directions; drain. Serve with sauce. **Yield:** 5 servings.

Nutritional Analysis: One serving (1 cup sauce with 1 cup vermicelli) equals 428 calories, 6 g fat (1 g saturated fat), 77 mg cholesterol, 752 mg sodium, 54 g carbohydrate, 5 g fiber, 37 g protein.
Diabetic Exchanges: 3 lean meat, 3 vegetable, 2-1/2 starch.

Mock Caesar Salad

1/3 cup fat-free plain yogurt
1/4 cup reduced-fat mayonnaise
1 tablespoon red wine vinegar *or* cider vinegar
2 teaspoons Dijon mustard
1 teaspoon Worcestershire sauce
1/4 teaspoon garlic powder
1/8 teaspoon pepper
6 cups torn romaine
1/2 cup fat-free salad croutons
2 tablespoons shredded Parmesan cheese

In a small bowl, whisk together the first seven ingredients. In a salad bowl, combine the romaine, croutons and cheese. Drizzle with the dressing; toss to coat. Serve immediately. **Yield:** 5 servings.

Nutritional Analysis: One serving (1-1/4 cups) equals 90 calories, 5 g fat (1 g saturated fat), 7 mg cholesterol, 299 mg sodium, 9 g carbohydrate, 1 g fiber, 4 g protein.
Diabetic Exchanges: 1 fat, 1/2 starch.

Chocolate Mousse

3/4 cup cold fat-free milk
  1 package (1.4 ounces) sugar-free instant
    chocolate pudding mix
1/2 cup reduced-fat sour cream
  3 ounces reduced-fat cream cheese, cubed
1/2 teaspoon vanilla extract
  1 carton (8 ounces) frozen reduced-fat whipped
    topping, thawed
  1 tablespoon chocolate cookie crumbs

In a bowl, whisk milk and pudding mix for 2 minutes (mixture will be very thick). In a mixing bowl, beat the sour cream, cream cheese and vanilla. Add pudding; mix well. Fold in whipped topping. Spoon into individual dishes. Sprinkle with cookie crumbs. Refrigerate until serving. **Yield:** 6 servings.

Nutritional Analysis: One serving (2/3 cup) equals 186 calories, 9 g fat (8 g saturated fat), 15 mg cholesterol, 263 mg sodium, 18 g carbohydrate, 1 g fiber, 4 g protein.
Diabetic Exchanges: *2 fat, 1-1/2 starch.*

Bountiful Breakfasts

BEGIN YOUR DAY by keeping nutrition in the spotlight "Try putting applesauce or pie filling over pancakes," relates Sue Yaeger. "This is a fast, easy and delightful way to increase your daily servings of fruit.

"Similarly, add fresh fruit or raisins to low-fat cereal for additional flavor and great health benefits," she suggests.

When Sue feels like topping her toast, muffin or bagel, she simply spreads on jam or jelly. "It's a lot less fattening than using butter or cream cheese.

"And when you want to end a special brunch with a sweet treat, consider angel food cake," recommends Sue. "Try a slice with fat-free pudding, sherbet, or caramel and chocolate syrups. They make tasty variations to reduced-fat whipped topping."

Southwestern Specialties

A BIG weight loss resulted in a tiny bundle of joy for Angela Oelschlaeger of Tonganoxie, Kansas.

"My husband, Michael, and I had been hoping to give our daughter, Tia, a brother or sister," says Angela. "But my doctor was concerned with my weight and high blood pressure.

"And I knew that I needed to be as healthy as possible—both for the baby's sake and for my own," she says. "Plus, I would need lots of energy to keep up with a second child and take care of my growing family. I took a look at my cooking and eating habits and realized I needed to make changes."

Angela admits to being a little concerned about lightening up her husband's favorite dishes. "Like most farmers, Michael was used to hearty down-home cooking. I wasn't sure I could get the same satisfying results with low-fat recipes.

"I wanted to make dishes that were good for us but didn't skimp on taste. I slowly began replacing ingredients in our favorite meals with healthier alternatives, and no one seemed to notice.

"I started with little things like making fresh veggies a staple in our house...and using fat-free refried beans in the Southwest dishes I often prepare.

"I adjusted my cooking methods, too, by using broth rather than oil for sauteing, and marinating and grilling pork and fish instead of frying them," she explains.

"Eventually, I brought my blood pressure down to normal and lost more than 70 pounds!" she says. "And when I reached my weight goal, I got a terrific reward. I found out I was expecting our second daughter!"

It was the gift of a lifetime for Angela—something that has much more valuable than her new reflection in the mirror.

"We were thrilled with the good news!" Angela says. "And I was glad that I knew how to eat right while carrying the baby because I had learned how to prepare nutritious meals for my family...and I also knew what foods to avoid."

With baby Sydnee in the house, Angela and Michael are busier than ever these days. The couple raises Black Angus cattle, and Michael grows soybeans, milo, wheat and corn in addition to working full-time for a parcel delivery service.

When she's not at home taking care of the kids, Angela works as a part-time administrator for a group of physicians. She enjoys getting involved with Tia's Girl Scout troop, baking bread and helping out on the farm.

Angela "wows" family and friends with one of her Southwestern specialties—Baked Chimichangas. For her mouth-watering entree, she fills tortillas with tender shredded chicken, then tops them with a thick, full-flavored sauce.

"To make the chimichangas healthier, I bake them instead of frying them. As a tasty change of pace, substitute lean ground beef for the chicken," she suggests.

For a simple but sensational side dish, Angela throws together refreshing Broccoli Raisin Salad. "I adjusted a friend's recipe to cut a few calories," she relates. "The raisins add sweetness, and the bacon gives it a nice crunch."

And what better way to end a meal than on a sweet note? Angela uses an ice cream maker to create delightful Pineapple Orange Sherbet that's low in fat and high in demand.

"My family looks forward to this meal each time I prepare it," Angela says, "and I promise yours will, too."

Baked Chimichangas

(Also pictured on page 254)

> 2-1/2 cups shredded cooked chicken breast
> 1 cup salsa
> 1 small onion, chopped
> 3/4 teaspoon ground cumin
> 1/2 teaspoon dried oregano
> 6 flour tortillas (10 inches)
> 3/4 cup shredded reduced-fat cheddar cheese
> 1 cup reduced-sodium chicken broth
> 2 teaspoons chicken bouillon granules
> 1/8 teaspoon pepper
> 1/4 cup all-purpose flour
> 1 cup fat-free half-and-half cream
> 1 can (4 ounces) chopped green chilies

In a nonstick skillet, simmer chicken, salsa, onion, cumin and oregano until heated through and most of the liquid has evaporated. Place 1/2 cup down the center of each tortilla; top with 2 tablespoons cheese. Fold sides and ends over filling and roll up. Place seam side down in a 13-in. x 9-in. x 2-in. baking dish coated with nonstick cooking spray. Bake, uncovered, at 425° for 15 minutes or until lightly browned.

Meanwhile, in a saucepan, heat the broth, bouillon and pepper until bouillon is dissolved. Combine flour and cream until smooth; stir into the broth. Bring to a boil; cook and stir for 2 minutes or until thickened. Stir in chilies and heat through. To serve, cut chimichangas in half; spoon sauce over the top. **Yield:** 6 servings.

Nutritional Analysis: *One serving (1 chimichanga with 1/4 cup sauce) equals 423 calories, 9 g fat (3 g saturated fat), 57 mg cholesterol, 1,326 mg sodium, 47 g carbohydrate, 7 g fiber, 32 g protein.*
Diabetic Exchanges: *3 starch, 3 lean meat, 1/2 fat.*

Broccoli Raisin Salad

(Also pictured on page 254)

> 4 cups fresh broccoli florets (1 medium bunch)
> 3/4 cup golden raisins
> 1 small red onion, chopped
> 1/2 cup fat-free mayonnaise *or* salad dressing

1 tablespoon white vinegar
2 teaspoons sugar
3 bacon strips, cooked and crumbled

In a large bowl, combine the broccoli, raisins and onion. In a small bowl, combine the mayonnaise, vinegar and sugar. Pour over broccoli mixture; toss to coat. Sprinkle with bacon. Refrigerate for at least 2 hours before serving. **Yield:** 6 servings.

Nutritional Analysis: One serving (3/4 cup) equals 116 calories, 2 g fat (1 g saturated fat), 3 mg cholesterol, 226 mg sodium, 23 g carbohydrate, 2 g fiber, 3 g protein.
Diabetic Exchanges: 1 vegetable, 1 fruit, 1/2 fat.

Pineapple Orange Sherbet

(Also pictured on page 254)

3 cans (12 ounces *each*) orange soda
2 cans (8 ounces *each*) unsweetened crushed pineapple, undrained
1-1/2 cups sugar
1 can (12 ounces) fat-free evaporated milk
1/8 teaspoon salt

In a large bowl, combine all ingredients. Fill ice cream freezer cylinder two-thirds full; freeze according to manufacturer's directions (refrigerate remaining mixture until ready to

freeze). Transfer to a freezer container; allow sherbet to firm up in the refrigerator freezer for 2-4 hours before serving. **Yield:** about 2 quarts.

Nutritional Analysis: One serving (2/3 cup) equals 175 calories, trace fat (trace saturated fat), 1 mg cholesterol, 73 mg sodium, 42 g carbohydrate, trace fiber, 3 g protein.

🍎 Pretty Presentations

"NO MATTER what new light recipe I've prepared, I found that if I made it *look* extra special, my gang was excited about trying it," says Angela Oelschlaeger.

"For example, when assembling a casserole that calls for light cheese, I mix half of the cheese into the casserole and melt the rest on top for a more attractive appearance."

Angela also pays attention to which plates best show off the food. "A plain white plate makes colorful foods such as grilled chicken with salsa look all the more attractive," she recommends.

"With something pale like low-fat fettuccine Alfredo, I'd suggest colorful dishes."

Chicken Dinner Made Lighter

LIGHTENING UP family-favorite recipes is so much fun for Elissa Armbruster that she almost thinks of it as a hobby! When she's not camping, biking or volunteering at her church, she spends her free time sorting through recipes, looking for ways to pare down the fat and calories.

"I love to play with recipes and make adjustments to the butter, oil, salt or sugar called for in the original recipe," says the Medford, New Jersey cook. "I think experimentation is the key to healthy baking and cooking.

"I used to believe that good nutrition just meant cooking meals from scratch and avoiding fast food," she says. "But after the birth of my second son, I realized the extra pounds I'd gained weren't going to go away by themselves. I began exercising regularly and tried to change my eating habits."

She wanted to cook good-for-you meals, but Elissa also knew that she needed to continue to prepare foods that would satisfy her husband, Mike, and sons Christian and Michael.

"I began by sorting through our favorite recipes, noting which ingredients could be substituted with lighter counterparts," explains Elissa. "I decided to try reducing the calories or fat in a few main courses without altering their tastes…and I gradually introduced these revamped dishes to my family."

Knowing that Mike was open to tasting new foods, Elissa was confident that he would take to the overhauled entrees. Her sons' opinions, on the other hand, were another concern.

"Because they were so young at the time, the boys were quite picky about what they ate," she says. "So I prepared foods I knew would appeal to them. They didn't complain about the changes I made because they were happy I served the foods they liked."

Elissa continued to work low-fat alternatives into her suppertime standbys and soon began noticing the benefits. The extra weight came off, she had more energy and, most importantly, her family was eating healthier.

Since having her third son, Ryan, she has also become mindful of the combination of foods she brings to the table.

"If a main dish is higher in calories or fat than what I normally serve," says Elissa, "I balance it with a slim side dish such as vegetables sauteed in broth.

"I now cook with more fruits and vegetables than ever before, mix my own salad dressings and marinades and prepare at least two protein-packed meatless dinners a week.

"By trial and error, I've even learned how to use reduced-fat yogurt and sour cream when baking breads, biscuits and muffins."

A former teacher, Elissa is a stay-at-home mom who keeps the books for the excavation company Mike owns and operates.

"Time can get pretty tight around here," she says, "but I don't let that interfere with nutrition. That's why I turn to Chicken Diane on busy nights."

In this classic dish, a luscious sauce of lemon juice, Dijon mustard and green onions ideally complements tender chicken breasts that are browned to a golden perfection on the stovetop.

"Try it with Basil Fettuccine," suggests Elissa. "The pasta is coated with a thick Alfredo sauce I make from plain yogurt. This keeps the sauce lower in fat than purchased varieties. Plus, you can easily double the recipe and serve it as a stand-alone supper rather than a side dish."

To round out this trimmed-down dinner in a dash, prepare palate-pleasing Peachy Pecan Salad. You'll only need a total of six ingredients—three for the refreshing citrus dressing and three for the colorful salad.

Notes Elissa, "You can replace the pecans in the salad with walnuts or almonds to better suit your tastes.

"Your family is sure to enjoy eating healthy as much as mine does when you put this quick-to-fix meal on the table," she adds. "You will be rewarded with smiles."

Chicken Diane

4 boneless skinless chicken breast halves (4 ounces *each*)
1/2 teaspoon salt
1/2 teaspoon pepper
2 teaspoons olive *or* canola oil
2 teaspoons butter *or* stick margarine
1 tablespoon lemon juice
1 tablespoon minced fresh parsley
2 teaspoons Dijon mustard
1/4 cup reduced-sodium chicken broth
3 tablespoons chopped green onions

Flatten chicken to 1/4-in. thickness; sprinkle both sides with salt and pepper. In a large nonstick skillet, brown chicken in oil and butter over medium heat for 3-5 minutes on each side or until juices run clear. Remove and keep warm.

In the same skillet, whisk the lemon juice, parsley and mustard until blended. Whisk in broth and green onions; heat through. Serve over chicken. **Yield:** 4 servings.

Nutritional Analysis: One serving (1 chicken breast half with 4-1/2 teaspoons sauce) equals 169 calories, 6 g fat (2 g saturated fat), 71 mg cholesterol, 490 mg sodium, 1 g carbohydrate, trace fiber, 27 g protein.
Diabetic Exchange: 3 lean meat.

Basil Fettuccine

8 ounces uncooked fettuccine
1 cup (8 ounces) fat-free plain yogurt
1/4 cup grated Parmesan cheese
2 tablespoons chopped fresh basil
or 2 teaspoons dried basil

1/2 teaspoon salt
1/4 teaspoon white pepper
  2 garlic cloves, minced
  1 tablespoon olive *or* canola oil

Cook fettuccine according to package directions. Meanwhile, in a bowl, combine the yogurt, Parmesan cheese, basil, salt and pepper; set aside. In a small nonstick skillet, saute garlic in oil for 1 minute. Drain fettuccine and place in a large bowl. Add garlic and oil; toss. Add the yogurt mixture; toss until well coated. Serve immediately. **Yield:** 4 servings.

Nutritional Analysis: One serving (1 cup) equals 290 calories, 7 g fat (2 g saturated fat), 6 mg cholesterol, 447 mg sodium, 47 g carbohydrate, 2 g fiber, 13 g protein.
Diabetic Exchanges: 3 starch, 1 fat.

Tasty Veggie Tactics

GETTING little ones to eat their vegetables can be difficult. Just ask Elissa Armbruster!

Since her three sons are all under the age of 10, she keeps a few nutrition tricks up her sleeve.

"Baby carrots are a staple in our refrigerator," she says. "Not only are they great snacks, but I let the boys substitute them for any vegetables they don't like at dinner.

"And salads are an easy way to sneak in extra vegetables," she adds. "For example, my kids like cucumbers in salads, so I toss in sliced zucchini, too. They never notice the healthy addition."

Peachy Pecan Salad

  8 cups torn mixed salad greens
  1 can (11 ounces) mandarin oranges, drained
1/4 cup coarsely chopped pecans, toasted
1/2 cup reduced-fat peach yogurt
  3 tablespoons reduced-fat mayonnaise
  1 tablespoon cider vinegar

Divide salad greens, oranges and pecans among individual salad plates. In a small bowl, combine yogurt, mayonnaise and vinegar; drizzle over salads. **Yield:** 4 servings.

Nutritional Analysis: One serving (2 cups salad with 3 tablespoons dressing) equals 169 calories, 10 g fat (1 g saturated fat), 6 mg cholesterol, 119 mg sodium, 19 g carbohydrate, 3 g fiber, 4 g protein.
Diabetic Exchanges: 1 fat, 1 vegetable, 1 reduced-fat milk.

Slim Down for Summer

MOST OF US think of high cholesterol as a health risk that comes with age. Not so for Michelle Smith's young daughter, Casey.

"When Casey was 5 years old, we learned she had a cholesterol level of over 400!" Michelle states from her home in Eldersburg, Maryland. "Although my husband, Dean, and I both have a family history of high cholesterol, we were shocked by the news. It was such a high number for someone so young.

"I immediately changed the way I cooked, the foods my family ate and, eventually, the way we thought about nutrition.

"I knew I needed to lighten up our meals but couldn't gradually work healthier foods into our menus," she says. "Changes needed to be made right away."

Michelle admits that her family had grown accustomed to fast food. "Dean is a lieutenant with the local fire department and also holds two part-time jobs," she explains. "Between trying to accommodate his changing meal schedule, getting Casey to karate and ballet classes, and caring for our second daughter, Anney, I often used drive-thrus as a last-minute meal option."

Michelle cut out the fast food in a hurry once Casey's doctors had made their diagnosis. And she started preparing meals from scratch.

"Ground turkey, lean cuts of pork and seafood became integral to my meal planning," shares Michelle. "We probably have fish four times a week. And the girls have learned to love turkey burgers.

"I try to boost nutrition wherever I can—by hiding chopped spinach in turkey meat loaf and bits of zucchini in mashed potatoes. I also serve steamed vegetables with every dinner.

"I depend on my grill and rotisserie, too," she adds. "I love how those cooking methods drain fat from the meat while bringing out their natural flavors.

"I also realized that if the girls grew up in a home that focused on nutrition, they'd have an easier time making good food choices later in life," notes the stay-at-home mom. "So I stopped buying junk food and started educating my daughters about healthy-eating options.

"We no longer keep sweets and salty snacks in the house. Instead, the kids enjoy low-fat yogurt, granola bars and dried fruit. They actually prefer milk and water.

"Popcorn is a favorite snack to munch on. And when I make cookies, I usually add oatmeal, since it's known to lower cholesterol."

By tweaking her family's eating habits, Michelle eventually helped lower Casey's cholesterol to a more manageable 271. Although we have to continually monitor her cholesterol, it's under control," Michelle reports.

"Eating right has been a learning experience for the whole family. Even though we're still learning, the process has made us all healthier, happier and wiser."

While Michelle continues to lighten up meal plans, she's already created plenty of mouth-watering family favorites, including Honey-Garlic Pork Chops.

"Whether or not you're keeping a close eye on your cholesterol level, you'll love the robust taste of these tender chops. They will be as popular at your home as they are at mine," she confirms. "The honey and garlic sauce is so good, I sometimes double it so there's extra for dipping."

The savory supper is impressive enough for company, too, especially when paired with Spaghetti Squash with Tomatoes.

"It's a wonderful alternative to pasta and a great way to show how tasty vegetables can be," Michelle notes.

Topped with Parmesan cheese, the sensational side dish combines onions, tomatoes and chopped sweet red pepper with seasonal squash for an unforgettable addition to any meal.

And nothing cools down a hot summer night like Michelle's refreshing Minted Raspberry Lemonade. "I guarantee this colorful beverage will be a hit whenever it's served.

"I try to cook the healthiest, tastiest foods possible for my family," Michelle adds. "And with this meal, you will have no problem doing the same."

● Slim and Speedy Snacks

FIXING a good-for-you treat doesn't have to eat up your time. Michelle Smith has some swift specialties that easily keep the spotlight on healthy snacking.

"To create a quick veggie dip, try combining fat-free mayonnaise with an envelope of ranch salad dressing mix," she suggests. "Add milk a teaspoon at a time until you achieve a consistency that's good for dipping carrot sticks and broccoli florets.

"Fruit smoothies are another staple at our house. I simply combine fat-free yogurt, cubed fruit and skim milk in my blender to whip up cool, refreshing and satisfying beverages."

Honey-Garlic Pork Chops

4 bone-in pork loin chops (6 ounces *each*)
1/4 cup honey
1/4 cup lemon juice
2 tablespoons reduced-sodium soy sauce
1 garlic clove, minced

In a large nonstick skillet coated with nonstick cooking spray, brown pork chops on both sides. Cook over medium heat for 10-12 minutes or until juices run clear and a meat thermometer reads 160°. In a bowl, combine the honey, lemon juice, soy sauce and garlic. Remove chops and keep warm. Add honey mixture to the skillet; cook over medium

heat for 3-4 minutes, stirring occasionally. Pour over chops. **Yield:** 4 servings.

Nutritional Analysis: *One serving (1 pork chop with 2 tablespoons sauce) equals 220 calories, 5 g fat (2 g saturated fat), 71 mg cholesterol, 361 mg sodium, 20 g carbohydrate, trace fiber, 25 g protein.*
Diabetic Exchanges: *3 lean meat, 1 starch.*

Spaghetti Squash with Tomatoes

  1 **medium spaghetti squash (2-1/2 pounds)**
  2 **tablespoons water**
1/2 **cup chopped sweet red *or* green pepper**
1/2 **cup sliced green onions**
  2 **large tomatoes, seeded and chopped**
  2 **tablespoons minced fresh parsley**
  2 **teaspoons minced fresh dill *or* 3/4 teaspoon dill weed**
  2 **teaspoons minced fresh basil *or* 3/4 teaspoon dried basil**
1/2 **teaspoon salt**
  2 **tablespoons grated Parmesan cheese**

Cut squash in half lengthwise; discard seeds. Place squash cut side down in a baking dish. Fill dish with hot water to a depth of 1/2 in. Cover and bake at 350° for 30-40 minutes or until tender. Meanwhile, in a nonstick skillet, heat water over medium heat; add pepper and onions. Cook and stir for 2 minutes. Stir in the tomatoes, parsley, dill, basil and salt. Bring to a boil. Reduce heat; simmer, uncovered, for 5 minutes or until tender.

When squash is cool enough to handle, scoop out pulp, separating strands with a fork; place in a large bowl. Add tomato mixture and toss to combine. Sprinkle with cheese. **Yield:** 6 servings.

Nutritional Analysis: *One serving (3/4 cup) equals 86 calories, 2 g fat (1 g saturated fat), 1 mg cholesterol, 266 mg sodium, 17 g carbohydrate, 3 g fiber, 3 g protein.*
Diabetic Exchange: *1 starch.*

Minted Raspberry Lemonade

1/2 **cup unsweetened raspberries**
  1 **cup lemon juice (about 4 medium lemons)**
3/4 **cup sugar**
  1 **teaspoon minced fresh mint *or* 1/4 teaspoon dried mint flakes**
  6 **cups water**

Mash and strain raspberries, reserving juice; discard pulp and seeds. In a large container or punch bowl, combine the lemon juice, sugar and mint. Stir in water and reserved raspberry juice. Serve over ice. **Yield:** 7 servings.

Nutritional Analysis: *One serving (1 cup) equals 88 calories, 0 fat (0 saturated fat), 0 cholesterol, 1 mg sodium, 23 g carbohydrate, trace fiber, trace protein.*
Diabetic Exchange: *1-1/2 fruit.*

Soup and Salad Always Satisfies

WHEN IT COMES to encouraging her family to eat healthy, home-school teacher Connie Thomas of Jensen, Utah gets high marks!

"Several years ago, I was ready to try anything to feel better," reports the stay-at-home mom. "I was always tired and seemed to catch any bug that was going around.

"I wanted to be as healthy as possible, and decided to try lightening up our meals. It was important to me that my husband, Don, and the rest of my family begin eating the right foods as well."

Connie, who teaches the couple's three children, Andrew, Alicia and Kyle, decided to practice what she preached on a daily basis.

"Just like I'm always telling the kids to do, I hit the books and studied," she says. "I worked my way through nutrition books, gradually changing our eating habits as I learned.

"One of the first things I did was focus on grains like wheat and brown rice," Connie explains. "I bought whole wheat bread…and eventually started to use whole wheat flour in most of my baking. And brown rice became a staple in our house. Not only is it nutritious, but the entire family enjoys it."

Next, Connie set out to reduce the amount of fat in family favorites.

"I started out slowly," she says. "I made small changes in the way I cooked, like steaming vegetables and using smaller amounts of meat. I began using my slow cooker once again, too. Slow-cooked foods are delicious, and since the moisture stays in the cooker, there's no need to add much fat.

"Plus, I began experimenting with light products. I discovered that fat-free sour cream is a good substitute for the heavier variety in many recipes. Similarly, skim milk can be used in place of whole milk in nearly any recipe.

"The last change we made was to focus on eating more fruits and vegetables. I made a point of keeping a green salad on hand in the refrigerator, having fresh fruit available and cooking with more vegetables.

"It took us a while to make and accept all of these changes, but they were well worth it," Connie notes. "We've all adapted and are healthier for it.

"I rarely get sick anymore, and I have the energy to do the things I love, such as gardening, crocheting and volunteering at my church. Best of all, I'm still serving great-tasting food."

Appropriately enough, all of Connie's recipes have to pass three tests before they've earned a permanent place in her recipe file. "They must taste good, be nutritious and come together easily," she says. "Chicken Vegetable Soup scores high on all three counts."

Not only is the recipe extremely low in fat, but it's as convenient as it is delicious. Chock-full of corn, lentils and tender chunks of chicken, the thick satisfying soup simmers to a heartwarming perfection in the slow cooker.

"Try it on a cool night with a loaf of bread or my golden Pumpkin Dinner Rolls," recommends Connie.

Connie rounds out her meal with Cucumber Buttermilk Salad Dressing draped over salad greens. A few ingredients are all you'll need.

"I extended bottled salad dressing to come up with this refreshing combination," relates Connie. "Full of cucumber flavor, it's wonderful over dark greens and fresh vegetables. It's a recipe I turn to time and again.

"Whenever I try a new dish, everyone in the family gets to vote on whether or not we should have it in the future," she concludes. "This meal gets thumbs-up approval from my whole gang."

Chicken Vegetable Soup

- 1 can (28 ounces) diced tomatoes, undrained
- 2 cups reduced-fat reduced-sodium chicken broth
- 2 cups cubed cooked chicken breast
- 1 cup frozen corn
- 2 celery ribs with leaves, chopped
- 1 can (6 ounces) tomato paste
- 1/4 cup dry lentils, rinsed
- 1 tablespoon sugar
- 1 tablespoon Worcestershire sauce
- 2 teaspoons dried parsley flakes
- 1 teaspoon dried marjoram

In a slow cooker, combine all ingredients. Cover and cook on low for 6-8 hours or until vegetables are tender. **Yield:** 8 servings (2 quarts).

Nutritional Analysis: One serving (1 cup) equals 140 calories, 1 g fat (trace saturated fat), 27 mg cholesterol, 388 mg sodium, 18 g carbohydrate, 3 g fiber, 15 g protein.
Diabetic Exchanges: 1 starch, 1 vegetable, 1 very lean meat.

Pumpkin Dinner Rolls

- 2 teaspoons active dry yeast
- 1-1/2 cups warm water (110° to 115°)
- 1-1/4 cups cooked or canned pumpkin
- 1/2 cup butter *or* stick margarine, softened
- 1/3 cup sugar
- 2 eggs
- 2 teaspoons salt
- 2-1/2 cups whole wheat flour
- 4-1/2 to 5 cups all-purpose flour

In a large mixing bowl, dissolve yeast in warm water. Add the pumpkin, butter, sugar, eggs, salt and whole wheat flour; beat until smooth. Stir in enough all-purpose flour to make a soft dough. Turn onto a lightly floured surface; knead until smooth and elastic, about 6-8 minutes. Place in a greased bowl, turning once to grease top. Cover and let rise in a

warm place until doubled, about 1 hour.

Punch dough down. Turn onto a lightly floured surface; divide into three portions. Roll each portion into a 12-in. circle; cut each circle into 12 wedges. Roll up wedges from the wide end and place pointed side down 2 in. apart on greased baking sheets. Curve ends to form crescents.

Cover and let rise until doubled, about 30 minutes. Bake at 400° for 12-15 minutes. Remove to wire racks. **Yield:** 3 dozen.

Nutritional Analysis: One roll equals 134 calories, 3 g fat (2 g saturated fat), 19 mg cholesterol, 161 mg sodium, 23 g carbohydrate, 2 g fiber, 4 g protein.
Diabetic Exchanges: 1-1/2 starch, 1/2 fat.

Cucumber Buttermilk Salad Dressing

1/2 cup 1% buttermilk
1/2 cup reduced-fat sour cream
1/4 cup prepared cucumber ranch salad dressing
  1 teaspoon dried minced onion
1/4 teaspoon sugar
  2 tablespoons grated peeled cucumber, patted dry
Salad greens and vegetables of your choice

In a small bowl, whisk the first five ingredients until blended. Refrigerate overnight. Stir in cucumber. Serve over a tossed salad. **Yield:** 1-1/4 cups.

Nutritional Analysis: One serving (2 tablespoons dressing) equals 50 calories, 4 g fat (1 g saturated fat), 4 mg cholesterol, 69 mg sodium, 3 g carbohydrate, trace fiber, 1 g protein.
Diabetic Exchange: 1 fat.

🍎 Crazy for Carrots

CARROT STICKS are a snacking staple for Connie Thomas' family. But if your bunch isn't keen on munching the vitamin-packed veggie, consider a few of her tips.

"Carrots are a great source of vitamin A, fiber and potassium," she says, "so I add them to several foods. For example, I stir a few finely grated cooked carrots into mashed potatoes with great results. I even add some to brownies and no one notices a difference in taste.

"Or try adding a shredded carrot to your next fruit smoothie," suggests Connie. "Blend it with sliced bananas, pineapple chunks and cold milk for a nutritious treat."

A Festive Turkey Dinner

THE KEY TO VICTORY on the playing field for sports enthusiast Nancy Zimmerman is plain old nutrition.

"I run about 40 miles per week and participate in a women's volleyball league year-round," she explains. "In the summer, my husband, Ken, and I play together on co-ed softball and volleyball teams.

"I wanted to improve my performance in all of the sporting activities I'm involved with...it's important to me to keep trim and feel good. So I began cooking and eating healthier."

The Zimmermans live in the small town of Swainton, located in Cape May County in New Jersey. Nancy works part-time as an account executive for a Christian radio station, and Ken is a CAT scan technician at a hospital.

"I was a real novice in the kitchen when I married Ken 7 years ago," Nancy confides. "I didn't know how to cook or bake. It's taken me a while to learn how to lighten up recipes."

"Ken and I have different tastes," shares Nancy. "Because I'm a vegetarian and he is not, I prepare separate main courses to suit each of our preferences.

"I eat mostly fruits and vegetables, but I prepare meat and poultry for Ken. I usually marinate his entrees in fruit juices before baking or roasting them. No matter what I'm cooking, I rely on colorful produce to keep everything attractive, nutritious and tasty."

While the couple may have different preferences when it comes to dinner, one thing they agree on is dessert. "We both look forward to homemade treats from time to time," Nancy writes. "I also enjoy contributing baked goods to fund-raisers and charity sales.

"Because eating right has now become a way of life in our home, I've learned to reduce the fat, calories and cholesterol in some of the recipes for our favorite sweets. "For instance, I often substitute two egg whites for every whole egg that a recipe calls for," she says. "I've also found that applesauce can be used in place of butter in many baking recipes, especially in cookies and sweet quick breads. Similarly, adding honey to a recipe is a wonderful way to cut back on sugar."

Nancy enjoys entertaining and hosts an annual New Year's Day gathering. "We have eight to 10 family members over, and none of them suspect that the meal I serve is low in fat," she notes.

One of Nancy's special-occasion dinners features Turkey Breast with Apricot Glaze. "I stuff the turkey breast with onion, cloves and an orange before baking it," she reports.

"The result is a wonderful aroma as the turkey is roasting...and great flavor! Removing the skin from the bird before serving helps trim the fat...and the sweet glaze drizzled over individual slices makes a fantastic alternative to gravy."

Nancy serves her four-ingredient Cranberry Sauce as an accompaniment to the turkey. "I turn to this recipe fre-quently because I can prepare it a day ahead—it's so convenient when company's coming," she adds. And with only a trace of fat, the fruity side dish is nutritious and delicious!

Dried apricots add sweetness and color to Nancy's Apricot-Pecan Wild Rice, a perfect pairing to her tender turkey. Seasoned with sage and thyme, the down-home dish is sure to have guests asking for seconds at your house, too.

"Share this special meal with your family and friends some time soon," Nancy suggests. "I'm sure you'll be as pleased with its good-for-you flair as with its traditional time-tested flavors."

Turkey Breast with Apricot Glaze

> 1 small onion
> 2 whole cloves
> 1 small orange, halved
> 1 bone-in turkey breast (4-1/2 pounds)
> 1 cup apricot preserves
> 1/2 cup unsweetened apple juice
> 1 teaspoon Dijon mustard

Peel onion and insert cloves. Stuff onion and orange into the neck cavity of turkey. Place on a rack in a shallow roasting pan. Bake, uncovered, at 325° for 2 to 2-1/2 hours or until a meat thermometer reads 170°.

Let stand for 10-15 minutes before slicing. Meanwhile, in a saucepan, combine the preserves, apple juice and mustard. Bring to a boil. Reduce heat; simmer, uncovered, for 4-5 minutes or until slightly thickened. Remove skin, onion and orange from turkey. Slice turkey; drizzle with glaze. **Yield:** 12 servings.

Nutritional Analysis: One serving (4 ounces cooked turkey with 4 teaspoons glaze) equals 228 calories, 1 g fat (trace saturated fat), 97 mg cholesterol, 82 mg sodium, 18 g carbohydrate, trace fiber, 35 g protein.
Diabetic Exchanges: 4 very lean meat, 1 fruit.

Cranberry Sauce

> 1 cup cranberry-raspberry juice
> 1 cup sugar
> 1 package (12 ounces) fresh *or* frozen cranberries, thawed
> 1 tablespoon lemon juice

In a large saucepan, bring juice and sugar to a boil. Add cranberries; return to a boil. Reduce heat; cover and simmer for 10-15 minutes or until the berries pop, stirring occasionally. Remove from the heat; stir in lemon juice. Cool. Cover and refrigerate for 1 hour or until chilled. **Yield:** 11 servings.

Nutritional Analysis: *One serving (1/4 cup) equals 101 calories, trace fat (trace saturated fat), 0 cholesterol, 1 mg sodium, 26 g carbohydrate, 1 g fiber, trace protein.*
Diabetic Exchange: *1-1/2 fruit.*

Nutritional Analysis: *One serving (3/4 cup) equals 204 calories, 6 g fat (trace saturated fat), 0 cholesterol, 282 mg sodium, 35 g carbohydrate, 4 g fiber, 5 g protein.*
Diabetic Exchanges: *1 starch, 1 fruit, 1 vegetable, 1 fat.*

Apricot-Pecan Wild Rice

1-1/2 cups finely chopped onions
1-1/2 cups finely chopped celery
    4 teaspoons canola oil
    5 cups cooked wild rice
    3/4 pound dried apricots, coarsely chopped
1-1/3 cups reduced-sodium chicken broth
    1/2 cup coarsely chopped pecans, toasted
    1/2 cup minced fresh parsley
    2 teaspoons dried thyme
    1 teaspoon rubbed sage
    1 teaspoon salt
    1/4 teaspoon pepper

In a nonstick skillet, saute onions and celery in oil for 5 minutes or until tender. Transfer to a large bowl. Stir in the remaining ingredients. Spoon into a 13-in. x 9-in. x 2-in. baking dish coated with nonstick cooking spray. Cover and bake at 350° for 30 minutes. Uncover; bake 10-15 minutes longer or until lightly browned. **Yield:** 12 servings.

🍎 Helpful Honey Hints

IF YOU'RE looking to reduce the amount of sugar in baked goods, consider using honey, recommends Nancy Zimmerman.

"I replace each cup of sugar with about 1/2 cup honey when baking," she says. "I've found this formula works most of the time, but occasionally, I still use a little sugar in some recipes. Try experimenting to see what works best for you with a particular recipe."

Nancy also adds 1/2 teaspoon baking soda for each cup of honey in a recipe.

"In addition, I reduce the amount of liquid by 1/4 cup for every cup of honey I use. And I decrease the oven temperature by 25° during baking to prevent over-browning," Nancy concludes.

Trimmed-Down Dishes for Two

Turn to this chapter if you're cooking
for just two and neither of you
cares to eat leftovers. These lighter
recipes yield smaller quantities
without sacrificing the flavor.

Baked Pineapple Chicken and Carrot 'n' Celery Amandine (page 270)

Apple Pie in a Glass

For a cool sweet treat with the flavor of apple pie,
sip on this satisfying milk shake.
—Dorothy Smith, El Dorado, Arkansas

  1/2 cup fat-free milk
    1 cup reduced-fat frozen vanilla yogurt
  1/2 cup apple pie filling
  1/4 teaspoon ground cinnamon

Place all ingredients in a blender or food processor; cover and process until smooth. Pour into glasses; serve immediately. **Yield:** 2 servings.

Nutritional Analysis: One serving (1 cup) equals 189 calories, 1 g fat (1 g saturated fat), 6 mg cholesterol, 120 mg sodium, 39 g carbohydrate, 1 g fiber, 7 g protein.
Diabetic Exchanges: 1-1/2 fruit, 1 reduced-fat milk.

Skillet Ham and Rice

(Pictured below)

This homey stovetop dish is very quick to fix. Ham, rice
and mushrooms make a tasty combination.
—Susan Zivec, Regina, Saskatchewan

    1 medium onion, chopped
    1 teaspoon olive *or* canola oil
    1 cup cubed fully cooked lean ham
    1 cup sliced fresh mushrooms
  1/2 cup reduced-sodium chicken broth
  1/4 cup water
  1/8 teaspoon pepper
  3/4 cup instant rice
    2 green onions, sliced
  1/4 cup shredded Parmesan cheese

In a nonstick skillet, saute onion in oil until tender. Add the ham, mushrooms, broth, water and pepper; bring to a boil. Add the rice. Reduce heat; cover and simmer for 5 minutes or until rice is tender. Gently fluff rice. Serve with green onions and Parmesan cheese. **Yield:** 2 servings

Greek Lamb Kabobs

Nutritional Analysis: One serving (1-1/4 cups) equals 341 calories, 10 g fat (4 g saturated fat), 31 mg cholesterol, 1,192 mg sodium, 37 g carbohydrate, 3 g fiber, 26 g protein.
Diabetic Exchanges: 3 lean meat, 2 starch, 1 vegetable.

We have a gas grill and use it year-round, especially to make these tender juicy kabobs. The lamb marinates overnight, and the skewers can be quickly assembled the next day. The recipe can easily be doubled.
—Kathy Herrola, Martinez, California

  1/4 cup lemon juice
    2 teaspoons olive *or* canola oil
    1 tablespoons dried oregano
    3 garlic cloves, minced
  1/2 pound boneless lean lamb, cut into 1-inch
      cubes
    8 cherry tomatoes
    1 small green pepper, cut into 1-inch pieces
    1 large onion, cut into 1-inch wedges

In a bowl, combine lemon juice, oil, oregano and garlic; mix well. Remove 1/8 cup for basting; cover and refrigerate. Pour remaining marinade into a large resealable plastic bag; add lamb. Seal bag and turn to coat; refrigerate for at least 8 hours or overnight, turning occasionally.

Coat grill rack with nonstick cooking spray before starting the grill. Drain and discard marinade from lamb. On four metal or soaked wooden skewers, alternately thread lamb, tomatoes, green pepper and onion. Grill kabobs, uncovered, over medium heat for 3 minutes on each side. Baste with reserved marinade. Grill 8-10 minutes longer or until meat reaches desired doneness, turning and basting frequently. **Yield:** 2 servings.

Nutritional Analysis: One serving (2 kabobs) equals 226 calories, 9 g fat (3 g saturated fat), 74 mg cholesterol, 83 mg sodium, 13 g carbohydrate, 2 g fiber, 25 g protein.
Diabetic Exchanges: 3 lean meat, 2 vegetable.

Pineapple Orange Slush

This tart, refreshing drink hits the spot, and you don't have to make a lot. And with just four ingredients whirred in a blender, it's ready in a jiffy!
—Roni Goodell, Spanish Fork, Utah

    1 cup orange juice
  1/2 cup unsweetened pineapple juice
    2 tablespoons lemon juice
    2 cups crushed ice cubes

In a blender, combine all ingredients; cover and process until thick and slushy. Pour into chilled glasses; serve immediately. **Yield:** 2 servings.

Nutritional Analysis: One serving (1-1/2 cups) equals 95 calories, trace fat (trace saturated fat), 0 cholesterol, 2 mg sodium, 23 g carbohydrate, trace fiber, 1 g protein.
Diabetic Exchange: 1-1/2 fruit.

Carrot 'n' Celery Amandine

(Pictured above and on page 268)

When I prepare a rather plain entree like baked chicken for dinner, I try to make an interesting side dish like this one. The crisp-tender veggies, seasoned with soy sauce and garlic, get added crunch from the toasted almonds.
—Carol Gaus, Itasca, Illinois

 1 garlic clove, minced
 1 teaspoon canola oil
 1 tablespoon water
 1 tablespoon reduced-sodium soy sauce
 1/2 teaspoon sugar
1-1/4 cups sliced carrots
 1/2 cup chopped onion
 1/3 cup chopped celery
 2 tablespoons sliced almonds, toasted

In a large nonstick skillet, saute garlic in oil for 1 minute or until tender. Stir in the water, soy sauce and sugar. Bring to a boil. Add carrots, onion and celery; cook until crisp-tender. Sprinkle with almonds. **Yield:** 2 servings.

Nutritional Analysis: One serving (3/4 cup) equals 133 calories, 7 g fat (1 g saturated fat), 0 cholesterol, 350 mg sodium, 15 g carbohydrate, 4 g fiber, 4 g protein.
Diabetic Exchanges: 3 vegetable, 1-1/2 fat.

Baked Pineapple Chicken

(Pictured above and on page 268)

Ginger and crushed pineapple flavor tender juicy chicken in this main dish recipe. Orange marmalade and lemon juice add just a hint of refreshing citrus

tang. It's simple to put together, low in fat and tasty, too.
—Marcille Meyer, Battle Creek, Nebraska

 1/4 cup chicken broth
 3 tablespoons reduced-sodium soy sauce
 1 teaspoon ground ginger, *divided*
 2 bone-in chicken breast halves (6 ounces *each*), skin removed
 1 can (8 ounces) unsweetened crushed pineapple, undrained
 1 teaspoon cornstarch
 2 teaspoons orange marmalade
 1 teaspoon lemon juice

In a large resealable plastic bag, combine the broth, soy sauce and 1/2 teaspoon ginger; add chicken. Seal bag and turn to coat; refrigerate for 2 hours, turning occasionally.

Drain pineapple, reserving 1/2 cup juice; set aside 1/4 cup pineapple (refrigerate remaining pineapple and juice for another use). In a saucepan, combine cornstarch and reserved pineapple juice until smooth. Stir in the pineapple, orange marmalade, lemon juice and remaining ginger. Bring to a boil; cook and stir for 1-2 minutes or until thickened.

Drain and discard marinade. Place chicken in a 9-in. square baking dish coated with nonstick cooking spray. Top with pineapple mixture. Bake, uncovered, at 350° for 45-50 minutes or until juices run clear. **Yield:** 2 servings.

Nutritional Analysis: One serving equals 207 calories, 3 g fat (1 g saturated fat), 68 mg cholesterol, 330 mg sodium, 18 g carbohydrate, 1 g fiber, 26 g protein.
Diabetic Exchanges: 3 lean meat, 1 fruit.

Baked Stuffed Zucchini

You don't have to fuss to make a special side dish for two, as this recipe proves. It's so easy to dress up zucchini halves with a flavorful mushroom stuffing.
—Sarah Rodgers, West Mifflin, Pennsylvania

 1 medium zucchini
 6 large fresh mushrooms, finely chopped
 1 green onion, finely chopped
 1 tablespoon butter *or* stick margarine
 1/2 cup white wine *or* chicken broth
 1/8 teaspoon salt
Dash white pepper
 2 teaspoons grated Parmesan cheese

Cut zucchini in half lengthwise. Scoop out pulp, leaving a 1/4-in. shell. Chop pulp; set shells aside. In a nonstick skillet, saute the zucchini pulp, mushrooms and onion in butter for 3-4 minutes or until tender. Add wine or broth. Reduce heat; simmer, uncovered, for 10-12 minutes or until liquid has evaporated. Stir in salt and pepper.

Place zucchini shells in a saucepan and cover with water; bring to a boil. Cook for 2 minutes; drain. Fill shells with mushroom mixture. Sprinkle with cheese. Broil 3-4 in. from the heat for 3-4 minutes or until lightly browned. **Yield:** 2 servings.

Nutritional Analysis: One serving (1 stuffed zucchini half) equals 133 calories, 7 g fat (4 g saturated fat), 17 mg cholesterol, 254 mg sodium, 7 g carbohydrate, 2 g fiber, 4 g protein.
Diabetic Exchanges: 2 vegetable, 1 fat, 1/2 starch.

Italian Bread Salad

This twist on the typical tossed salad combines garden-fresh veggies with bread cubes and herbs... and is terrific when tomatoes are at their peak. I first tasted this salad when I worked for a caterer. I experimented with different combinations until I came up with this version.
—Kathleen Hufstedler, Kerrville, Texas

   1 cup cubed fresh tomato
   2 tablespoons minced fresh basil *or* 2 teaspoons dried basil
   1 tablespoon chopped green onion
   2 teaspoons olive *or* canola oil
   2 teaspoons balsamic vinegar
1/8 teaspoon salt
1-1/4 cups cubed French *or* sourdough bread
   2 tablespoons minced fresh parsley

In a bowl, combine the tomato, basil, green onion, oil, vinegar and salt. Cover and let stand for 30 minutes. Place bread cubes in a 15-in. x 10-in. x 1-in. baking pan. Bake at 325° for 8-10 minutes or until lightly browned, stirring occasionally. Stir into tomato mixture. Add parsley. Serve immediately. **Yield:** 2 servings.

   Nutritional Analysis: One serving (1 cup) equals 168 calories, 6 g fat (1 g saturated fat), 0 cholesterol, 387 mg sodium, 25 g carbohydrate, 2 g fiber, 4 g protein.
   Diabetic Exchanges: 1-1/2 starch, 1 vegetable, 1 fat.

Blueberry Betty

Cubes of toasted raisin bread top this yummy blueberry treat that has just the right degree of sweetness. I concocted the recipe years ago for a weight-loss group I belonged to. It also tastes great on a cold morning!
—Nancy Baylor, Nixa, Missouri

   2 eggs, lightly beaten
3/4 cup fat-free evaporated milk
Sugar substitute equivalent to 1/3 cup sugar*
   1 teaspoon vanilla extract
1/2 teaspoon ground cinnamon
1/4 teaspoon salt
   1 cup fresh *or* frozen blueberries
   2 slices raisin bread, toasted and cubed
Dash ground nutmeg

In a bowl, beat the eggs, milk, sugar substitute, vanilla, cinnamon and salt. Stir in the blueberries. Pour into two 1-cup baking dishes coated with nonstick cooking spray. Top with toast cubes; sprinkle with nutmeg. Bake at 350° for 20-25 minutes or until bubbly. **Yield:** 2 servings.
   *Editor's Note: This recipe was tested with Equal Sweetener. Look for it in the baking aisle of your grocery store.

   Nutritional Analysis: One serving equals 278 calories, 6 g fat (2 g saturated fat), 220 mg cholesterol, 583 mg sodium, 41 g carbohydrate, 3 g fiber, 15 g protein.
   Diabetic Exchanges: 2 fat-free milk, 1 fruit, 1 fat.

Chicken and Julienned Veggies

(Pictured below)

Thyme seasons this quick skillet entree. I serve the tender browned chicken breasts, colorful sliced carrot and zucchini and savory sauce over spaghetti for a pleasing pasta meal.
—Lois Crissman, Mansfield, Ohio

   2 boneless skinless chicken breast halves (4 ounces *each*)
   2 teaspoons olive *or* canola oil
1/2 cup plus 2 tablespoons reduced-fat reduced-sodium condensed cream of chicken soup, undiluted
1/4 cup fat-free milk
1/4 teaspoon dried thyme
1/4 teaspoon salt
1/8 teaspoon white pepper
   1 medium carrot, julienned
   1 cup julienned zucchini
Hot cooked spaghetti, optional

In a nonstick skillet, brown chicken in oil. In a bowl, combine the soup, milk, thyme, salt and pepper until smooth; pour over chicken. Add carrot. Reduce heat; cover and simmer for 5 minutes, stirring occasionally. Add zucchini; cover and simmer 5 minutes longer or until chicken is no longer pink. Serve over spaghetti if desired. **Yield:** 2 servings.

   Nutritional Analysis: One serving (1 chicken breast half with 2/3 cup vegetable mixture, calculated without spaghetti) equals 261 calories, 9 g fat (2 g saturated fat), 74 mg cholesterol, 955 mg sodium, 13 g carbohydrate, 2 g fiber, 30 g protein.
   Diabetic Exchanges: 3 lean meat, 1 vegetable, 1/2 starch, 1/2 fat.

General Recipe Index

This index lists every recipe by food category, major ingredient and/or cooking method, so you can easily locate recipes to suit your needs.

APPETIZERS & SNACKS

Cold Appetizers
Crab-Filled Veggie Bites, 36
Deviled Eggs/Makeover
  Deviled Eggs, 33
Ranch Tortilla Roll-Ups, 31

Dips and Spread
Apple Salsa with Cinnamon
  Chips, 30
Beef 'n' Cheese Dip, 29
Creamy Fruit Dip, 34
Cucumber-Dill Shrimp Dip, 30
Fabulous Fruit Spread, 25
Feta Olive Dip, 23
Gazpacho Salsa, 24
Hot Spinach Artichoke Dip, 32
Mandarin Orange Fruit Dip, 23
Meaty Salsa Dip, 34
Mediterranean Salsa, 36
Texas Caviar, 21

Hot Appetizers
Asparagus Spanakopita, 22
Baked Sausage Wontons, 20
Blue Cheese Appetizer Pizza, 27
Cauliflower Hors d'oeuvres, 18
Cheese-Stuffed Jalapenos, 35
Cheesy Bagel Bites, 23
Couscous-Stuffed
  Mushrooms, 250
Frank 'n' Swiss Crescents, 20
Grilled Pork Appetizers, 25
Phyllo Turkey Egg Rolls, 28
Red Pepper Bruschetta, 24
Saucy Turkey Meatballs, 26
Seafood Nachos, 18
Turkey Crescent Wreath, 26

Snacks
Breakfast Sundaes, 110
Cereal Crunchies, 32
Cheesy Pita Crisps, 34
Chili Popcorn, 19
Cinnamon Toasties, 22
Fruity Granola, 35
Fruity Yogurt Ice Pops, 19
Granola Fruit Bars, 20
Healthy Snack Mix, 19
Mini Rice Cake Snacks, 27
Mock Strawberry Cheesecake
  Treat, 28
No-Bake Almond Bites, 28

APPLES
Apple Gingerbread, 234

Apple Halibut Kabobs, 176
Apple in a Glass, 269
Apple Pie Coffee Cake, 213
Apple Pockets, 196
Apple Salad, 66
Apple Salsa with Cinnamon
  Chips, 30
Apple Squash Soup, 41
Apple Thyme Chicken, 133
Apple-Topped Pork Chops, 162
Apple Wheat Muffins, 193
Apples and Onion Beef Roast, 114
Apricot Apple Compote, 216
Bavarian Apple Tart, 233
Cake-Topped Apple Cobbler, 208
Cran-Apple Crisp, 221
Cranberry-Apple Bread, 194
Microwave Apple Crisp, 226
Moist Apple Cake, 206
Pork with Apples and Sweet
  Potatoes, 161
Scalloped Squash and Apples, 99
Sweet 'n' Savory Apple Stuffing, 99
Sweet Potato Apple Scallop, 96

APRICOTS
Apricot Apple Compote, 216
Apricot-Pecan Wild Rice, 267
Turkey Breast with Apricot
  Glaze, 266

ASPARAGUS
Asparagus Avocado Medley, 68
Asparagus Chicken
  Sandwiches, 138
Asparagus Frittata, 105
Asparagus Spanakopita, 22
Asparagus Tomato Stir-Fry, 86
Asparagus Tossed Salad, 246

Beefy Broccoli Asparagus
  Salad, 55
Roasted Asparagus with Balsamic
  Vinegar, 90
Salmon-Wrapped Asparagus, 164
Scallops and Asparagus
  Stir-Fry, 174

AVOCADOS
Asparagus Avocado Medley, 68
Avocado Salad Dressing, 60
Gingered Citrus-Avocado
  Salad, 50

BACON
Bacon 'n' Veggie Pasta, 91
Barbecue BLT Chicken Salad, 54

BANANAS
Banana Mocha Cooler, 21
Banana Nut Bread/Makeover
  Banana Nut Bread, 195
Banana Split Dessert, 240
Creamy Banana Pudding, 222
Patriotic Banana Split, 244
Strawberry-Banana Ice Cream/
  Makeover Strawberry-Banana
  Ice Cream, 227

BARLEY
Barley and Rice Pilaf, 92
Barley Radish Salad, 50
Barley Vegetable Stew, 180
Lentil Barley Stew, 190
Multigrain Stuffed Pepper
  Cups, 149
Mushroom Barley Soup, 44

BARS & BROWNIES
Caramel Brownie Pizza, 210
Caramel Fudge Brownies, 214
Crimson Crumble Bars, 225
Delightful Brownies, 202
Granola Fruit Bars, 20
Rocky Road Fudge Brownies/
  Makeover Rocky Road Fudge
  Brownies, 205

BASIL
Basil Fettuccine, 260
Basil Tomato Soup, 39
Basil Turkey Burgers, 152
Buttermilk Basil Salad Dressing, 53

PORK (continued)
Pork with Apples and Sweet
    Potatoes, 161
Pork with Garlic Cream Sauce, 156

POTATOES (also see Sweet Potatoes)
Main Dishes
    Breakfast Pizza, 106
    Microwave Potato Ham
        Dinner, 157
    Polish-Style Sausage 'n'
        Potatoes, 154
Side Dishes
    Balsamic Roasted Red
        Potatoes, 100
    Buttermilk Mashed Potatoes, 94
    Garlic Potato Wedges, 79
    Garlic Twice-Baked
        Potatoes, 244
    Grilled Vegetable Potato
        Skins, 88
    Oven-Baked Country Fries, 84
    Roasted Spicy Mustard
        Potatoes, 95
Soups and Salad
    Cheesy Ham 'n' Potato Soup/
        Makeover Cheesy Ham 'n'
        Potato Soup, 43
    Crunchy Potato Salad, 52

PUDDING & BREAD PUDDING
Baked Pumpkin Pudding, 230
Creamy Banana Pudding, 222
Peanut Butter Bread Pudding, 204
Sugarless Rice Pudding, 210

PUMPKIN
Baked Pumpkin Pudding, 230
Pumpkin Dinner Rolls, 264
Pumpkin Spice Cookies, 225
Pumpkin Squares, 232
Pumpkin Trifle, 226
Pumpkin Vegetable Soup, 48

RAISINS & DATES
Anise Raisin Bread, 102
Broccoli Raisin Salad, 258
Carrot Raisin Pilaf, 79
Chewy Date Cookies, 202
Raisin Cinnamon Rolls, 108

RASPBERRIES
Chocolate-Filled Raspberry
    Meringues, 238
Cool Raspberry Peach Pie, 214
Minted Raspberry Lemonade, 263
Pork Loin with Raspberry
    Sauce, 155
Raspberry Chicken Salad, 61
Raspberry Pie with Oat Crust, 220
Raspberry Thyme Chicken, 129
Slow-Cooker Berry Cobbler, 224
Three-Berry Sauce, 80

RICE & WILD RICE
Main Dishes
    Cheesy Beans and Rice, 186
    Gaucho Casserole, 117
    Glazed Cornish Hens with Rice
        Pilaf, 242
    Jambalaya, 174
    Lentil Loaf, 188
    Peppery Shrimp and Rice, 178
    Pork Fried Rice for Two, 162
    Red Beans and Rice, 184
    Skillet Ham and Rice, 269
    Three-Cheese Rice
        Lasagna, 182
    Wild Rice Chicken Bake, 140
Salads
    Chicken Rice Salad, 76
    Paradise Rice Salad, 61
    Wild Rice Chicken Salad, 56
Side Dishes
    Apricot-Pecan Wild Rice, 267
    Barley and Rice Pilaf, 92
    Italian Rice, 80
    Meatless Hopping John, 97
    Southwestern Rice, 95
Soup and Sandwiches
    Great Grain Burgers, 180
    Lentil Vegetable Soup, 40

ROLLS
Apple Pockets, 196
Jumbo Pineapple Yeast Rolls, 110
Pumpkin Dinner Rolls, 264
Raisin Cinnamon Rolls, 108
Sweet Potato Yeast Rolls, 198

SALADS & DRESSINGS (also see Coleslaw)
Bean and Lentil Salads
    Creamy Bean Salad, 73
    Dijon-Four Bean Salad, 58
    Mediterranean Lentil Salad, 74
Dressings
    Avocado Salad Dressing, 60
    Buttermilk Basil Salad
        Dressing, 53
    Creamy Herb Dressing, 76
    Cucumber Buttermilk Salad
        Dressing, 265
    Dijon Herb Salad Dressing, 72
    Hold-the-Oil French Dressing, 74
    Honey-Mustard Salad
        Dressing, 56
    Strawberry Salad Dressing, 70
Fruit and Gelatin Salads
    Almond Sunshine Citrus, 105
    Apple Salad, 66
    Carrot-Pineapple Gelatin
        Salad, 53
    Peachy Fruit Salad, 74
    Pineapple Waldorf Salad, 62
    Seven Fruit Salad, 60
    Simply Fruit, 73
    Spiced Fruit, 67
    Summertime Yogurt Salad, 68
Green Salads
    Asparagus Tossed Salad, 246
    Fennel Orange Salad, 59
    Fruit 'n' Feta Tossed Salad, 68
    Gingered Citrus-Avocado
        Salad, 50
    Mock Caesar Salad, 256
    Orange Cucumber Tossed
        Salad, 62
    Peachy Pecan Salad, 261
Main-Dish Salads
    Barbecue BLT Chicken
        Salad, 54
    Beef 'n' Black-Eyed Pea
        Salad, 59
    Beefy Broccoli Asparagus
        Salad, 55
    Chicken Rice Salad, 76
    Cranberry-Chutney Turkey
        Salad, 70
    Grilled Salmon Salad, 52
    Pineapple Chicken Paradise, 55
    Raspberry Chicken Salad, 61
    Tarragon Turkey Salad, 71
    Warm Chicken Spinach
        Salad, 73
    Wild Rice Chicken Salad, 56
Pasta and Potato Salads
    Black-Eyed Pea Salad, 54
    Cranberry Couscous Salad, 66
    Crunchy Potato Salad, 52

Alphabetical Index

*This handy index lists every recipe in alphabetical order
so you can easily find your favorite dish.*

Reference Index

Use this index to locate the many healthy cooking hints located throughout the book.